95

FAX

The Principles and Practice of Facsimile Communication

By DANIEL M. COSTIGAN

The Principles and Practice of Facsimile Communication

CHILTON BOOK COMPANY

PHILADELPHIA NEW YORK LONDON

Published in Philadelphia by Chilton Book Company
and simultaneously in Ontario, Canada,
by Thomas Nelson & Sons, Ltd.
ISBN: 0-8019-5641-2
Library of Congress Catalog Card Number 76-169584
Designed by William E. Lickfield
Manufactured in the United States of America

For *Dorothy*, *Drew*,
and *Christopher*

Preface

ACCORDING to a recent estimate, some 55,000 facsimile devices (presumably of all sorts) are in use in the United States at the present time. From this it would seem a safe estimate that several times that number—or at least a few hundred thousand—are in use throughout the world. These numbers are small compared with the number of other, more familiar telecommunication devices, such as telephones and teletypewriters, but they appear to be growing at a healthy pace.

Possibly the most impressive thing about facsimile (fax, for short) when you have examined it in some depth is its enormous potential. Without looking much beneath the surface you may get the impression that it is slow and somewhat unsophisticated by modern standards, and expensive compared with some of the competing media. However, when you penetrate the surface, you see a communications tool that is extremely versatile and self-sufficient, and one for which the economic picture has, in fact, been steadily improving during the past few years.

It is true, of course, as it is of any communications medium, including the postal service, that, depending on requirements and conditions, fax may prove impractical for a given application. It is also true that in some ambitious past attempts to gain a foothold it has been prone to failure in selling itself to the prospective user. But possibly the main reason fax has been slow to catch on is that so many people, probably including a considerable number of otherwise astute businessmen, simply do not know it exists. Or perhaps they have heard of it but are unaware of its ready availability, or of what it might be able to do for them as a communications tool.

Even if one were consciously to set out to learn what he could of facsimile, where would he look? If he were lucky, he might come across a reasonably comprehensive magazine article on the subject, written recently enough to have some validity.

My main objective in writing this book is to provide a single source from which the student—or practitioner—of the facsimile art can conveniently assess most of the basic information for which he might otherwise have to search, often in vain, through many scattered books and journals. Charles R. Jones had essentially the same objective some twenty years ago when he wrote his excellent book *Facsimile.* Much progress has been made in the facsimile field since then. But, as has been the habit with this bashful giant, the advances for the most part have not been conveniently documented or adequately publicized. I hope that this book will help to fill an obvious void.

* * *

A book of this sort could never have been put together without the help of those who possess the materials, facilities, and first-hand knowledge of the subject necessary to ensure completeness and accuracy. The following individuals and organizations deserve special thanks for their generous assistance:

E. B. Kimball of the Associated Press; Tom Benewicz and Ed Christiansen of the AT&T Co.; Gene Gartner of AT&T's Long Lines Department; J. J. Mahoney, Jr., and Les Spindel of Bell Labs; Lee Grove of the Council on Library Resources; A. M. Wilson of the Electronic Industries Association; Jack Herbstreit, J. Lalou, and J. Rouviere of the International Telecommunications Union; Don Avedon and Dr. Carl Nelson of the National Microfilm Association; W. Carl Jackson, Director of Libraries at Pennsylvania State University; Dr. G. K. Weiss of the World Meteorological Organization; John Carlson and Fred Simpkins of Alden Electronic & Impulse Recording Equipment Company; "Mac" Reader of Computerpix Corporation; Robert Meltzer of Dacom, Inc.; G. W. Kaye, W. L. Kelker, and Ken McConnell of Litton's Datalog Division; Charles E. Sack of the HCM Corporation; John Clark and Joseph Verruso of International Scanatron; Richard Doelger and Frank Miles of Muirhead; and G. H. Ridings and Susan Tyrrell of Western Union.

Also worthy of acknowledgment for the assistance they provided are the American Library Association; the American Newspaper Publishers Association; the Department of Defense; the Federal Communications Commission; the IEEE; the National Bureau of Standards; NASA; RCA; UPI; the U.S. Weather Bureau; the firm of Dr.-Ing. Rudolf Hell of Kiel; Graphic Sciences, Inc.; the Magnavox Company; Nippon Electric Company; the Stewart-Warner Corporation; Toshiba; Xerox; and the several other manufacturers whose products are described in Chapter 8.

Finally, my thanks to Dorothy Costigan for her help with the original sketches and to Ida Hagan for assisting with the typing of the manuscript.

—Daniel M. Costigan
November 1970

To the Reader

IF you are an electrical engineer seeking guidance in the design of facsimile terminal equipment, you will no doubt find portions of this book useful to you, but, frankly, it was not written with you in mind. If you are accustomed to the level of technical book in which virtually every page abounds in equations, you will find that this book tends for the most part to be simplistic.

If, on the other hand, you are . . .

- a systems engineer seeking guidance in the planning of a whole system, or . . .
- a technician (or student technician) who is interested in facsimile and is eager to learn all he can about it without getting hopelessly entangled in engineering particulars, or . . .
- a businessman who feels that facsimile may have a place in his office or plant, and who wants to learn more about it before talking to a salesman—

then this book should be of value to you.

You will naturally be expected to have some knowledge of mechanics and electronics to begin with. The level of knowledge required will become evident as you begin to read. The book would obviously have to be three times its size if it were to attempt to teach the facsimile art to a layman whose only previous experience with communications gear consisted of the twisting of knobs and the pushing of buttons.

Among the things the book *will* do is acquaint you with facsimile's past history, survey some of the many ways in which it is being applied today, and explain (in reasonable detail) how it works and why it sometimes does not work as it should. It will also discuss standards, specific commercial systems, the variety in types of systems, and the inevitable trade-offs between cost, quality, and speed within a system.

And, finally, it will examine current trends and speculate on what the future holds for this enduring medium with its remarkable capacity for remaining young and modern in spite of its age.

—DMC

Contents

Preface vii

To the Reader ix

1 HISTORY 1
Evolution, 2
Newspapers by Radio, 8
A New Generation, 9

2 FAX TODAY 12
Current Applications, 12
Virtues, 28
Limitations, 34
Trends, 37

3 HOW IT WORKS 47
Scanning, 47
Recording, 56
Amplification, 66
Phasing and Synchronization, 69
Index of Cooperation, 75

4 TRANSMISSION 79
D.C. and Subaudio, 80
Modulation, 81
Transmission Impairments, 91
Other Facilities, 97
Couplers and Modems, 102
Redundancy Reduction, 108

5 QUALITY 119
Resolution, 119
Contrast, Gray Scale, and Polarity, 133
Impairments Due to Digitizing, 137
Legibility Criteria, 141
Pictorial Criteria, 147

6 ECONOMICS 154
Cost Factors, 154
Trade-offs, 160
Cost per Copy, 161
Economic Trends, 169

7 STANDARDS 172
Domestic Standards, 173
International Standards, 181

8 COMMERCIAL HARDWARE AND SYSTEMS 191
Section 1—"Message," or General Purpose: Low-Speed to Medium-Speed Systems, 193
Section 2—General Purpose: High-Speed (and Multispeed) Systems, 209
Section 3—Telephotographic (Phototelegraphic or Photofacsimile) Systems, 221
Section 4—Special Purpose and Miscellaneous Systems, 231

9 THE FUTURE 256
Speed, 256
Fax in the Home, 257
Fax in Color, 259
The Question of Paper, 261

Index 263

The Principles and Practice of Facsimile Communication

1 History

TWO significant events in the field of telecommunications took place within the first four months of 1926. One was the first public demonstration of television—by John Baird, in a little laboratory in London's Soho district in January. The other was the inauguration of commercial transatlantic radio facsimile service—for the transmission of news photos—by the Radio Corporation of America three months later.

That the two events occurred within a few months of each other is perhaps not in itself significant. What is interesting is the relative state of development of these two loosely related picture transmission media at that time. They were technologically similar, both employing essentially the same electromechanical techniques of dissecting and reconstructing pictures. But while TV remained confined to the laboratory bench, its static counterpart (static in the sense that it was concerned with still, as opposed to moving, images) already had several decades of practical application behind it, in the course of which it had steadily progressed to a high state of refinement.

Although TV was to enjoy a somewhat more rapid technological growth than facsimile in the ensuing years, it was not for another two decades that it finally caught up in the sense of having become a full-fledged commercial reality. And it was not until the advent of communications satellites in the 1960s that it was able to span the seas on even a limited commercial basis.

As late as 1949 it was still believed in some quarters that facsimile could compete actively with TV as a home news and entertainment medium. Although that dream has not materialized, facsimile has nevertheless managed to maintain—and, in fact, gradually reinforce—its position as an indispensable telecommunications medium.

At this point it might be well to clarify exactly what the word facsimile means as a telecommunications term. There are conflicting definitions. To some, the word is confined to describing what is essentially a "message" medium through which written or printed messages and sketches are exchanged via wire or radio and are visibly recorded by *non*photographic means—i.e., by electrochemical or electromechanical means not requiring further processing. By this definition, the systems customarily used for transmission of news photographs are excluded.

To others, facsimile refers to any system by which printed *or* pictorial matter (graphics material, in general) is transmitted electrically from one place to another and a reasonably faithful copy permanently recorded at the receiving end in any one of several forms.

This book takes the latter view, lumping together the news photo and so-called "message" or "document" facsimile systems simply as variations in facsimile recording technique, which is, in fact, the only genuine distinction existing between them.

EVOLUTION

The origin of facsimile—or *fax,* as it is often referred to today—dates back well beyond the 1926 event mentioned at the beginning of this chapter. Its birth, curiously enough, was not so much the result of a conscious quest for a new telecommunications medium as it was an offshoot of the invention of the electric clock.

In 1842 Scottish inventor Alexander Bain[1] fashioned an electrically controlled pendulum mechanism that formed the basis for a master-slave system of interconnected synchronized clocks, a later refinement of which is still widely used in schools, office buildings and the like. From this novel time-keeping system evolved Bain's pioneering device for the transmission of visible symbols over telegraph lines.

The inventor had shrewdly observed that, inasmuch as each of the synchronized pendulums of this clock system was in the same relative position at a given moment of time, if the master pendulum could somehow be rigged to trace a pattern of intermittent electrical contacts in its travel, the pattern could simultaneously be reproduced (by a means that had yet to be devised) at one or more locations remote from the sending device.

The result of the ensuing experiments was an "automatic electrochemical recording telegraph," on which Bain received British Patent 9745 in 1843.

Basically three modifications had been necessary to convert the synchronized clock to a graphics transmission device. One was the addition of a stylus to the pendulum of each device. The second was the addition of a clockwork-actuated "message block," and the third was the development of a suitable electrosensitive recording medium.

In the SEND mode, the added stylus functioned as a brush contact arranged to sweep over a message block containing a group of words formed of raised metallic lettering. Each sweep of the pendulum intermittently disrupted and

[1] Not to be confused with Alexander Bain, the noted Scottish philosopher-psychologist, with whom inventor Bain was contemporary.

completed a circuit, producing, in effect, a series of pulses corresponding to the metal protrusions the stylus contacted within the breadth of the pendulum's stroke. With each full swing of the pendulum, the message board was caused to drop down a notch so that, on the next swing, the stylus would contact a fresh segment of the message.

The resulting serial stream of d.c. pulses was sent by wire to the receive device, where, in place of raised metal lettering, the message board accommodated a sheet of electrosensitive paper. As the RECEIVE stylus swept over the face of the recording paper, it formed a dark mark wherever a pulse occurred. After several sweeps the dark marks formed a facsimile of the raised metal lettering at the SEND terminal.

Synchronization was achieved by an automatic correcting action in which a pendulum tending to lead its remote mate would be electromagnetically "locked" at the end of a swing cycle, and released by a momentary opening of the circuit when the lagging pendulum caught up (Figs. 1.1 and 1.2).

Bain's device enjoyed a moderate success but was unable to compete with the electromechanical printing telegraph, which had meanwhile been perfected and which surpassed the Bain system in speed and reliability.

Having originated in Europe, it was only natural that facsimile's early commercial applications should be centered in Britain and on the continent. The first commercial system on record was established in France in 1865 by an Italian expatriate, Giovanni Caselli, who had patented an improved version of Bain's device. The system, which connected Paris with several other French cities, remained in operation for about five years.

Meanwhile, in 1850, Frederick Bakewell of England had successfully demonstrated the forerunner of the "cylinder-and-screw" arrangement that was eventually to replace Bain's pendulum and was to reign for many years as the standard fax mechanism (Fig. 1.3). Many present-day fax systems are of the cylinder type.

The next contributor of consequence was Germany's Dr. Arthur Korn, whose principal contribution was the introduction of photoelectric scanning. For nearly 60 years facsimile had been tied to Bain's contact scanning technique with, at best, a few subtle variations. In 1902 Korn publicly demonstrated the first practical photoelectric fax system for the transmission and reproduction of photographs. Five years later he established a commercial picture transmission system that was at first confined to Germany, but which, by 1910, linked Berlin with London and Paris.

In 1922 Korn successfully transmitted a picture to America by radio. The picture, a photograph of Pope Pius XI, was sent from Rome and received at Bar Harbor, Maine. It was published in the New York *World* on the same day it was transmitted: June 11, 1922.

Other European innovators of note were Clement Ader, a versatile French inventor who contributed one of the first electromagnetic light valves for photographic recording (similar in principle to the one later to be perfected

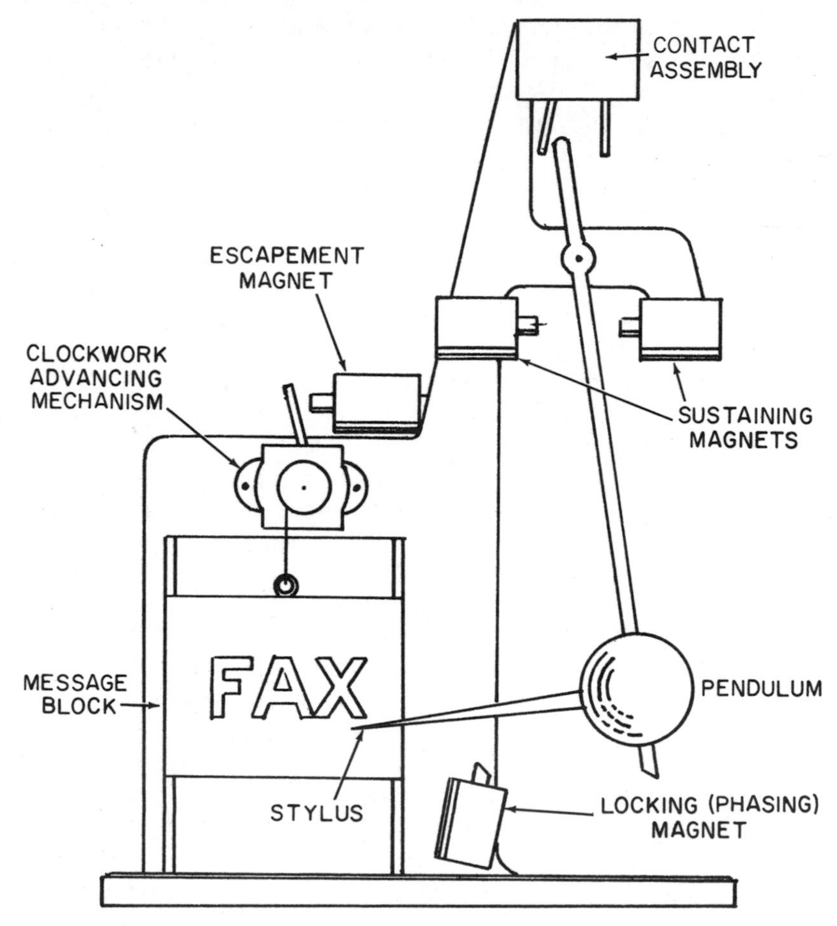

Fig. 1.1. Basic mechanics of Bain's electrochemical recording telegraph. In the SEND mode, the message block contained raised metallic letters, and in the RECEIVE mode, a piece of electrolytic paper. An electrically actuated escapement lowered the message board one notch for each swing of the pendulum, thus effecting line-by-line scanning by the oscillating stylus. (Original sketch by the author, based loosely on an old patent drawing.)

by E. C. Wente in the United States); Edouard Belin, also of France, who made a variety of contributions; and Bartholomew and Macfarlane, two Britons who codeveloped the Bartlane system of tape transmission, utilizing a technique that anticipated the present-day PCM (Pulse Code Modulation) system of encoding discrete amplitude levels of an analog signal.

In this country serious experimentation with fax did not begin until the 1920s, when three telecommunications giants—American Telephone & Telegraph, RCA, and Western Union—set about developing picture transmission systems chiefly for press use. All three separately developed systems came to fruition in 1924.

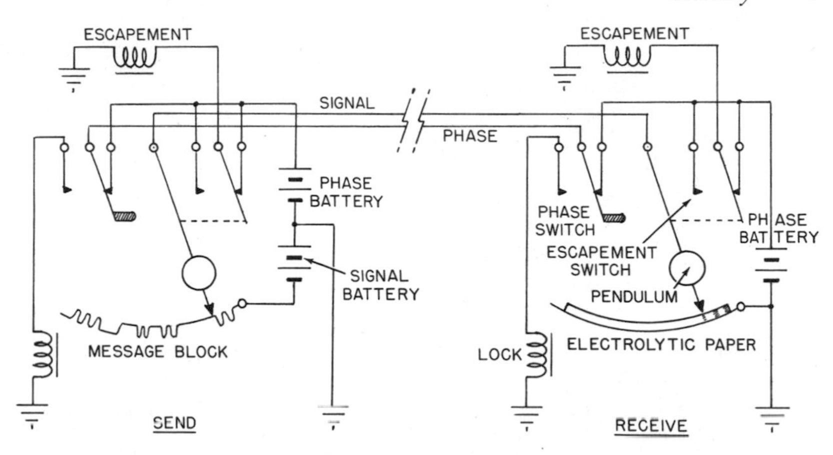

Fig. 1.2. Schematic representation of Bain's telegraph, illustrating (a) the basic scheme for visual electrolytic recording of a d.c. pulse train, and (b) the scheme for synchronizing, or "phasing," two pendulums by holding a leading pendulum at the start position while its lagging mate catches up. For simplicity, pendulum-sustaining circuitry has been omitted, and signaling and phasing are shown as isolated functions. (Original sketch—and circuit—by the author.)

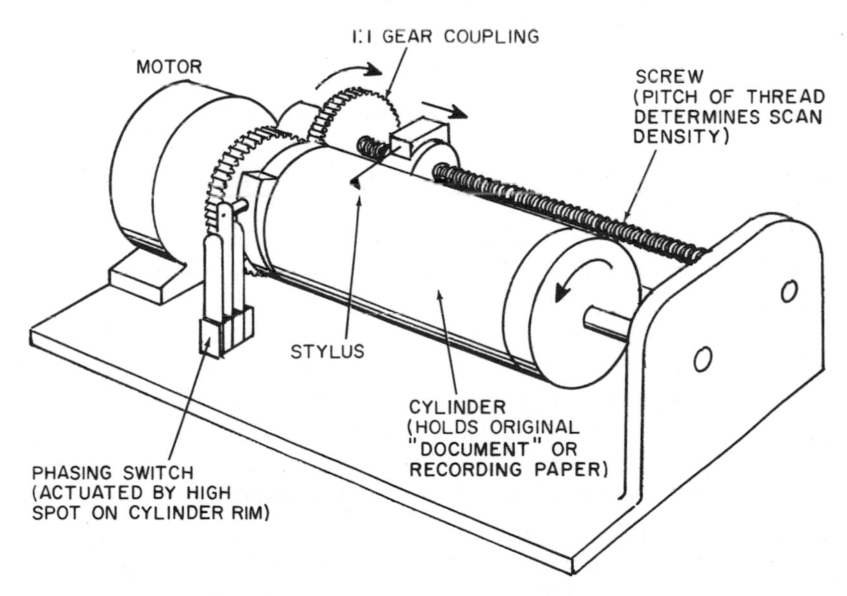

Fig. 1.3. Successor to Bain's pendulum was the still familiar "cylinder-and-screw" mechanism (c. 1850) usually attributed to Bakewell. Scanning and recording were done lathe fashion, with the stylus (or light beam in a later innovation) progressing slowly along the screw, tracing a continuous helical scan around the face of the revolving cylinder. (Original sketch by the author.)

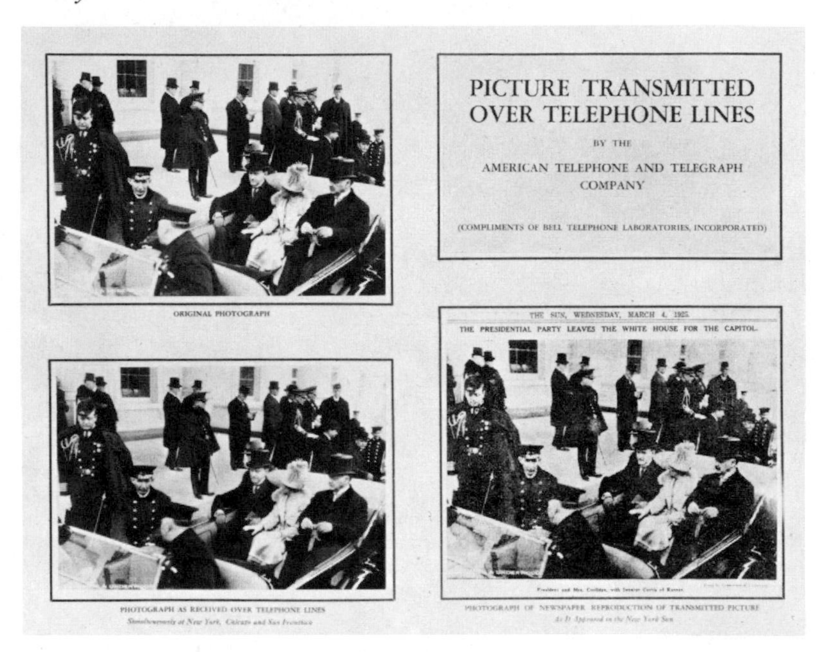

Fig. 1.4. Evolution of a newspicture, 1925. Original picture (upper left) was transmitted from Washington, D.C.; received simultaneously in New York, Chicago, and San Francisco (lower left); and published in the New York *Sun,* Wednesday, March 4, 1925 (lower right). (Courtesy Bell Telephone Labs.)

In May AT&T transmitted a 5 × 7-inch picture from Cleveland to New York (a distance of over 500 miles) in 4½ minutes. And, in July, RCA successfully sent a picture by radio to England and back. Meanwhile, Western Union established a limited commercial service called "Telepix," which, however, it was shortly to abandon for lack of customer interest.

It is an interesting sidelight that the AT&T "telephoto" system was developed by Dr. Herbert Ives,[2] a Western Electric Company (and, later, Bell Labs) engineer, whose father, Frederic Ives, had invented the halftone photoengraving process in 1878. The elder Ives' invention had figured prominently in a number of earlier (prephotoelectric) fax experiments, here and abroad, by having provided the necessary means for transmitting photographs by contact scanning. The younger Ives was later to conduct the first public demonstration of television in America—in New York City, April 7, 1927.

The AT&T domestic system went commercial in 1925, and RCA's international radiophoto system followed suit a year later.

[2] For a comprehensive account of Ives' work in picture transmission, see Ives, Horton, et al., "The Transmission of Pictures Over Telephone Lines," *The Bell System Technical Journal*, April 1925, pp. 187–214.

At about this time Western Union, while continuing to develop circuits and equipment for phototransmission, began to explore fax's potential as a message-sending medium to supplement the firm's telegraph service. In the process, it developed a new, nonelectrolytic direct recording paper called Teledeltos,® introduction of which contributed notably to the success of the automatic facsimile telegraph system the firm inaugurated in the early 1930s. The development of this system culminated, in 1948, in introduction of the Desk-Fax, a compact, desk-top fax message transmitter, of which thousands of units have since been installed.

Another important departure from the newspicture application was fax's adoption, in 1930, as a means of distributing weather data. Earlier short-range experimental transmissions (by C. F. Jenkins and others) had culminated, that year, in RCA's pioneering transmissions of weather maps to ships at sea via radiofacsimile. Since then, fax's role in weather forecasting has grown steadily.

After having developed its picture transmission system to a high degree of refinement (at a cost of about two million dollars), AT&T sought to interest a major news agency in taking over the operations aspect of it. The Associated Press did so in 1934, dubbed it "Wirephoto," and, within a year, had made such a success of it that a mad scramble ensued among other newspaper interests to develop picture transmission systems of their own. AT&T continued to provide circuits—and, for a time, terminal equipment

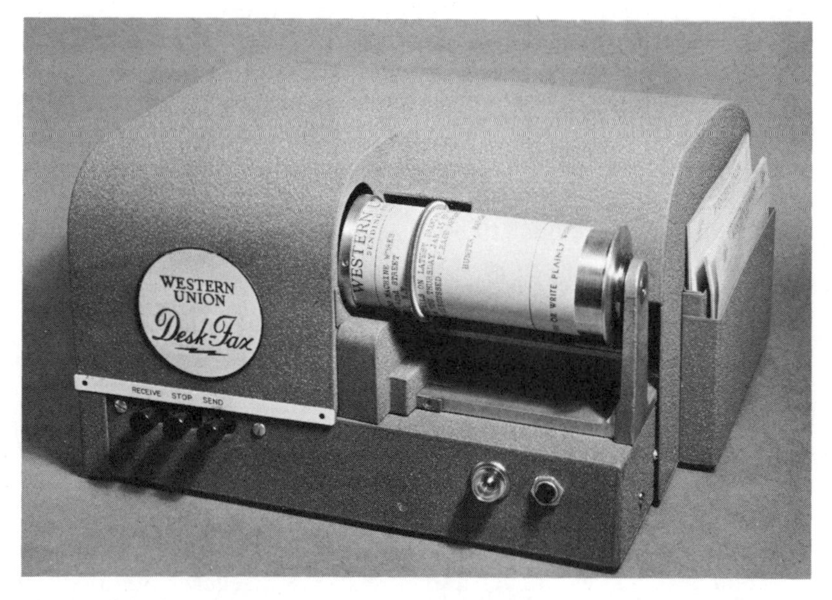

Fig. 1.5. Western Union's Desk-Fax, one of the most compact fax transceivers ever developed. Some 30,000 are currently in regular use. (Courtesy Western Union.)

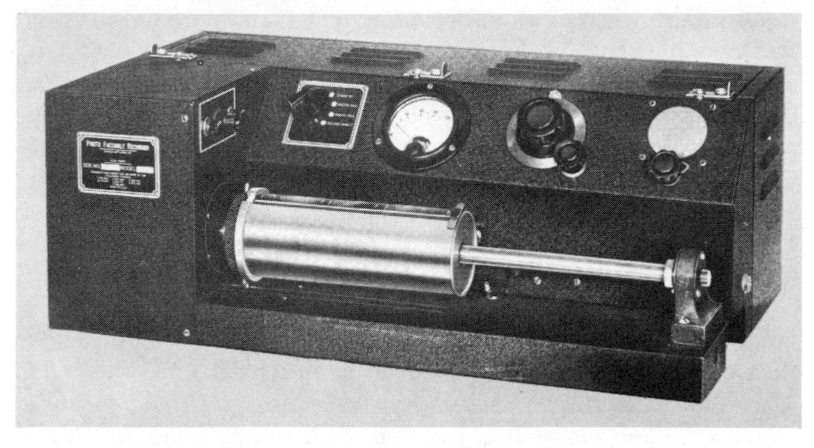

Fig. 1.6. The classic Times Facsimile Model CF portable photofacsimile transmitter. Introduced some 30 years ago, this venerable piece of fax gear was still commercially available, along with its mate the Model RF recorder, from the Westrex Corporation (successor to Times Facsimile Corporation) in the early 1960s. (Courtesy Datalog Division, Litton Industries.)

as well—to implement the private newspicture networks operated by the AP and others.

Out of the scramble emerged at least three new fax equipment manufacturers: Acme (manufacturing offspring of Acme Newspictures), Times Facsimile, and Finch Telecommunications. Along with RCA, Western Union, and another pioneering firm called Radio Inventions, Inc. (founded in 1929 by radio pioneer John V. L. Hogan),[3] these firms pretty much constituted the nucleus of the American facsimile industry until the 1950s. The Bell System (specifically Bell Labs and the Western Electric Company) had meanwhile phased itself out of the development and manufacture of fax equipment. However, AT&T, the parent firm, has remained quite active to this day in the development and leasing of fax transmission facilities.

NEWSPAPERS BY RADIO

As early as 1937 a newspaper had been successfully delivered by radio facsimile—first by Station KSTP in St. Paul, Minnesota, and then by WOR in New York. This was to be fax's long-awaited bid for public recognition. In the eyes of a small but growing fraternity of visionaries, the day was fast approaching when a fax recorder would be a household fixture no less common than a radio set—to which, in fact, it would be an indispensable appendage.

By the close of the '30s the idea had caught on to the extent that one manufacturer alone (RCA) had already sold several hundred radio fax receivers. But, unfortunately, results of public demonstrations had left much

[3] See *Proceedings of the IRE,* March 1956, p. 296.

to be desired and, by the time fax joined the war effort in 1941, interest had flagged considerably.

Interest was rekindled after the war, however, and on June 9, 1948, the FCC officially authorized commercial fax broadcasting. Prior to that, by the spring of the year, no fewer than four major newspapers—the Miami *Herald*, the Chicago *Tribune*, the Philadelphia *Inquirer*, and the New York *Times*—had experimentally broadcast special fax editions via their respective FM radio outlets. The St. Louis *Post-Dispatch* had already transmitted a special fax edition via UHF radio as early as December 1938.

Of these pioneering papers, the Miami *Herald* took the venture most seriously and had gambled considerable money and developmental effort on the belief that the fax newspaper would catch on.

It never did. For, in the meantime, upon the scene had come a rival with apprcciably greater popular appeal: commercial TV. For the venture to have succeeded under the circumstances, the fax recorders for home use would have had to be marketed at less than cost. And even then it is doubtful that a public preoccupied with the long-awaited debut of TV would have accepted fax with sufficient enthusiasm to make it a paying proposition as a consumer item.

So fax quietly retreated to its behind-the-scenes role as a strictly utilitarian communications medium—a role in which it has continued to grow in stature and in variety of applications, despite strong competition from younger and more sophisticated systems.

A NEW GENERATION

Several of the names that once formed the nucleus of the fax industry have since vanished, and several new—and in some cases more familiar—ones have appeared.

The assets of Acme Telectronix, heir to the fax manufacturing activities of the old NEA-Acme news organization, were purchased by the Fairchild Camera & Instrument Corporation in the early 1960s. Prior to that, in 1951, Acme Newspictures had been acquired by the United Press Associations, which subsequently (1959) were absorbed by International News Service to form the present United Press International. Fairchild has since divested itself of its facsimile product line, but UPI has continued to produce picture transmission equipment in the Acme tradition for internal use in its Telephoto system.

Times Facsimile Corporation, with fax pioneer Austin Cooley at the helm, was acquired by Litton Industries in 1959. Some of the Times-developed apparatus remained available briefly under the name "Westrex" (a Litton division; formerly the Western Electric Export Company). More recently, Litton's entire facsimile line, including separate systems for eleven different applications—some of the equipment embodying original Times Facsimile designs, some of it brand new, and some of it of foreign manufacture—bore the name *Litcom.* Late in 1970, the Litcom Division of Litton Industries was renamed *Datalog,* and the fax line renamed accordingly.

Finch Telecommunications had contributed notably to fax's progress, but had banked heavily on the success of the ill-fated fax news venture of the late 1940s and, as a result, quietly lapsed into total obscurity sometime thereafter.

Radio Inventions was reorganized in the early 1950s as Hogan Laboratories Inc., which, with its "Faximile" manufacturing division, was subsequently acquired by Telautograph, Inc. The latter is currently a producer of a line of fax equipment, while its Hogan Faximile Division concerns itself primarily with supplying its (Hogan's) patented electrolytic FAXpaper® to the news wire services for the direct recording of transmitted photographs.

Both RCA and Western Union have remained active in the fax field, though not as producers of apparatus for the general market. Both firms maintain facilities for fax transmission and both have engineered a number of novel systems, such as RCA's system for sending fax signals over commercial TV channels by utilizing the blanking period between frames. Western Union, in addition to developing new transmission facilities and leasing lines to fax customers—as does the Bell Telephone System—maintains a uniquely equipped fax "message" network which it makes available to subscribers. It also leases facsimile equipment, some of it of its own manufacture.

Of the names that currently lead the roster of manufacturers of fax equipment for the general market, that of Alden[4] is perhaps the best established. The Alden Company was a maker of radio parts when it entered the fax field during World War II. Since then it has matured steadily in the broad field of electronic graphics recording and is today one of the leading producers of specialized fax gear.

RCA, General Electric, and the Stewart-Warner Corporation were conspicuous among the handful of industrial giants who had briefly joined the regular fax manufacturers—notably Alden, Finch, and Radio Inventions—in the design and building of experimental broadcast fax equipment during the late 1930s and 1940s. Stewart-Warner returned to fax manufacture in 1956, when it took out a license agreement with Hogan Laboratories and acquired the facsimile business of the Allen D. Cardwell Electronics Production Corporation. The Stewart-Warner Datafax equipment has ranked high in the document fax field for the past several years.

Another currently popular item is the desk-top, telephone-coupled transceiver, variations of which are produced by the Magnavox Company, Xerox Corporation, Stewart-Warner, and two relatively new firms, Graphic Sciences, Inc., and Shintron. The name Telecopier,® which has become almost synonymous with this new breed, is Xerox's registered name for the particu-

[4] Alden Electronic & Impulse Recording Equipment Co., Westboro, Mass.

lar units it produces and markets. The original Telecopier was developed and produced by the Magnavox Company, whose Magnafax® units have competed with it on the low-lease, fax rental market.

Other domestic firms currently engaged in fax manufacture are International Scanatron (a portion of whose fax product line had formerly been that of Fairchild Camera and Instrument Corp.), Addressograph-Multigraph Corporation, Decitron Communications Systems, Inc., Electronic Transmission Systems, Inc., Comfax Computerpix Corp., and Graphic Transmission Systems, Inc. Among the leading foreign makers of fax gear are Muirhead of England (whose products are marketed extensively in this country), Rudolf Hell of Germany, and Matsushita Graphic Communication Systems (formerly Toho-Denki) and Nippon Electric of Japan. Chapter 8 contains descriptive data on a sampling of current facsimile products of leading domestic and foreign producers.

BIBLIOGRAPHY

"AP," *Fortune,* Feb. 1937, pp. 88–93.

Baracket, A. J., "Demonstrating Broadcast Facsimile at the N.Y. World's Fair," *RCA Review,* July 1940, pp. 3–7.

Bell, J., et al., "Some Recent Developments in Phototelegraphy and Facsimile Transmission," *Proceedings of the Institute of Electrical Engineers* (London), Part 3, Nov. 1952, pp. 344–359.

Bond, D. S., and V. J. Duke, "Ultrafax," *RCA Review,* March 1949, pp. 99–115.

Bond, F. F., *An Introduction to Journalism,* New York, Macmillan, 1954 ("Miracle of Transmission," pp. 259–263, and "Milestones in 'Facsimile' Transmission," pp. 286–287).

Byrnes, I. F., "Radio Weather Map Service to Ships," *Radio Facsimile,* Vol. 1, New York, RCA Institutes Technical Press, 1938, pp. 294–304.

Costigan, D. M., "FAX . . . ," *Popular Electronics,* Feb. 1969, pp. 33–41.

Feldman, S., "Facsimile is Coming of Age," *Electronic Industries,* May 1964, pp. 38–42.

"Filling the Blanks" (item), *Electronics,* Nov. 13, 1967, pp. 305–306.

Freebody, J. W., *Telegraphy,* London, Sir Isaac Pitman & Sons, 1958 (esp. p. 32).

Hills, L., and T. J. Sullivan, *Facsimile,* New York, McGraw-Hill, 1949.

Hogan, J. V. L., "The Early Days of Television," *Journal of the SMPTE,* Vol. 63, Nov. 1954, pp. 169–172.

———, and G. M. Stamps, "A New Continuous-Feed Facsimile Scanner," *Electrical Engineering,* July 1954, pp. 615–619.

Jones, C. R., *Facsimile,* New York, Murray Hill Books, 1949.

Kane, J. N., *Famous First Facts* (3rd ed.), New York, H. W. Wilson, 1964, pp. 416 and 501.

"Knudsen's System of Wireless Transmission of Photographs," *Electrician,* May 1, 1908, pp. 89–90.

Marland, E. A., *Early Electrical Communication,* London, Abelard-Schuman, 1964 (esp. p. 115).

Moseley, S. A., and H. J. B. Chapple, *Television Today & Tomorrow,* London, Putnam & Sons, 1934.

"Newspictures Ignore Profits and Loss," *Fortune,* Sept. 1930 (esp. "Science and Newspictures: Telephoto," p. 108).

"Photographic Transmission Over Wires Is Accomplished" (item), *Telephone Engineer,* June 1924, p. 30.

"Portable Facsimile Device," *Mechanical Engineering,* June 1966, pp. 58–59.

Ranger, R. H., "Transmission and Reception of Photoradiograms," *Proceedings of the IRE,* April 1926, p. 177.

2 Fax Today

THERE is virtually no limit to the variety of applications to which facsimile uniquely lends itself as a communications medium. In the spectrum of communications techniques, it bridges the gap between mail and so-called "data" transmission—or, at a higher level of graphic complexity, between mail and closed-circuit TV.

In situations where delays of a day or more, as imposed by the postal system, are prohibitive, fax stands ready to get the message through in a matter of minutes—or seconds. It costs more, but the economic gap has been gradually narrowing.

As for its speedier and more sophisticated competitors, fax is preferable to data transmission from the standpoints of error rate and required operator training, and to closed-circuit TV from the economic standpoint. (This does not necessarily include slow-scan TV systems, or limited range systems intended for referencing of remotely stored documents.) What's more, fax has a decided edge over pure digital (nonfacsimile) techniques when it comes to the faithful—and economic—reproduction of complex graphics such as photographs, engineering drawings, signatures, and fingerprints.

Some current fax applications are briefly examined in the paragraphs that follow.

CURRENT APPLICATIONS

NEWSPICTURES

Historically, the distribution of newspictures ranks as one of the earliest fax applications (Chapter 1). It is also probably the only one that has assumed an independent identity, namely, as *telephotography,*[1] the generic name by which the newspicture process is known technically in the United

[1] Not to be confused with the taking of pictures through a telescopic lens, which is also called telephotography.

States, or *phototelegraphy,* as it is known in Europe. But while telephotography is often spoken of as a technique distinct from facsimile, it is in fact merely a branch of the fax art.

Through a complex communications network consisting of perhaps 40,000 miles of wire circuits alone, the two big American wire services—the Associated Press (AP) and United Press International (UPI)—furnish member newspapers throughout the United States with about 250 fax-transmitted news photos daily. The AP alone has more than 1000 recorders installed and in regular use.

In addition to wire circuits, both services exchange pictures with the rest of the world via transoceanic cable and radio facilities. The public telephone network is also used on occasion for special transmissions (or retransmissions) to individual papers.

A typical newspaper installation consists of one photographic recorder for each of the wire services to which the paper subscribes (typically, two machines—one for AP and one for UPI). These are usually located in a room convenient to the darkroom facilities in the paper's picture section. Larger papers may have two machines per service, to ensure that there is always one ready to record an incoming picture.

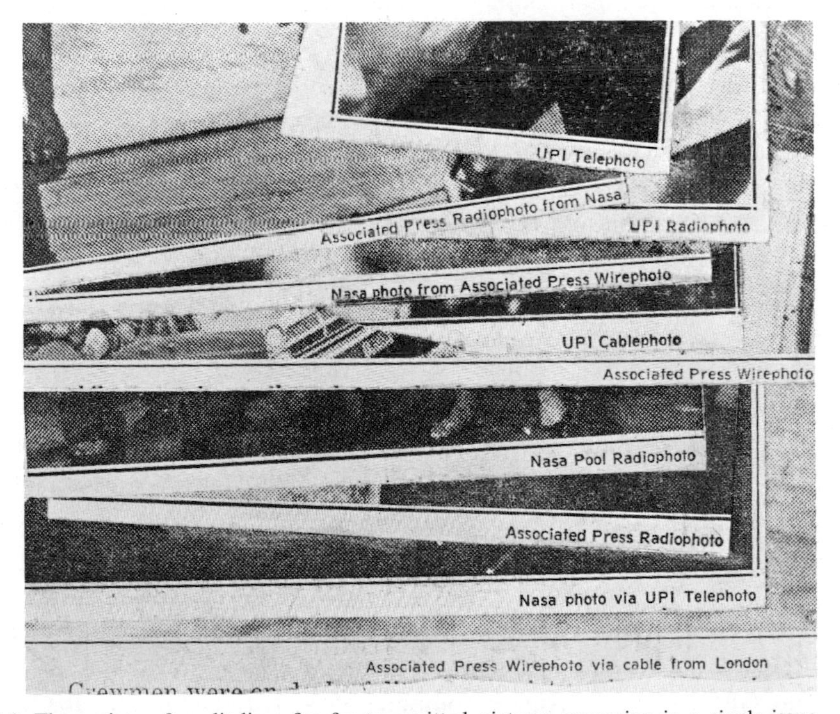

Fig. 2.1. The variety of credit lines for fax-transmitted pictures appearing in a single issue of a major daily newspaper should dispel any doubts as to the influence of facsimile in the field of journalism. (Source: New York *Daily News*.)

Pictures to be transmitted are usually briefly described over a loudspeaker via an auxiliary voice link with the wire service control desk. The loudspeaker may be placed near the picture editor's desk to enable him to decide in advance whether to bother loading a recorder to receive a given picture. Pictures are transmitted complete with captions.

Typically, although the paper may actually record and process 80 to 100 pictures a day, only a small fraction of these will actually be used. Roughly a third of all the pictures used in one edition of a large metropolitan daily are wire service pictures. Certain periods of the day are set aside for limited range transmission of pictures that are only of local or regional interest.

Direct fax recorders (no chemical processing required) have come into fairly wide use for the reception of newspictures. Where time is tight, they have proved useful in minimizing the delay between picture reception and photoengraving. Further, they are comparatively inexpensive to operate in terms of material costs. Picture editors have found direct recording useful as a way of "monitoring" a photographic machine in the sense that the completed picture can be rejected without taking the time to process the actual photographic recording.

Another fairly recent development is the automatic photographic recorder, which has its own chemical photo-processing facilities built in. These are becoming increasingly popular for newspicture reception.

WEATHER FORECASTING

Radio weather map service to ships at sea via facsimile was initiated experimentally in this country in 1930. From this important beginning evolved today's worldwide facsimile weather network.

Within the continental United States alone there are, at present, three principal facsimile weather map networks: the National Network (largest of the three); the High Altitude Network, or Aviation Meteorological Network (AMFAX), which provides up-to-the-minute upper atmosphere weather data to airports; and the Forecast Office Network (FOFAX), which dispatches raw data from a variety of sources, including earth-orbiting weather satellites. This composite of networks ties in, via shortwave radio, with ships at sea and with similar networks throughout the world.

At the hub of the three U.S. national fax networks is the National Meteorological Center (NMC) at Suitland, Maryland, just outside Washington, D.C. Into the NMC pours a daily volume of some 30,000 encoded reports representing raw data gathered by a vast complex of observation stations. The "stations" range from fixed land installations (from which the bulk of the reports are received) to ships at sea and commercial aircraft in flight.

The data collected by the NMC is methodically decoded and analyzed, and becomes the basis for plotting the maps. The maps are produced both manually and by high-speed computer-plotters. In either case, the finished product is the input to the fax nets.

Fig. 2.2. Location of terminals on the national facsimile network, largest of three fax networks maintained by the U.S. National Weather Service. (Courtesy U.S. National Weather Service.)

Fig. 2.3. Map transmission room at the Weather Service's National Meteorological Center in Suitland, Maryland. A comparative handful of fax scanners serve several hundred receiving terminals across the country. Transmission is monitored by the bank of recorders visible in the background and at the extreme right of the picture. (Courtesy Alden Electronics.)

Principal recipients of the fax-transmitted maps are local Weather Service offices and Forecast Centers all over the United States. In addition, certain maps and charts are dispatched by radio facsimile to ships at sea and to foreign countries. At the Forecast Centers, the facsimile maps are supplemented with additional data, and forecasts are prepared for the various news media, for airports, and for ocean-going vessels.

An exact count of the number of fax terminals in use within and around the United States (including ships at sea) for weather chart purposes would be difficult to obtain, but it can be reasonably estimated that there are a few thousand. The national network alone serves more than 900 receivers.

Supplementing the work of the NMC is the World Meteorological Organization's Regional Center for Tropical Meteorology in Miami. Through its Tropical Regional Analyses (TROPRAN) fax circuit, it provides tropical weather data to forecast offices in the southern states and Puerto Rico, and it serves as a link in the radioing of appropriate fax charts to the Caribbean-South America areas.

Means of speeding up the distribution of maps and of cutting transmission costs are constantly being explored by the U.S. National Weather Service. In the past few years, for example, a number of bandwidth compression devices have been installed at fax terminals to permit a doubling of the speed with which maps can be transmitted over ordinary telephone circuits.

COMMERCIAL

Facsimile has established itself in a variety of commercial applications, its capacity for improving communication efficiency having been demonstrated in at least three general areas:

1. the shipping of goods,
2. the expediting of customer orders,
3. the expediting of monetary transactions.

In the shipping of goods, fax is used effectively to transmit waybills, bills of lading, trucking manifests and the like from the point of origin to freight destinations along extensive rail, air, and highway shipping routes, or to central control locations.

At least one major freight-carrying airline fax-dispatches all of its air freight waybills from originating and receiving points within a limited geographic area to a main operations center, thus making it easier for shippers to track down cargoes. One advantage is that the operations center has an exact copy on hand, making it easier not only to answer questions, but also to make additions or corrections when necessary. Another is that no special training, as would be required of a teletype operator, is required to operate the fax equipment. In between waybills, the fax transmitters at the air terminals can be used to send periodic reports of operations to the center.

Similarly, railroads have found fax useful for the dispatching of "train consists"—lists of rolling stock constituting the various trains, formerly sent by mail or teletype. When mail was used, shipments frequently arrived ahead

Fig. 2.4. Bank of high-speed fax recorders at a rail freight control center. Waybills are dispatched here from key points along a 10,000-mile rail network. (Courtesy Xerox Corp.)

of the "consists," resulting in further delays. And while teletype is fast and relatively inexpensive, fax eliminates the need for data conversion and minimizes the chance for error in conversion and transmission. One U.S. railroad operates a waybill-dispatching fax system covering over 10,000 rail miles, and another uses a number of special, high-speed terminals (ten documents a minute) for the same purpose in a private microwave network covering 900 miles.

As for the expediting of customer orders, fax systems are used for this purpose by a number of manufacturing and service firms whose operations are, by nature, decentralized. One major eastern steel firm, for example, maintains more than 50 fax terminals to link its 18 district sales offices to its general offices. Formal orders received on the customer's own letterheads are fax-dispatched by the district offices to the main office, along with forms containing pertinent supplementary information, which the district offices provide. Within six minutes of insertion of an order into the fax scanner at the district office, processing of the order can begin at the main office. Errors are virtually eliminated.

The system also permits more effective communication of inquiries and order changes, each of which formerly consumed the time of two people engaging in a long-distance phone conversation in which the risk of communication errors ran comparatively high.

This system is more or less typical of similar ones in use in other industries, but fax is also finding considerable use in the expediting of orders for service, as opposed to commodities. Utilities, in particular, have discovered that in some ways it is more practical to relay customer service orders by fax than

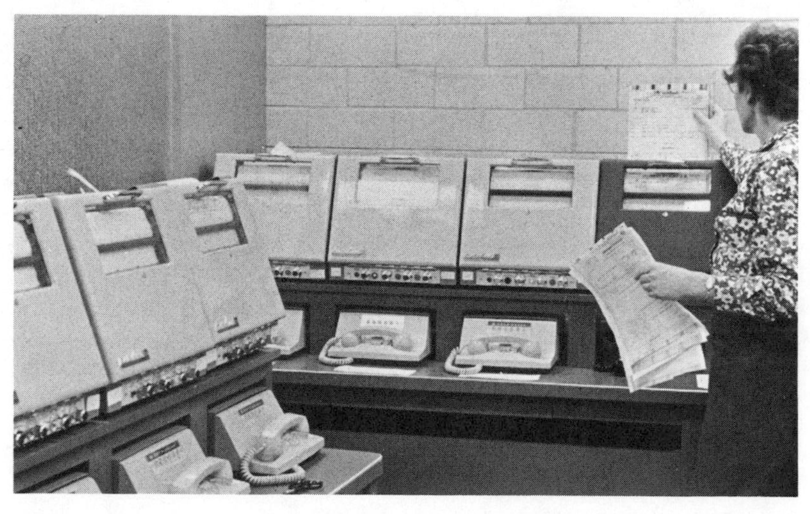

Fig. 2.5. Customer orders are received via fax at the main office of a big steel firm from scattered district offices. (Courtesy Bethlehem Steel.)

Fig. 2.6. Special fax scanner used by banks for signature verification. The system makes centrally stored customer signature cards readily available to outlying branches. (Courtesy Alden Electronics.)

by the more conventional method of teletyping them to the various departments concerned. For one thing, it eliminates the need for trained teletype operators, and for another, it minimizes errors and therefore expedites the satisfactory completion of service obligations.

Legend has it that, as far back as the late 1920s, a million dollar transatlantic business deal was saved by the successful transmission of some vital signatures from New York to London via radiofacsimile. Since then, the use of facsimile in the expediting of monetary transactions has become almost commonplace.

A number of banks use fax regularly today to verify signatures on withdrawal slips or other transaction forms where comparatively large sums of money are involved. Verification can be made while the customer waits, even though the depositors' signature file may be located several miles away. Special fax equipment has been developed for the purpose and is sold commercially.

Fax lends itself to a variety of other banking applications as well. A Chicago bank, for example, uses it to dispatch stop payment notices on checks from the bookkeeping office where the notice is received to the main office in another part of the city. And, in another Midwestern city, several auto dealerships maintain fax links with a local bank in connection with the bank's auto financing program. A car buyer completes an application for financing, which is then fax-dispatched direct from showroom to bank to be examined and processed. Within a little over an hour, the dealer—and the customer, if he chooses to wait—will know whether the application has been approved or denied.

PUBLISHING

The publishing industry uses facsimile in essentially three ways:

1. to expedite graphic communication between editorial offices and printing facilities,
2. to dispatch news copy from satellite offices or bureaus to a paper's main newsroom,
3. to eliminate duplication of typesetting effort between separate printing facilities.

A number of periodical publishers have found fax well suited for the interchange of material between geographically separated departments. Typically, manuscripts ready to be set in type are transmitted from the editorial offices to the printer, who, in turn, wires back proofs ("galleys," page proofs, etc.) of the typeset material for proofreading. If there are corrections or revisions to be made, and if the fax system is capable of producing a readable second generation facsimile of its own output, the marked proofs can then be fax-transmitted back to the printer.

Assuming that the material formerly had to go by mail, fax can save a publisher several days of production time—a saving that could prove vital when there are last-minute revisions to be made in the face of a fast-approaching deadline.

Besides connecting editorial offices with printing facilities, fax is also used to some extent as the link between a newspaper's main news room and its satellite offices. The *Wall Street Journal,* for example, uses fax to dispatch copy from its Washington Bureau to the newsroom in New York. And in Quincy, Massachusetts, the *Patriot-Ledger* maintains a similar link with its news office in Norwood, some 15 miles away.

One of the more highly specialized fax applications in the publishing industry—and one that appears to be catching on quite rapidly—concerns the operation of satellite printing plants by large periodical publishers. Again, the *Wall Street Journal* is a case in point. It maintains satellite plants for its Eastern and Pacific Coast editions. To avoid having to duplicate all of the various steps associated with letterpress printing, the main and satellite plants in each case are linked together by a special fax system that permits final page proofs from the main plant's presses to be transmitted to the satellite plant and recorded as photographic masters for a less involved printing process. That way, typesetting is necessary at only one plant, and page proofs from that plant can be sent simultaneously to any number of

Fig. 2.7. Fax transmitter for full-size newspaper pages. A companion recorder at a satellite printing plant reproduces the transmitted page proof as a photographic printing master. (Courtesy Muirhead.)

satellite plants. The *Journal's* two fax-linked West Coast plants are separated by about 400 miles, and the two East Coast plants by about 150 miles.

A Japanese newspaper, *Asahi Shimbun,* pioneered the use of such systems, having established the first one in 1959, linking its main Tokyo plant to a satellite plant in Sapporo, some 500 miles away. The equipment was developed and produced by Muirhead of England. Since then, other Asian papers and several in Europe and other scattered parts of the world have adopted the system, and at least three other fax manufacturers around the world have developed (and are presently producing) equipment to implement it. Data compression devices have recently been introduced to make the broad bandwidth transmissions more economical over long distance.

Besides the *Wall Street Journal,* other users of such systems in the United States include *Business Week* and a southwestern newspaper chain—the Palmer Newspapers of Camden, Arkansas.

ENGINEERING AND MANUFACTURING

Liaison between a manufacturer's engineering and production facilities, or between separated engineering facilities working on different aspects of the same project, has been greatly enhanced by the use of facsimile. An aircraft concern in California, for example, exchanges engineering data via fax with subcontractors in two southern states and in Canada. The graphic data transmitted, such as engineering sketches, columns of figures, or curves representing test data, supplement telephoned technical discussions between engineers at the separated facilities. The result, in this particular instance, is a far more efficient exchange of complex information than would otherwise be possible.

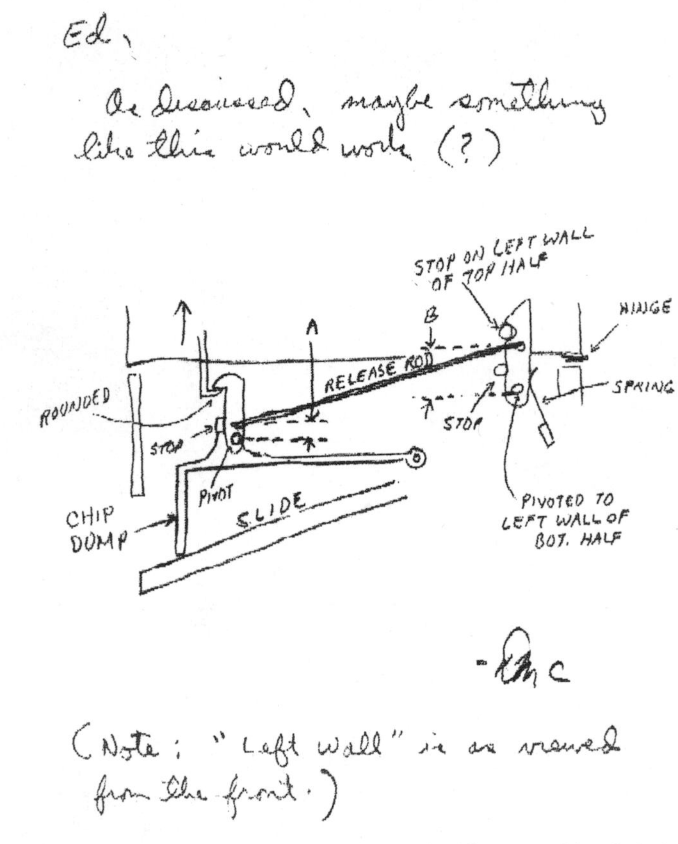

Fig. 2.8. Fax-transmitted engineering sketch. Imagine trying to describe even this relatively simple sketch orally by phone.

Once a product is in production, or a plant is being tooled for production, fax can also be quite useful for dispatching engineering *change orders* from the firm's engineering department to the distant plant—particularly if the product is very complex.

Let us assume that the engineering department has discovered a flaw in the design of a new electronic device that is being mass-produced on a rush basis in a plant 1000 miles away. An engineering change has been worked out that will effectively eliminate the flaw. The units are being turned out at the rate of ten an hour and, for each unit already produced, the change will cost about $50 to make (in manpower and wasted components).

The question is, do you stop production and leave an entire production unit idle for the time it takes to get the change order to the plant? Or do you keep producing at the risk of losing several thousand additional dollars in modification costs? Or do you utilize a fax system to dispatch the necessary paperwork to the plant in a matter of minutes?

The choice will depend, of course, on the operating cost of the fax system as compared with the cost of occasional production delays that might result without it.

Still another application of fax in the engineering realm is its use by oil companies in the drilling of offshore wells. A drilling foreman on a platform some 75 miles from shore sends drilling logs by radiofacsimile to a land-based geologist to determine whether to begin installing a casing in a well. The offshore rig, with its 45-man crew, costs the oil company an estimated $14,000 a day to operate. So, every minute saved is worth about $10.

One oil company reportedly maintains nearly 100 radiofacsimile links to drilling platforms in the Gulf of Mexico.

LAW ENFORCEMENT

Facsimile has proved quite effective for the dispatching of fingerprints and "mug shots" from one location to another by law enforcement agencies. The Police Department of the City of Chicago, for one, has maintained, for the past several years, a fax net between its Central Headquarters Identification Section and 19 outlying districts.

The system works like this: a criminal suspect, upon being booked at a local precinct house, is photographed with a Polaroid camera and fingerprinted. Within minutes, the combined mug shot and fingerprint are fax-dispatched to Central Headquarters, where, with the aid of efficient file retrieval techniques, a quick check can be made as to whether the suspect has a past record. By speeding up the checking process, the use of facsimile helps reduce detention time and expedites the administration of justice.

In New York State a statewide fax law enforcement network is operated by the State Police, and, in England and Germany, police departments have experimented with a system in which mug shots of suspects are radioed from headquarters directly to patrol cars. Similar mobile fax systems were experimented with in this country some 25 years ago, but were found impractical because of the state of the technology at that time. However, as this is being written, at least two fax equipment manufacturers—Datalog (formerly Litcom) and Muirhead—are preparing to market newly developed mobile systems.

The same two firms presently offer stationary police facsimile systems as part of their commercial line. The systems are designed to afford the comparatively high resolution needed for the faithful reproduction of fingerprints—about 200 scan lines to the inch—and therefore lend themselves to other applications where high-definition reproduction is required.

MESSAGES

The term "message facsimile" probably originated with fax's adoption by the Western Union Telegraph Company in the 1930s as an automatic message-sending medium, the main object of which was to permit the

MISSING PERSON FAX DISPATCH

DATED November 1, 1970

NAME Bruno Nagitsock

LAST SEEN (DATE) October 31 (6 p.m.)

IN VICINITY OF Pendleton and Wyndmoor, in Edison

LAST SEEN WEARING black trousers, long black coat

BUILD slender HAIR black

EYES hazel HEIGHT 6' 7"

AGE 63 SEX M RACE cauc.

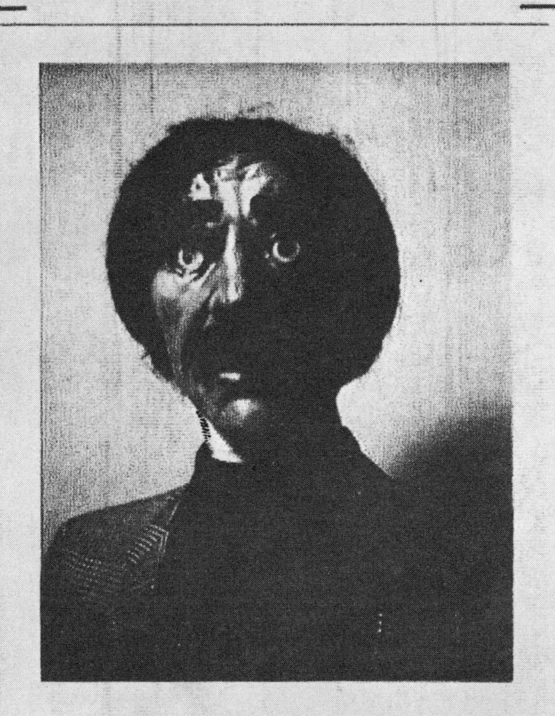

MISSING PERSON

Fig. 2.9. A police application of facsimile. Reports such as this can be dispatched via radio to hundreds of patrol cars simultaneously and received automatically (with about the same quality as you see here) on compact, dashboard-mounted recorders. (The report illustrated is, of course, fictitious.)

sending of hand-written "messages" to the nearest WU office via scanners (some of them coin-operated) in bus terminals, apartment house lobbies, etc. Upon receipt at the telegraph office, the message could then go out over the wire in the usual manner. The idea of exchanging urgent messages by facsimile subsequently caught on in the business community, and today it ranks as one of the principal uses of the medium.

To say that the sending of messages is a principal use of facsimile is perhaps a rather equivocal statement to make in view of the difficulty of drawing a clear distinction between simple messages and commercial or technical communications. "Will arrive Penn Station at 5:30" and "Try substituting these values: . . ." are both messages, the basic distinction being that one is personal and the other technical.

The author's concept of a true message facsimile system, as the term is generally applied in business and industry today, is a system that is used for graphic communications *in general* and does not have any one specific function, like the dispatching of weather maps or customer orders. A great many decentralized businesses today maintain fax systems for the exchange of everything from budget reports to engineering sketches.

Although an occasional remnant of it may still be found in a hotel lobby or airline terminal here and there, Western Union's original automatic message facsimile system has been essentially phased out. One of the

Fig. 2.10. Receive and transmit units for an automatic facsimile telegraph system. (Courtesy Western Union.)

problems with it, according to G. H. Ridings, who had helped develop it, was the vulnerability of slot-type transmitters to abuse of various sorts. Besides their convenience as receptacles for gum and candy wrappers, hairpins, and similar refuse, Ridings points out that the design of the units ". . . made it easy for hoodlums to shock our central office personnel by sending sketches and poetry of the type found on public washroom walls."[2]

On the other hand, Desk-Fax, a later Western Union development that has made it possible for a businessman to send short messages via a telegraph central office direct from his desk, has been eminently successful. As of August 1970 there were nearly 30,000 of the compact Desk-Fax transceivers in operation throughout the United States.

In Japan, a telegraph message system employing conventional fax scanners is currently in operation by the Nippon Telegraph & Telephone Corporation for relaying telegrams between collecting offices and main stations.

LIBRARIES

While the idea of facilitating interlibrary loans by use of facsimile has great appeal, the fact is that, to date, most such systems that have been tried have, at best, proved only marginally feasible. Among the major library systems that have run trials, and were apparently not sufficiently satisfied with the results to adopt the trial system as a regular service, are those of New York State, the University of California, and the University of Nevada. One of the few that is presently operating, apparently to the full satisfaction of its administrators, is the one in the library system of the Pennsylvania State University.

One reason library fax systems—or telefacsimile systems, as library people prefer to call them—have failed is that there is usually a great deal of time lost in manually processing the requests at both ends of the system, a factor that remains unchanged with the adoption of facsimile. In addition, where the average single request is for a number of pages (of a book, document, etc.), the problem of queuing is introduced, and a traffic jam ensues at the transmit station—especially where a straight, voice-grade fax system is used and transmission is therefore relatively slow.

But the biggest reason for failure is that the systems generally cannot be economically justified. The University of California trial of March 1967, involving a high-speed fax system between two campus libraries 65 miles apart, is a case in point. While the average turnaround time between a request and its fulfillment was reduced from six or seven days to about a day by initiation of the trial system, the cost of each 10-page transaction at a volume of 500 transactions a month came to about $10. At 100 transac-

[2] Quoted from Ridings' article, "Facsimile Communications, Past, Present, Future," in the November 1962 issue of *Signal,* official journal of the Armed Forces Communications and Electronics Association.

tions a month, the cost per transaction would have been $40. A survey of users of the service indicated that the need for the transmitted material was not urgent enough to justify the high cost.

The library fax system that is currently in regular operation at Penn State does not have the usual objective of facilitating research by students and faculty, but rather is intended to support the teaching program by supplementing the limited book collections available at a given campus library. The faculty member is thus aided in the preparation of his courses by having a much broader range of material quickly available to him than he would have if he had to rely on what was available locally. The system adopted is by no means an elaborate one, consisting as it does of inexpensive transceivers coupled to telephone sets. However, it serves its purpose and has been judged successful by its administrators.

Perhaps the most sophisticated library fax trial conducted to date is that currently in progress as part of Project Intrex at the Massachusetts Institute of Technology. Intrex is an experiment in information retrieval that could lead to an actual working system, capable of making a wide variety of research material available on demand through human interaction with a computer. As part of the project, a high-speed electronic fax system has been developed to deliver the requested material in the form of strips of microfilm, which must be placed in a viewer to be read. Preliminary demonstrations of the system have been impressive, and its further development is being closely watched by other large university libraries and by all who are concerned with the current information explosion. Once Intrex has evolved into an operating system and has proved its utility, it may well become the model for similar systems in other large libraries and information centers.

So, while there may not be many working library fax systems at the present time, it is an application that has potential.

MISCELLANEOUS

Fax is also used in a number of ways that are not sufficiently widespread to warrant general classification. Just a few of these need be mentioned to complete the picture of the medium's innate versatility.

A big electric utility uses it to relay trouble reports to emergency service crews, the original incoming report being written on a card by a telephone contact clerk, who thereupon promptly inserts the card into the appropriate fax transmitter. The report reaches its destination in about the same time it would take to relay it by phone—but with less chance of error, and with the advantage that, while it is being transmitted, the clerk is left free to handle other calls.

A widely marketed office machine utilizes the fax principle to produce stencils for stencil duplicators. The machine is, in essence, a fax scanner and recorder, mechanically and electrically coupled in a single compact unit.

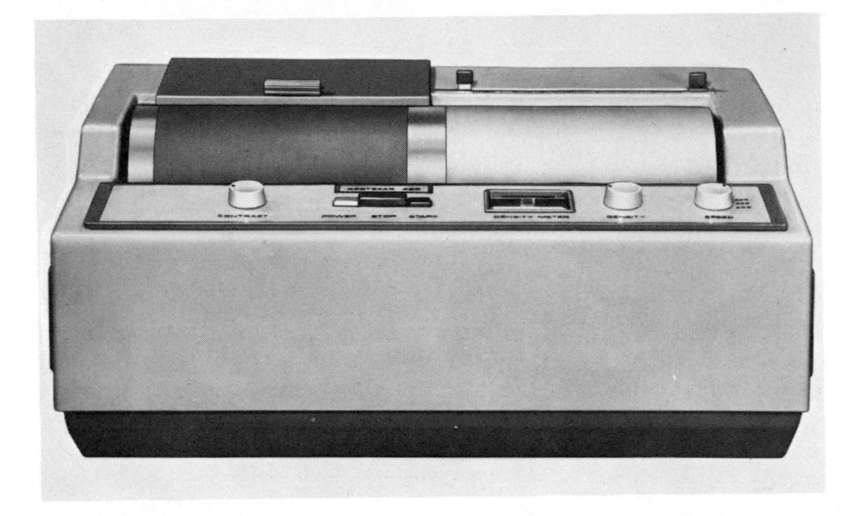

Fig. 2.11. Fax stencil maker. The scanner portion at the right "transmits" the original document to the recorder portion at the left, where it is reproduced as a duplication master. (Courtesy Gestetner Corp.)

The original item to be duplicated is scanned photoelectrically and reproduced on the special stencil paper by a kind of arcing process. Scanning and reproduction take place side by side. (It is often possible, incidentally, to produce reproduction masters for various duplicating processes on conventional fax recorders, in place of the usual "hard copy.")

There are also military applications. Polaroid photos of enemy positions, for example, are radioed to command posts from fax transmitters mounted in reconnaissance vehicles. And, from central microfilm files in a protected area, drawings and parts lists are remotely retrieved by fax, *as needed,* to facilitate the repair of helicopters at the fringes of a battle zone.

Fax has also been used to transmit x-ray photos from hospitals to analysis centers, to record the output of electron microscopes, to dispatch railroad passenger tickets from a main reservation office to local agencies, and to provide the crews of fishing boats with print-outs of fishing conditions and other pertinent information. Both technically and functionally, it is a versatile tool whose potential for new and unusual applications remains practically limitless.

VIRTUES

Most of fax's advantages over competing media have already revealed themselves in the preceding pages. It might be useful, however, to review these briefly and, at the same time, to examine them in more detail.

FASTER THAN MAIL

Herein lies one of fax's prime justifications for existence: its ability to deliver a document or picture (or at least a reasonable facsimile thereof) in minutes or seconds as compared with days. A quick glance down the list of specific applications described in the preceding section will reveal that better than 75 percent of them involve the need to expedite delivery of the items involved. It is hard to imagine newspictures or weather maps, for example, ever having been delivered by any means except fax.

One might argue that, if electrical transmission is to be adopted anyway as the means for delivery, there are faster and possibly cheaper techniques available. The argument has merit, but much depends on the nature of the material being sent—which brings us to another of facsimile's prime attributes.

INPUT FLEXIBILITY

True, documents can be sent by digital techniques at the rate of more than 300 characters a second over ordinary telephone lines, which amounts to sending the contents of a typical, one-page, single-spaced business letter in about four seconds. To send the same item, a fax system roughly comparable in cost and transmission bandwidth would require about six *minutes*.

So, for pure alphanumeric material we can say that, from the standpoint of speed, digital techniques have an edge over fax. Let us be sure, though, to qualify this by pointing out that the speed advantage really applies only to machine-originated communication, e.g., telemetry, or the output of a computer. Anytime conversion to an encoded form is required prior to actual communication, the time so consumed must be included in any speed comparison between fax and digital (or so-called "data") techniques.

Human beings seldom, if ever, originate communication in coded form. Where an $8\frac{1}{2} \times 11$-inch page of information must be encoded via a manual keyboard for transmission, the time consumed is normally about twice that for sending the same material via one of the slower fax systems.

But it is in the area of graphic communication—the sending of maps, diagrams, photographs, etc.—that fax really proves its worth. Although digital techniques have advanced to the point where they can be used to transmit simple graphics as well as alphanumerics with relative ease and economy, the general rule has been that, as the graphics increase in complexity, these techniques become sharply less economical and reliable.

In the simplest digital systems for the transmission of graphics, symbols must usually be rigidly standardized, limited in number, and inputted manually with a keyboard. More elaborate (and expensive) systems may employ Optical Character Recognition (OCR) or other highly sophisticated techniques to permit insertion of the original item directly into a scanner. But, in the present state of the art, even these systems are limited in the variety of symbols they can recognize and accurately reproduce. (Redundancy reduction techniques, which are also usually digital, will be discussed later.)

By contrast, the same comparatively simple fax system that is used to exchange business correspondence and other types of alphanumeric material can, without alteration, faithfully reproduce a reasonably complex sketch, chart, map, or photograph as well. It is this intrinsic indifference to complexity or variety of input that, perhaps more than anything else, makes fax hard to beat as a graphic communications medium.

ERROR IMMUNITY

There are two characteristics of the fax process that make it inherently less susceptible to error than competing digital communications media. One is that, although it segments copy into lines in the process, it subsequently reconstructs its input as a unified whole; that is, as a camera or office copier would reproduce it, making no distinction between essential and nonessential details. And the other, very closely related to the first, is that it analyzes and reproduces its input on an element-by-element basis, and not as a sequence of codes representing the components of which the input consists. These characteristics generally apply whether the transmitted fax signal is analog or digital in nature (with the exception of systems in which "digitizing" is for the purpose of compressing the signal).

The distinction between elements and components is significant here. Component, in this instance, means a character (number or letter) which is, in turn, composed of a number of elements. In a conventional fax system having a scan density of 96 lines per inch, a $\frac{1}{8}$-inch-high letter A would be dissected by 12 scan lines, and would be represented in the transmitted signal by a total of about 22 *elemental* pulses (Fig. 2.12).

In a data system the same letter A would be translated into a binary code, such as 1000001, which would be represented in the transmitted signal by only seven pulses (one for each of the *bits* in the code). If any of these binary pulses were lost in transmission, or if, as a result of external electrical interference, one or more pulses were incorrectly recognized, a different code would result and an entirely different character would be printed at the receiving end of the system.

However, if one, or even a few, of the 22 pulses representing the character in the *fax* signal were changed, the effect on the reproduced character would be scarcely detectable.

Although the data system has the capability of indicating when it has made an error, it usually cannot report the nature of the error. Thus, where errors are indicated, and they are significant, retransmission is generally necessary, a fact that must be considered in assessing the data system's speed advantage.

With a fax system, even when the transmitted signal is in digital form,

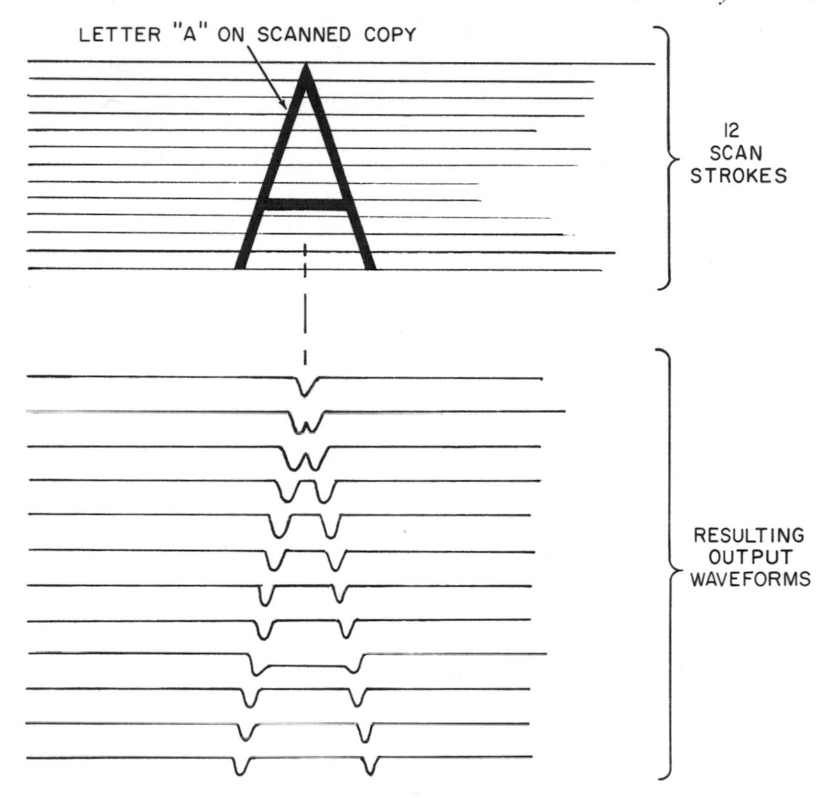

Fig. 2.12. Letter "A," dissected by 12 scan strokes, takes the form of some 22 electrical "blips" in the transmitted picture signal. The blips constituting a single character may be spread out over several seconds of time.

with codes representing gray levels, as long as it is on an element-by-element basis, errors will not have a significant effect on output integrity. In fact, tests performed in connection with the trial of an all-digital newspaper page facsimile system, in February 1968, revealed that the effect of error rates as high as one in 100 in a digital fax system may not even be perceptible in the output.[3]

NO SPECIAL TRAINING

There have been, and no doubt still are, facsimile machines that require a measure of skill to operate. The trend, however, has been toward a steady improvement in simplicity of operation. Most of the fax gear in use today can be operated by nonskilled personnel after only a few minutes of instruction.

[3]See ANPA Research Institute's *R. I. Bulletin* #949, March 18, 1968.

This is an attribute that makes fax especially attractive in situations where the dispatching of high volumes of alphanumeric data is required, and where an employee turnover problem makes it difficult to retain a staff of suitably skilled operators of keyboard type transmitting equipment. The problem of securing skilled personnel to perform comparatively menial tasks has been growing increasingly acute throughout industry. But, at least in this one area—data communications—fax has proved effective as a ready and relatively inexpensive solution.

ESSENTIALLY AUTOMATIC

Fax's simplicity of operation is due largely to the fact that it is essentially an automatic process. Apart from the training required, operation of a keyboard type data transmitter keeps an individual occupied throughout transmission (or throughout the preparation of a tape, which amounts to the same thing), whereas operation of a fax transmitter requires only as much of the individual's time as is needed to insert the copy.

Many modern fax systems have been automated to the point where they can operate completely unattended. Recording paper is automatically fed from a roll long enough to produce a few hundred $8\frac{1}{2} \times 11$-inch copies, and an automatic feeding accessory at the transmitter permits loading of a stack of documents, for feeding into the scanner one at a time. In addition,

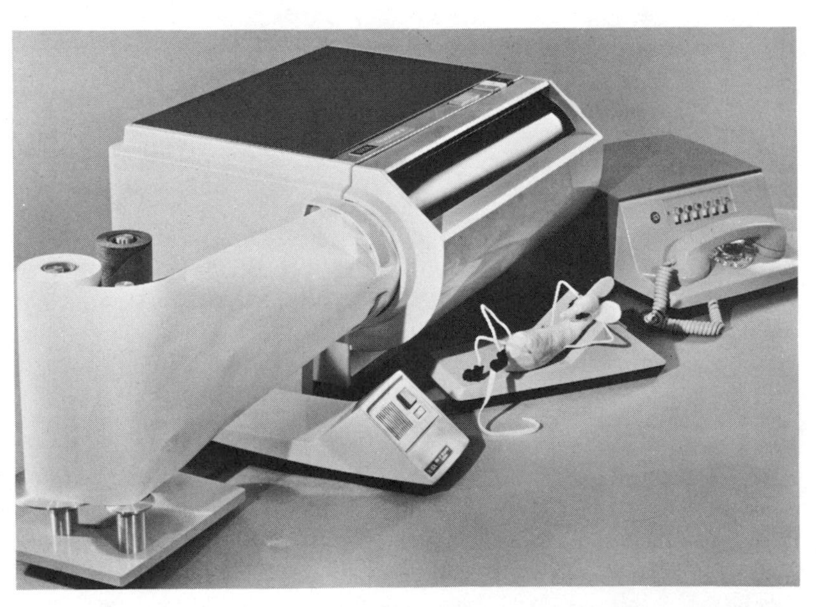

Fig. 2.13. Automatic paper feed permits a fax recorder to continue receiving after an office has closed down for the day. (The mouse suggests an office vacant of people.) (Courtesy Xerox Corp.)

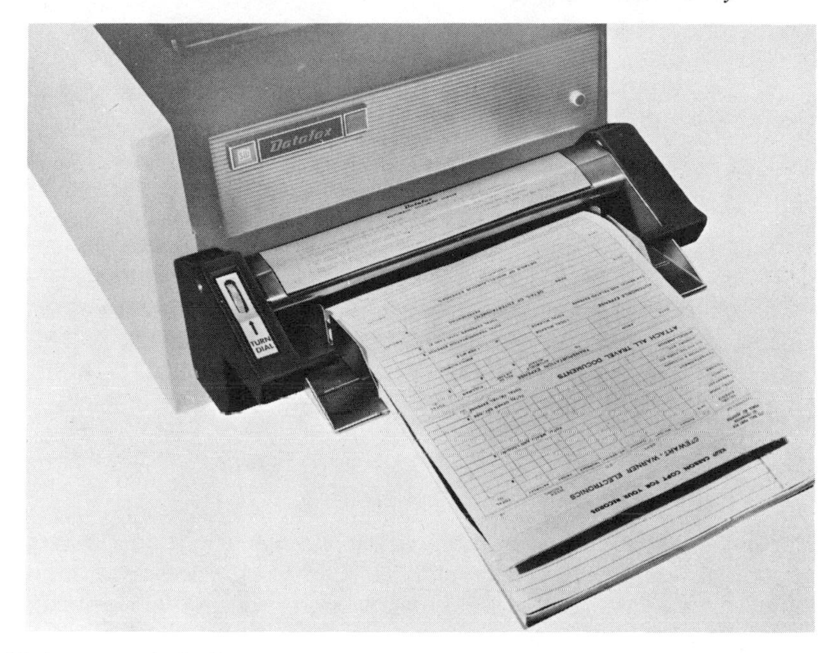

Fig. 2.14. An automatic feeding accessory attached to a fax scanner is usually all it takes to make a modern fax system completely automatic. (Courtesy Stewart-Warner.)

most modern fax receivers feature automatic answer and "hang-up" capabilities.

Besides saving on labor, a fully automated system of this sort makes it possible to take advantage of the lower nighttime phone rates, utilize leased lines more efficiently by keeping them in use at times when they would normally be idle, and continue communicating with a branch office in a different time zone after one location or the other has closed down for the day.

FLEXIBILITY THROUGH TRADE-OFFS

Facsimile is not a live medium as is voice communication and conventional TV. In other words, it is not committed to recreating a sequence of changes with respect to a time frame. Like other so-called "data" communication systems, it can be operated as slowly as is tolerable or as rapidly as transmission and economic parameters will permit, so long as it preserves proper spatial relationships and reasonable fidelity of dark-light—or mark-space—transitions.

It is thus a comparatively flexible medium. If a fax user wants to utilize an existing phone line as his transmission medium, he can obtain equipment compatible with that choice. However, he must be willing to trade quality and/or transmission speed for the bandwidth economy he gains.

If, on the other hand, speed is desired, fax systems are available for a variety of transmission speeds. Here again, some trading is necessary, and it is usually bandwidth economy that is sacrificed. With sufficient funds to pay for the broad bandwidth required, one can have a system that is both fast and capable of high resolution output.

Trade-offs will be discussed at greater length in subsequent chapters.

LIMITATIONS

So far in this chapter, fax has been represented as a kind of paragon of perfection among communications media. Obviously, along with its many virtues, it has certain limitations. The important ones are examined in the next several paragraphs.

REDUNDANCY

It is the nature of a conventional fax system to examine every square fraction of a millimeter of the physical item transmitted (with the possible exclusion of upper and lower margins), and to transmit an electrical analog of what it sees, even when it sees absolutely nothing. In other words, a large portion of the transmitted signal represents the blank space in margins and between characters, words, and lines of information.

In the transmission of a typical one-page business letter, for example, containing a total of about 250 words, the proportion of the total signal representing the actual "marks" necessary to reconstruct the letter at the recorder is roughly five percent. (This is based on 9350 scan-inches for the entire $8\frac{1}{2} \times 11$-inch sheet, of which 1520 contain "pulse trains" whose "black" elements represent an estimated average of $\frac{10}{32}$ of each pulse train inch.) The proportion for a simple sketch would be less yet.

It was pointed out that fax and voice communication differ basically with respect to the comparative significance of time as a transmission variable. However, from the standpoint of transmission efficiency, the two have much in common. Both demand considerably more channel space than they actually need for the amount of information they convey. In information theory terminology, their signals are said to be *redundant.*

A number of techniques have been devised to reduce transmission redundancy or required bandwidth, but while these techniques improve efficiency from the standpoint of reducing transmission time or permitting use of lower grade facilities, they usually impose a higher terminal cost, which, depending on the volume of messages transmitted, can result in a net loss economically. Moreover, in most such systems, binary codes are substituted for all, or part, of the original analog signal, and the margin for error decreases accordingly.

More will be said of redundancy reduction in subsequent sections.

RELATIVE SLOWNESS

Fax has capitalized appropriately on the fact that it is considerably faster and more direct than mail. But, measured against our conditioned space-age expectations—particularly as they concern anything electronic—it often gives the impression of being a ponderously slow way of communicating electrically. The characteristic redundancy of its signaling process, and what this means in terms of bandwidth requirements, does, in fact, place fax among the more sluggish of the electrical communications media.

Its comparative slowness becomes apparent when we compare two hypothetical information retrieval systems in which the material transmitted is limited to the contents of a central store arranged for remote access by phone or by telegraphed retrieval codes. In one system, the central store consists of the actual documents containing the original data, an arrangement that makes facsimile the logical transmission medium. In the other system, the data has been extracted from the documents and stored in binary form on magnetic tape, which permits use of a straight digital transmission mode with high-speed teleprinters or CRT display units as the output hardware.

Both systems use regular telephone circuits as links between the inquiry stations and the central store. But in the fax system, the information contained on a single document page takes from three to six minutes to transmit, whereas in the digital system, the same information is sent in a matter of seconds.

Speed is, of course, only one consideration in choosing between fax and digital systems. Other factors influencing the choice would be the degree to which graphics are to be handled along with alphanumerics; the comparative terminal costs; and, in the case of the digital system, the costs associated with data conversion and storage.

VULNERABILITY TO TRANSMISSION IMPAIRMENTS

When we hook an oscilloscope to the output of an audio system, we are likely to see a certain amount of "hash" and other imperfections that are not apparent to the ear. Likewise, transmission impairments that go essentially unnoticed in voice communication may have a drastic effect on the quality of a fax recording.

Much has been done in recent years to minimize the effects of transmission impairments on fax signals. FM has been adopted, for example, to reduce the effect of characteristic variations in transmission level in telephone circuits, and *amplitude quantizing* techniques have been applied to permit reshaping of fax signals into discrete pulses that are unaffected by moderate amounts of "noise."

But, in spite of these efforts, fax signals remain vulnerable to the effects of a variety of transmission phenomena, the more important of which will be explored in some detail in subsequent chapters.

SERVICING DIFFICULTIES

Locating the source of trouble in an erratically operating facsimile system can be a problem, particularly where the system contains only two terminals. Typically, the terminals are separated by a matter of miles, and the connecting link is controlled by someone other than the firm responsible for servicing the terminals. Relatively few of the troubles normally encountered in such a system can be predictably isolated to a given point.

Of course, this is not a unique problem; it is common to all electrical communications systems where two or more separated terminals are interconnected by wire or radio. In most cases, however, it is a problem that we (as customers) have come to take for granted. In the case of the telephone, for example, where servicing is the common carrier's problem, we tend to ignore the fact that a huge force of technicians is constantly at work keeping the system going. And in the case of commercial radio and TV, the customer himself can usually determine whether the trouble is at the transmit or receive ends of the system simply by a twist of the station selector knob.

Locating the source of trouble in a fax system is usually not quite that simple. True, some terminals lend themselves to "self-testing" by the ability to hook send and receive units back-to-back to help isolate the trouble. This is possible even with some transceivers. But, self-test features notwithstanding, it is usually advisable that a firm providing fax terminals for lease, or selling service on purchased gear, be prepared to provide *coordinated* service between geographically separated terminal locations.

LACK OF STANDARDS

Of the various makes of commercially marketed facsimile terminal units (transmitters, receivers, and transceivers), few are compatible with each other. Unfortunately, standardization has been somewhat lax in the fax industry.

Within large fax networks, certain basic standards have naturally had to be adopted. Networks for the gathering and distribution of weather data are an example. At least within each of the various aspects of the overall system—e.g., map distribution and the reception of cloud cover photos from satellites—there is standardization, and we find fax equipment of several different makes linked together within a network.

Also, within the Associated Press's national network for the distribution of news pictures, there are several different makes and types of receivers in use, all of which must conform to established transmission standards. (There is less of this in the competing UPI net, inasmuch as UPI produces much of its own terminal equipment.)

But, outside of these long-established and inherently widespread networks, the standardization situation is generally disappointing. Suppose, for example, the personnel at one terminal of a fax network within a decentralized business concern are dissatisfied with some characteristic of the recordings they have to handle. Perhaps there is a tendency for the copy to smudge, or it may have a chemical odor that some persons find objectionable. Chances are the choice of an alternative piece of equipment that will be compatible with the rest of the machines in the system will be extremely limited—if, indeed, there is any choice at all.

Similarly, when someone with a telephone-coupled fax terminal wants to communicate via the dial network with a party at another location, he first has to ascertain that the two terminals are compatible. This can be as much a problem within a company as between companies. Imagine how it would be if a similar situation prevailed for voice communication by phone!

It has been something of a problem that, whenever a fax manufacturer introduces a significant technological advance, such as an appreciable boost in transmission speed with existing communication facilities, it tends to make obsolete (in spirit, at least) a good many existing installations. Unquestionably, the stimulation of product improvement through competition is to be encouraged, but where it concerns the multiple terminals of a relatively large network, which, *collectively,* may be periodically rendered obsolete by new advances, it can confront systems planners with an uncomfortably unstable situation.

Actually, considerable standards work *has* been done in the facsimile field by several organizations, and certain formal standards have been adopted and are strictly adhered to in various areas of fax communication. (More on this in Chapter 7.) It is in the broad area of general purpose, or so-called "message," fax that standardization has been perhaps least effective.

The Electronic Industries Association's standard of 96 scan lines per inch (LPI) and 180 lines per minute (LPM) for message fax systems has been widely adhered to by manufacturers. But the problem often facing the customer or user is that, while a transmitter and receiver—or two transceivers—of different makes may both conform to the 96/180 standard, each may use a different system of modulation (one may be FM and the other AM), or each may employ different phasing and synchronizing schemes. Any such variations will make the units incompatible, despite adherence to established resolution and scan rate standards.

Further, there has been a notable trend lately toward the adoption of scan rates higher than 180 LPM, usually accompanied by some degree of resolution degradation. Popular alternative speeds are 240 and 360 LPM, and scan resolutions of 90 and fewer lines per inch appear to be gaining in acceptance.

TRENDS

In the first section of this chapter we examined some of the areas in which fax is actively utilized at the present time. Now, to round out the picture, it might be well to examine briefly some current and emerging trends, to get some idea of what new dimensions the medium is beginning to assume and in what new directions it appears to be headed.

FAX BY PHONE

The use of the public switched telephone network—the dial network—for facsimile communication is not entirely new. Phone couplers for the purpose have been around since the 1930s, although they were seldom used until quite recently. In 1963, the common carriers made available devices to interface electrically with fax machines and condition their signals for transmission over the telephone network.

What had already begun to develop as a trend, facsimile via the dial network, was given fresh impetus in the middle and late 1960s by the emergence of a new breed of relatively compact, desk-top transceiver, specially designed for the purpose. At the same time, restrictions on connection of "foreign" (noncommon-carrier) devices to telephone lines were eased, with the result that simpler, less expensive direct hookup arrangements have become available and more of the signal conditioning is now integrated into the fax machine.

Continuation of the present trend should see a steadily expanding use of the telephone as a convenient coordinating device and interface for the selective communication of graphic materials via the dial network. The trend may be retarded somewhat by lack of compatibility between fax machines, but at the same time it may be nourished by a renewed emphasis on miniaturization and improved portability of the machines.

Supplementing the regular dial network are common carrier switched *broadband* nets, permitting reductions in fax transmission time down to a minute or less per page (see Chapter 4). These facilities are in relatively limited use at the present time, but are expected to grow in proportion to the increasing demand anticipated for such services.

SOLID STATE

The fax equipment industry has been comparatively slow at adapting to solid state electronics. Until 1965 or thereabouts, most new fax gear being marketed still used vacuum tube circuitry. By the end of the 1960s, however, the situation had pretty much reversed. While no doubt there is still, as of this writing (late 1970), a good deal of vacuum tube equipment in service, and some still being sold "off the shelf," it would be difficult to find anything currently in production that is not at least nominally solid state.

In fax, as in everything else electronic, solid state technology has permitted a substantial reduction in equipment bulk. Portability was mentioned as a feature that could well enhance the utility of phone-coupled fax transceivers. Along with its potential for miniaturization and weight reduction, solid state's inherent ruggedness has made possible the design of compact

Fig. 2.15. Phone coupler (small device behind phone) permits use of the telephone for fax transmission and reception without direct hookup. (Courtesy Magnavox.)

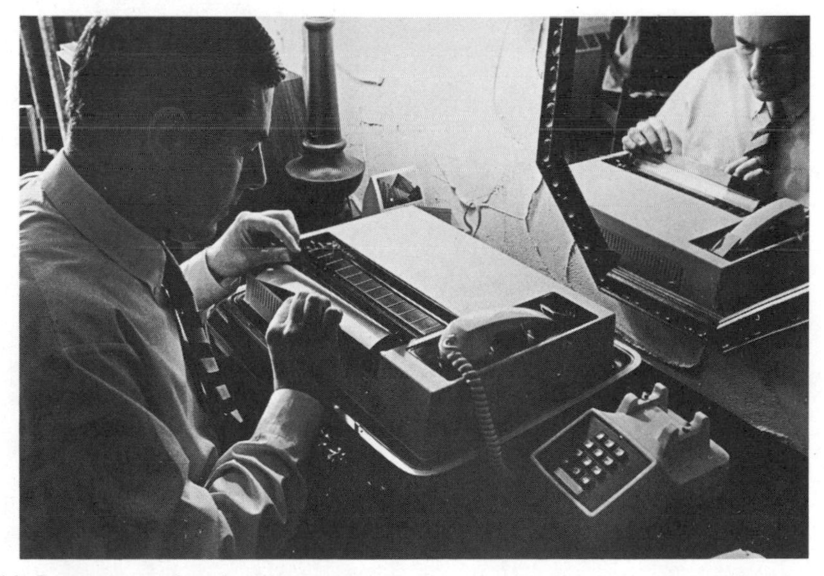

Fig. 2.16. Compactness of modern fax transceivers gives the traveling businessman the capability to file daily reports to the home office from any convenient phone, wherever he may happen to be. (Courtesy Xerox.)

transceivers about the size of an attaché case, that can be carried about in the trunk of a car without being jounced out of commission.

CATHODE RAY TECHNIQUES

The increasing use of cathode ray techniques for fax scanning and recording—in place of the more conventional electromechanical techniques—is generally not so much a matter of modernization as it is an expedient in the design of higher speed systems. An electron beam can be made to move extremely fast and to undergo very rapid changes in speed and direction of movement without being subject to the effects of friction and inertia that might afflict a mechanical system under like conditions. In fact, its extreme quickness of response makes it almost a must in some data compression systems.

Other features offered by these newer techniques are quieter operation, reduced mechanical wear and tear, and an improved ability to scan an item while it remains absolutely stationary. Various cathode ray scanning and recording processes are discussed in the next chapter.

DATA COMPRESSION

A trend that is rapidly gathering steam is the abandonment of straight, cycle-by-cycle signaling in fax transmission in favor of data compression—or

Fig. 2.17. Data compression fax terminal. The electronics in the lower section consist of what amounts to a minicomputer, its function at the send terminal to convert the scanner's output signal to a form that can be transmitted more efficiently. At the receive end, the re-formatted signal is converted back to a form suitable for conventional recording. (Courtesy Stewart-Warner.)

redundancy reduction—schemes that permit speedier transmission over existing facilities, or transmission at the same speed over less costly facilities. For some time the trend was confined to the fax manufacturers' drawing boards, but by the end of 1969 at least three compression systems had become available on the commercial market (namely, *Pacfax, Datafax 9000D,* and *Bandcom*). By mid-1970 at least three others were being readied for market, and no doubt several more are currently under development.

The schemes vary widely in principle, although most of them have in common their reliance on digital techniques to modify the signal format. Among the drawbacks of such systems are the increased risk of error through the use of digital encoding, and the boost in terminal costs imposed by the increased complexity. On the other hand, continued technological advances, together with the economic effects of competition, should comprise a generally improving picture from the fax user's viewpoint.

In any event, from the standpoint of transmission efficiency, data compression is a welcome trend. Some of the more popular techniques are explored in Chapter 4.

DIGITAL TRANSMISSION

Apart from their value as a means of compressing transmitted intelligence, digital techniques offer significant advantages in the bulk handling of electronic communications of all sorts. For one thing, a digital signal, consisting as it does of discrete pulses instead of complex analog waveforms, can be regenerated at intervals along a long-distance circuit with devices much simpler and less expensive than the precision amplifiers required in analog circuits. Moreover, the signal can be regenerated any number of times without the risk of accumulating noise and distortion in the process, as is usually the fate of repeatedly amplified analog signals.

For these reasons, digital transmission is expected eventually to replace analog as the norm for electronic communication. This does not mean that terminal devices such as telephone sets and fax scanners, which are analog by nature, will become obsolete. Where such devices are used, the conversion to digital and back to analog will usually be the responsibility of the common carrier. In the case of fax and other visual systems, however, the customer may have the option of doing his own converting and, in that way, possibly gaining some transmission efficiency and reproduction fidelity in the process.

Many fax applications lend themselves to *two-level,* or binary (black-white), "digitizing." Alphanumeric material—text, tables, etc.—is a good example. Other examples are weather maps, graphs, and engineering sketches. Once digital transmission facilities have been established, it should be possible to send two-level fax signals quite a bit faster and more economically than these signals can now be sent over existing analog facilities.

INCREASING AUTOMATION

Time was when fax machines had to be manually phased before recording could commence. (Phasing is explained in the next chapter.) Happily, that day is past, and now the machines phase themselves and a receiving machine will "answer a call" from a sending machine and "hang up" when transmission is completed.

As was mentioned earlier in this chapter, many (if not *most*) fax recorders are arranged for continuous roll-feeding, with enough paper on a roll in most cases to accommodate upwards of 200 $8\frac{1}{2} \times 11$-inch documents. And, to complement this continuous reception capability, many scanners can be equipped with automatic document feeders to permit uninterrupted transmission.

These facts are reviewed here merely to point out that automation is a continuing trend in the fax field.

MICROFACSIMILE

An allied trend that has already begun to influence the further automation of facsimile systems is the increasing use of microfilm for the storage of documents and engineering drawings. So far (late 1970), at least one fax equipment manufacturer—namely, Alden—has heeded the call by making available scanners designed to accept microfilm as the input. Another, Comfax/Computerpix, has developed and successfully tested a microfacsimile scanner which it plans to market. Other organizations have developed microfacsimile scanners, though not necessarily for the commercial market.

The tie-in with automation is that microfilm is often the first step toward total mechanization of a document or drawing file. Optical codes can be added to a reel of film, for example, to enable automatic selection of any one of over a thousand documents recorded on it; or frames of microfilm mounted in tab cards or in sheet form ("microfiche") can be automatically selected by punchings or notches in the code portion of each card or film sheet. In either system, the selected microimages, instead of merely being projected on a screen for viewing, can be scanned, and the resulting signal transmitted to a distant fax recorder. The output of such a system will ordinarily be an enlarged paper reproduction of the scanned microimage, although special recorders can easily be designed to produce duplicate microfilm output if that is desired.

Both the Alden and Computerpix scanners are designed for ease of interfacing with automatic microfilm retrieval devices. In fact, Alden offers a complete *Dial-a-Document* system, embodying a Kodak automatic microfilm retrieval subsystem, a microfacsimile scanner, and a magnetic tape unit to permit high-speed scanning and temporary storage (in magnetic form) of the selected microimage, followed by a lower speed read-out over limited bandwidth transmission lines.

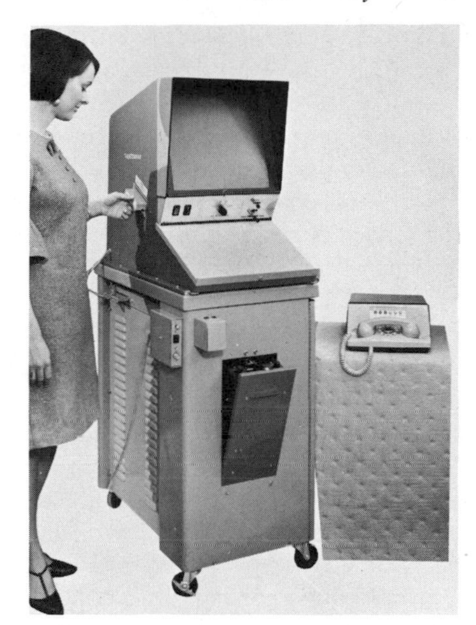

Fig. 2.18. Microfilm input fax scanner. From a film cartridge inserted into the side of a microfilm "reader," an image is selected, centered on the screen, and then transmitted by phone to a distant fax recorder. (Courtesy Alden Electronics.)

At the Massachusetts Institute of Technology, *Project Intrex* is paving the way for systems to make technical reference materials of all sorts instantly available to students and researchers by remote automatic retrieval, by subject, from a central mechanized microfilm library. A key component of this unique experimental system is the microfacsimile subsystem, which has microfilm as both its input and output. A special viewer is used to enlarge the tiny fax-recorded microimages on the delivered strips of automatically processed film.

These initial developments of microfacsimile systems as appendages to mechanized data banks are indicative of a trend that definitely bears watching.

FAX NETWORKS

A recent trend in fax usage has been the establishment of service centers in major cities, between which documents of all sorts can be speedily interchanged—for a fee. The operator of a network of such centers leases blocks of telephone lines between cities and buys or rents the necessary quantities of fax terminal units. Since the cost per transmitted copy for a given distance is determined by volume of use, the service center is able to send material from city to city more economically than would a business concern with its own private system and a lower volume.

At last count there were at least half a dozen such networks in operation throughout the United States. They range in size from about 30 stations to over 1000, and the fee per transmitted page ranges anywhere from $2.50

to $10 or more, depending on distance, among other things. The concept is still too new for a safe prediction to be made as to how successful these networks will prove to be eventually.

Supplementing the service center nets is Western Union's *Info-Fax 100* dial facsimile net, a complete commercial fax service including installation of terminals on the subscribers' premises. Using existing microwave facilities, the service permits transmission of letter-size (8½ × 11-inch) documents at less than four minutes a page between subscribers in 46 major cities.

RISING MAIL COSTS

Only a very few years ago, the suggestion that facsimile might someday be more economical than mail would have been ridiculed. The fact is that, by 1969, it was already possible to send documents relatively short distances by fax for as little as 8½ cents a page, which includes the bonus of being able to receive a letter within only a few minutes of its being sent. The only catch is that to realize so low a unit cost would require that transmission be confined within a telephone exchange area and that it be maintained almost steadily for eight hours a day. (The 8½ cents is based on the lease of a transceiver at $65 a month, coupled to a dedicated telephone set, and transmitting about 70 copies a day—at a material cost of 4 cents a day—via the dial network to other terminals within the same exchange area.)[4]

Of course, where a point-to-point system is concerned—which, for fax, is generally more economical at high volumes than a dial-up system—a valid comparison would have to take into account the fact that mailing could be on a bulk basis, thus widening the unit cost gap considerably. The fact remains, however, that, as mail costs have risen, there has been a simultaneous general decline in message fax terminal and transmission costs.

The U.S. Post Office Department, itself, has financed studies to determine the feasibility of dispatching mail by various electronic means, including facsimile. Meanwhile, the actual use of fax systems for that purpose continues to grow steadily within private industry.

Besides these general trends, there are a number of subsidiary ones. In the publishing industry alone, for example, we see the use of fax not only steadily growing, but finding new niches as it grows. The dispatching of proofs and corrections by fax, the direct (nonphotographic) recording of news photos, and the transmission of photographic masters to satellite printing plants are all trends of fairly recent inception. Unquestionably, there are others beginning to emerge, not only in publishing, but also in other areas.

Projected trends and speculation on future developments are the subject of Chapter 9. The next chapter examines fax's vital organs and provides a comparative look at some of the many variations in technique that have evolved over the years.

[4] See Chapter 6.

BIBLIOGRAPHY

9th, 11th, 12th and 13th Annual Reports of Council on Library Resources.
Axner, D. H., "The Facts About Facsimile," *Data Processing,* May 1968, pp. 42–53.
Badler, M., "New System Transmits Microfilm Cross Country in Seconds," *Information and Records Management,* Aug./Sept. 1969, pp. 60–61.
Becker, F. K., et al., "An Experimental Visual Communication System," *Bell System Technical Journal,* Jan. 1959, pp. 141–176.
Bell, E. J., and R. Everett, *Facsimile Transmission and Reception of Weather Charts by Radio,* booklet published by Muirhead & Co., Ltd., 1965.
Bello, F., "The Information Theory," *Fortune,* Dec. 1953, pp. 136–141.
Bliss, W. H., "Advancements in the Facsimile Art During 19—" (ann.), IEEE *International Convention Record,* Wire and Data Communic. Sec., 1964–67.
Complete Newspaper Page Transmission, booklet published by Muirhead & Co., Ltd., 1965.
Costigan, D. M., "FAX . . . ," *Popular Electronics,* Feb. 1969, pp. 33–40 and 102.
"Datafax Speeds Steel Orders," *Iron Age,* Jan. 28, 1965, p. 122.
"Dictafax Speeds Car Credit . . . ," *American Banker,* Dec. 27, 1967.
Dow Jones Services, brochure published by Dow Jones & Co., N.Y., 1965.
"Entire Newspaper Page Facsimile Sent Via Telephone Data Link" (item), Bell Laboratories *Record,* Sept. 1968, p. 277.
"Facsimile a Late Bloomer . . ." (item), *Electronic News,* May 13, 1968, Sec. 2, p. 35.
"Facsimile Links Widespread Steel Empire," *Business Automation,* Feb. 1965.
Floyd, H. A., "Instant Mail by Facsimile," *Reproductions Review,* Aug. 1969, pp. 8 and 46, and Sept. 1969, pp. 38 and 53.
Ideas For Industry (flyer series distributed by Datafax Division, Stewart-Warner Corp.).
"Mail by Phone Picks Up New Speed," *Business Week,* Dec. 13, 1969, pp. 120–122.
Morehouse, H. G., "Telefacsimile Services Between Libraries with the Xerox Magnavox Telecopier," Dec. 20, 1966; and "Equipment for Facsimile Transmission Between Libraries; a Description and Comparative Evaluation of Three Systems," Dec. 29, 1967 (studies prepared for Council on Library Resources, Inc., published by University of Nevada Library, Reno).
"Nationwide Facsimile Transmission System" (item), *Micro-News Bulletin* #6, National Microfilm Association, Oct. 1968, p. 2.
"Networks Spark Facsimile Field" (item), *Data System News,* Nov. 1968, p. 12.
Project Intrex (Semiannual Activity Report PR-5, Massachusetts Institute of Technology, Mar. 15, 1968).
"Publisher, Printer Linked to Facsimile" (item), *Publishers Weekly,* Feb. 6, 1967, p. 117.
Report of Telefacsimile Operations During the Fiscal Year 1968–1969, Pennsylvania State University Libraries.
"Reward For Copying," *Chemical Week,* May 29, 1965.
Ridgway, F., "By Using Facsimile Network, Coordination Becomes Easier" (item), *Product Engineering,* June 5, 1967, pp. 196–197.
Ridings, G. H., "Facsimile Communications, Past, Present, Future," *Signal,* Nov. 1962, pp. 34–40.
R. I. Bulletins 949 (Mar. 18, 1968) and 978 (Dec. 31, 1968), ANPA Research Institute.
Rothstein, A., *Photojournalism,* New York, American Photographic Book Publishing Co., 1965.
Schatz, S., "Facsimile Transmission in Libraries: A State of the Art Survey," *Library Resources and Technical Services,* Winter 1968, pp. 5–15.
Schieber, W. D., and R. M. Shoffner, *Telefacsimile in Libraries* (report published by Institute of Library Research, University of California), Feb. 1968.
Smith, F. D., "Error Considerations in Data Transmission," *Data Processing,* Nov. 1969, pp. 32–36 and 41.
"Speedup" (item), *The New Yorker,* Nov. 25, 1967 ("The Talk of the Town"), pp. 51–52.
Spielman, H. S., *Electronics Source Book,* New York, Hayden, 1965 (Vol. II, Sec. 28, "Facsimile and Related Systems," pp. 998–1015).
Stark, G., "Sending Records by Phone," *Information and Records Management,* Oct/Nov. 1969, pp. 37–39.
Thomas, A. G., and J. F. Verruso, "Fingerprint Identification and Facsimile Communications," *Technique* (Muirhead & Co., Ltd.), April 1967, pp. 11–16.

Transmission Systems for Communications (4th ed.), Bell Telephone Laboratories, 1970.
Verruso, J. F., "NYSIIS: A New Era in Law Enforcement," *Fingerprint and Identification* (Instit. of Applied Science), April 1967, pp. 3–7 and 15–16.
"War on Crime" (item), *New York Sunday News* Coloroto Section, Mar. 16, 1969, p. 54.
"Weather (Forecasting and Prediction)," *McGraw-Hill Encyclopedia of Science and Technology,* Vol. 14.
Weather Bureau Tech. Memo. T & EL-4: "Final Report—Test and Evaluation of a Facsimile Bandwidth Compression Technique," U.S. Weather Bureau, April 1968.
"Why Ma Bell Chops Up the Signals," *Business Week,* Jan. 13, 1968, pp. 82–84.
"With the Weather Nets," *Instant Graphic Recording News,* Alden Co., Vol. 2, No. 3, July 1969, pp. 5 and 6.

3 *How it Works*

THE facsimile process consists of converting visual details of a diagram, document, etc., to an analogous electric current, conditioning the current for transmission by wire or radio to a receiver, restoring it to its original form at the receiver, and amplifying it sufficiently to drive a reproducer, which converts the current variations to a visual facsimile of the transmitted item.

Of course, it is not that simple. The transmission aspect is a study in itself, let alone the need for perfect (or near perfect) synchronism of the scanning and recording mechanisms, which may be separated by thousands of miles.

This chapter will briefly explore all aspects of the basic process except the actual transmission of a picture signal from one terminal to another. The transmission aspect is covered separately in Chapter 4.

SCANNING

Modern commercial fax systems generally use electromechanical scanning techniques to convert visual tonal variations on the input copy to electrical variations for transmission to a receiver/recorder. With one or two possible exceptions, all fax scanners in use today are photoelectric and are arranged to bounce light from the input material (or "subject copy," as it is officially defined)[1] to a photocell or photomultiplier tube for conversion to electricity.

The object of photoelectric scanning is to produce an electrical analog of the tonal variations that make up the image details to be transmitted. The scanner unravels the subject copy into a serial stream of light intensity variations, which it simultaneously converts to a varying electric current. The unraveling is accomplished by the movement of a spot of light over the copy surface—or conversely, by the movement of the copy surface

[1]IEEE No. 168, "Standards on Facsimile: Definitions of Terms."

relative to a fixed spot of light—in such a way that the spot progressively covers the entire copy area. The subject copy is the mirror by which the source light is bounced to the photoelectric transducer (photocell or photomultiplier), and it is a mirror that varies constantly in reflectance throughout scanning. The reader should not infer from the above that fax scanners are exclusively bounced-light devices. There are scanners designed for use with transparencies as well—e.g., a microfilm scanner.

There are two basic requirements a photoelectric transducer must meet to qualify for use in fax scanning. One is that its electrical output at reasonable light levels be sufficient to overpower electrical "noise." (The electronics of a fax system will be discussed in more detail in subsequent sections.) The other is that its spectral sensitivity be broad enough to make the device responsive to all but the palest of colors, interpreting them as gray levels. It is also desirable that the gray scale (or color) response be reasonably linear, although this is not necessarily a requirement.

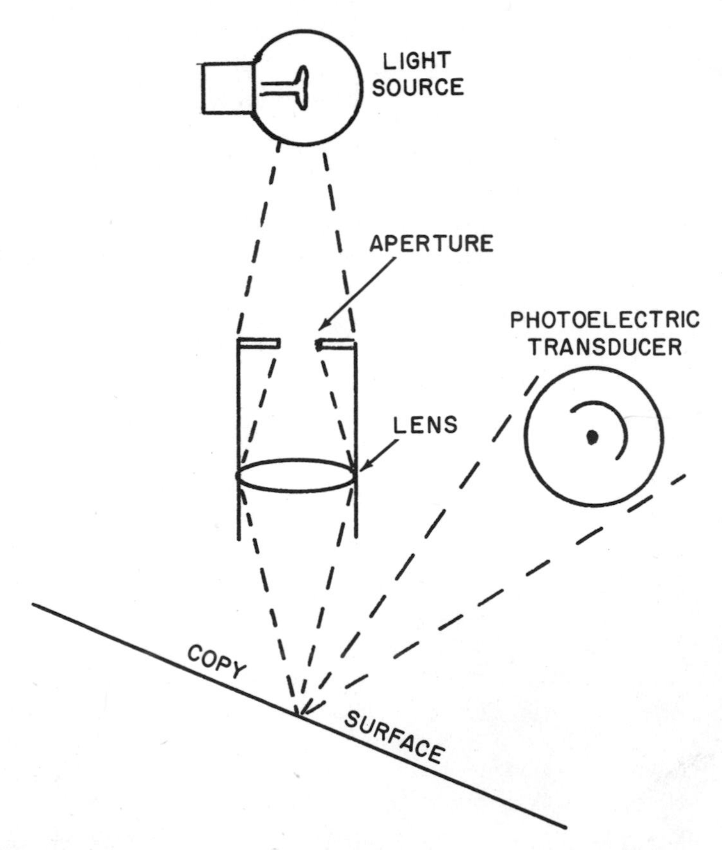

Fig. 3.1. Spot projection. Illuminated aperture is optically projected onto the copy surface, from which the image is bounced to the transducer.

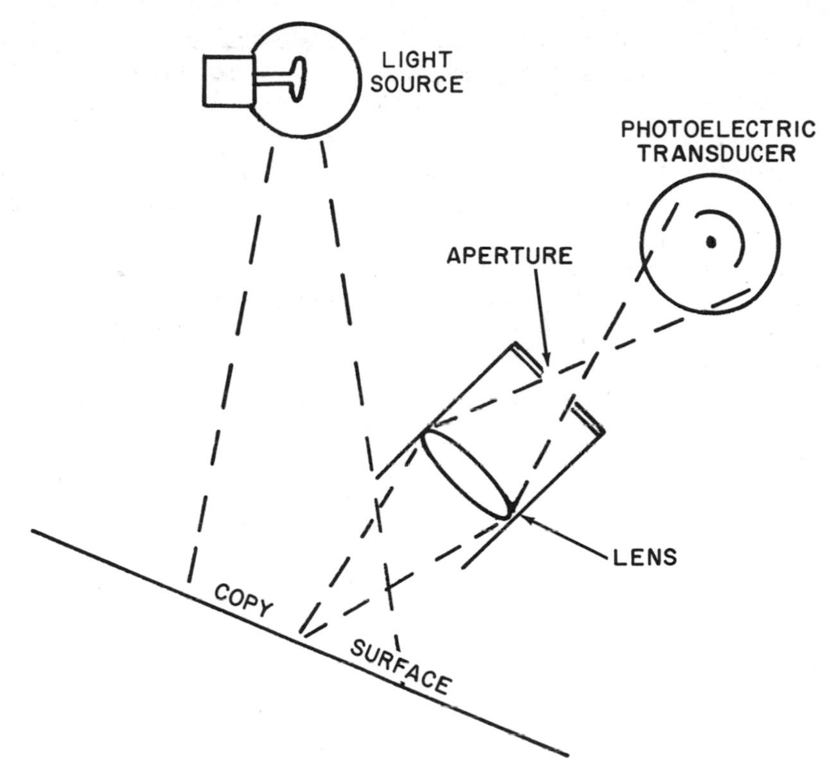

Fig. 3.2. Flood projection. Floodlit copy surface is optically projected, through an aperture, to the transducer.

Scanning methods vary both optically and mechanically. Optically, the basic variation is between flood and spot projection, which have to do with the manner in which the optical path connects the light source to the transducer via the copy surface. Mechanically, there are three variations:

1. the subject copy alone may move relative to the scan spot;
2. both the subject copy and scan spot may move—at right angles to each other and at different speeds;
3. the scan spot alone may move.

SPOT VS FLOOD

Spot projection in fax scanning is the optical projection of a tiny spot of light onto the surface of the subject copy, the bounced spot being picked up directly by the photoelectric transducer (Fig. 3.1). This approach is akin to the "reading" of an optical sound track in a motion picture projector. The only real difference is that, in the projector, the spot is sent through the graphic medium instead of being bounced off it.

In flood projection (Fig. 3.2), the subject copy is illuminated by diffused light in the general area where it is being scanned, and the bounced light is optically projected through a tiny aperture onto the cathode of the photoelectric transducer.

Both approaches are used in modern fax scanners, and each has its advantages and disadvantages. Spot projection utilizes the available light more efficiently, but it requires a more sensitive photoelectric transducer than does flood projection. The chief drawback of flood projection is its need for a relatively high-intensity light source, which may impose restrictions on the physical compactness of the scanner. With spot projection, the scan head usually embodies the light source and transducer in a fixed relationship and in close proximity to each other. Flood projection allows the illuminating lamps to be separate from the scan head, although they need not necessarily be.

Scanning mechanisms fall into two general categories with regard to the scanner in which the subject copy interfaces with the scanning beam. The two are cylinder and flat bed.

CYLINDER SCANNING

Cylinder (or drum) scanning dates back more than a century, but it is still widely used in both newspicture and document transmission applications. It requires that the subject copy be wrapped around a cylinder and rotated to effect a continuous helical scan of the entire copy. Usually, the scan head, containing the photoelectric transducer (and possibly the light source as well), advances slowly along the axis of the cylinder, like the cutting tool of a lathe, as the cylinder spins (Fig. 3.3). However, the cylinder can

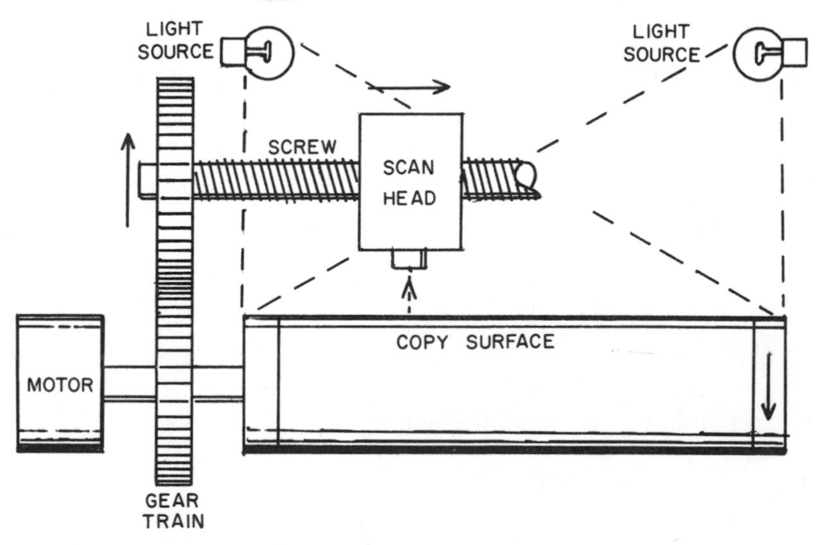

Fig. 3.3. "Lathe-style" scanning. Copy is mounted on a rotating drum. The scan head moves laterally, the space of one scan interval (or spot width) for each rotation of the drum.

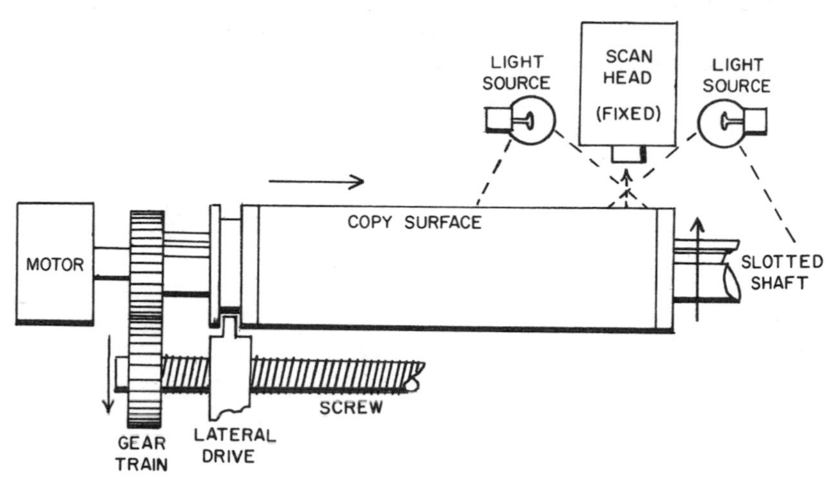

Fig. 3.4. Drum scanner in which the copy moves both radially and axially while the scan head remains stationary.

do all the moving—radial and axial—while the scan head remains stationary, or the scan head may even rotate on a fixed plane *within* a cylinder (or semicylinder), while the copy is caused to move laterally across the scan grain. The latter two schemes are illustrated in Figs. 3.4 and 3.5.

Traditionally, the chief drawback of cylinder scanning has been the bother of having to affix the copy to the cylinder. However, methods have been devised to minimize this difficulty, and it is no longer a factor in comparative

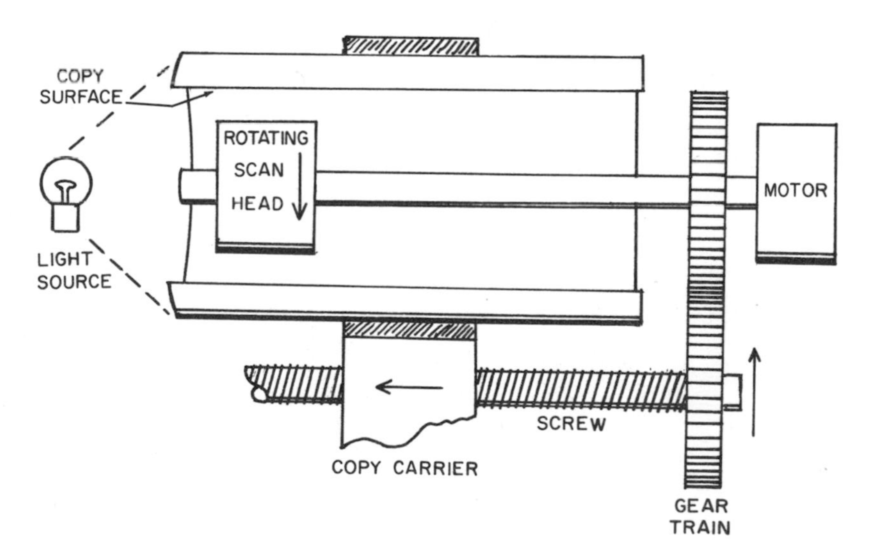

Fig. 3.5. Laterally moving copy has been curved to form a semicylinder, within which the scan head rotates.

operating convenience. Current examples of automatic loading cylinder scanners are the *Messagefax* transmitter produced by Litton's Datalog Division (formerly Litcom), and the *DEX* (Decision EXpediter) transceivers produced by Graphic Sciences, Inc.

The fact remains that, in spite of these loading improvements, cylinder type fax scanners do not readily lend themselves to automated sequential stack-loading of subject copy as does the flat-bed variety.

FLAT-BED SCANNING

Flat-bed scanning permits insertion of the subject copy into a slot, in which a feed mechanism takes over. In most flat-bed scanners, the inserted copy can be observed slowly being "swallowed" as it advances over the scanning area within the machine (Fig. 3.6), eventually to be released through a return slot. Figure 3.6 also illustrates one of the more common scanning techniques used in flat-bed scanners. The lateral scanning action is achieved by rotation of a spiral aperture relative to a fixed slit.

Another means of converting rotary to lateral motion in a scanner is by "piping" the light from the flat subject copy to a rotary scan head via optical fibers. Nippon Electric of Japan is one firm that has successfully employed the technique in commercial fax gear.

In other flat-bed scanners, particularly those employing electronic *flying spot* scanning, the copy is merely laid on a platen where it remains at rest throughout the scanning process, while the scan spot does all the moving (Fig. 3.7), and, in yet another variety (Fig. 3.8), the so-called "flat" bed is curved to conform to the sweep of a rotating scan head.

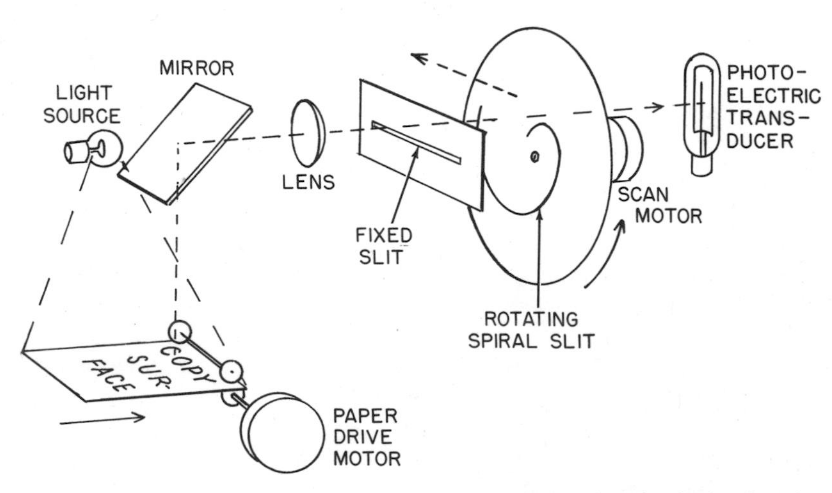

Fig. 3.6. Flat-bed scanning by the fixed/spiral slit technique. An image of the slowly advancing copy is optically projected onto the fixed slit. The spiral slit effects a lateral scan in the direction indicated by the dotted arrow.

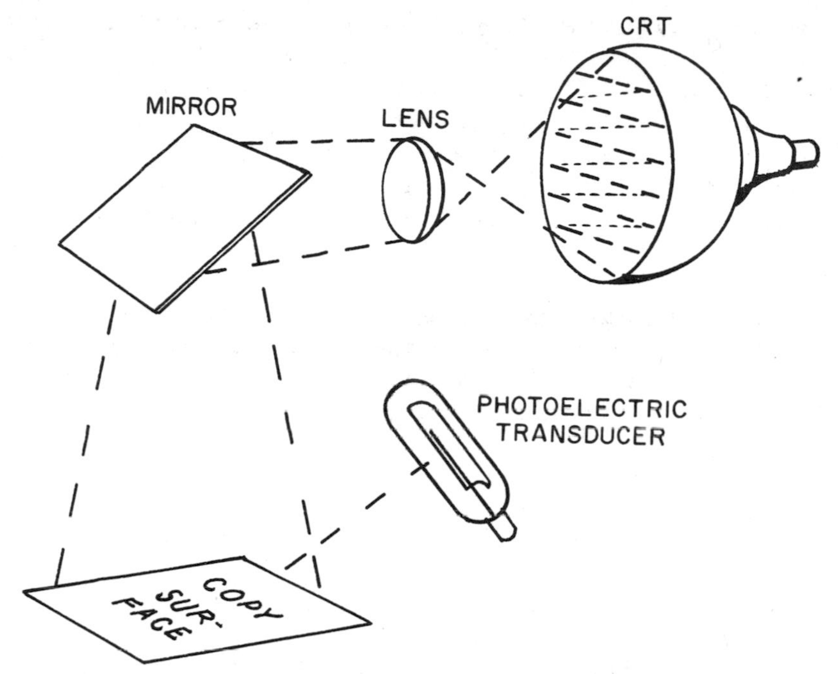

Fig. 3.7. Stationary copy is scanned by an optically projected "flying spot" from the CRT screen.

THE ELECTRONICS OF SCANNING

Historically, the generation of a fax signal has been an electronic process ever since around the beginning of this century, when scanning first embodied photoelectric principles. Prior to that, it was strictly an electromechanical, interrupted contact process—a form of telegraphy. With the more recent advent of "flying spot" scanning, in which a CRT and its associated circuitry replaces all mechanical moving parts (Fig. 3.7), the term electronic scanning has taken on a new meaning.

Conventional (non-CRT) scanning is a mechanical process only up to the point where the scan beam is intercepted by the photoelectric transducer. Thereafter it becomes electronic. The transducer may be either a photocell or a photomultiplier tube, the principle difference being in the relative strength of its output.

Typically the current in the output circuit of a straight, two- or three-element[2] photocell is in the microampere range—or a maximum of about a volt across a high resistance load—and therefore requires substantial amplification. The photomultiplier, on the other hand, contains a number

[2]Three-element (twin anode) photocells have been used in some scanners to simplify modulation by energizing the photocell through a bridge circuit associated with the modulating oscillator. Modulation is discussed in Chapter 4.

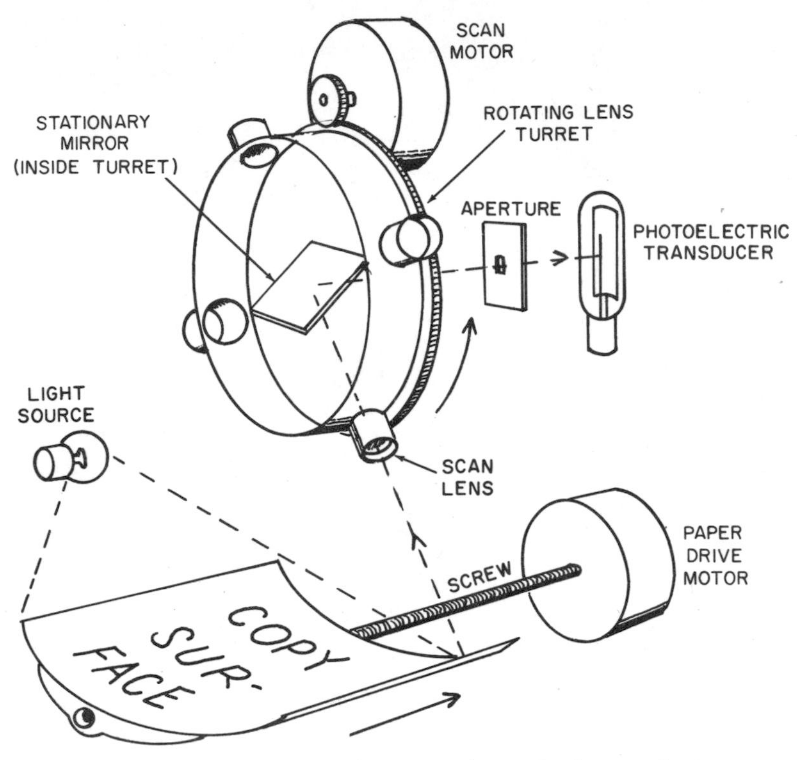

Fig. 3.8. Laterally fed copy must be curved slightly to permit scanning by a rotating lens turret. The turret makes one complete turn for every four scan strokes. (This is similar to the technique illustrated in Fig. 3.5.)

of elements called *dynodes,* the surfaces of which have the property of emitting more electrons than they receive from the adjacent emitting element. An ascending series of positive—or descending series of negative—potentials from one dynode to the next instigates a relaying of electrons from the cathode to the anode, with the stream being reinforced at each step of the way. The result is an output current that may be as much as 100,000 times greater than that from a simple photocell. Figures 3.9 and 3.10 show basic circuits for the two types of transducers.

One apparent disadvantage of the photomultiplier is its higher cost, although this is largely compensated for by the reduction its use affords in total amplifier circuitry. Its high voltage requirements might also be viewed as a limitation on its use but will usually not pose a problem if the equipment has been properly designed.

It bears mentioning, incidentally, that, whether the transducer is a photomultiplier or straight photocell, its output contains a d.c. component, and therefore cannot, without prior alteration, be processed through a conven-

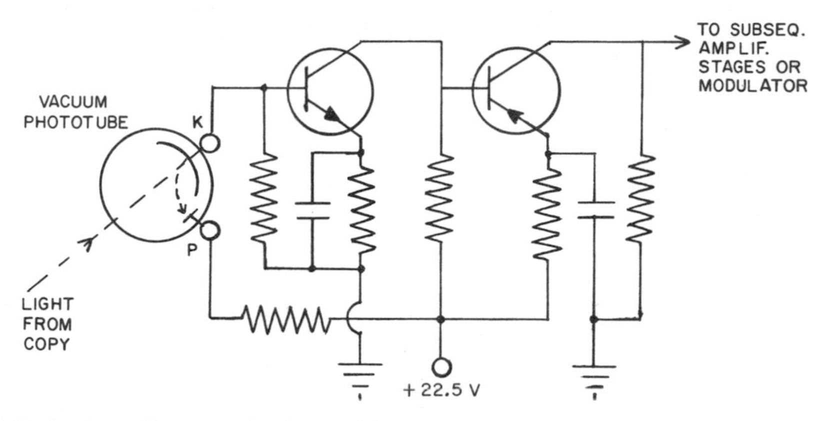

Fig. 3.9. Basic photocell scanner circuit. Amplifier stages are direct-coupled to permit passage of d.c. components characteristic of fax baseband signals.

tional capacitor or transformer-coupled amplifier. This will be discussed further in a later section.

In electronic flying spot scanning, the moving spot on the face of the CRT is merely the source of illumination, which, upon being modified by density variations in the subject copy, impacts on the cathode of the photoelectric transducer, just as in conventional scanning. The electronics associated with

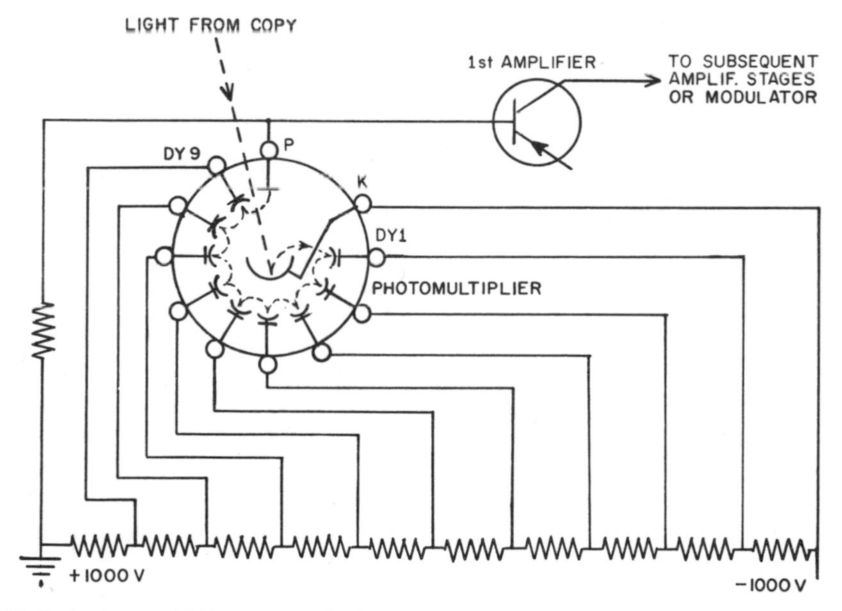

Fig. 3.10. Basic photomultiplier scanner circuit. Dotted arcs indicate the path of the multiplying electron flow from cathode (K), through the dynode chain (DY 1-9), to anode (P). High voltage is required because each dynode, from 1 to 9, must be progressively less negative, in increments of about 100 volts.

the CRT consist of power and sweep circuits virtually identical to those in a standard TV set. This scan technique is particularly applicable where the subject copy is in the form of a transparency, as in the case of a microfilm input fax system.

One somewhat critical requirement concerning the electronics of scanning is that the d.c. power energizing the scan circuitry be properly stabilized. Slight fluctuations in voltage level, which would go unnoticed in an audio system, could easily result in false gray level representations in a fax recording. The power to the scanner, including that used for illumination, must therefore be regulated within fairly tight tolerances.

RECORDING

As with scanning, most modern fax systems use electromechanical techniques for recording (visually reproducing) the received picture information. The prevalence of these techniques imposes certain speed limitations on the fax process, but the ceiling on speed is sufficiently high for most purposes. There are cylinder recorders (and scanners) in operation capable of speeds as high as 3600 rpm. To some extent, the recording process used will influence the system's maximum speed.

Recorders, like scanners, exist in both the cylinder and flat-bed varieties, the former requiring that the recording medium be in the form of precut sheets to be wrapped around a cylinder, and the latter permitting continuous feeding of the recording medium from rolls.

In recent years, a compromise technique has been employed in certain desk-top transceivers, namely, Magnavox's Magnafax® and the Xerox Telecopier,® in which the recording paper is fed from a roll and formed into a semicylinder for continuous passage *through* the terminal unit, while the recording head spins *within* the semicylinder (Fig. 3.11).

As applied to the actual recording process, electromechanical may be considered as denoting any system in which the recording transducer is in direct physical contact with the recording medium. There are four basic processes that fit this category, within each of which there are mechanical variations. The most popular is electrolytic, which is actually an electrochemical process. The others are electrothermal, electropercussive, and electrostatic.

The one established recording process that lies outside the electromechanical category (as defined above) is photographic recording, traditionally used in the facsimile reproduction of newspictures. In addition, there has recently emerged a variation of photographic recording called electron beam recording, in which accelerated electrons, rather than light, impact directly on the photographic emulsion to produce a latent image.

Two processes that do not exactly fit either of the two categories are the

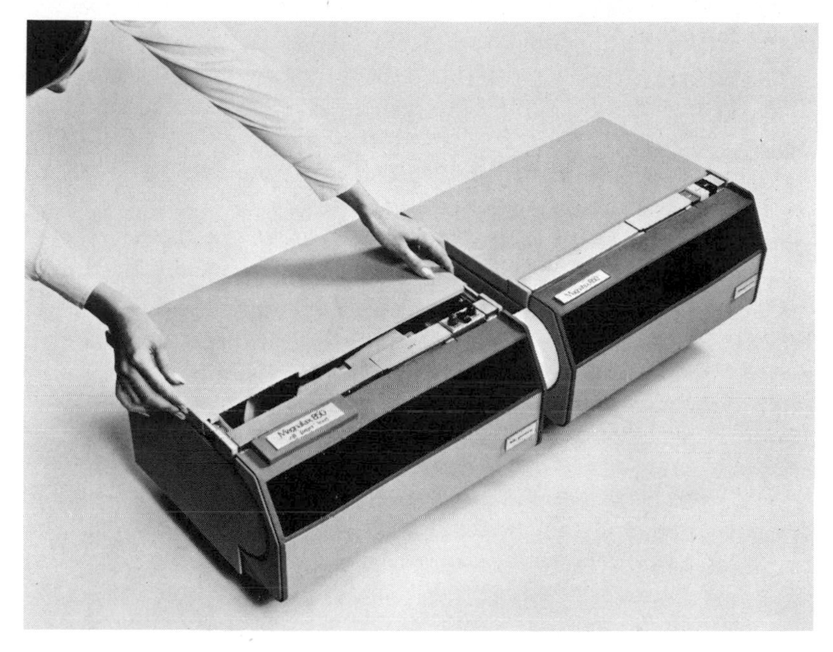

Fig. 3.11. Desk-top transceiver designed to permit continuous paper feed from a roll while operating in the RECORD mode. Paper is formed into a semicylinder as it passes through the unit. Continuous feeding permits fully automatic reception of transmitted copy. (Courtesy Magnavox.)

Hellfax offset process and ink vapor recording, both of which have in common the use of wet ink and ordinary paper. In the Hellfax process the transmitted "marks" are recorded in ink on a moving plastic ribbon and then transferred to plain paper, a line at a time. And in the ink vapor process, a combination of electromechanical and electromagnetic (or electrostatic) principles is utilized to modulate a fine spray of ink and direct it to the surface of plain paper.

The Hellfax process will be briefly described later. All that need be said further about ink vapor recording is that, since its introduction some thirty years ago, its use in facsimile has been very limited. In recent years, a variation of it has found application as a substitute for impact printing in computer output devices.

All recording processes except photographic fall under the general heading of *direct recording,* to distinguish them as requiring no additional processing (chemical or other). Electrostatic recording rightfully belongs somewhere between photographic and direct, inasmuch as it involves creation of a latent image, followed by one or two processing steps. But, since the electrostatic method invariably includes automatic processing, it may be loosely regarded as a direct recording process.

ELECTROLYTIC RECORDING

Electrolytic is the oldest and still the most popular fax recording process. It makes use of the discoloration produced in a material saturated with a special electrolyte when an electric current passes through it. The color change is from natural to a darker shade, is permanent, and usually varies in relative darkness in proportion to the strength of the current.

Applying this effect to fax recording is merely a matter of placing the electrolyte-saturated material (paper) between a fixed electrode and a moving stylus and applying the amplified fax signal current as a potential between the electrode and stylus. As the stylus sweeps across the paper, the variations in current are recorded on the paper as a line of varying darkness. If each subsequent sweep of the stylus is displaced by the width of the recorded line, the variations in darkness will begin to form a pattern. With proper synchronism between the fax scanner and recorder, the pattern should form a facsimile of the scanned copy.

The first electrolyte used for fax recording—by inventor Alexander Bain in 1842 (Chapter 1) consisted of water, sulfuric acid, and a saturated solution of yellow prussiate of potash.[3] The marks made by the recording stylus on the electrolyte-impregnated paper were the result of decomposition of the iron stylus by electrolysis. Since Bain, a number of different electrolytes have been used successfully and patents have been secured by fax manufacturers on paper impregnated with the firms' own specially concocted solutions.

There is some diversity in marking characteristics among the various commercial electrolytic papers. The Alden Company's Alfax paper, for example, is instantly recognizable by the soft brown coloration of recorded details. Another brand produces marks that appear, at times, to contain a violet component. Others produce dark brown or black marks on a white background. Suppliers usually offer several paper types by name or number, each having different characteristics.

Some electrolytic papers are *archival*—meaning that the images will not fade appreciably over a period of time, or that the paper will not deteriorate in storage. Others may not have the desired archival property.

The stylus/backplate technique of electrolytic recording lost favor some years ago to a somewhat more practical technique called helix-and-blade, which is used almost exclusively today in electrolytic recorders. The principle is illustrated in Fig. 3.12. The special drum containing the helix makes one complete revolution for each scan line. To the recording paper, the laterally moving pressure point between the rotating helix at the rear and the stationary blade in the front has the same effect that a laterally moving stylus in the front would have were it pressing the paper against a stationary backplate. As the electrical potential between blade and helix varies during each rotation of the helix, marks of corresponding darkness are recorded

[3] *Automatic Printing and Telegraph Systems,* Part 1 (Western Union/American School of Correspondence, 1918), p. 9.

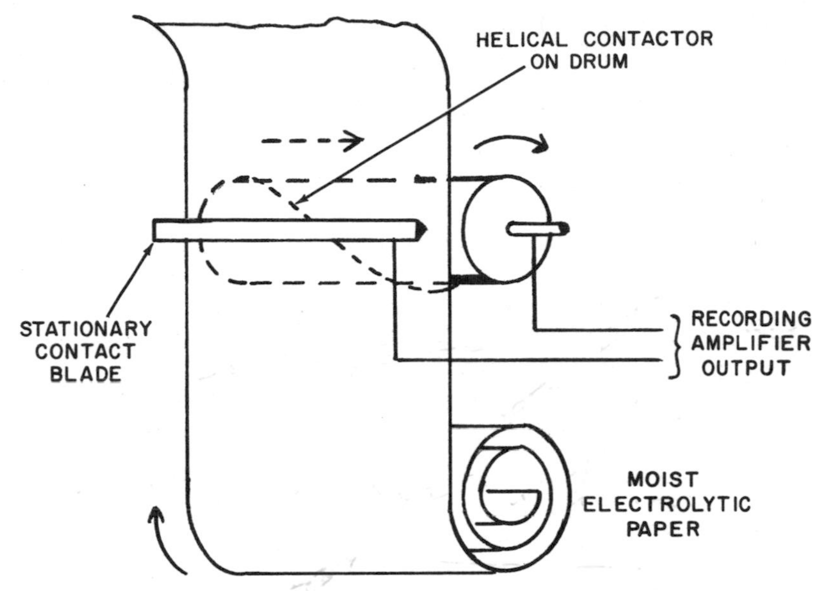

Fig. 3.12. Electrolytic recording by helix-and-blade technique. The drum containing the single-turn helical contactor makes one revolution per scan stroke. The junction of the helix and a stationary blade constitutes a laterally moving stylus (dotted arrow).

along the length of the laterally moving pressure point. The stationary printing blade requires frequent replacement because of the eroding effect of electrolysis.

Although the natural state of electrolytic paper is moist, and it must remain so prior to and during recording, it usually emerges dry from the recorder because of a heating element just beyond the recording point. The change from moist to dry after recording may result in some shrinkage of the recorded image.

ELECTROTHERMAL RECORDING

For lack of a better descriptor, *electrothermal,* or *thermal,* will suffice to identify this next process, although a chemist will tell you that heat has nothing directly to do with it. The connection is that electrical arcing—and occasionally even a wisp of smoke—occurs as a by-product of the reproduction of marks on the paper. For that reason, it is sometimes also loosely referred to as a "burn-off" process.

The process is similar to electrolytic in that the conductive recording paper is interposed between two electrodes, one of which is the recording stylus. It differs in that the marks made by the stylus on the paper are the result of the paper's white coating having been decomposed by the electric current passing through it.

By far the best known thermal—or electrosensitive—paper for fax recording is Teledeltos,® developed by Western Union nearly 40 years ago and still in wide use in both fax and laboratory instrument recorders. The active ingredient of Teledeltos is a copper compound. Mixed with it is titanium oxide, which gives the paper its normal white coloration and which permanently discolors at the point where the current from the stylus passes through it.

Thermal paper is durable and generally unaffected by temperature changes, but it is usually slightly more expensive than electrolytic paper. Perhaps the chief characteristic of a thermal recording is its high contrast. As for tonal rendition, it does a fair job of reproducing halftones.

ELECTROPERCUSSIVE RECORDING

Electropercussive recording, also known variously as *impression, impact,* or *pigment transfer* recording, has been in use on and off since the early 1930s. It has been popularized in recent years through its use in certain desk-top transceivers, notably Magnavox's Magnafax® 850 and the Xerox Telecopier.® It is also used extensively in weather map recorders.

The process is basically the same as that used in audio disk recording. The amplified signal is fed to a transducer in which a stylus is electromagnetically actuated in response to the signal current variations. In the facsimile application, visual recording is effected by interposing a sheet of carbon paper between the stylus and a sheet of plain paper. As the stylus vibrates during scanning it produces a carbon impression on the paper, the darkness of the impression varying in proportion to the variations in strength of the picture signal (Fig. 3.13).

The technique produces good contrast recordings on nonchemical paper and permits recording in duplicate or triplicate through use of additional transfer sets. A possible disadvantage, depending on the mechanical design

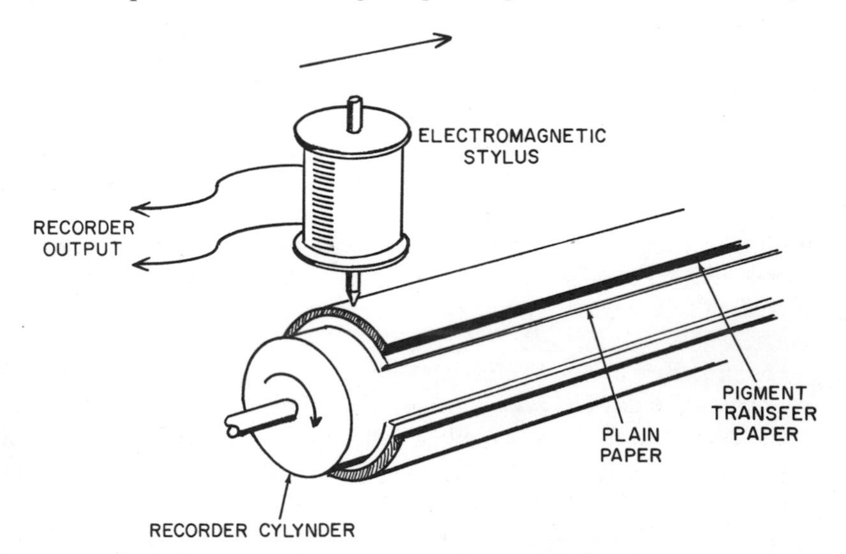

Fig. 3.13. Impression (or pigment transfer) recording utilizes a vibrating stylus in conjunction with ordinary carbon paper to produce fax recordings on plain paper.

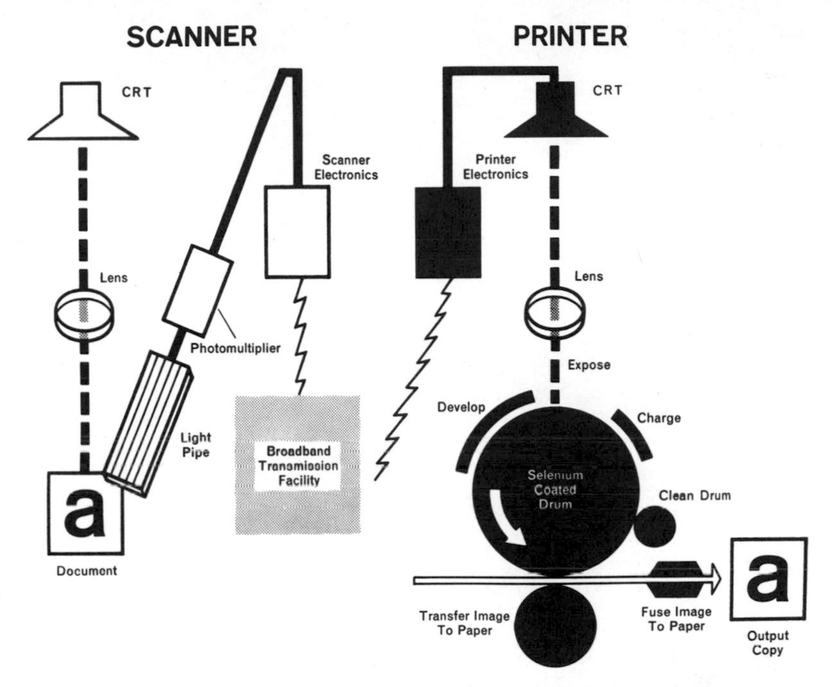

Fig. 3.14. Xerox's LDX system combines CRT scanning and reproducing with xerographic recording. At the transmitter, the CRT's "flying spot" bounces from the copy to a photomultiplier via a light pipe. At the recorder, the electronically reconstructed light variations vary the static charge on a selenium drum. The image is "developed" by electrostatic powder (toner), clinging to the charged portions of the drum; then it is transferred and heat-fused to plain paper. (Courtesy Xerox Corp.)

of the recorder, is that a malfunction resulting in obliteration of a recording—or possibly no recording at all—may go undiscovered until completion of transmission.

ELECTROSTATIC RECORDING

There are two basic electrostatic recording techniques. One is transfer xerography, which is somewhat analogous to offset printing and which permits recording on ordinary paper; and the other is a direct technique (also essentially a xerographic process), requiring specially coated recording paper.

Transfer xerography is used in the Xerox Corporation's LDX® (Long Distance Xerography) facsimile system. The LDX reproducer is a more or less conventional cathode ray tube on whose screen the received picture signal is reconstructed as a train of light variations. The image is projected onto a selenium drum, where it is converted to a "latent image" in the form of a varying electrostatic charge pattern. The drum is "dusted" with heat-sensitive powdered resin called *toner,* which clings by static electricity to the charged portions of the drum. The pattern formed by the toner is then transferred from the drum to paper and is fused to the paper by heat (Fig. 3.14).

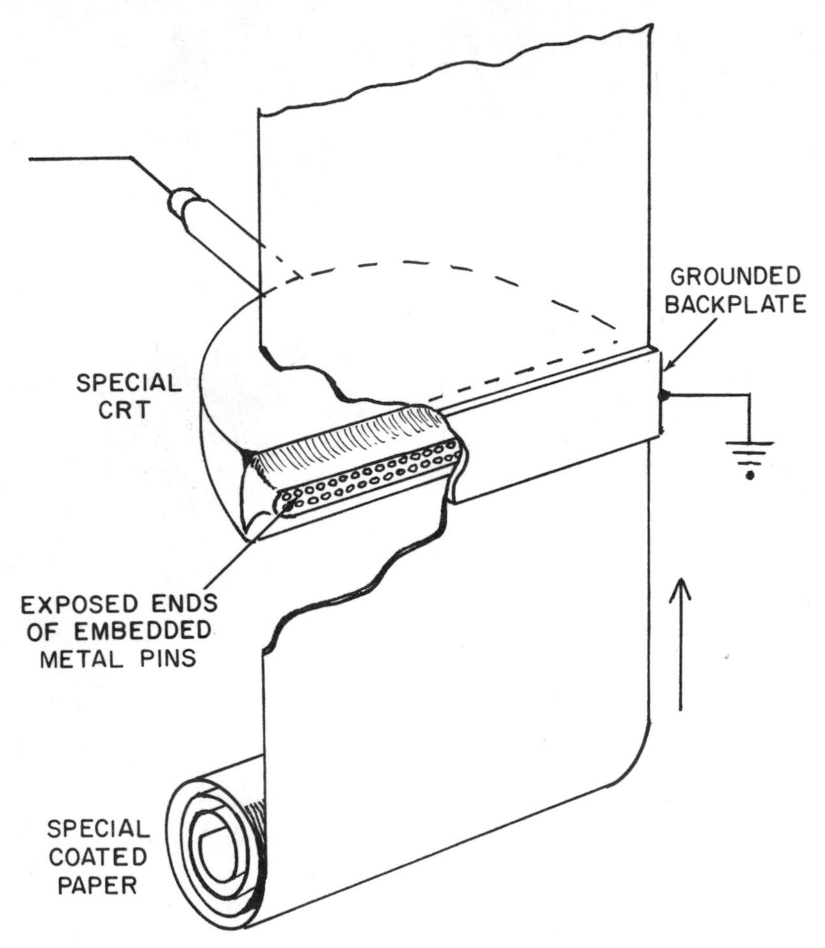

Fig. 3.15. "Videograph" recording technique uses a special, conducting faceplate CRT to put a latent image directly on coated electrostatic paper. The image is then developed by application of electrostatic ink to the paper.

In the direct technique, the reproducer is also a cathode ray tube, which may be either the conventional type with a phosphor screen, or one specially designed to permit direct "electronic" contact with the oxide-coated recording paper. The latter has no screen, but has metal pins imbedded in its faceplate, permitting the electron beam to extend through the glass to the outside for transfer of the signal energy directly to specially coated paper (Fig. 3.15). With the conventional type tube, the scan spot may be either projected or "piped" (by fiber optics) from the phosphor screen to the paper (Fig. 3.16).

In the direct process, toner is applied directly to the signal-charged paper, and, as in transfer xerography, it is permanently fused to the parts where it clings.

The use of a CRT is not in any way essential to this or other electrostatic recording techniques. With suitable scan mechanisms, a crater tube or other type of light-modulating device could also be used.

HELLFAX OFFSET RECORDING

The wet-ink offset technique developed by Hell of Germany ranks as one of the more unique fax recording processes currently in use in commercial equipment (Fig. 3.17).

First, for the process to work properly, the received analog signal must be converted to a series of discrete black marking pulses. The transducer

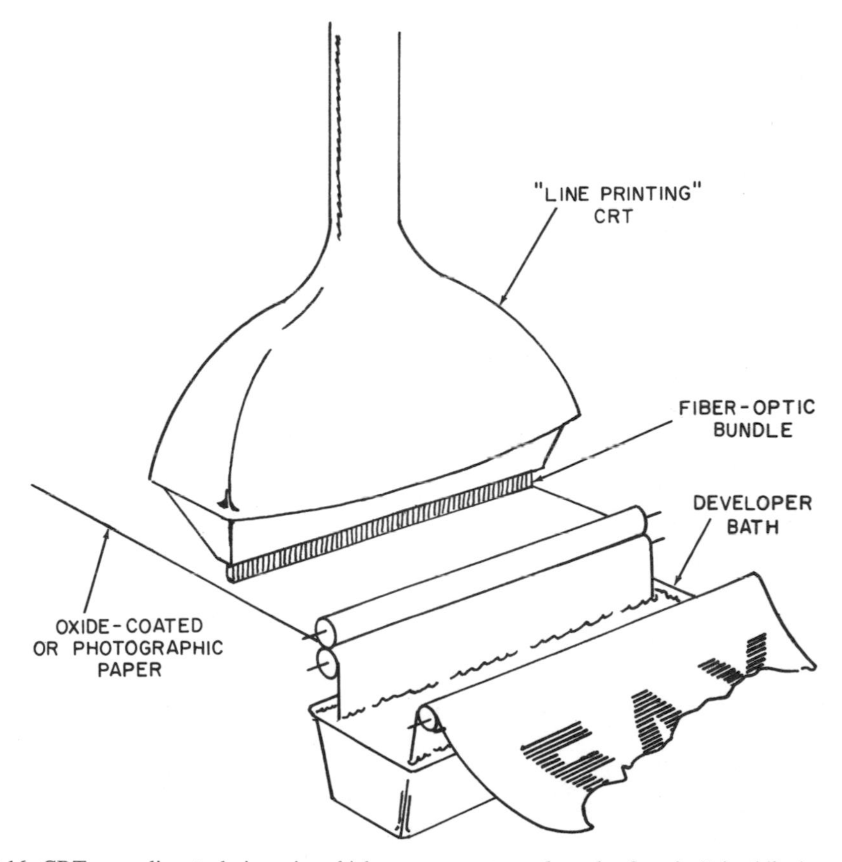

Fig. 3.16. CRT recording technique in which a scan spot on the tube face is "piped," via fiber optics, to the surface of specially coated paper within a lightproof enclosure. A latent image is formed on the paper and made visible by passing the paper through a liquid developer. The fiber-optic faceplate extension minimizes the effects of diffusion and reflections, and eliminates distortion due to curvature of the tube face.

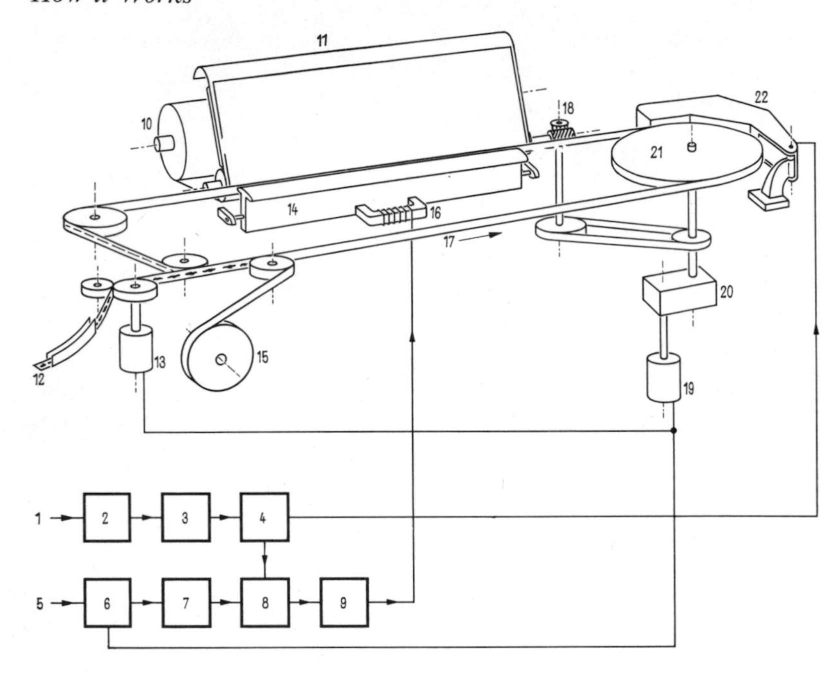

Schematic Representation of Operation

1	Signal input	9	Printing bar amplifier	17	Recording belt
2	Automatic gain control	10	Paper supply roll	18	Paper feed gearing
3	Demodulator	11	Paper guide	19	Main drive motor
4	Output stage	12	Erasing belt exit	20	Motor gear box
5	Power network	13	Erasing belt motor	21	Recording drum
6	Power supply	14	Printing bar	22	Recording system
7	Frequency divider	15	Erasing belt roll		
8	Automatic phasing circuit	16	Printing magnet		

Fig. 3.17. Hellfax wet-ink offset recording. Ink marks corresponding to black picture elements are printed by the transducer on a plastic belt and transferred to the plain recording paper by pressure. (See text.) (Courtesy Dr.-Ing. Rudolf Hell of Kiel.)

(22), which responds directly to the processed signal, consists of a mechanically actuated inked roller, which reproduces the marking pulses visually, as they occur, on a moving belt of plastic ribbon (17). When one complete line has been thus reproduced, an electrically actuated printing bar (14) automatically transfers it from the ribbon to the paper on which the full recording is to be reproduced. Before the transfer belt completes a cycle, it comes in contact with a strip of consumable blotting paper (15), which removes any remaining ink and prepares that portion of the belt for reproducing a subsequent line.

The somewhat elaborate nature of the process has to do with the machine's ability to record flat-bed fashion on paper fed from a roll. In Hellfax cylinder-type recorders utilizing the wet-ink process, the transducer contacts the paper directly. The ink used, incidentally, is a type that dries rapidly once it is applied to the paper.

PHOTOGRAPHIC RECORDING

The photographic process has been traditionally associated with the facsimile distribution of news photos, although it has been—and is—used in other fax applications as well. It differs mechanically from direct recording in two ways: (l) recording must be done within a lightproof enclosure, and (2) the transducer does not directly contact the recording medium (photographic paper or film). We should perhaps qualify the latter by pointing out that the transducer may contact the recording medium indirectly via a fiber optic "light pipe" (Fig. 3.16).

Traditionally, there has also been an added step in the recording process, namely the necessity for darkroom development of the latent photographic image. Recently, however, photographic recorders have been introduced in which processing is automatic within the recorder. The simplest way of achieving this has been through use of Polaroid film packs as the recording medium, but there are also more complex recorders in which the paper containing the latent image is automatically fed through a chemical bath and ejected from the machine as a processed photograph within seconds after recording is completed (Fig. 3.18).

The transducer for photographic recording may be either a conventional

Fig. 3.18. A photographic recorder featuring automatic processing. There is a slight time delay between completion of reception and emergence of the finished recording from the processing section. (Courtesy Muirhead.)

projection lamp combined with a light valve (e.g., a Kerr cell) or a special lamp capable of rapidly varying its brilliance in response to picture signal fluctuations. The latter method is the more prevalent and the lamp commonly used is a *crater* or *glow modulator tube,* which provides a concentrated gas discharge light source, the intensity of which is variable directly by amplified signal currents. Figure 3.19 shows a typical photographic recording arrangement.

Electron beam recording, a variation of photographic, has not as yet (late 1970) been used in a commercial fax system. It employs cathode ray scanning principles and is capable of much finer resolution than conventional scanning techniques (Fig. 3.20). The chief drawback is that the recording medium—film on paper—must be placed within a vacuum.

AMPLIFICATION

Except for very high-speed systems, the frequencies involved in facsimile transmission are usually within the audio range. The basic difference between the output of a fax scanner and that of the optical sound head of a movie projector (the two devices have much in common mechanically) is that, while the projector sound head output consists entirely of measurable audio frequencies, the fax scanner output usually consists of a more or less haphazard sequence of transitions. Unless the scanned subject copy consists

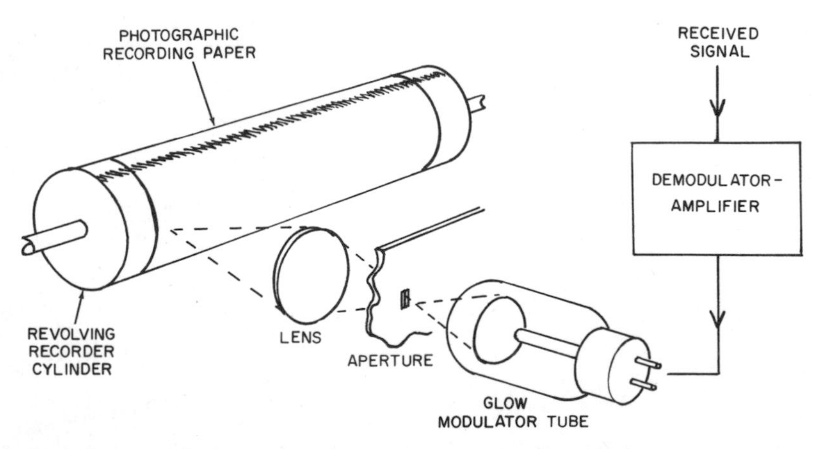

Fig. 3.19. Typical photographic recording scheme. The recovered baseband signal is amplified sufficiently to vary the illumination of the glow tube. The light variations, optically focused onto photographic paper, form a latent image, later made visible by conventional chemical processing. The cylinder must be in a lightproof enclosure during recording.

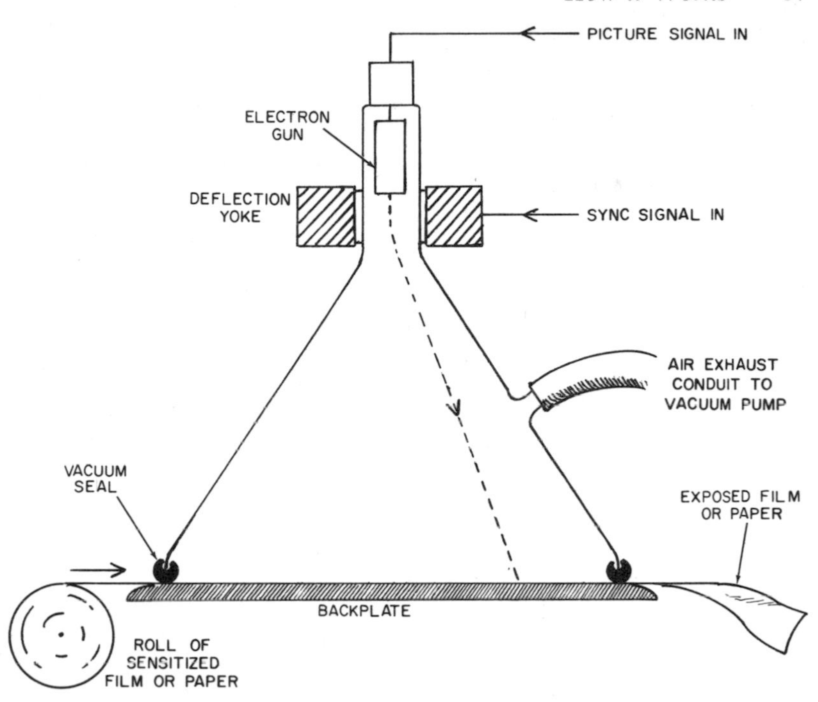

Fig. 3.20. Electron beam recording substitutes sensitized film or paper for the phosphor screen within the evacuated interior of a CRT. The electron beam impinges directly on the sensitized surface. The latent image is developed by normal processing.

of a reasonably symmetrical pattern of lines arranged obliquely or at right angles to the scan grain, the scanner output is in the audio range only in the sense of the number of transitions that normally occur within a second.

Another distinction—a more significant one—is that, while the audio range seldom extends below 20 Hz, the fax scanner output frequencies can range all the way down to zero, a fact that presents a problem with respect to amplification and coupling. The answer to the problem is modulation—the superimposing of the scanner output on an a.c. carrier signal of comparatively high frequency. This aspect of the facsimile process is explored further in Chapter 4.

Suffice it to say, for the moment, that amplification of the modulated fax signal involves use of conventional Class A amplifier circuits not unlike those found in audio systems, whereas the scanner output prior to modulation and the demodulated signal delivered to the recorder require direct coupling of amplifier stages (i.e., no capacitors or transformers in the signal path). Examples of the two types of amplifier circuits are shown in Figs. 3.21 and 3.22.

See page 80

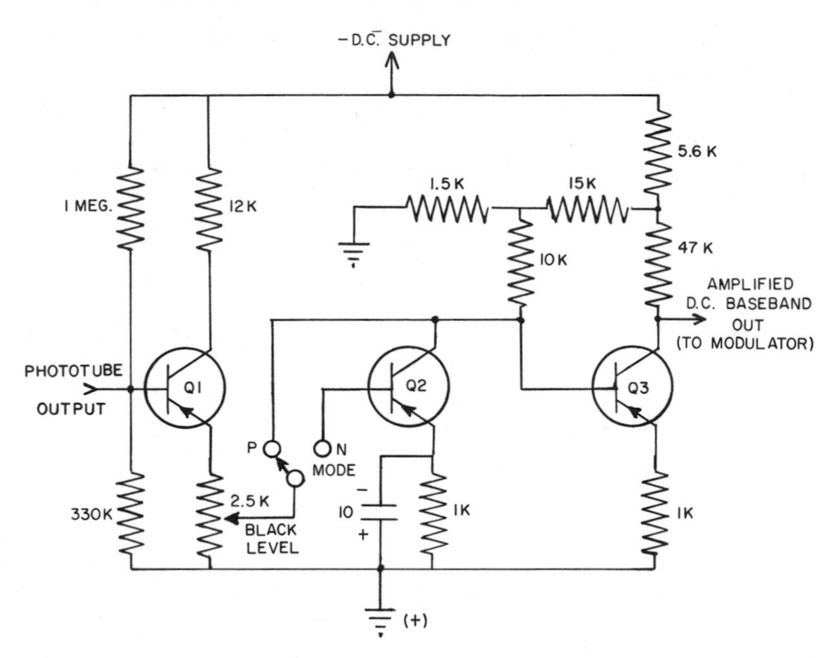

Fig. 3.21. Amplifier stages preceding the modulator in a fax transmitter must be direct-coupled because of d.c. components in the scanner output. The same applies to stages following demodulation in the receiver. The *Mode* switch determines whether the signal will be transmitted with peaks representing black (positive) or white (negative) elements of the picture. (Courtesy Alden Electronics.)

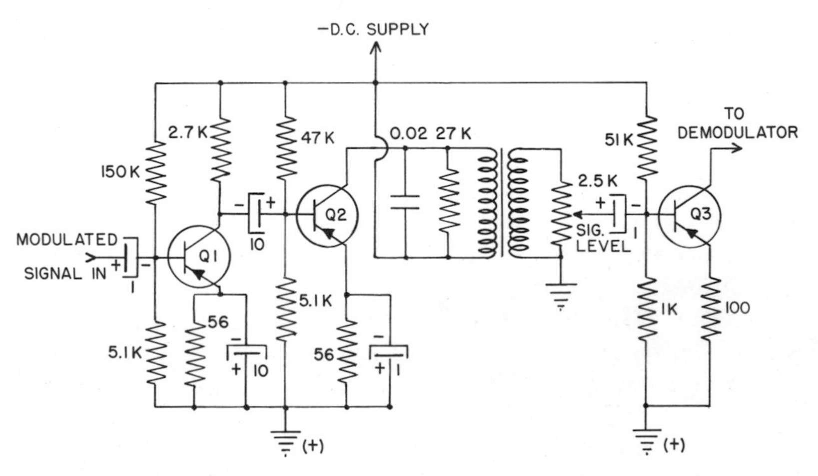

Fig. 3.22. Input stages of a typical fax receiver closely resemble a conventional audio amplifier. (Courtesy Alden Electronics.)

PHASING AND SYNCHRONIZATION

It is one thing to get a picture signal from point A to point B, but the received signal is worthless unless provision has been made to reassemble the picture elements at point B in the same spatial order in which they were unraveled by the scanner at point A. To ensure this, two things are necessary: (1) at the commencement of transmission of image details, the positions of the scan and recording beams—or scan beam and recording stylus—must exactly coincide with respect to their relative positions within a stroke, and (2) the relationship must be maintained throughout transmission.

The first of these requirements is called phasing; the second, synchronization.

PHASING

Phasing can be accomplished in a number of ways, all of which employ the same general principle, namely, that of retarding the mechanism at one end of a system—in standard practice, the receiving end—until the start-of-stroke occurs at precisely the same instant at both—or all—terminals of the system. (A single transmitter can simultaneously serve a number of receivers.) It will be recalled from Chapter 1 that, in Bain's original facsimile system, which used stylus-equipped pendulums for scanning and recording, a leading pendulum was "grabbed" and locked by an electromagnet at the height of its stroke, to be released through a switching arrangement when the lagging pendulum caught up. This was the forerunner of the stop-start technique used in numerous facsimile systems right up to the present era.

The more popular method today is to retard, rather than completely halt, the recording mechanism until the start of a recording stroke coincides with that of a scan stroke. Depending on the design of the equipment, this may require several strokes prior to the actual transmission of image detail. In modern equipment, the preliminary phasing step is completely automatic.

All conventional fax scanners are designed to transmit some form of phasing signal for a certain interval—usually several seconds—prior to the commencement of actual picture signal transmission. The signal is generally in the form of a pulse of fixed amplitude and duration, occurring at scan line intervals. It may vary in form from one system to another, but that shown in Fig. 3.23 is fairly typical.

Whatever the form, the object is to utilize the received pulse, in conjunction with a start-of-stroke pulse generated locally at the recorder, to free the temporarily retarded recording mechanism. Thus freed, the mechanism speeds up so that it is now in step with the scanner.

A common way of accomplishing this "catching up" is to temporarily alter, through a switching circuit, the electrical characteristics of the recorder drive motor so that it runs at a slightly reduced speed for as long as the local

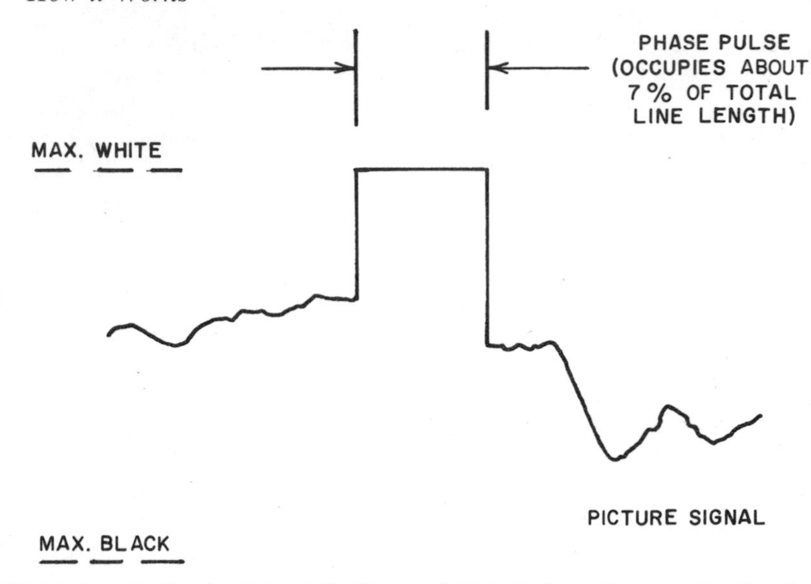

Fig. 3.23. Typical phasing signal is a full white (or full black, depending on polarity) pulse between scan strokes, occupying about seven percent of each scan cycle. During pretransmission phasing, the white pulse shown would be preceded and followed by a steady black signal.

and remote pulses remain out of phase. As soon as the pulses occur together, a relay closes and the motor is switched to normal operation.

Another way is to utilize the coincident occurrence of the two pulses to release an electromechanical or magnetic brake. Figure 3.24 shows one way that coincident pulses might be used to bring a receiver into phase. It is a typical pulse-comparing circuit arranged to operate a switch when the pulses coincide, and it may be applied to either of the phasing methods just described.

SYNCHRONIZATION

Synchronizing the scan and recording mechanisms of a fax system so that they remain in perfect step throughout transmission is usually achieved in one of three ways:

1. reliance on unification of commercial a.c. power sources serving system terminals;
2. use of matched precision power supplies;
3. transmission of a sync signal, or sync pulses, along with the picture signal.

The first two require the use of frequency-matched (normally 60 Hz) a.c. synchronous drive motors in scanners and recorders. Where the transmit and receive ends of the system operate from the same a.c. power grid, method (1) is applicable, and synchronization after initial phasing is automatic. This is by far the simplest, and therefore the most popular, method of synchronization.

Where, on the other hand, the separate terminals must operate from isolated commercial power sources, it is necessary to resort to one of the other two methods. Method (2) requires that the scanner and recorder drive motors be operated from matched, tuning-fork-, or crystal-controlled a.c. power supplies—or *frequency standards,* as they are sometimes called. Accessory precision power supplies are available for most commercial fax systems (excluding, of course, those in which the terminals are designed for operation on integrated precision supplies. The Magnafax 850 is an example.)

For most purposes, the output frequencies of the separate precision supplies must be matched within 0.001 percent (one part in 100,000) to ensure adequate synchronization. Greater differences may cause a noticeable *skewing* of recorded details, with elements normally at right angles to the scan axis appearing to lean consistently one way or the other, the direction of skew depending on whether the recorder is running slower or faster than the scanner. The circuit of a typical standard frequency power supply is shown in Fig. 3.25.

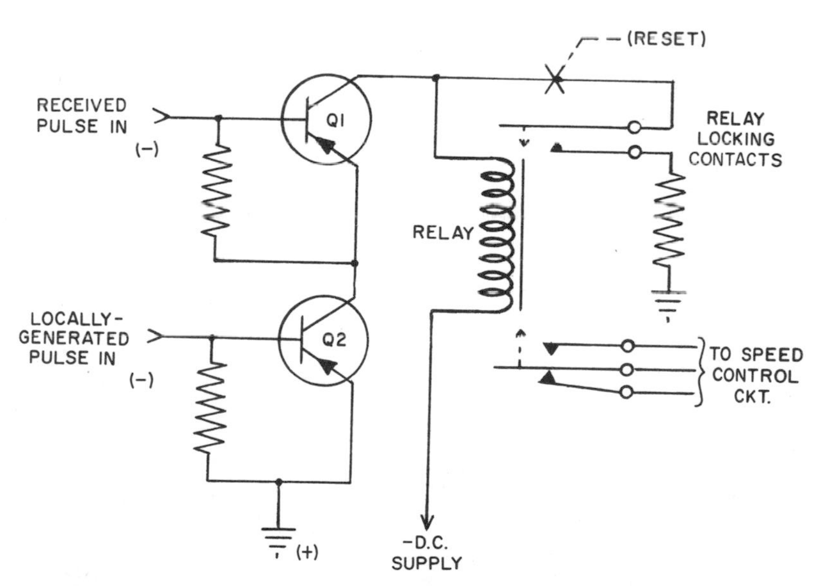

Fig. 3.24. Familiar "AND gate," or "coincidence detector," illustrates one approach to the automatic phasing of scanner and recorder mechanisms. With the system at rest, transistors Q1 and Q2 are cut off by lack of forward bias. Current cannot flow through the relay until coincident negative pulses at the inputs simultaneously unblock *both* links in the series path. The operated relay removes a temporary "drag" from the recorder mechanism.

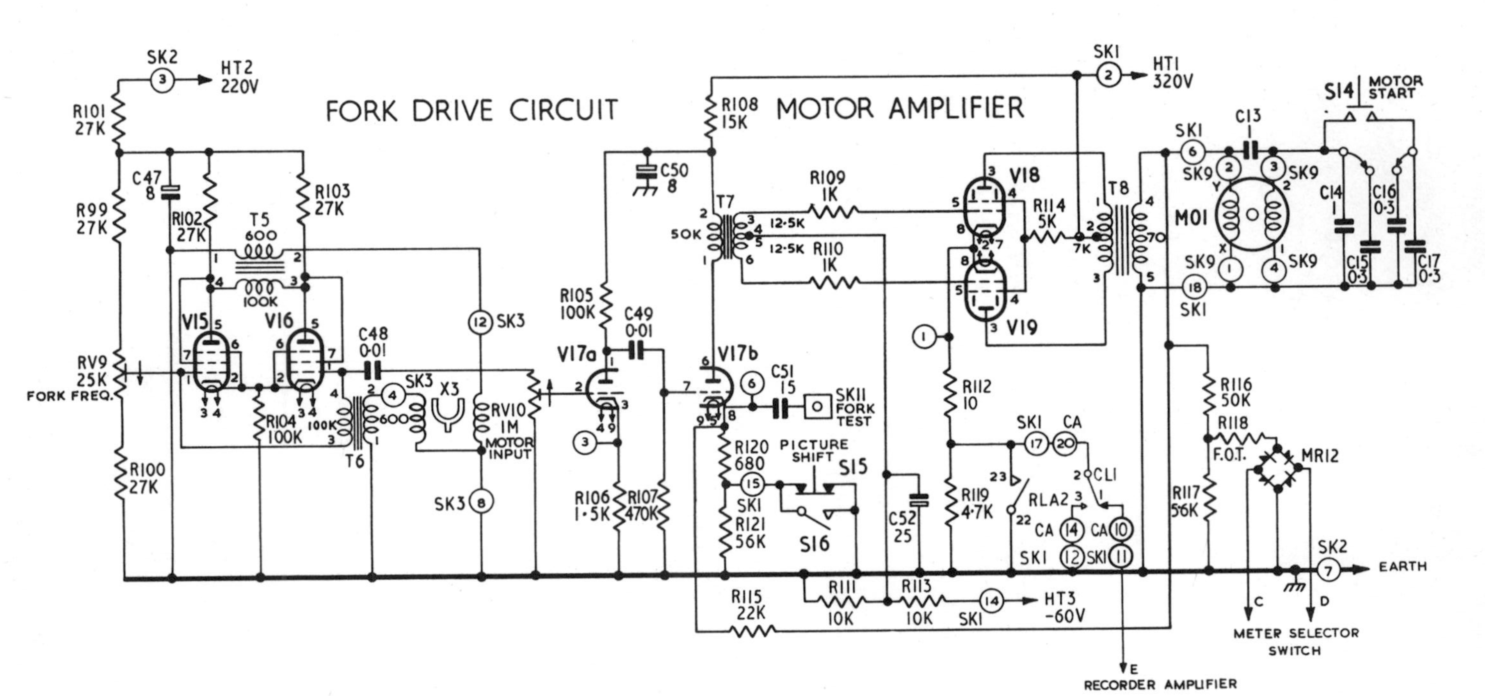

Fig. 3.25. Circuit of a "fork-drive" frequency standard for operation of fax terminal drive motors at a constant speed. Through use of a precision, tuning fork oscillator, the circuit permits local synchronization of terminals that cannot be synchronized with each other via a common commercial power grid. (Courtesy Muirhead.)

Method (3), the "slaving" of the receiver to the transmitter by provision of a special sync signal, may be implemented in one of several ways. One is to transmit a continuous signal of constant frequency that is either below or above the highest picture signal frequency transmitted. Amplified, the signal becomes the a.c. current on which the scanner and recorder drive motors operate. Where a high frequency is chosen, it will probably be a multiple of some standard motor operating frequency (e.g., 60 Hz), so that commercially available synchronous motors may be employed, the frequency being appropriately reduced through dividers.

This method requires effective filtration and separation of frequencies to ensure that the sync and picture signals do not interact. Design of the circuitry to accomplish this could be critical, depending on the amount of separation allowed by signal and channel bandwidths. An alternative is to separate by amplitude rather than frequency, by maintaining the sync signal at an amplitude below the white level (or black level, depending on polarity) of the picture signal.

Another way of implementing method (3) is the sending of either a continuous frequency or short pulses to be utilized as a check on the speed of the recorder drive motor. The approach is similar to phasing, except that it is continuous throughout transmission of picture detail. It has the advantage of permitting use of d.c. drive motors, or various other nonsynchronous types, the one at the recorder being designed (or geared) to run slightly faster than that at the scanner.

Where a continuous frequency is used in the latter approach, its function will be to control an inductive "governor" on the motor drive shaft. There are several ways of doing this, the most basic of which is illustrated in Fig. 3.26. In a more complex arrangement, the inductive device might function

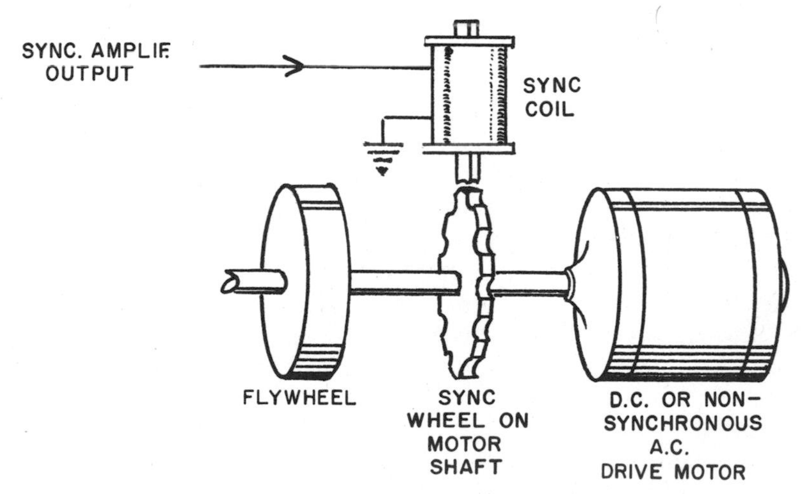

Fig. 3.26. Method of synchronizing scanner and recorder drive motors by means of inductive "governors" on drive shafts. The method permits use of nonsynchronous motors. A steady sync signal is transmitted along with the picture signal.

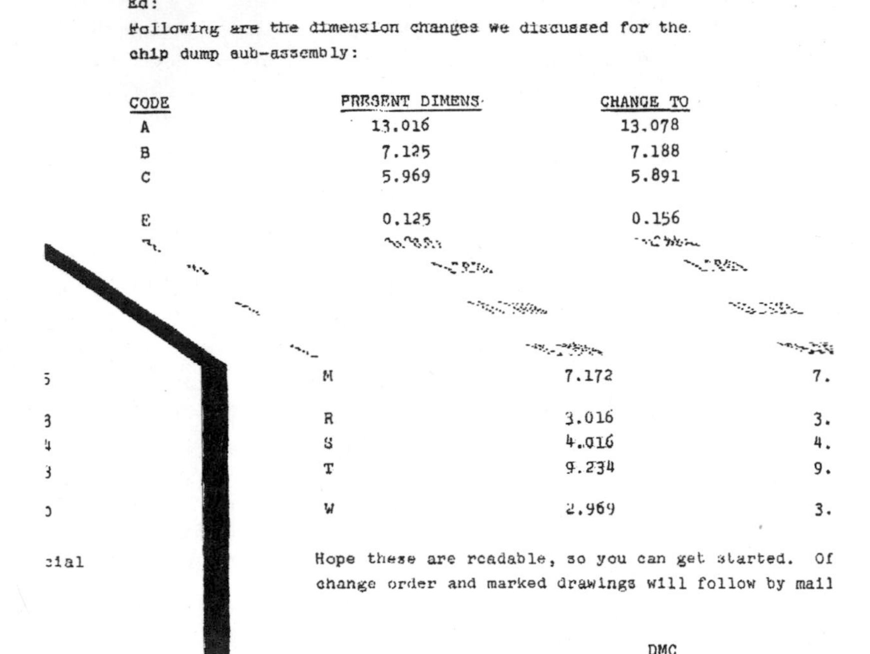

Ed:

Following are the dimension changes we discussed for the chip dump sub-assembly:

CODE	PRESENT DIMENS.	CHANGE TO
A	13.016	13.078
B	7.125	7.188
C	5.969	5.891
E	0.125	0.156

5	M	7.172	7.
3	R	3.016	3.
4	S	4.016	4.
3	T	9.234	9.
ɔ	W	2.969	3.

cial

Hope these are readable, so you can get started. Of change order and marked drawings will follow by mail

DMC

Fig. 3.27. Effects of synchronization and phasing malfunctions on a fax recording. Sync loss produces "tearing" similar to that resulting from loss of horizontal hold in a TV system. Recovery of synchronization without rephasing causes the recording stroke to start at the wrong point with respect to the paper. (Simulated.)

as an alternator, generating an a.c. current whose phase is constantly compared with that of the received synchronizing frequency in a special comparing circuit. Differences in phase will result in variations in supply voltage to the drive motor, thus varying its speed to maintain equilibrium.

Similarly, intermittent pulses, transmitted at scan line intervals, may be used to control either an inductive or mechanical brake at the recorder. The latter is a variation of the old stop-start technique of Bain, in which the faster-running recorder is stopped momentarily by an automatic clutch at the end of each stroke while the scanner catches up.

One other variation of method (3) is the use of between-the-line pulses to control the frequency of a motor drive oscillator at the recorder in much the same manner that transmitted sync pulses in a TV system control the sweep frequency of a local oscillator at the receiver.

There are several situations in which reliance on the commercial power grid for automatic synchronization is intrinsically precluded. Among them are ship-to-shore and air-to-ground transmission, mobile operations, temporary military field installations, and most international facsimile operations. In each of these situations, some variation of methods (2) and (3) is required.

Figure 3.27 illustrates the effects of phasing and synchronization malfunctions on a fax recording.

INDEX OF COOPERATION

What if the length of stroke at a recorder is less or greater than that at the scanner? Or what if the number of scan lines within a given linear dimension varies between the scanner and recorder? The effect depends on the degree of disparity, but if the scan length varies without a proportional variation in scan line density (scan lines per inch), or vice versa, the result is a distorted recording.

Associated with every fax transmitter and receiver is an index of cooperation, which is the product of scan density (in lines per inch) times effective stroke length.[4] If a transmitter and receiver have the same index, they are

[4] The international (CCITT) index of cooperation is based on cylinder diameter rather than stroke length, and it is equal to 0.318 multiplied by the IEEE stroke length index.

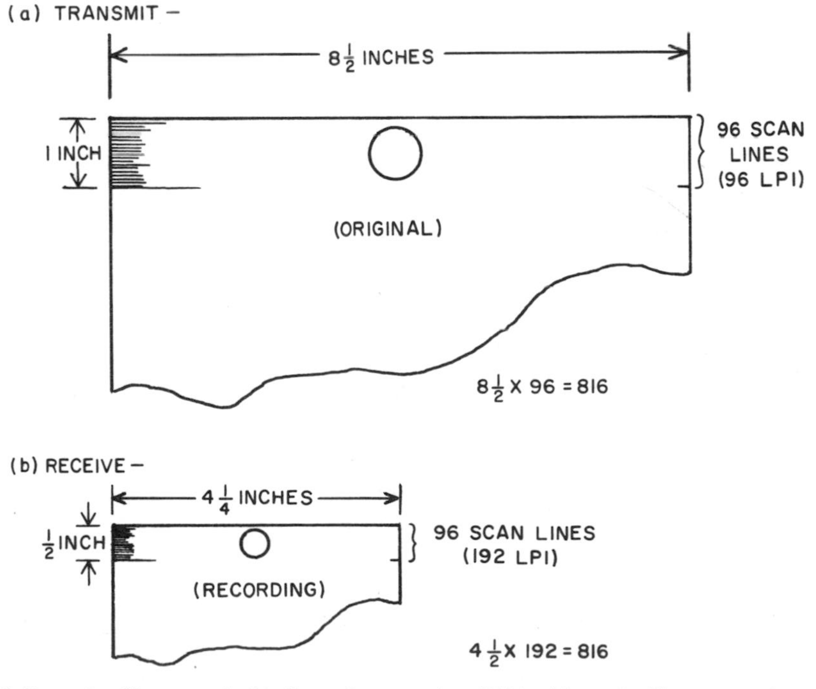

Fig. 3.28. Example of how matched indices of cooperation (816 in this case) will ensure against geometric distortion while permitting wide variations in relative size of original and recording. The scan *rate* (LPM) must be the same for scanner and recorder.

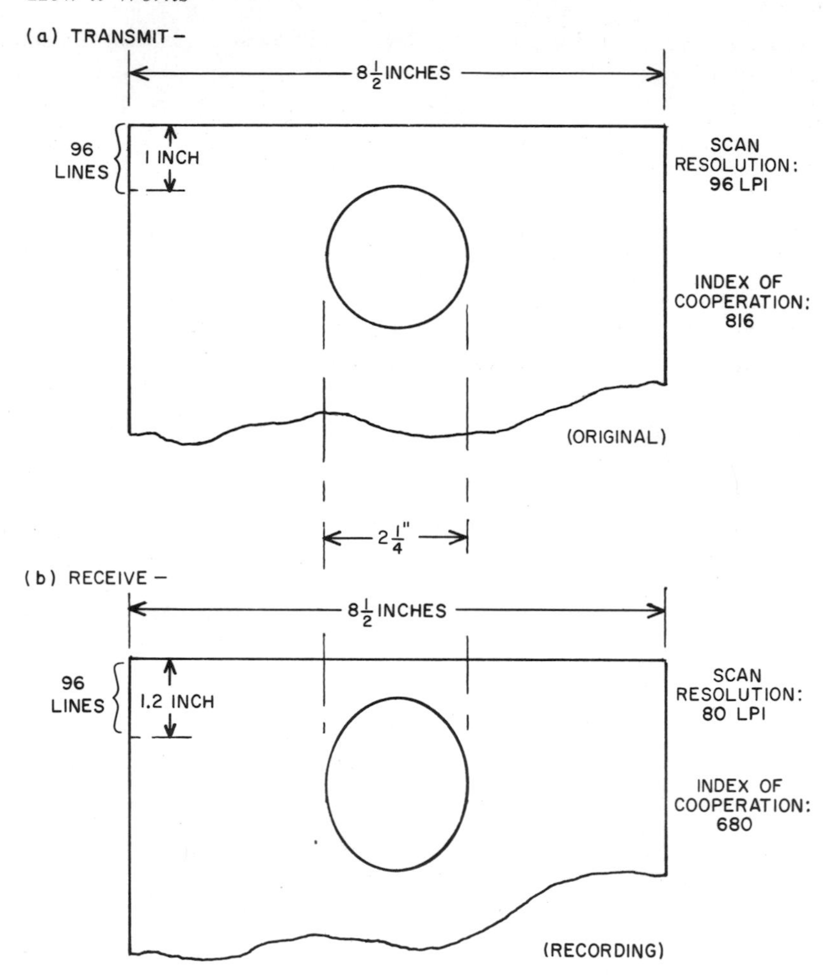

Fig. 3.29. A lower index of cooperation at the receive end of a system will result in stretching of image details in the direction normal to the scan axis.

considered compatible and the recording produced at the receiver will be a geometrically faithful reproduction of the subject copy transmitted. However, the reproduction will not necessarily be of the same size as the original.

Consider, for example, a transmitter and receiver each having an index of 816. This could mean that the scanner and recorders each produce an equal number of strokes of a given length within a given linear dimension—e.g., 96 strokes per inch; 8.5 inches per stroke ($96 \times 8.5 = 816$)—or it could mean that one produces fewer strokes of a greater length or more strokes of a shorter length than the other, the product in any case equaling 816. Regardless of the combination, the number of strokes necessary to result in a product of 816 will occur within the same length of time.

Assume that the scanner produces 96 $8\frac{1}{2}$-inch strokes in about half a minute, and the recorder, operating in synchronism with the scanner, produces 96 $4\frac{1}{4}$-inch strokes in the same amount of time. If both units have an index of 816, the scanner's 96 strokes will occupy an inch of space (at right angles to the stroke length), and the recorder's 96 strokes will occupy only $\frac{1}{2}$-inch of space (192 strokes per inch). The result will be as illustrated in Fig. 3.28. While the recording is one-fourth the size of the original, the vertical-to-horizontal relationship of image elements has been preserved.

Figure 3.29 illustrates one possible result of the linking together of a recorder and scanner with different indices of cooperation, but equal scan rates. As noted, the scanner's index is 816, while the recorder's is 680. In

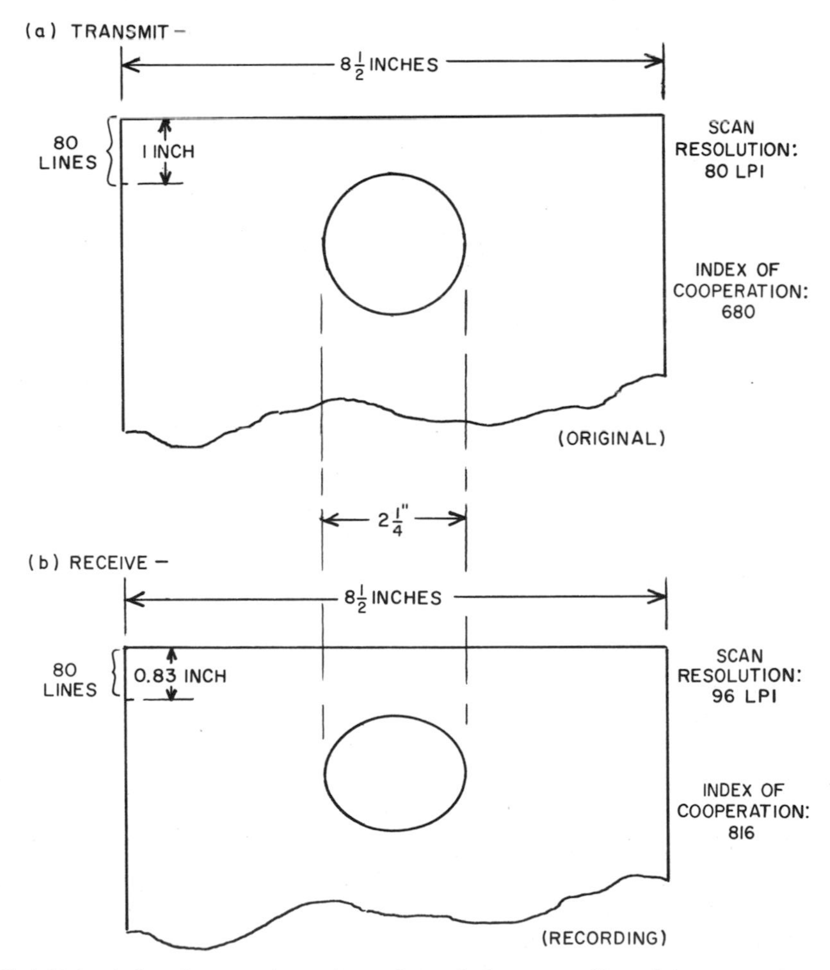

Fig. 3.30. A higher index of cooperation at the receive end of a system will result in compressing of image details in the direction normal to the scan axis.

this particular example the 680 index is the product of 80 strokes per inch and 8.5 inches per stroke. But regardless of whether it is that particular combination, or 85 8-inch strokes—or any other combination that results in a product of 680—the distortion pattern and the degree of distortion will be the same. Figure 3.30 illustrates what the result would be if the indices were reversed between scanner and recorder.

The next chapter will discuss technical considerations and special problems involved in the actual transmission of a picture signal between the separated terminals of a fax system.

BIBLIOGRAPHY

Axner, D. H., "The Facts About Facsimile," *Data Processing,* May 1968, pp. 42-53.

Bliss, W. H., "Advancements in the Facsimile Art During 19—" (ann.), IEEE *International Convention Record,* Wire and Data Communic. Sec., 1964-67.

Costigan, D. M., "FAX . . . ," *Popular Electronics,* Feb. 1969, pp. 33-40 and 102.

Floyd, H. A., "Instant Mail by Facsimile," *Reproductions Review,* Aug. 1969, pp. 8 and 46, and Sept. 1969, pp. 38 and 53.

Goldsmith, A. N., et al., *Radio Facsimile* (Vol. I), New York, RCA Institutes Technical Press, 1938.

IEEE No. 168, "Standards on Facsimile: Definition of Terms," New York, Institute of Electrical and Electronics Engineers, 1966.

Jones, C. R., *Facsimile,* New York, Murray Hill Books, 1949.

Plevy, A. L., "Facsimile Techniques and Equipment," *Electronics World,* Aug. 1962, pp. 21-24 and 93.

Ridings, G. H., "Facsimile Communications, Past, Present, Future," *Signal,* Nov. 1962, pp. 34-40.

R. I. Bulletin 949, March 18, 1968, ANPA Research Institute.

Spielman, H. S., *Electronics Source Book,* New York, Hayden, 1965 (Vol. II, Sec. 28, "Facsimile and Related Systems," pp. 998-1015).

4 *Transmission*

THE output of a facsimile scanner is comparable to that of a record player in the sense that it is an electrical analog, varying in both amplitude and frequency, and that the frequencies it contains are usually within the audio range. Further, the amplitude transitions constituting the outputs of both devices may be sinusoidal or essentially square and can therefore vary widely in harmonic content.

There are, however, also two significant distinctions between the two outputs. One, already briefly mentioned in the preceding chapter, is that the fax signal does not ordinarily contain "clean" frequencies such as those that would identify a flute or a bell in an audio signal. Having resulted from a succession of generally random light reflectance variations, the scanner output consists primarily of an irregular chain of transitions that constitute audio frequencies only in the sense of the number of times they may occur within a second (Fig. 4.1).

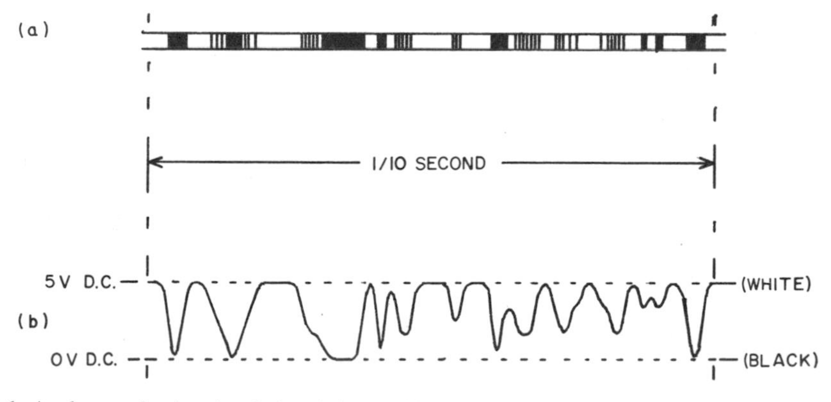

Fig. 4.1. Analogous fax baseband signal (b) resulting from random light variations within a scanned segment (a) of a subject copy.

The other basic distinction is that the scanner output can vary in frequency from several thousand hertz all the way down to zero. It is this latter characteristic more than any other that necessitates altering the form of the fax signal before it can be sent out over a transmission circuit engineered to handle voice currents.

D.C. AND SUBAUDIO

To say that the fax scanner generates "zero frequencies" is to say that its output contains very slow variations that can approach a d.c. component, a fact which presents a problem in that there is virtually no communication transmission system in operation today that will accept or pass subaudio frequencies. Transmission has evolved into a highly sophisticated art since the day when the d.c. telegraph was the dominant means of communicating electrically.

If the d.c. component of the scanner output represented only the white space of the copy being transmitted, there might not be a problem. Assuming an output polarity of maximum on black,[1] a steady white level would be analogous to a silent passage in an audio signal (e.g., a pause in a telephone conversation). The problem is that broad expanses of black—underscoring on a document, for example—and shades of gray, as in a photograph, are each represented by an analogous d.c. level.

Even if the fax signal frequency did not go to zero but contained very low frequencies, say in the neighborhood of 20 to 50 Hz, there would still be a problem in sending it over telephone circuits because of their characteristically poor low-frequency response (which, to some extent, is deliberate, to avoid a.c. power hum and to provide separation between channels). The response curve for a single voice path in the telephone network is, in general, reasonably flat between 300 and 2500 Hz, but tends to fall off sharply beyond these points (Fig. 4.2).

In actuality, if a solid black, gray, or white area were to extend through several scan strokes, the resulting scanner output would not be a steady d.c. level—or a steady zero—because of the regular occurrence of phasing, or "dead sector," pulses between strokes. Nevertheless, the resulting waveform would be such that it would present problems in transmission and, even if viewed as pulsating d.c., would represent a subaudio frequency in all but the highest speed fax systems.

[1] Depending on the manner in which it is accessed and the type of photoelectric transducer used, the output of a scanner may represent white portions of the copy as zero and the black as maximum signal, or vice versa.

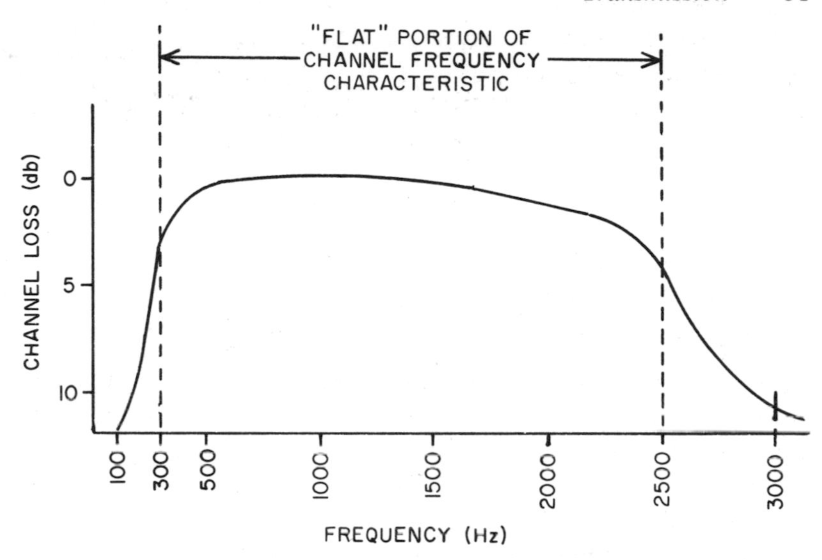

Fig. 4.2. Frequency characteristic of a typical telephone circuit.

MODULATION

The subaudio problem is solved in practice by impressing the scanner output on an audio frequency carrier. In that way the various d.c. levels are converted to audio rate a.c. of discrete frequencies or of corresponding amplitude levels of a fixed frequency, depending on the kind of modulation used. In addition, since the carrier frequency is customarily higher than the highest anticipated picture signal frequency, modulation has the effect of shifting the entire picture frequency range upward so that it is wholly within the flat portion of the transmission circuit's response curve.

BASEBAND, HARMONICS, AND SIDEBANDS

In a conventional 96 LPI/180 LPM[2] message fax system, assuming equal vertical and horizontal resolution, the required picture signal frequency range—or *baseband*—is from 0 to about 1300 Hz. The 1300 Hz maximum assumes a 9-inch stroke interval, within each of which a total of 432 black-to-white transitions can be detected and reproduced. (It takes two scan lines to reproduce one black-to-white transition at right angles to the scan grain. Since each transition is a complete cycle and there are 96 scan lines per inch, the system should be capable of resolving 48 cycles per inch horizontally and vertically.) At 180 strokes per minute, there are 3 strokes per second. $3 \times 9 \times 48 = 1296$ (1300) cycles per second (Hz).

[2] Ninety-six lines (or strokes) per inch and 180 lines per minute, in accordance with the Electronic Industries Association message facsimile standard RS-328.

The next consideration is how much additional channel capacity has to be allowed for harmonics and sidebands, the latter being the by-products of modulation. Just as a reproduced violin sound will lack fidelity if the audio system fails to reproduce the instrument's natural overtones or harmonics, a recorded image detail in a fax system will theoretically lack fidelity if harmonics are suppressed by provision of too narrow a transmission channel.

Some purists have contended, in fact, that faithful reproduction of a modulating waveform requires a channel bandwidth sufficient to include the third harmonic of the highest fundamental frequency generated by the scanner. Moreover, it is a rule of thumb that the carrier frequency be at least double the highest baseband frequency to be transmitted. Any less of a gap between carrier and baseband will result in an overlap of the latter and the lower sideband produced by modulation (Fig. 4.3), resulting in a distortion known as the *Kendall effect.* It will usually manifest itself as a kind of fuzziness at the edges of recorded picture details.

In the case of the conventional $^{96}/_{180}$ system, the third harmonic would be 3.9 kHz (3 × 1296 Hz), which would amount to a carrier frequency of 7.8 kHz (2 × 3.9). Even ignoring allowance for sidebands, 7.8 kHz far exceeds the capacity of a telephone voice circuit.

The sidebands produced as a by-product of modulation consist of a range of frequencies below and above the carrier frequency, extending from the carrier *minus* the highest baseband frequency to the carrier *plus* the highest baseband frequency. (This pertains to *amplitude modulation* (AM) only. The sideband situation is somewhat different for frequency modulation (FM). The distinction will be discussed further on in this chapter.) In the example just given the lower sideband would range from 3.9 to 7.8 kHz, and the

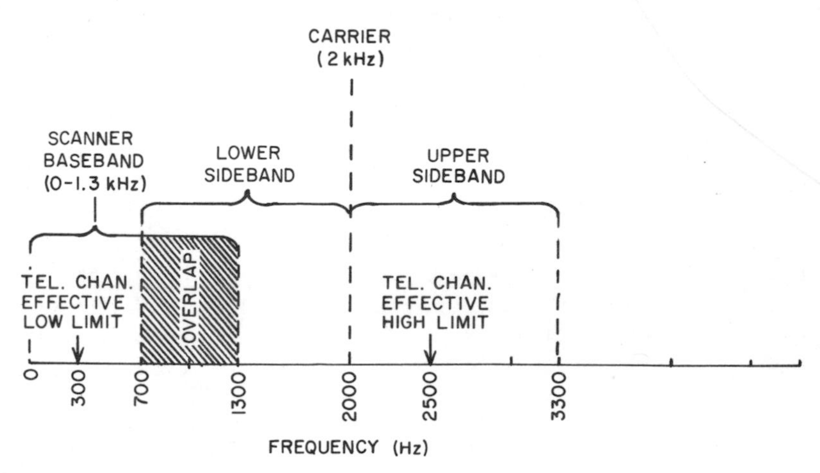

Fig. 4.3. Overlap resulting when the carrier frequency is less than twice the highest baseband frequency.

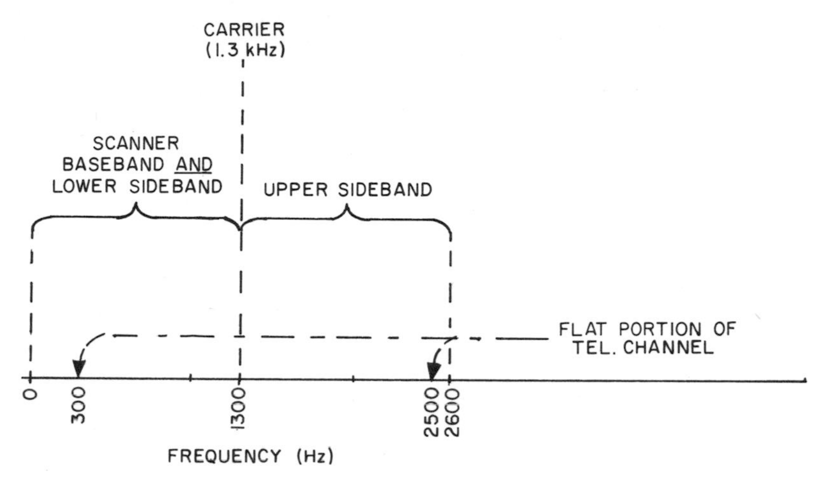

Fig. 4.4. Heavy channel space requirements make double-sideband AM a generally unsuitable fax transmission technique for the telephone network.

upper from 7.8 to 11.7 kHz. Theoretically, then, the transmission circuit for a conventional message facsimile system would have to be capable of handling frequencies as high as 11.7 kHz—which would, of course, completely rule out the use of conventional voice grade telephone facilities for fax transmission.

So much for theory. In actual practice it has been found that harmonics can be pretty much ignored without having any obvious degradation of recording fidelity in a fax system. Thus, from a practical standpoint, about the highest baseband frequency we need concern ourselves with in the 96/180 system is 1300 Hz. Experience has also shown that, Kendall effect notwithstanding, the carrier frequency can be substantially less than double the highest baseband frequency, and recording fidelity will still be adequate for most purposes.

But, even ignoring harmonics and allowing no margin at all between the top baseband and carrier frequencies, the modulated carrier plus sidebands will just barely fit within the flat portion of the telephone network bandpass (Fig. 4.4). The bandspread of the fax transmitter has still somehow to be further reduced.

SIDEBAND SUPPRESSION

The one further step necessary to fit the fax signal into a voiceband channel is sideband suppression. In 1915, John R. Carson, an AT&T Company engineer, made some important observations regarding the role sidebands play in modulated carrier transmission. He established that identical information was conveyed by each of the two sidebands produced when a carrier was amplitude-modulated, and that each contained all of the

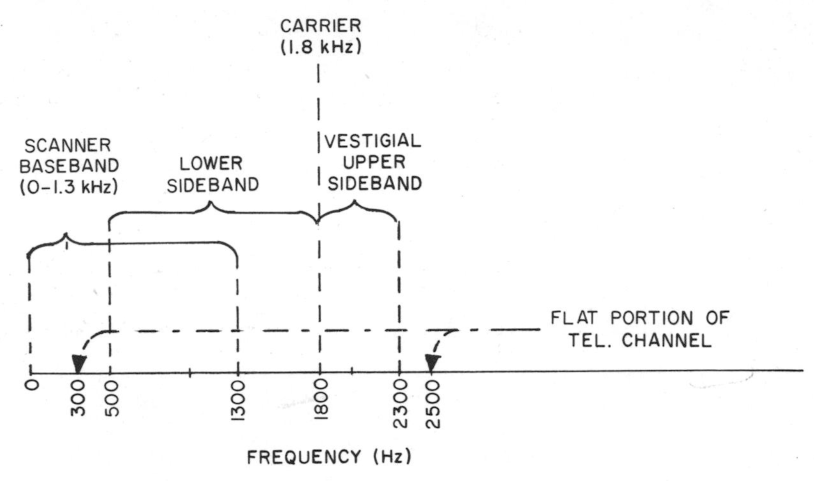

Fig. 4.5. Vestigial sideband AM transmission provides a practical compromise between single and double sideband techniques.

intelligence present in the modulating signal. This being the case, it followed that one of the two sidebands could be suppressed, theoretically with no effect on the intelligence being transmitted.

In practice, both an entire sideband (usually the upper) and the carrier itself can be suppressed by bandpass filtration without seriously affecting the fidelity of the received signal. The carrier frequency must, of course, be restored at the receiving end. However, while this *single sideband technique* makes the most efficient use of a transmission channel, it is difficult in practice to suppress the upper sideband and carrier frequencies without also sacrificing a portion of the lower sideband. The portion lost will contain lower frequency baseband components and will therefore result in total distortion of relatively broad picture elements in a fax recording.

A good compromise technique, and one that has been resorted to in a number of commercial fax systems, is *vestigial sideband transmission.* Here, the entire lower sideband, the carrier, and a small portion of the upper sideband are transmitted. Using a carrier slightly higher in frequency than the top baseband frequency—e.g., 1800 Hz in the aforementioned $^{96}/_{180}$ system—and retaining the portion of the upper sideband extending to, say, 2300 Hz, we have an audio frequency signal of a range that will fit most telephone circuits with room to spare (Fig. 4.5). A possible difficulty with this technique is that positioning of the carrier and design of the bandpass filters may be critical.

LIMITATIONS OF THE "SWITCHED NETWORK"

In the foregoing paragraphs, occasional reference has been made to the "telephone network." By this is meant the switched, or dial, network to which a telephone subscriber has access only for the duration of a call. It is termed a switched network because the trunks connecting two telephone central offices are shared by all subscribers served by each office. When a party in one city phones someone in another, automatic switching equipment at the originating central office selects an interconnecting trunk that does not happen to be in use at the moment. A subsequent call placed between the same two points will very likely go over a different trunk.

Telephone lines can also be privately leased and specially conditioned for fax transmission. A major disadvantage of the switched system for fax is that, while slight differences in transmission quality between two trunks may not be detectable audibly, they may result in fax recordings of unpredictably different visual quality. In addition, there are present in switched trunks a variety of electrical "noises" that can normally be overlooked because of their negligible audible effects, but which can produce significant degradation in a visual recording.

So far, only amplitude modulation has been discussed as a fax transmission technique. There is also frequency modulation, which offers certain technical advantages that have made it a generally preferred modulation technique for systems designed to interface with the switched network. Private line systems use AM almost exclusively, but switched network systems tend to use FM predominately.

FM

The fundamental distinction between AM and FM is that AM converts the varying modulating voltage to corresponding amplitude variations in a fixed-frequency carrier, whereas FM converts it to variations in carrier frequency. The distinction is illustrated in Fig. 4.6.

Ordinarily, the chief advantage of FM over AM is its relative immunity to the effects of electrical noise. Unfortunately, it is an advantage usually gained only at the expense of additional bandwidth—which, needless to say, the telephone network cannot afford.

It is nevertheless "noise" of a sort that makes FM somewhat preferable to AM where the switched network is concerned. We generally think of noise as the random, more or less constant, low level voltage fluctuations that find their way into a transmission circuit and become an unwanted part of the transmitted signal. Amplifier tube noise, power line induction, and crosstalk are typical examples.

But there is also noise in the form of changes in signal level during transmission. These are particularly prevalent in the switched network, where they can have a variety of causes, including the switching of batteries or other circuit components at any of the several exchanges a call may have to pass through enroute to its destination. They can have a significant and unpredictable effect on the quality of fax transmission in an AM system. FM, with its relative insensitivity to amplitude fluctuations, is largely unaffected by them.

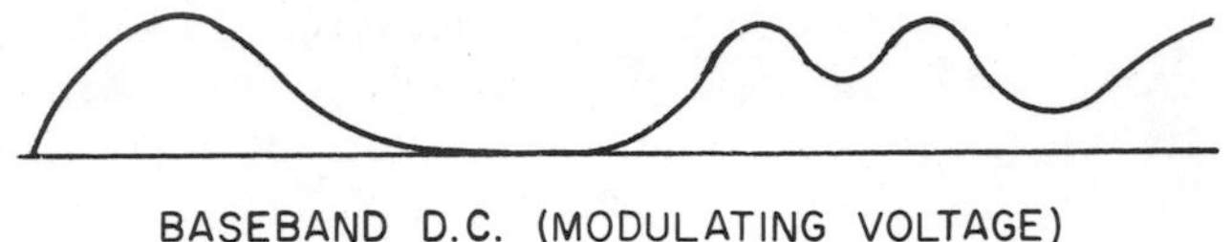

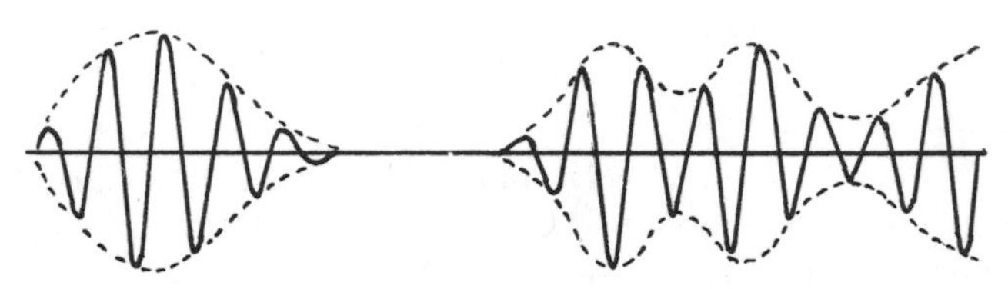

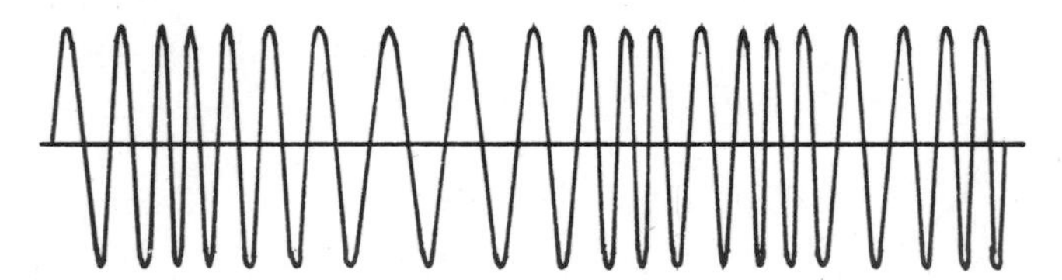

Fig. 4.6. Baseband d.c. from the scanner can modulate either the amplitude or frequency of the carrier.

Another kind of amplitude fluctuation is the fading encountered in long-range radio reception, an atmospheric phenomenon that is unpredictable and generally unavoidable. Where fax signals are transmitted via long-range AM radio, the effects of fading—notably, "rushes" of noise in the recording—might be disastrous, were it not for the expedient of employing an FM subcarrier (more on this in the discussion of radio facilities, later in the chapter).

As for bandwidth, which FM normally needs plenty of, requirements are governed by two variables. It is an unfortunate peculiarity of FM that it produces not just two sidebands, as does AM, but a proliferation of them, each containing a portion of the signal energy. Their spacing is in direct proportion to the instantaneous baseband frequency, and their number and relative significance in terms of energy content varies in proportion to the strength of the input signal (and thus the degree of carrier swing (Fig. 4.7).

By constraining and balancing each of these variables (among other special design twists), it has been possible to perfect FM modulators that function quite effectively in "fax-by-phone" systems. A basic requirement is that the ratio of maximum carrier swing to maximum baseband frequency be as small as effective operation of the system will permit. A small ratio results in a low *modulation index,* which makes the FM signal practically indistinguishable from AM in terms of required bandwidth and resistance to noise other than changes in signal level.

Through skillful engineering (and some judicious compromising of quality), 96 LPI FM fax systems are now available that can transmit at the rate of 240 LPM over the switched network, without apparently penalizing output legibility.

MODULATION SCHEMES

What are the actual mechanics of modulation in a facsimile transmitter? There are probably more different schemes than there are makes of fax terminal gear in use, but a quick review of some of the more venerable methods plus a brief analysis of a couple of modern circuits should suffice to give the reader a general idea of what is involved.

During the reign of the vacuum tube, analog modulators (in general) were classified as either plate or grid, the grid being generally favored in facsimile because it permitted use of a lower level modulating voltage and thus minimized the required number of preamplifier stages. With vacuum tubes, baseband amplification required relatively high d.c. supply voltages because the amplifier stages had to be directly coupled to preserve the d.c. component of the transducer output (see Chapter 3, Amplification). In some vacuum tube fax transmitters, the transducer output was fed directly to the modulator, thereby eliminating preamplification entirely.

Another method employed in some older fax transmitters to eliminate the need for d.c. preamplification was to mechanically interrupt, or "chop,"

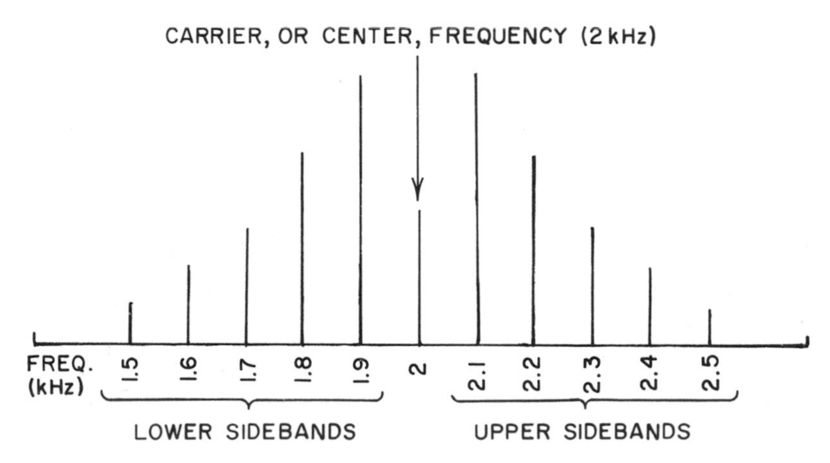

Fig. 4.7. Sideband proliferation is a characteristic of FM. Shown here is a partial array resulting from an instantaneous modulating frequency of 100 Hz.

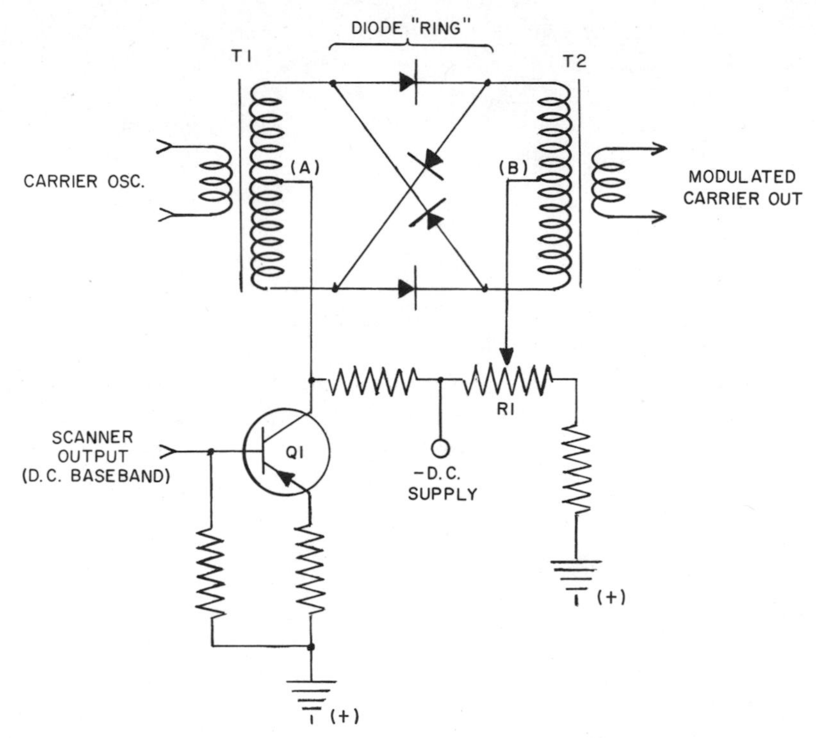

Fig. 4.8. "Ring" modulator for AM is simple and reliable. Balancing of d.c. bias between points (A) and (B) prevents flow of carrier from Tl to T2. D.C. signal fluctuations at the collector of Q1 produce a varying bias differential, controlling the flow of carrier in accordance with the baseband variations.

the scanner light beam at a carrier rate (approximately twice the highest baseband frequency to be transmitted). Modulation thus actually *preceded* the generation of the baseband signal, permitting the latter to be processed through a conventional capacitor- or transformer-coupled amplifier.

Transistors have lent themselves much more readily to the design of direct-coupled amplifiers capable of operating at the low supply voltages characteristic of solid state circuits, and have, in general, simplified the design of modulators.

A basic AM modulator circuit is shown in Fig. 4.8. It is a conventional *ring* modulator, so named for the arrangement of the four diodes in a kind of ring, or electrically circular configuration, which functions as a bridge. Adjustment of R1 balances the d.c. bias on the four diodes, in which state the diodes constitute a short circuit which blocks the carrier frequency from getting to T2 from T1. The biases become unbalanced with each change in voltage at the collector of Q1, due to the scanner output variations applied to the base. The bridge thus unbalances at the baseband rate and controls the flow of carrier current to T2 accordingly, resulting in an amplitude-modulated carrier at the output.

The FM modulator shown in Fig. 4.9 is essentially a free-running, symmetrical multivibrator (Q2 and Q3), the output frequency of which is controllable by varying the d.c. supply voltage. Modulation is accomplished by using the amplified baseband d.c. to vary the supply voltage (via Q1). The multivibrator is isolated from the transmission line by Q4, preventing unwanted frequency shifts due to possible stray currents and line impedance changes.

DEMODULATION (DETECTION)

In a basic AM system, restoration—or detection—of the baseband signal at the receiver is principally a matter of rectification. As transmitted, the baseband is the *envelope* of the a.c. carrier and is electrically self-canceling.

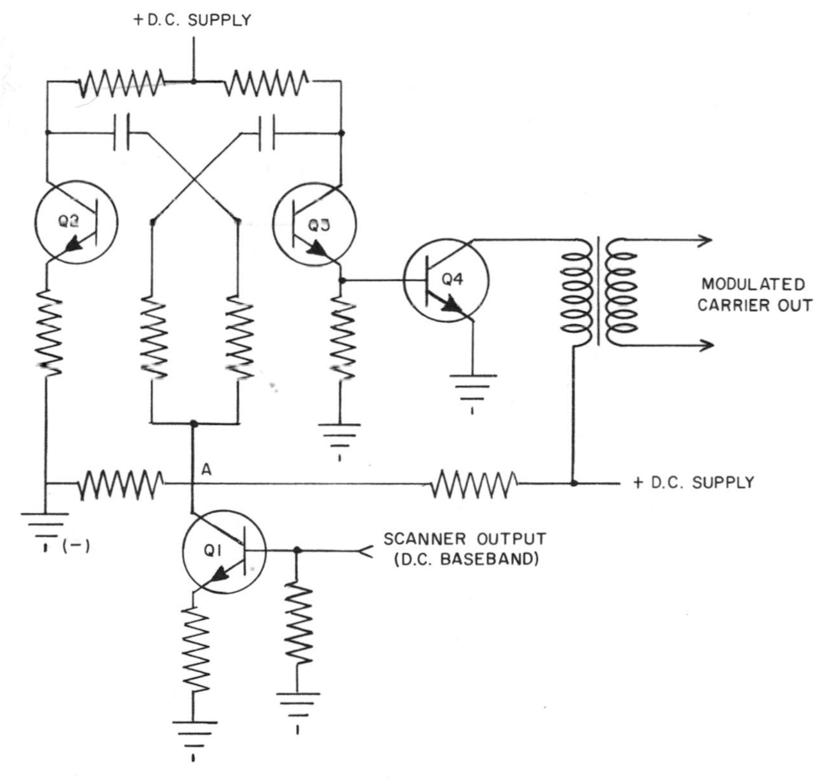

Fig. 4.9. FM modulator employing a free-running multivibrator (Q2 and Q3), the frequency output of which varies with supply voltage fluctuations. Baseband current flow through Q1 varies the supply voltage at point (A) at the baseband rate, thereby frequency-modulating the multivibrator output. Q4 isolates the multivibrator from the transmission line.

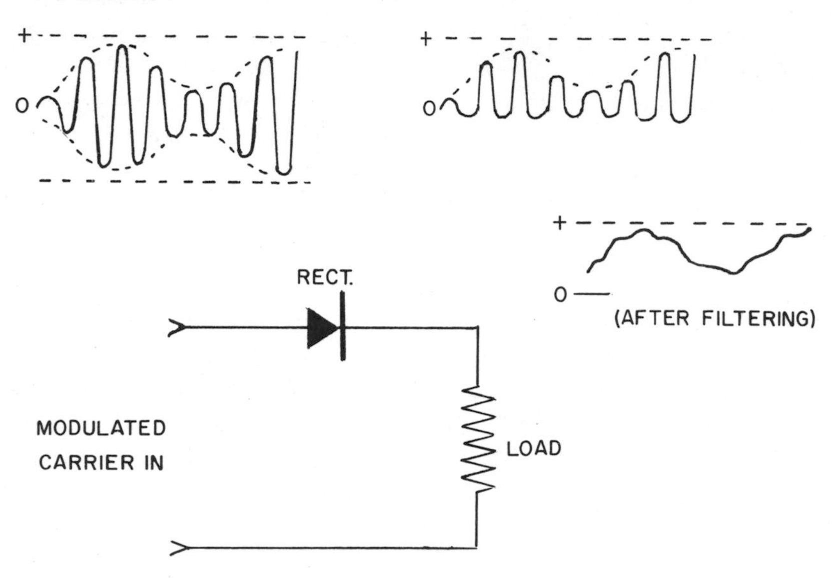

Fig. 4.10. An AM detector is basically a rectifier, its purpose to convert the a.c. carrier to pulsating d.c. Subsequent filtering effectively eliminates carrier pulses, leaving only the restored d.c. baseband variations contained in the carrier envelope.

The first step in restoration, therefore, is to eliminate either the positive or negative half-cycles of the carrier (Fig. 4.10).

In practice, the retained carrier half-cycles also are smoothed (by filtering) so that only the broader d.c. fluctuations represented by the envelope remain. The latter are, in effect, the restored scanner output, which is amplified and fed to the recorder.

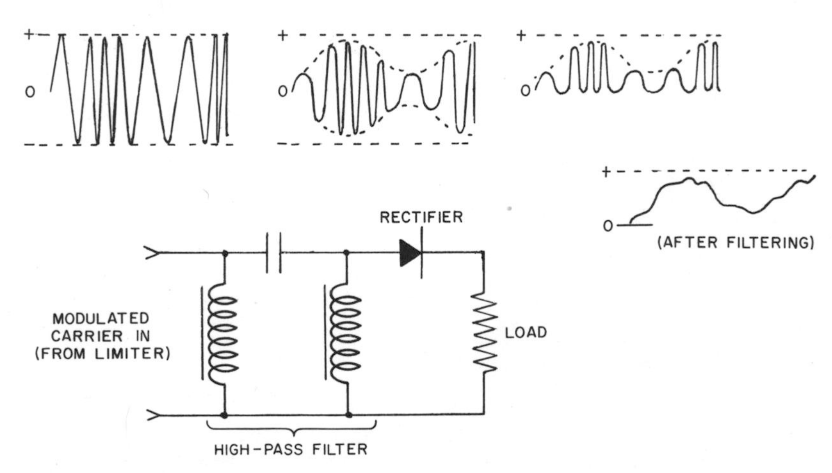

Fig. 4.11. FM detection is a combination of "slope" filtering and rectifying. The circuit shown illustrates the basic principle. The modulated carrier emerges from the high-pass filter with its amplitude attenuated at lower frequencies. It thus acquires an equivalent AM envelope, enabling recovery of the baseband by conventional rectifying and filtering.

Whereas AM signals are detected by rectification, FM detection is basically a filtering action, the object being to attenuate the carrier's constantly shifting frequency on a sloping curve so that the higher frequencies (for example) will be passed more freely than the lower ones. Thus processed, the carrier now varies in strength with frequency and can be treated as an AM signal. Rectified and filtered, it becomes a faithful reproduction of the scanner output. The general principle is illustrated in Fig. 4.11.

Immediately before detection, the received FM carrier passes through a *limiter,* which clips its amplitude peaks, eliminating unwanted level variations that may have been picked up in transmission. As pointed out earlier, it is this aspect of the FM technique that makes it attractive for fax transmission via the public telephone network, where level variations can be a problem. In principle, the limiter is really nothing more than a conventional amplifier stage that is overdriven by an excessive input signal level.

TRANSMISSION IMPAIRMENTS

Some of the sources of impairment of a fax recording have already been broadly discussed, particularly as they relate to the use of the public switched telephone network as the transmission medium. It might be well at this point to briefly review some of those already mentioned and to explore others that are likely to be encountered regardless of the transmission medium employed.

EXTERNAL INTERFERENCE

Lightning, power line induction, and "crosstalk" are among the principal external interferences that can blemish a fax recording. Lightning and other "arcing" interferences are usually momentary, but their spasmodic occurrence can obliterate essential details of the transmitted copy. Here is an essential distinction between voice and fax transmission: with voice, if a word is marred by a momentary "crackle," it need only be repeated; with fax, retransmission can be time-consuming and costly.

AM radio systems and open-wire telephone lines are most vulnerable to atmospheric disturbances, but all telephone connections are subject to impulse noise from arcing interferences.

Single frequency interference such as power line induction, unlike interference from spasmodic arcing, is usually continuous and symmetrical, and therefore will generally result in a kind of herringbone or diagonal stripe pattern over the entire fax recording (Fig. 4.12).

Crosstalk is a problem almost as old as the telephone. Despite elaborate measures taken to minimize it, it persists as an elusive malady in most transmission systems having parallel paths. It occurs when the transmission level in a wire circuit or carrier channel exceeds prescribed limits and causes

Fig. 4.12. Single-frequency a.c. interference produces a herringbone pattern in a fax recording.

transmission paths to overlap.[3] Its effect on a fax recording is somewhat like that of single frequency interference (Fig. 4.12), but without the clean symmetry.

There is actually no fixed limit in signal strength beyond which crosstalk will definitely occur in all cases. The tolerable maximum signal current can range anywhere from $\frac{1}{20}$ to 1 milliwatt. The coupling units generally required for connection of privately operated terminals (including fax transmitters) to the telephone network are designed to hold the maximum signal energy within prescribed limits for a given installation.

[3] The reference to *carrier* here concerns the multiplexing systems by which multiple signals are sent simultaneously over a single wideband facility. Most long distance telephone calls today are transmitted via carrier systems.

INTERNAL NOISE

Various "noises" can originate within a transmission path as well. Typical examples are contact noise in a switching system, tube and transistor noise within terminal amplifiers and repeater (or relay) stations, and intermodulation noise caused by nonlinear circuit elements.

Some, if not all, of these noises are likely to be present in varying degrees in almost any transmission system. Naturally, the more complex the system, or the longer the transmission link, the more the variety of noises and the greater their potential effect.

For the purposes of this book, all that need be said further of these unwanted, but usually unavoidable, noises—and this applies, in general, to external interference as well—is that, in a typical system, they can generally be ignored if their level remains 30 decibels (db) or more below the maximum picture signal level. If they are of a single frequency, such as the "singing" that sometimes results from feedback in two-wire telephone circuits, the signal/noise separation may have to be slightly greater.

LEVEL FLUCTUATIONS

Fluctuations in transmission level can occur for a variety of reasons, some of them associated with intrinsic characteristics of long telephone circuits, others with natural phenomena that are beyond human control (specifically, the fading encountered in long-range radio reception), and still others that are purely accidental. The last category consists of intermittent trouble conditions that can occur anywhere within the system, including the fax terminal equipment. These need not be discussed since they are not inherent conditions.

An inherent (though not necessarily critical) source of level fluctuations in the telephone system is the in-service substitution of equipment—batteries, amplifiers, etc.—at telephone exchanges. The longer the circuit and the more exchanges it passes through, the greater the chance that such fluctuations will occur. These abrupt changes in transmission net loss are small enough to go unnoticed in aural communication, but sufficient to visibly blemish a fax recording (Fig. 4.13). A tiny fraction of a decibel of amplitude change can have a visible effect on a fax recording, while it takes at least 3 db of change to be detectable in speech transmission.

As already mentioned in the discussion of modulation, FM is practically impervious to transmission level changes and has therefore become popular for systems utilizing the switched network, as well as for long-range, broadcast-type radio systems. In leased wire systems, where the problem is less likely to be encountered, AM is generally preferred.

ECHO

A telephone user will occasionally have the annoying experience during a long distance call of hearing an echo of his own voice whenever he speaks.

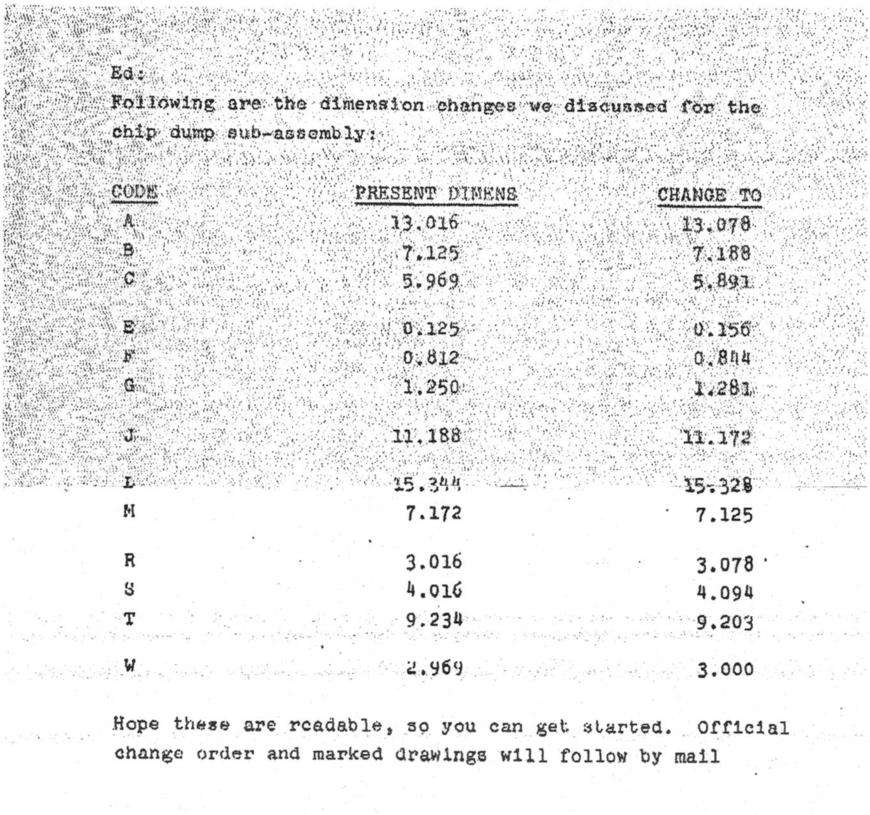

Ed:
Following are the dimension changes we discussed for the chip dump sub-assembly:

CODE	PRESENT DIMENS	CHANGE TO
A	13.016	13.078
B	7.125	7.188
C	5.969	5.891
E	0.125	0.156
F	0.812	0.844
G	1.250	1.281
J	11.188	11.172
L	15.344	15.328
M	7.172	7.125
R	3.016	3.078
S	4.016	4.094
T	9.234	9.203
W	2.969	3.000

Hope these are readable, so you can get started. Official change order and marked drawings will follow by mail

DMC

Fig. 4.13. Effect of a sudden change in transmission amplitude level in an AM fax system. The weak signal portion at the top also illustrates the effect of random noise. (Level change is simulated.)

The effect is the result of somewhat the same conditions that produce acoustic echoes in large empty halls: each time a sound wave encounters a physical obstacle, a portion of it bounces back toward the source. The greater the distance of the obstacle from the source, the longer the delay between original sound and echo, and the more detrimental the effect on acoustical communication.

Likewise, in a long telephone circuit consisting of the linking together of several separate facilities, any significant mismatch in impedance at a circuit juncture can cause a portion of the signal current to bounce back toward the source. Since a two-way communication path is, in essence, a loop, the echo can travel completely around the circuit to be picked up at the receiving end as well as at the originating terminal.

In practice, long circuits include special design features intended to prevent echo. One preventive device is a *balancing network,* whose function it is to optimize impedance matching at circuit junctures. Another is a *voice-controlled echo suppressor,* through which additional attenuation is introduced into the return path of a two-way circuit during transmission and automatically switched to the transmit path during reception.

The first of these, the balancing network, is only partially effective because, through switching, it has to match a number of different circuits, all varying slightly in impedance. Hence, at best, the impedance match it provides can only be a compromise. The second method may pose a potential problem in fax transmission because of the possibility of suppression elements being switched in during a low level interval in the transmitted signal. However, with modern terminal equipment and the provision for disabling the suppressors by transmission of a special signal, the occurrence of the problem is minimized.

In leased line systems, it is possible to tailor the balancing networks at circuit junctures to exactly match the impedances involved and thus improve the networks' effectiveness in preventing echo. This is easily achieved since no switching of lines is involved in these systems.

Figure 4.14 illustrates the effect of echo on a fax recording.

DELAY DISTORTION

Somewhat akin to echo is envelope delay distortion, one of the more chronic of transmission impairments—particularly in fax systems. It is a distortion of signal frequencies near the low and high cutoff points of the channel's response curve, resulting from a retarding effect that can slow the fringe frequencies of a signal and thereby deform the signal envelope. The free-space velocity of electrical signals is 186,000 miles a second, the same as that of light. However, telephone circuits contain a variety of inductive and capacitive characteristics that have a decelerating effect on signal currents.

In voice transmission, the effect of excessive low-frequency delay is somewhat like that of shouting into a well, while an excess at the high end will cause sharp sounds to be accompanied by a "pinging" effect, like the plucking of a high-pitched string. The visual effect on a fax recording is similar to that of echo except that it is more a *smear* than a *ghost* and may not manifest itself uniformly throughout a recording (Fig. 4.15).

Experience has shown that, for effective fax transmission within the voice band, delay must be held uniform for all frequencies within ±300 microseconds within the full frequency range of the transmitted signal. This is accomplished by installation of devices called delay equalizers at intervals along the length of a circuit.

It is a relatively simple matter to equalize leased lines to ensure good fax transmission. However, in the switched network, circuits are equalized on an "as needed" basis, and there can be no assurance that equalization will in all instances be adequate to produce good quality fax recordings.

Other transmission impairments already briefly discussed are those resulting from the Kendall effect and from synchronization and phasing errors and the mismatching of indices of cooperation (Chapter 3). All that need be said further about these is that all are usually avoidable through proper engineering of the system terminals.

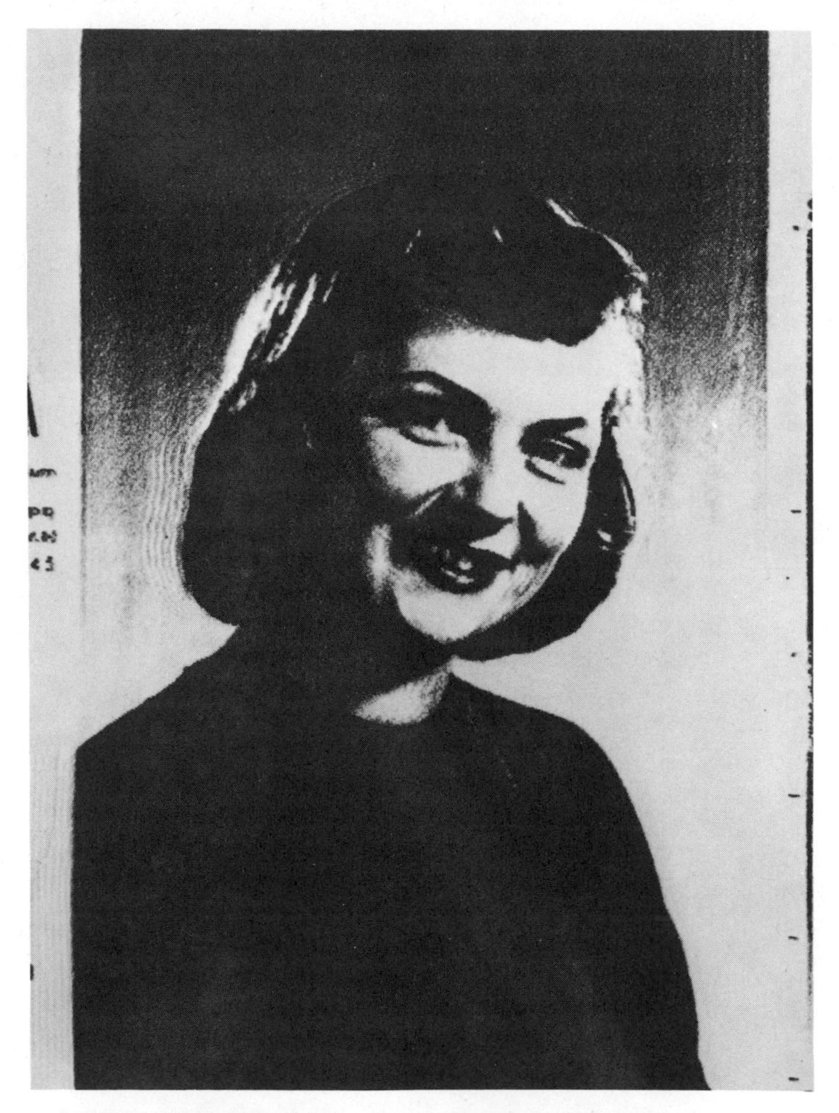

Fig. 4.14. Ripples, or "ghosts," discernible at the left of the picture were caused by multiple echoes in the transmission line.

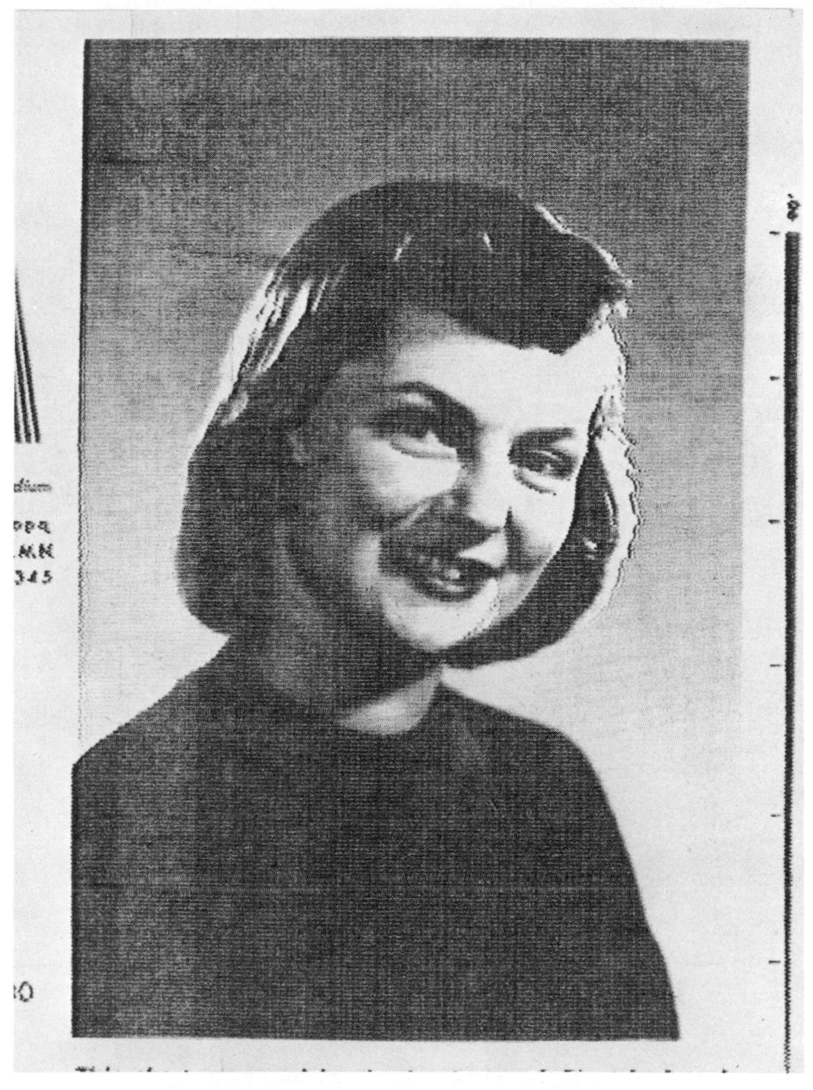

Fig. 4.15. Envelope delay in the transmission circuit was the probable cause of the distortion noticeable along the right periphery of the girl's head in this fax recording.

OTHER FACILITIES

So far the emphasis of this chapter has been on voice-grade fax transmission. There are, of course, broader bandwidth circuits available from common carriers like the telephone companies and Western Union for use with higher speed fax systems. And not to be overlooked is the use of radio, where wire service is impracticable.

The heading "Other Facilities" may be somewhat misleading in one respect, namely, the fact that conventional phone lines frequently form the basis for broader bandwidth wire links. The distinction lies chiefly in how *existing* facilities are utilized and in how they are augmented by special amplifying and equalizing devices.

Some commercial facsimile systems have bandwidth requirements lying somewhere between voice-grade and broadband—e.g., 5–15 kHz. Such facilities are not now generally available and would be quite expensive to provide on a custom engineering basis. For that reason, channel requirements beyond the limits of voice-grade or *Telephoto* facilities will usually require the purchase of transmission service on a "grouped" basis, which will be explained further on in this section.

TELEPHOTO

Telephoto facilities, known also as "Schedule II," or "Type 4002," facilities, are specially conditioned voice grade wire links leasable from common carriers and intended primarily for the transmission of photographs. They have a practical maximum bandpass of about 800 to 2800 Hz, which is generally adequate for distortion-free transmission of newspictures (about 120 scan lines to the inch at 90 lines a minute, using AM double sideband transmission), or for "message" systems of higher-than-average speed—e.g., 96 LPI at 360 LPM.

As might be expected, Telephoto facilities are somewhat more expensive to lease than conventional voice grade facilities: in the neighborhood of $460 a month for a 100-mile private link, as opposed to $275 a month for a voice grade, Series 3002 facility for the same distance (based on rates as of late 1970, including special conditioning in both cases). While the additional cost is usually justified for transmission of photographs, where quality requirements are critical, some of the benefits of the special engineering of the Telephoto facility are lost on general purpose systems that merely take advantage of the increased bandwidth to effect a modest gain in speed or resolution.

Western Union offers Schedule II circuits on a switched, "dial-up" basis, permitting the customer access to the facilities only as needed, rather then lease them on a full-time basis. In most cases, the dial-up mode will afford savings to the customer compared with leased line service. The economic crossover point will be determined principally by the average copies-per-month volumes involved. It will vary with mileage and with the customer's objective in going to a higher bandwidth in the first place—i.e., whether he uses the extra bandwidth to gain *speed* or *quality*.

One potential disadvantage of the dial-up mode is that the customer does not have the same assurance he has with a dedicated facility that results will be consistent from one transmission to the next.

As of this writing,[4] Western Union's Broadband Exchange service, as it is officially called, costs the customer a flat rate of $30 a month, plus a per-call charge of anywhere from 20 to 75 cents a minute, depending on mileage. (The range is roughly 0 to 3000 miles.)

"GROUPED" CIRCUITS

Where it is absolutely necessary, a local phone company or other communications common carrier will specially engineer a transmission circuit for a customer when no standard service exists that can meet the particular specifications. Such special engineering, however, is expensive and can usually be done only within a restricted geographic area. The usual alternative where a broadband facility is required is to lease channel space on the basis of the number of voice channels being displaced. Twelve full, 4-kHz voice channels is considered a *group,* and 60 voice channels, a *supergroup.*

In terms of interstate tariff, a 48-kHz group (or "8000 type" channel) is the next step—after telephoto—in ascending bandwidth for common carrier wire links. A group can also be subdivided into two *half groups,* each with a usable bandwidth of about 20 kHz. But the smallest grouping a customer can lease is still 12 voice channels (a full 48-kHz group), which he can use as a single broadband facility or, with proper terminal equipment, subdivide as required.

At present, a 48-kHz group, leased between two points 100 miles apart, costs the customer $2350 a month, including the required terminal interfaces. A 240-kHz supergroup leases for a flat $30 a mile per month, plus a "station charge" of $650 a month at each system terminal. Rates include provision of a voice grade coordination or control channel.

Of available commercial fax systems, Xerox's high-speed, high-resolution LDX (Long Distance Xerography) system is one of few requiring the full group or supergroup channel space. The 135 LPI/2520 LPM and 190 LPI/1800 LPM configurations of the system each require a full 48-kHz group, and the 135 LPI/12,600 LPM and 190 LPI/9000 LPM configurations require a full 240-kHz supergroup. Most message fax systems of the "copy-a-minute" variety (96 LPI/960 LPM, for example) require the leasing of a 48-kHz group, even though only a portion of the full bandwidth may actually be needed.

SWITCHED BROADBAND

"Dial-up," or switched, broadband service (50 kilobits per second) is now being offered on a trial basis in and between a limited number of major cities. It is expected that before very long a service of this general type will become standard.

[4] References to the time of writing, including such phrases as "at present" or "to date," or the word "now," may be interpreted as meaning the last quarter of 1970.

As with the public switched telephone network, or Western Union's Broadband Exchange service, switched broadband permits the user to buy the service on a per-call, or message rate, basis, in addition to which he must pay a fixed monthly charge for the special terminal equipment required. Transmit time thus becomes the controlling factor in the economics of the switched service. Leased facilities, on the other hand, become more economical the greater the average monthly volume of copies transmitted.

Distance, of course, also enters the picture, its influence on the per-copy cost in a leased line system becoming more pronounced the lower the average volume of copies involved. At terminal separations of less than 100 miles, a volume of from 75 to 100 copies a day might suffice to make the leased facility the more economical, provided the broader bandwidth is used primarily to gain transmission speed—e.g., 96 LPI at 960 instead of 180 LPM. For distances of 500 miles or more, daily volumes at the same resolution and speed would probably have to exceed 200 copies before the leased group service would become more economical than the switched broadband service.

Where the primary objective, on the other hand, is to gain improved output resolution rather than speed—e.g., 200 LPI (instead of 96) at 180 LPM—the crossover would occur at a much lower point in terms of volume (roughly 20 to 40 copies a day for the example given).

Transmission economics are covered in somewhat greater detail in Chapter 6.

RADIO FACILITIES

Theoretically, the factors affecting required bandwidth for distortion-free transmission by wire facilities should apply to radio as well—and for the most part they do. As a rule, however, an additional modulation step is required for radio transmission of fax signals. For convenience (and to some extent for technical reasons), the modulated carrier output of the fax transmitter is usually applied as a *subcarrier,* which means that it becomes the wavering audio "tone" by which the radio frequency carrier is, in turn, modulated.

Another distinction between wire and radio is radio's potentially greater susceptibility to external interference. AM systems in particular are affected by lightning and other atmospheric and cosmic disturbances, while radio systems in general—with the possible exception of microwave—are vulnerable to harmonic and crosstalk interference from each other. Fading, caused indirectly by atmospheric temperature inversions, is a common problem in shortwave and microwave systems. Such systems are also subject to high power losses between stations and, at very high frequencies, can even be affected by rain.

An advantage of radio is that, because of the higher frequencies involved, bandwidth is not so much a limiting factor as it is in wire systems. Its chief advantage is that it can reach places that cannot be reached by wire.

In modern common carrier communications there is no longer a meaningful distinction between wire and radio facilities, particularly from the customer's point of view. Within the telephone network, for example, long distance calls (including fax and data signals) may on one occasion go by wire, and on another by radio—and the customer will not know the difference. In fact, nearly half of all long distance carrier telephone nets existing today are in the form of microwave radio relays.

With proper licensing and sufficient capital for the initial equipment investment, and a willingness to sustain continuing maintenance costs, a business concern can install its own microwave network between separated branches. However, maintenance alone can be a major problem. Even if the need for repairs is infrequent, specially trained technicians have to be on call in the event of a system breakdown and for the making of periodic tests and adjustments. This is one of the reasons—possibly the principal one—why, to date, relatively few private businesses have attempted to operate their own communications networks.

One of the more venerable commercial applications of radio to facsimile transmission is the so-called *Radiophoto* service for international dispatching of news photos. Introduced by RCA in the 1920s, Radiophoto was later taken over by the wire services themselves (AP and UPI), which today lease the radio facilities from common carriers on a full-time basis. It operates in the 4–27 MHz HF band, and its operation is governed by FCC regulations. Picture signals are transmitted via an FM subcarrier to minimize the effects of fading.

Another area in which radiofacsimile has proved particularly useful is the gathering and distribution of weather data. Since 1930 weather maps have been transmitted to ships at sea via land-based radio stations. Present-day equipment operates in the 1.5–25 MHz HF band and uses the popular *frequency shift* method of two-level transmission (1500 Hz for black, and 2300 Hz for white). Conventional fax gear is used for scanning and recording.

Of more recent vintage is the Automatic Picture Transmission (APT) system by which television views of segments of the earth's cloud cover are transmitted at regular intervals from orbiting satellites several hundred miles high and reconstructed by facsimile at ground stations all around the globe. The slow read-out signals from the spaceborne vidicon storage tubes amplitude-modulate an audio subcarrier, which is then transmitted by compact, 5-watt FM transmitters operating in one of two frequency ranges: 4–30 MHz (HF), or 135–139 MHz (VHF). Transmission is at the rate of 240 lines a minute, with a full 800-line picture being sent in a little more than three minutes.

Newspicture and weather data dissemination are among the fax applications that have been discussed in a more general way in Chapter 2.

COUPLERS AND MODEMS

To prevent excessive signal levels that may present hazards for maintenance personnel and cause trouble for other customers, connection of communication terminals to a common carrier network have to be made through an appropriate interface. The form may range from a simple coupling device to a relatively elaborate service terminal, frequently referred to as a *data set.*

Common carriers offer a selection of interfaces to accommodate various system configurations. In most cases, the units are separately leased at a fixed monthly rate per terminal. Alternatively, for voice-grade systems only, there are special couplers which do not require direct electrical connection to the phone line. These are usually furnished by the fax equipment manufacturer either as an integral part of the equipment or as an optional extra.

"INDIRECT" COUPLERS

While the rules governing "interconnection" specifically forbid direct electrical connection of customer-provided terminals to the switched network, *indirect* coupling by acoustical or inductive means is permitted, provided certain requirements are met regarding the level and frequency content of the transmitted signal. Recognizing this, the fax industry has developed special couplers to permit use of a standard telephone set as a "mechanical" interface between the fax terminal equipment and the dial network (Fig. 4.16). In recent years these devices have been improved to the point that they have become almost standard equipment with the new family of compact, desk-top transceivers.

Use of the indirect couplers—or "phone couplers," as they are sometimes called—requires that the sender place a call through a standard telephone set to the receiving party, whom he knows to possess a fax transceiver compatible with his own. Having established voice contact (which may be optional, depending on the kinds of automatic features the terminal units have), both parties place their telephone handsets in the coupler units, which are physically designed to accept all standard handsets.

Electrically, the coupler is so designed that, in the SEND mode, a built-in reproducer induces its output into the telephone handset, either acoustically—by literally "speaking" into the mouthpiece of the handset—or inductively, by transformer action. In the RECEIVE mode, the coupler functions as an acoustic or inductive pickup, relaying the incoming audio signal present in the handset to the fax transceiver for recording.

A disadvantage of the indirect coupler is its susceptibility to external acoustic and (or) inductive interference and to impairments introduced by the telephone set. Moreover, its method of transferring signals is not the most efficient and can result in losses, both in quality and strength of the

Fig. 4.16. Phone coupler permits interfacing of fax terminal gear to the telephone network by inductive and/or acoustic means, as opposed to direct hookup. (Courtesy Magnavox.)

processed signals. However, in a well-designed coupler, the effects of these shortcomings can be minimized.

DATA ACCESS ARRANGEMENT

For a slight increase in his monthly phone bill, the fax user can hook up directly to the switched network through what is called a Data Access Arrangement (DAA). In its simplest form (Fig. 4.17) it consists of the addition of a protective coupling circuit to a standard telephone set, along with a manual key through which the instrument can be switched from its normal operating mode (voice) to a data input mode, in which it functions as a passive interface between the fax equipment and the line. More elaborate couplers are also available to provide for automatic origination and answering of calls.

In addition to permitting direct hookup of the actual fax terminal equipment to the switched network, DAA opens the door to the customer's use of his own (noncommon-carrier) *modems* (modulator-demodulators) and compression devices. With the strides currently being made in the area of bandwidth and data compression, fax users should have a choice, in the very near future, of a variety of auxiliary devices that will permit increased transmission speeds, or transmission of greater image detail (or both), over the switched telephone network. Compression techniques are discussed in more detail in a separate section at the end of this chapter.

Fig. 4.17. Basic Data Access Arrangement (DAA) consists of a wall-mounted coupler to which both the telephone set and fax terminal gear are "hard-wired." (Courtesy Bell Telephone Labs.)

602 DATA SET

The Bell System's 602 Data Set (Fig. 4.18) is basically an analog modem for conversion of the d.c. output of a fax scanner to an audio FM signal suitable for transmission over the switched telephone network, and reconversion of the received signal to the original d.c. analog for recording. Introduced in 1962, the 602 provided industry with a standard means for transmitting low-speed, or "message," facsimile signals over regular telephone lines on a dial-up basis.

In addition to its primary function as a modem, the 602 provides all necessary filtering and equalizing circuitry to effectively adapt the fax signal to the switched network; it provides an optional synchronizing—or control—channel at the low end of the circuit passband (550–660 Hz); and it provides the means for unattended operation of the fax receiver.

As a modulator in the SEND mode, the unit converts the d.c. variations of the scanner output to a linear carrier frequency swing of 1500 to 2450 Hz, 1500 Hz corresponding to 0 volts of scanner output and 2450 Hz corresponding to the upper limit of +7 volts. In the RECEIVE mode, the FM carrier is *clipped* by a limiter to remove amplitude variations due to noise acquired in transmission, *rectified* to convert it from an a.c. signal to a series of positive pulses, and *reconverted* to the original baseband signal by an "averaging" technique. This last step is accomplished by the combination

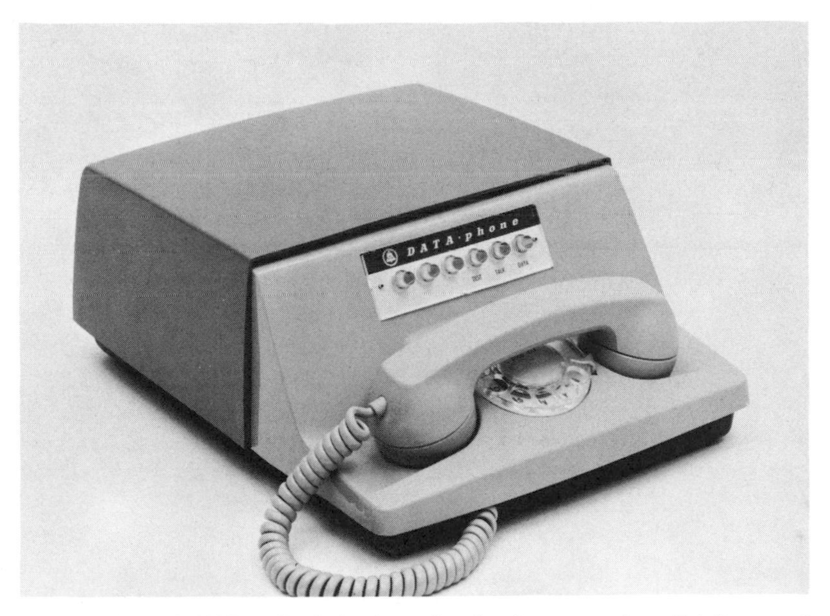

Fig. 4.18. The Bell System's 602 Data Set is the pioneering signal converter that officially opened the public telephone network to facsimile use in the early 1960s. (Courtesy Bell Telephone Labs.)

of a *monopulser,* which emphasizes the alternate "bunching" and separating of the positive pulse train by adjusting all pulses to uniform width, and a *low-pass filter,* which filters out the actual separate pulses and passes only the lower frequency average d.c. variations, thus recovering the original baseband frequencies. Figure 4.19 illustrates the sequence of signal-processing steps involved in modulation and demodulation.

Since fax terminal equipment normally includes its own modulating and demodulating circuitry, connection to the 602 Data Set requires that certain portions of the fax equipment's built-in circuitry be bypassed, or, alternatively, that the d.c. analog baseband be recovered by a converter at the output of the fax transmitter. Most modern message fax equipment is designed to facilitate selection of either an independent operating mode, or hookup through a 602 Data Set.

When the 602 is used, one unit is required at each terminal of a system. As of this writing, the average lease rate for each unit (it may vary somewhat from one telephone company to another) is about $35 a month.

303 DATA SET

For group and supergroup service, the Bell System's 303 Data Set (Fig. 4.20) is the standard interface between terminals and transmission facilities. It is a versatile piece of equipment and one of considerably different design than the 602 Data Set. For one thing, it is designed to operate in a *digital* rather than an analog mode.

In the use of this data set with analog facsimile equipment, digital operation means that the analog output of the fax scanner is converted to a sequence of ON or OFF pulses, the distinction being whether a given point along the signal envelope is interpreted as black or white. In other words, regardless of what gray tones may exist on the original, the scanner output is transmitted as a binary, or two-level (black and white), signal.

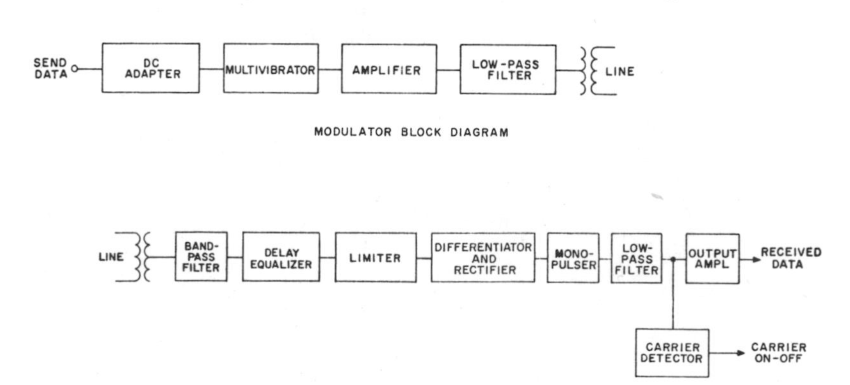

Fig. 4.19. Functional scheme of the 602 Data Set. Each set has both transmit and receive capabilities. (Courtesy Bell Telephone Labs.)

Fig. 4.20. The Bell System's 303 Type wideband data station permits displacement of up to 60 voice channels for high-speed fax transmission. The station is of modular design and consists of a composite of individual terminal devices. (Courtesy AT&T Co.)

Part of the 303's versatility is that it can be operated in either a synchronous or nonsynchronous mode. In the synchronous mode, precision oscillators, or "clocks," at each terminal are synchronized with each other so that the rapid switching from ON to OFF conditions at the transmitter can be accurately followed and regenerated at the receiver and at repeater stations along the way. This is roughly analogous to the use of standard frequency power supplies in fax systems when the terminal mechanisms are served by different commercial power grids. It is also somewhat analogous to the use of sync pulses in TV systems, except that in digital transmission the sync pulses and the data being transmitted are more directly interrelated.

The synchronous mode is intended primarily for the linking together of business machines—e.g., a tape reader at a computer center with a high-speed printer at a distant office. As an interface for fax gear, the 303 is normally used in the nonsynchronous mode because of the characteristic randomness of picture signal elements.

In the SEND mode, the input to the 303 is the d.c. scanner output, taken directly from the scanner or recovered at the fax transmitter output by an accessory converter. An *amplitude quantizing* circuit in the 303 provides a threshold above which all d.c. signal levels represent an ON, or black, condition, and below which all represent an OFF, or white, condition. The resulting random stream of ON and OFF pulses goes out on the line to the nearest exchange, where it is then modified to conform to the requirements of the broadband carrier facility.

In the RECEIVE mode, the 303 samples and interprets the demodulated pulses and feeds them to the fax recorder, which translates them to a two-level graphic reproduction of the original.

Two other features that contribute to the 303's versatility are (a) its applicability to half-group, group, or supergroup operation with minor options, and (b) its provision for simultaneous voice or code coordination over a separate channel included for that purpose in the group service package. The 303 Data Set, incidentally, is generally included as part of the monthly station charge for this class of broadband service (approximately $300 for switched 48 kHz service, $425 per 48 kHz private line terminal, and $650 per 240 kHz terminal, as of January 1970).

OTHER TERMINAL INTERFACES

In addition to the interfaces described above, all of which are either designed specifically for facsimile use or have at least proved their adaptability to it, there are a variety of digital modems available that lend themselves to use in conjunction with fax systems requiring digital encoding prior to transmission (e.g., certain data compression systems; see next section). The Bell System's new 203 Data Set is an example of one that is available for lease from common carriers for use in conjunction with voice grade facilities. It permits a bit rate of 4800 (bits per second) over the switched network. Other suitable digital modems are available commercially from a number of electronics firms specializing in communications equipment. Codex, Collins, Lenkurt, Rixon, and Sangamo are just a sampling of the names currently to be found on commercial digital modems.

For fax systems designed to transmit large printed masters, such as those for newspaper pages, from main printing plants to satellite plants, a common carrier terminal has been developed to permit interconnection of what is essentially an analog system to digital transmission facilities. The result is more economical transmission than is possible over analog facilities, and output quality that is comparable to that obtained with an all-analog system at the same scan resolution. Only short-haul digital facilities are available at the present time, but the same terminal will work with longer-haul digital systems when they become available, (presumably sometime in the early 1970s).

REDUNDANCY REDUCTION

Sideband suppression (discussed earlier in this chapter) was the first successful technique for reducing bandwidth in modulated carrier transmission systems. Transmission having always been a comparatively costly proposition, it is natural that engineers have persisted through the years in seeking new ways to conserve bandwidth in communication facilities.

Until the advent of data transmission in the 1950s, emphasis had been on *bandwidth compression,* the actual reducing of the total range of frequencies required for effective transmission. With the ensuing spectacular growth of data communications, the emphasis has shifted, naturally enough, to *data compression.* It is difficult to determine where one leaves off and the other begins, although bandwidth compression is usually thought of as being confined to analog systems, and data compression to digital systems. Whatever the distinction, both schemes fall under the general heading of *redundancy reduction.*

It would take nearly an entire book to discuss the whole gamut of compression techniques that have been developed to date. What follows is a condensed examination of some of the more noteworthy ones—past and present.

THE VOCODER

After sideband suppression, the next significant step in bandwidth compression technology was the development of the *Vocoder* at Bell Labs in the late 1930s. It is not applicable to facsimile but is described here merely to illustrate a basic redundancy reduction concept.

Basically, the Vocoder is a device for analyzing and artifically reproducing speech. It was developed for that purpose by Homer Dudley of Bell Labs in 1936, and its potentialities as a bandwidth compression system were not fully appreciated until sometime thereafter. As a compression device, instead of transmitting the actual pitches representing a series of spoken words, it transmits an electric current whose variations represent the *transitions* from one pitch to another. Since, in normal speech, there are fewer than ten such transitions per second, it is easy to see how this technique can conserve on bandwidth.

Inasmuch as the actual pitches are not transmitted, they must be recreated artificially by local oscillators in the receiver. The transmitted signal, then, merely determines what pitches are to be reproduced and in what sequence. In practice, there is more to it than that, but for the purposes of this chapter the foregoing will suffice as a basic description of the Vocoder.

The Vocoder has been successfully utilized in a few isolated applications, but facsimile has not been one of them. As noted earlier in this chapter, the baseband frequencies from a fax scanner, while in the audio range, are usually of a random, basically impure nature. The Vocoder is limited to reproducing pure, or nearly pure, oscillator-produced frequencies, as are more common to speech or music.

Figure 4.21 illustrates the Vocoder principle.

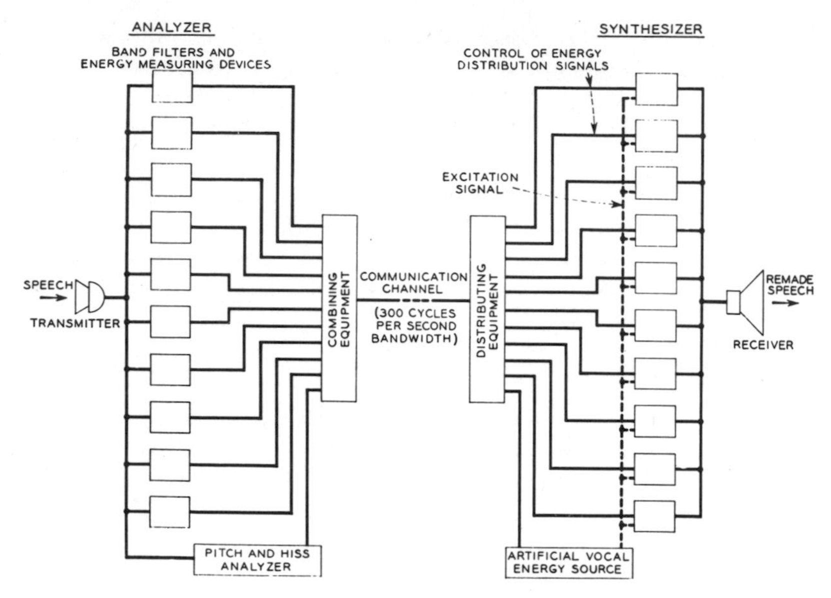

Fig. 4.21. Bell Labs' Vocoder introduced a basic redundancy reduction concept, namely, the transmission of data representing the *transitions* from one state to another in the original signal, rather than the signal itself. The original signal is artificially reconstructed at the receiver. (Courtesy Bell Telephone Labs.)

VARIABLE VELOCITY SCANNING

Various other analog type compression systems have been developed and demonstrated, but, for one reason or another, have not found application in fax transmission. An exception is variable velocity scanning, which may be applied to analog and digital systems alike and which may, in fact, combine both modes in a single system.

The object is to vary the scan rate in accordance with the density—or degree of congestion—of tonal transitions the scan beam encounters within a stroke. Typically, this is accomplished by momentarily storing the scanner output in a buffer (a recycling magnetic recorder), while its content is analyzed by a built-in computer.

The computer's function is two-fold: (1) to determine the pattern of speed variations at which the temporarily stored signal is to be "read out" onto the transmission line, based on variations in density of tonal transitions; and (2) to provide, along with the processed picture signal, the codes necessary to tell the recorder at the other end when and to what degree it must change speed to keep in step with the variations in read-out speed.

Variable velocity scanning is one of the simpler compression techniques—at least in principle. It is also a proven technique, inasmuch as variations of it have been successfully applied in commercial equipment.

For typical text type material, it can afford compression ratios up to about 6:1.

A pioneer in the use of this technique in a compression fax system is the Comfax/Computerpix Corporation, a relatively new firm in the fax field. Addressograph-Multigraph, an established manufacturer of business machines, also utilizes a form of variable velocity scanning in its *Telikon* system, which, however, is basically a run-length encoding system. (See next item.) Actually, in the Telikon system, the velocity of the scan spot remains constant within a stroke, but the speed with which the system "steps" from stroke to stroke varies.

Both systems—the Comfax/Computerpix (Fig. 4.22) and A-M's Telikon—use advanced electronic techniques for scanning, recording (Telikon uses a laser beam), signal processing, and encoding, and both can yield significant savings for the user, provided volume of use, urgency of need for fast service, or the savings realized through use of narrower bandwidth circuits over long distances are sufficient to offset the higher initial investment or lease rate for terminal equipment.

RUN-LENGTH ENCODING

Of the various scan compression techniques that are of a purely digital nature, run-length encoding was among the earliest to be developed and is perhaps the best known. It relies on the digital technique of viewing all image elements as either black or white, and of periodically sampling (at a very rapid rate) the content of a scan stroke to determine which of the

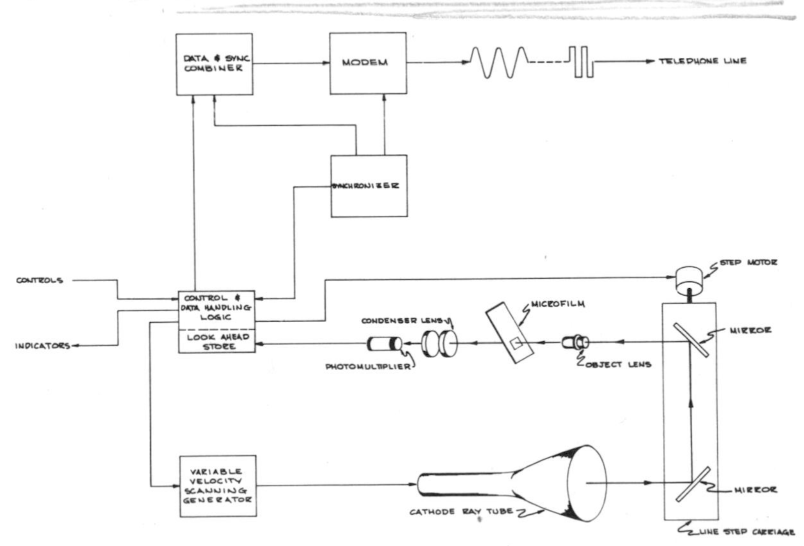

Fig. 4.22. Computerpix data compression scheme. The scan beam in effect "looks ahead" to determine the density of detail to be encountered, and the speed of the system varies accordingly. (Courtesy Computerpix Corp.)

two conditions obtain at a given instant. However, instead of the resulting serial bit stream being transmitted bit for bit, a START code is generated each time a black condition is encountered, and an END code when a white condition is encountered. (The system can be designed to accommodate a limited number of discrete gray tones as well, but at the expense of a reduced compression ratio.)

The START code is the cue for the system's logic to start counting black (ON) pulses, and the END code is the cue to start counting white (OFF) pulses. These "cueing" codes, plus a code representing the number of pulses occurring between cues, are all that is transmitted, and they can be sent at a comparatively high speed over a voice grade circuit or a greater number of them can be sent at a comparatively low speed.

The signal entering the fax receiver, then, is in the form of a sequence of codes which tell the recorder at what points it should start and complete each of a sequence of black marks within a stroke. At the SEND and RECEIVE ends of a typical system, the data must pass through a buffer stage to absorb the slight time lapses that ensue between detection of an image element and encoding at the SEND terminal, and subsequent interpretation and recording at the receiver. An alternative to buffers would be the use of variable velocity scanning, the scan speed being varied in accordance with the code generator's ability to keep pace.

Depending on the coding scheme used and the ratio of white space to image detail on the subject copy, run-length encoding is capable of a wide range of compression ratios. It can, in fact, range down to where it becomes totally impractical when the average subject copy contains an abnormally high degree of graphic detail—a page of a telephone directory, for example. The average number of transitions per scan stroke could conceivably reach the point where the descriptive codes would require greater transmission time, or bandwidth, than the actual picture elements. With a typical coding scheme, this situation is likely to obtain for runs of fewer than three sampling intervals in length.[5]

Although the technique has been widely discussed over the past few years, only a couple of commercial firms have succeeded, to date, in developing practical run-length encoding fax systems. One who has made it to the marketplace with a system is Dacom, of Sunnyvale, California, whose unique compression system will be discussed in more detail below.

ADAPTIVE TECHNIQUES

Effective compression of digital fax signals can be achieved through automatic adaptation of the signal characteristics to changes in information content of the scanned original. For example, *adaptive sampling,* used

[5] See Wyle, et al., "Reduced-Time Facsimile Transmission by Digital Coding" (*IRE Transactions on Communications Systems,* September 1961, pp. 215–222.)

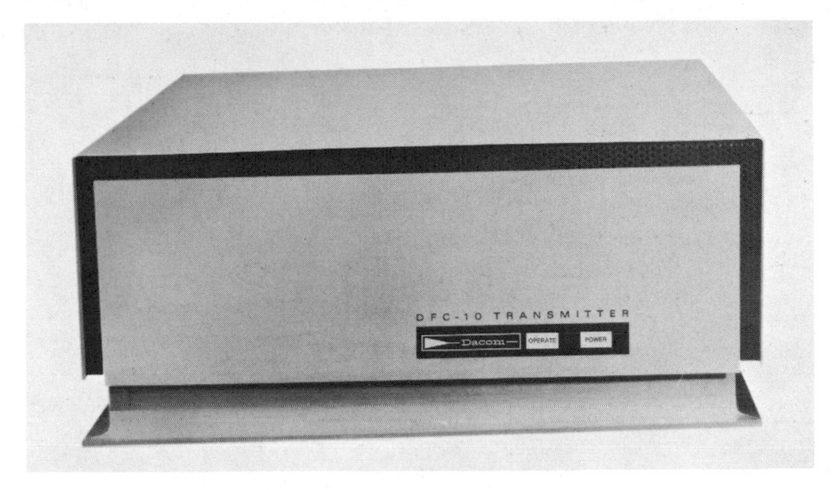

Fig. 4.23. The Dacom DFC-10 compression unit utilizes advanced digital techniques to reduce redundancy in the transmitted fax signal. (Courtesy Dacom, Inc.)

extensively in telemetry, entails continuous altering—or adapting—of the digital sampling rate in accordance with changes in characteristics of the input analog waveform. The result is something akin to the output of a variable velocity scanning system in the sense that what might otherwise be transmitted as an alternate bunching and dispersing of pulses is pulled together to form a pulse train of more or less consistent intervals.

The "pulling together" usually takes place in a buffer, and the technique involves not only continuous speed variations, but also the generation of appropriate codes to be transmitted to the receiver to produce synchronous variations through which original spacing of black-to-white transitions is recovered.

Another adaptive technique, *adaptive encoding*, is used in the Dacom DFC-10, a commercially available fax compression system designed to interface with high-speed mechanical terminal equipment (Figs. 4.23 and 4.24), and which the manufacturer has now also integrated into a self-contained compression fax system. As previously mentioned, the Dacom system is fundamentally a run-length encoding system.

In the Dacom transmitter, the fax scanner output is first modified by an automatic gain control (AGC) amplifier to equalize amplitude peaks. The spacing of the peaks is then automatically analyzed and codes generated to describe digitally the continuous changes that take place. A *data formatter* combines the encoded picture signal with special synchronization codes and, through a buffer, the composite code is transmitted as a compressed bit stream to the receiver.

At the receiver, the processing sequence is essentially reversed, but with one step eliminated—namely, the restoration of the picture signal to its

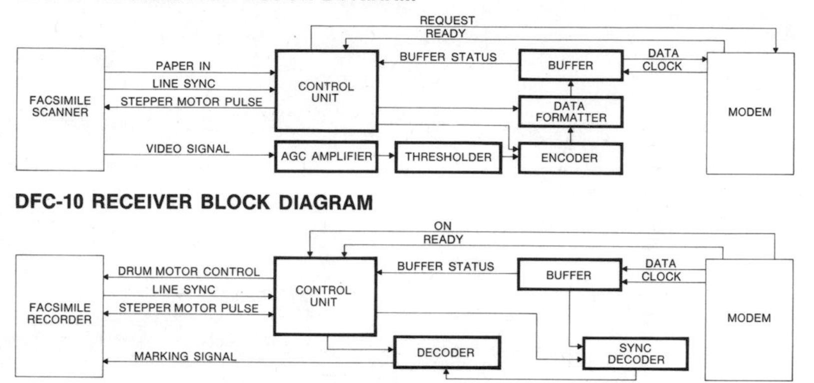

Fig. 4.24. Basic Dacom approach to data compression. Heavily outlined blocks are basic components of the DFC-10 compressor and reconstructor. In addition to the Dacom unit, a modem is required at each terminal as an interface between the DFC-10 and the transmission facility. (Courtesy Dacom, Inc.)

original continuously variable analog form. The signal fed to the recorder consists of discrete amplitude levels, the number normally being confined to two: ON and OFF, or black and white. With a proper adaptor, additional levels can be encoded at the transmitter, permitting the sending of photographs, but at the cost of a reduced compression ratio.

Although not technically a variable velocity scanning system, the Dacom technique entails a certain amount of speed variation of the associated scan and record mechanisms, an automatic acceleration occurring whenever broad white or broad black areas are encountered by the scan beam. The slight slowing down that occurs during "busy" intervals prevents the buffer from overloading.

THREE-LEVEL DIGITAL

A comparatively simple and inexpensive (and therefore increasingly popular) way of achieving an assured 2:1 bandwidth compression in a digital system, regardless of density of image detail, is by the addition of a second white level—or a second black level, depending on signal polarity—the object being to convert each white-black or black-white swing of the signal to a two-step *unidirectional* transition, thereby halving the number of zero-crossings. The scheme depicted in Fig. 4.25 will suffice to illustrate the basic principle, although there are variations in the way it may be applied.

For simplicity, the figure shows the principle applied to a three-level d.c. representation of the scanner baseband output. Zero-crossings are therefore represented by the dipping of the signal to zero level. In normal practice, it would be the modulated carrier that is processed by the compression modem. In any case, halving the number of zero-crossings means halving the transmitted frequencies, which permits the choice of either utilizing a narrower bandwidth transmission facility, or transmitting twice the data over a given facility.

The first commercial device to use the three-level principle is *Pacfax,* a bandwidth compression modem introduced in the mid-1960s and manufactured by the International Scanatron Systems Corporation of Wyandanch, New York.[6] The modems are used extensively by the U.S. National Weather Service in the transmission of weather maps.

Scanatron has more recently introduced a voice grade fax system in which the Pacfax circuitry is integrated into the separate scanner and recorder units. Meanwhile, at least two other fax manufacturers have entered the market with compression fax systems utilizing similar techniques.

OTHER SCHEMES

There are probably as many different compression schemes as there are communications engineers who have at one time or another said to themselves, "There ought to be a better way." For the purposes of this chapter, it will suffice to mention just two more.

In a system called RACE (Radiation Adaptive Compression Equipment), developed by Radiation, Incorporated, a Florida-based subsidiary of Harris-Intertype Corporation, compression ratios in the neighborhood of 5 : 1 are achieved by removal of redundant samplings in an analog-to-digital

[6]Early Pacfax units bore the name "HELAC Electronics." The Pacfax patents were transferred from HELAC to International Scanatron upon formation of Scanatron in 1968.

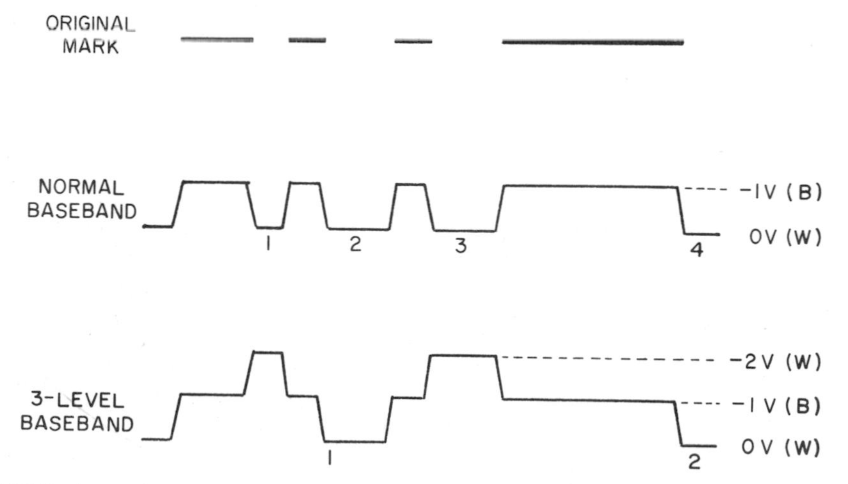

Fig. 4.25. Basic principle of the three-level digital technique employed in International Scanatron's *Pacfax* bandwidth compression modems. Reshaping the waveform in the manner shown has the effect of halving the frequency of the transmitted picture signal.

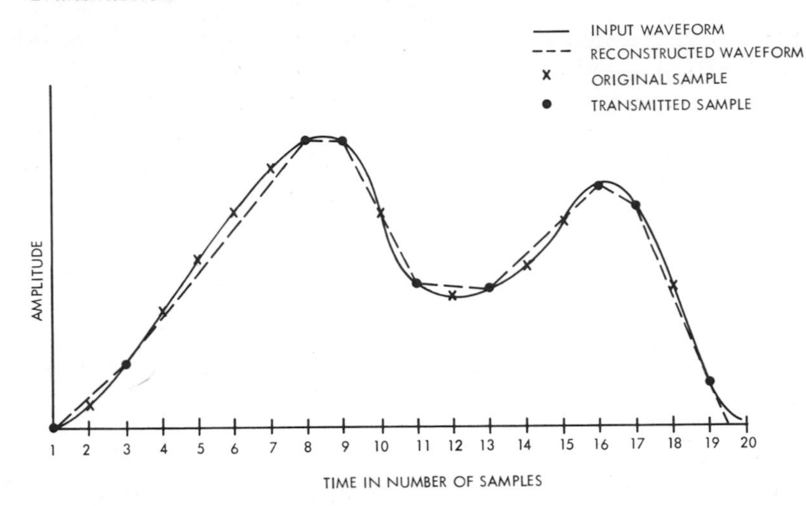

Fig. 4.26. Redundancy reduction by removal of redundant samplings in an analog-to-digital conversion process. (Courtesy Radiation, Inc.)

conversion process. Only those data points are retained that are necessary to reconstruct a straight line equivalent of the original waveform (Fig. 4.26). The system is somewhat complex in its circuitry and requires buffers at all terminals, but it is embodied in relatively compact equipment units.

By itself, RACE is capable of reducing the digital bit-rate from about 48 kilobits per second to 9.6 kilobits. It is designed to interface, in turn, with a commercial modem which enables transmission over a voice grade facility.

Another analog input compression technique—one that has been implemented through adoption of special equipment developed by Grundig of West Germany—makes possible the sending of closed-circuit television (CCTV) signals over a single voice grade circuit. The video input to the system is subjected to a "splitting" process, which results in a kind of scrambling of the signal, converting it to a composite of two signal halves 180 degrees out of phase with each other. The technique is said to permit transmission of a high-resolution video signal, normally requiring as much as a 20 MHz bandwidth, over a specially conditioned pair of phone lines for limited distances. Maximum transmission distances claimed for the system range from 1800 feet to several miles.

Other sophisticated digital systems have been devised that boast of ratios as high as 1000:1, for unlimited transmission distances over standard circuits. Such systems can be implemented right now by anyone willing to pay for the highly specialized hardware and logic required to make them work.

Meanwhile, the common carriers themselves have been working vigorously to increase the overall efficiency of electronic transmission, notably through adoption of advanced digital, or pulse code, techniques. Because of the number of inherent advantages (to the common carrier and customer alike), it is a primary objective of the communications industry to ultimately put all electronic communication on a purely digital basis.

One thing is certain: redundancy reduction and transmission efficiency in general are facets of communications technology that are definitely worth watching. They are the factors that will most influence the future course of facsimile developments.

BIBLIOGRAPHY

Badler, M., "New System Transmits Microfilm Cross Country in Seconds," *Information and Records Management,* Aug./Sept. 1969, pp. 60–61.

Bell System Data Communications, *Technical References:* "Data Set 602A Interface Specification," July 1963 (and Addendum 1 thereto, Jan. 1967); "Wideband Data Station 303 Type," Aug. 1966; "Transmission Specifications for Voice Grade Private Line Data Channels," March 1969; "Data Access Arrangement CDT for Manual Originating and Answering Terminals," July 1970; "Data Communications Using the Switched Telecommunications Network," Aug. 1970.

Benewicz, T. F., "Measuring Line Level in Telephoto Systems," Bell Laboratories *Record,* Mar. 1960, pp. 96–101.

"CCTV Signals Transmitted Over Conventional Phone Line," *Electronic News,* Aug. 20, 1969, p. 18.

De France, J. J., *Communications Electronic Circuits,* New York, Holt, Rinehart and Winston, 1966.

Dudley, H., "Synthesizing Speech," Bell Laboratories *Record,* Mar. 1956, pp. 81–85.

Electronic Industries Assoc. Standard RS-328, "Message Facsimile Equipment for Operation on Switched Voice Facilities Using Data Communication Terminal Equipment," Oct. 1966.

Erdmann, R. L., and A. S. Neal, "Character Legibility of Digital Facsimile Resolution," *Human Factors,* Oct. 1968, pp. 465–473.

Goldsmith, A. N., et al., *Radio Facsimile,* Vol. I, New York, RCA Institutes Technical Press, 1938.

Goodison, C. E., "Operational Weather Satellites," *Wireless World,* Dec. 1966, pp. 590–594.

Hartley, R. V. L., "Relations of Carrier and Side-Bands in Radio Transmission," *Proceedings of the IRE,* Feb. 1923, Vol. 11, No. 1, pp. 34–56.

James, R. T., "The Evolution of Wideband Services in the United States," IEEE *International Convention Record,* 1966, Pt. 1, pp. 180–184.

Kiver, M. S., *F-M Simplified,* New York, D. Van Nostrand Co., Inc., 1947.

Kock, W. E., "Speech Bandwidth Compression," Bell Laboratories *Record,* Mar. 1956, pp. 81–85.

Kretzmer, E. R., "Facsimile Communications via the Dialed Telephone Network," IEEE *International Convention Record,* 1965, Pt. 1, pp. 180–184.

Lattimer, I. E., *The Use of Telephone Circuits for Picture and Facsimile Service* (booklet), New York, AT&T Co., 1948.

"Mail by Phone Picks Up New Speed," *Business Week,* Dec. 13, 1969, pp. 120–121.

Michel, W. S., et al., "A Coded Facsimile System," IRE *WESCON Convention Record,* 1957, Pt. 2, pp. 84–93.

Press, H., and W. B. Huston, "Nimbus: A Progress Report," *Astronautics and Aeronautics,* Mar. 1968, pp. 56–65.

Ridings, G. H., "Facsimile Communications, Past, Present, Future," *Signal,* Nov. 1962, pp. 34–40.

Transmission Systems for Communications (4th ed.), Bell Telephone Laboratories, 1970.

Unrue, J. E., Jr., "Controlling Echo in the Bell System," Bell Laboratories *Record,* Aug. 1969, pp. 233–238.

Weber, D. R., "A Low Cost Facsimile Compression System," *Telecommunications,* June 1969, pp. 31–33.

———, "A Synopsis on Data Compression," *Proceedings* of the 1965 National Telemetering Congress, pp. 9–15.

Wier, J. M., "Telephone Circuits: a New Link in Data Communications," Bell Laboratories *Record,* Oct. 1960, pp. 368–372.

Wyle, H., et al., "Reduced-Time Facsimile Transmission by Digital Coding," *IRE Transactions on Communications Systems,* Sept. 1961, pp. 215–222.

5 *Quality*

BEFORE the planning of a facsimile system can properly proceed, at least two of three basic variables have to be tied down within reasonable limits. The three are *cost, speed,* and *output quality.* Given any two, the third can usually be derived without much difficulty.

There may, of course, be additional factors to complicate the task, such as size or portability of terminal gear, and availability of facilities capable of meeting transmission needs. Depending on how many are specified at the outset and how inflexible they are, the combined end requirements for a system might even conflict to the extent of making the system impossible to implement.

Of the three basic variables, output quality is perhaps the most involved—primarily because it cannot be computed or predicted with mathematical precision, as can the other two. This chapter will therefore confine itself to a discussion of various factors governing legibility and overall quality of a fax recording. The interrelationship of quality with other variables, particularly cost and speed, will be explored in Chapter 6.

Some of the factors influencing quality have already been discussed in preceding chapters. Chapter 3 described distortions produced as a result of phasing and synchronization errors and of mismatched indices of cooperation, while Chapter 4 covered the detrimental effects of various phenomena inherent in the transmission process.

In this chapter, the emphasis will be on conditions and principles that are fundamental to the scanning and recording processes—which takes us beyond the realm of straight mechanics into that of the individual's subjective judgment.

RESOLUTION

Before we can legitimately assess the output quality of a graphics communication system, it is necessary that we know something about resolution.

The general definition of the term as applied to optics is *the degree to which adjacent elements of an image are distinguishable as being separate.* As applied to scan systems (fax and TV), the term is used loosely to specify the *scan density*—i.e., the number of scan lines within a given linear dimension. In TV it is the number of lines constituting an entire image—e.g., 525 for American commercial TV—whereas in fax it is the number of lines per inch—e.g., 96 in conventional message fax. (The fax-equivalent resolution of a properly adjusted picture on a 21-inch, diagonally measured TV screen would be about 35 lines per inch.)

Actually, in scan systems, there are two kinds of resolution—or, more correctly, the resolution of the system is governed by two sets of variables, depending on whether we are talking about the width or height of the reproduced image. While resolution across the scan "grain" (i.e., at right angles or oblique to the scan axis) is controlled essentially by the number of scan lines within a given linear dimension, resolution *along* a scan line is governed by the speed with which the system, as a whole, can react to tonal transitions.

LINES VS "LINE PAIRS"

Careless use of the word "lines" in a discussion of resolution can lead to serious misunderstanding. A *scan line* is one kind of line, while the line that is a component of a resolution test pattern may be quite another, the distinction being that the latter may consist of a *line and space* of equal width, while scan lines are contiguous (theoretically). The significance is that it takes two scan lines to resolve one line and space—or *line pair,* as it is sometimes called—of test pattern resolution (Fig. 5.1).

Electrically, a visual line/space pair represents one cycle of a theoretically square waveform (why not actually square will be explained later in this chapter). However, even where there are no electronics involved, a visual line/space pair is, in itself, a *cycle of spatial frequency.* Throughout the

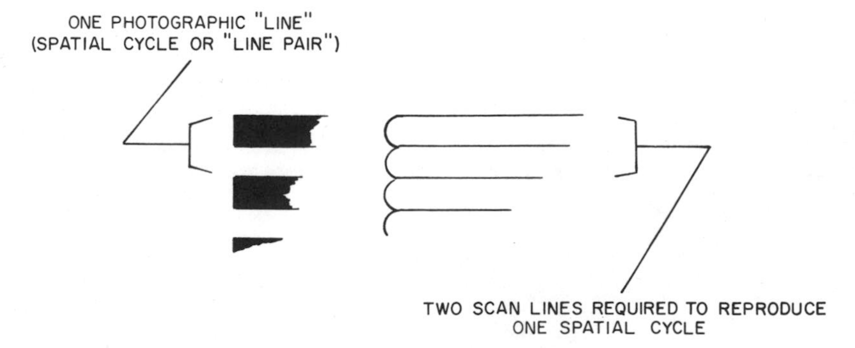

Fig. 5.1. It takes at least two scan lines to resolve one "line pair," or spatial cycle, of a resolution test pattern when the transitions occur along an axis normal to the scan axis.

remainder of this chapter, the word cycle will therefore be used interchangeably for a visual cycle and for its electrical counterpart. The term hertz will, of course, apply as a unit of measure when we speak of electrical cycles as occurring within a particular time frame.

The IEEE Facsimile Test Chart (Fig. 5.2) contains a variety of test patterns for measuring the resolution of a system. At the top of the chart are vertical bar patterns ranging from 10 to 96 contiguous lines (or 5 to 48 cycles) per inch. A bit farther down are clusters of triple-line groups known as repeating tri-bar patterns. These permit resolution readings ranging from 61 to 406 contiguous lines (30.5 to 203 cycles) in 12 steps.

Fig. 5.2. The IEEE Facsimile Test Chart, 1970 Edition. (*Note:* the chart as reproduced here cannot be used for actual tests.) (Courtesy Electronic Industries Association.)

The radial line pattern, which is enveloped in a square area at the left of the chart, near the center, permits resolution readings at any angle, ranging continuously from 50 contiguous lines per inch (outer circle) to 200 (innermost circle). The wedge or fan type pattern diagonally below it is calibrated in the number of contiguous lines (black *and* white) per inch.

The variety of type faces in the lower left quadrant of the chart are self-explanatory (more on character size later). The six rectangular gray scale patterns just below the left edge of the portrait photo consist of two halftone dot patterns—65 and 120—each reproduced in 10, 50, and 90% tints. These are useful in checking for the probability of encountering moiré patterns in the transmission of halftone material.

The National Bureau of Standards (NBS) microcopy resolution test target appears in two locations on the chart: between the radial line pattern and the portrait photo, and in the lower right-hand corner. It contains 23 patterns, each consisting of two sets of lines and spaces. The five lines and four spaces constituting each set are of equal width, and the two sets within a pattern are arranged at right angles to each other. The number associated with each pattern is the quantity of spatial cycles (lines and adjoining spaces) per millimeter.

This is actually a condensation of the standard NBS target, which consists of 26 patterns, ranging from 1 to 18 cycles per millimeter. However, in all other respects it is unaltered. It is a particularly valuable set of patterns inasmuch as it is standard for microphotography and therefore provides the basis for comparison of microfilm and facsimile quality standards. Such comparisons will become increasingly important as the growing use of microfilm—both for document storage and as a computer output medium—continues to impact on the input requirements for modern fax systems.

The angular positioning of the corner NBS target permits measurement of resolution along two axes oblique to the scan axis (by about 45 degrees).

About all that need be said further about the various resolution patterns constituting the IEEE chart is that, depending on whether scanning is vertical or horizontal, the patterns may be measuring either the effective system bandwidth (indirectly, of course), or the effect on resolution of the segmenting of the image by the scanning process. The radial line and NBS patterns measure both, regardless of scan direction.

LINES VS ELEMENTS

To avoid confusion, it is good practice to think of resolution in terms of elements rather than lines. Since there is ideally a 1:1 relationship between scan lines and image elements (in the across-the-grain direction), the distinction between vertical and horizontal resolution effectively disappears when each is expressed in elements.

The same 1:1 relationship exists between image elements and *bits* (binary digits) in a two-level ("mark and space") digital system. Thus we can talk about the reproduced subject copy as consisting of a total of so many thousands of elements, or *kilobits,* thereby facilitating the computation of transmission time and required channel capacity.

For example, let's say we are sending an 8½ × 11-inch document over a system having a scan resolution of 100 lines per inch. Assuming that resolution is to be equal horizontally and vertically, we will need a transmission facility capable of accommodating 850 × 1100 (or a total of 935,000) elements of picture information within a given amount of time. If we are willing to tolerate a transmission duration of six minutes, the required transmission bandwidth would be 2.6 kilobits per second (935 ÷ 360 seconds). For shorter durations, the bandwidth would be proportionately broader.

Expression of resolution in elements also provides a universal basis for comparison of various image-reproducing media. Some representative examples are shown in Table 5.A.

RESOLUTION DETERMINANTS

1. *Spot Size.* A fundamental factor limiting the resolution capabilities of a fax system is the size of the scan spot. Of course, it is a factor only insofar as it is consistent with the scan density, or *pitch* (scan lines per inch), of the system. The optimum relationship—assuming, for the moment, a round spot—is a spot diameter, in inches, equal to the reciprocal of the

Table 5.A—*Elemental resolutions of selected graphic reproductions.*

Image	*Resolution in Total Elements (or Bits)*
3¾ × 5-inch newspaper halftone (about 50 dots per inch)	50,000*
8-mm home movie frame	50,000**
525-line commercial TV	150,000†
3¾ × 5-inch "slick" magazine halftone (about 150 dots per inch)	420,000*
1000-line CCTV	550,000†
96 LPI fax recording of an 8½ × 11-inch document	630,000††
35-mm professional movie frame	1,000,000**
Frame of 35-mm microfilm (100 cycles/mm resolved in image)	50,000,000
8 × 10-inch glossy contact print from fine grain negative	150,000,000**

*D. G. Fink, *Television Standards and Practice* (N.Y., McGraw-Hill, 1943), pp. 62–63.
** *Ibid.,* pp. 5–6.
† Assumes equal horizontal and vertical resolution and various losses (to be discussed later in this chapter).
†† Assumes 850 elements per line (100 per inch) and an *actual* vertical resolution of 740 elements.

number of lines per inch. For example, in a 96 LPI system, the optimum spot diameter would be $\frac{1}{96}$-inch.

The greater resolution potential of a smaller spot would be wasted on a system having a scan pitch of significantly fewer lines than could be accommodated in the same space without overlapping—e.g., a spot of $\frac{1}{200}$-inch diameter in a 100 LPI system. Likewise, an oversized spot, resulting in overlapping strokes, would unfairly limit a system's potential resolution capabilities. In actual practice, to avoid overlap, the scan spot is usually somewhat smaller than the optimum for a given pitch.[1]

In existing commercial fax equipment, spot size may vary from $\frac{1}{50}$-inch (20 mils) down to $\frac{1}{1000}$ (1 mil), and even smaller. In fax scanners for special applications, it can extend down through fractions of a mil, all the way to the *micron* (thousandths of a millimeter) range. Alden's 35-mm microfilm scanner, for example, uses an optically reduced spot measuring about 0.6 mils, which permits the equivalent of 96 LPI scan resolution on a 16×-reduced microimage of the original subject copy. Special microfilm scanners have been developed that use electron or laser beams to produce spots as small as 5 microns (0.2 mils), a size which permits a scan resolution of better than 5000 LPI on the film.

2. *Shape of Scan Aperture.* While a round scan spot, or aperture, will produce images of adequate quality in most cases, the optimum shape from the fidelity standpoint is a rectangle, its long dimension defining the width of the stroke. Why a rectangle and not a square—or a circle—is best explained by referring to Fig. 5.3.

As illustrated, particularly in 5.3(a), the effect of an aperture of finite width passing across the juncture of dark and light picture elements is somewhat like that of a window shade being raised or lowered, except that the window moves with respect to the shade. From the viewpoint of the scanner's photoelectric eye, a sharp transition from black to white on the subject copy thus becomes a relatively gradual change because of the finite interval between the aperture's being obscured by the dark detail to its being fully bathed in light.

In other words, the faithfulness with which a sharp tonal transition is reproduced along the scan axis is a function of the relative amount of time it takes for the full width (w) of the aperture to pass the tonal juncture. The wider the aperture, the more sluggish the scanner's response to sharp transitions, and therefore the poorer the fidelity of reproduction. The phenomenon is commonly known as *aperture distortion.*

What this suggests is that the ideal aperture, from a fidelity standpoint, would be a slit of infinitesimal width. Obviously, such an aperture would

[1] However, according to Mertz and Gray ("A Theory of Scanning . . . ;" see references, end of chapter), there is something to be said for overlapping. While it reduces resolution, it may also minimize the occurrence of certain "extraneous patterns" such as the moiré patterns and the serrations that appear on oblique details of an image.

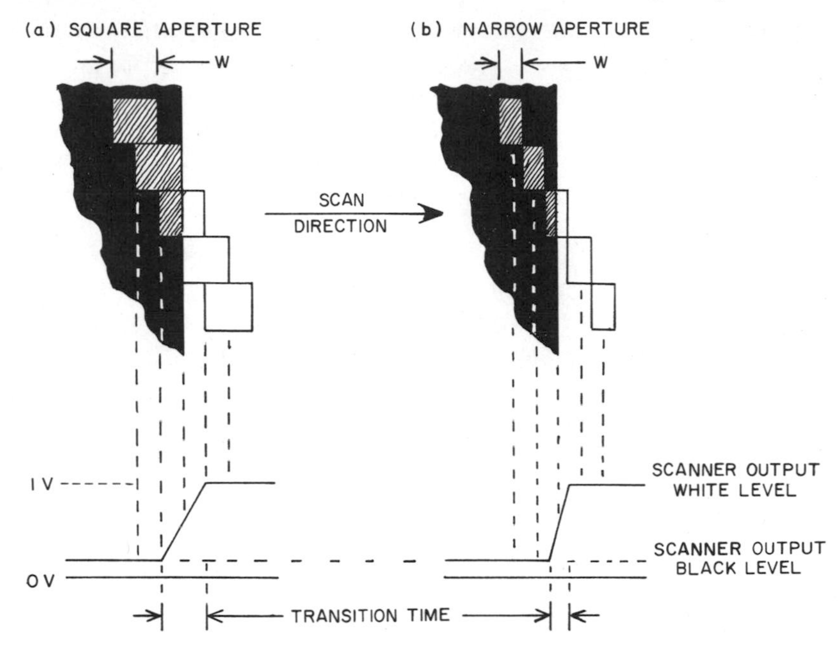

Fig. 5.3. Aperture distortion due to the finite width of the scanning aperture. The greater the width, the less sharp the transition from one contrasting brightness level to another. Note: the descending sequence of aperture positions in each sketch represents successive positions within a stroke.

be impractical because it would not admit sufficient light. Therefore, in practice, a compromise is struck, as illustrated in Fig. 5.3(b). The ratio of width to height for a given system will (or should) be governed by the fidelity of the system as a whole.

Where a system operates close to the upper frequency limitations of the transmission channel (as is often the case with systems utilizing the telephone network), it is perhaps just as well that the aperture shape does *not* approximate the ideal. In such cases, it is generally recommended that transmitted frequencies be limited in the scanning process, rather than by relying on the response characteristics of the transmission circuitry. The latter alternative may produce distortions even less desirable than the limiting of resolution. (See Chapter 4.)

It is also generally true that aperture shape becomes less critical as spot size decreases—consistent, of course, with an increase in scan resolution. Where, for example, an extremely fine scan grain can be achieved through application of a laser or cathode ray device, one should not be too concerned if the scan spot is round rather than rectangular or square.

3. Recording Process. In conventional ink printing and duplicating, quality is governed principally by the process involved and the quality of the paper. There is no question but that letterpress is superior to stencil duplication (for example), or that glossy paper stock produces better quality copy than coarse newsprint. The difference is perhaps as much aesthetic as it is physical.

Similarly, in fax recording, where process and print medium are more closely related, the combination of the two is among the factors influencing faithfulness of reproduction. Of the various processes, photographic recording is generally acknowledged as being superior to others from the standpoints of both resolution and tonal latitude. Beyond that, it is difficult to single out any one process as being totally superior to another, although each has its distinctive characteristics. (See Chapter 3.)

Figure 5.4 shows a picture segment reproduced by the photographic process and by a direct process. The scan line resolution is essentially the same—nominally 100 LPI—for both. Bear in mind that these are specimens selected more or less at random, and that they do not necessarily represent the best—or worst—that these processes can do.

4. *Axis and Direction of Scanning.* Experimenters have generally concluded that, from the resolution standpoint, there is no measurable basis for prescribing one scan axis, or direction, over another—i.e., horizontal vs

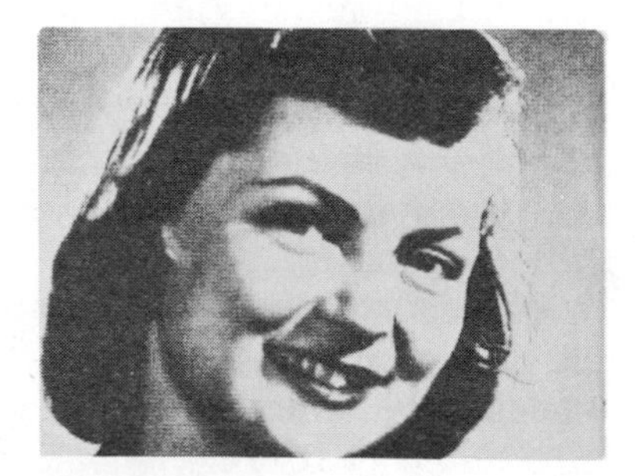

Fig. 5.4. Comparison of fax recordings made by the photographic process (lower left), as used by news agencies, for example, and by a popular direct recording process (lower right). Original photograph is shown at top.

vertical; left-right vs right-left; up vs down. The axis is generally controlled by the relationship of width to height of the subject copy and how it affects orientation of the copy with respect to the scan mechanism.

The prevalence of horizontal, left-to-right scanning—sometimes referred to as the "positive" or "normal" scan direction—in TV and flat-bed facsimile systems is best explained as having been influenced, originally, by the way the human eye scans a page of reading matter. (It is as good an arbitrary basis as any.) One may reasonably speculate that, had these arts been a product of eastern rather than western cultures, scan orientation and direction might have been influenced accordingly.

5. *Kell Factor.* It was pointed out that different factors control horizontal and vertical resolution in a scan system; that, within a scan stroke, resolution is a function of speed of response, while, across the scan "grain," it is determined *basically* by the relative coarseness of the grain, as measured in scan lines per inch (LPI). The word *basically* is emphasized here because, while there should be a 1:1 relationship between scan lines and image elements on the "cross-grain" axis, effectively the number of elements resolvable per inch is *less* than the LPI. The loss, generally estimated to be 30 percent of the ideal elemental resolution (equivalent to the LPI), is called *Kell factor.*[2]

In simple terms, what Kell factor represents is a loss that is inherent in the scanning process. It has to do with the fact that scan lines are of finite width, across which there can be no discrimination between light values. For example, if a stroke of the scan spot just catches the edge of a dark image element on the subject copy, the resulting recording stroke will register a dark mark across its entire width at that point. (Fig. 5.5). Thus, the scanning process tends to have a spreading effect on elements along the cross-grain axis.

The spreading effect also applies in the case of lines of image detail that are ostensibly parallel to the scan axis but are actually slightly oblique to it. Rarely will an image line lie exactly coincident with a scan line. The spreading effect on oblique lines is illustrated in Fig. 5.6.

The degree of loss represented by Kell factor has been derived both subjectively and statistically by different researchers. All that is important to know, from a practical standpoint, is that the effective cross-grain output resolution of a fax system, in *elements per inch,* is the LPI $\times$ 0.70.

6. *"Square" Resolution.* For all practical purposes, the optimum condition with regard to relative vertical/horizontal resolution in a fax system is equality. When the two are equal, we say that the element area resolved by the system is *square,* or that we have *square resolution.*

[2]Named for R. D. Kell, RCA engineer who introduced it as the "K factor" in a coauthored 1934 technical paper titled, "An Experimental Television System" (*Proceedings of the IRE,* Vol. 22, p. 1247).

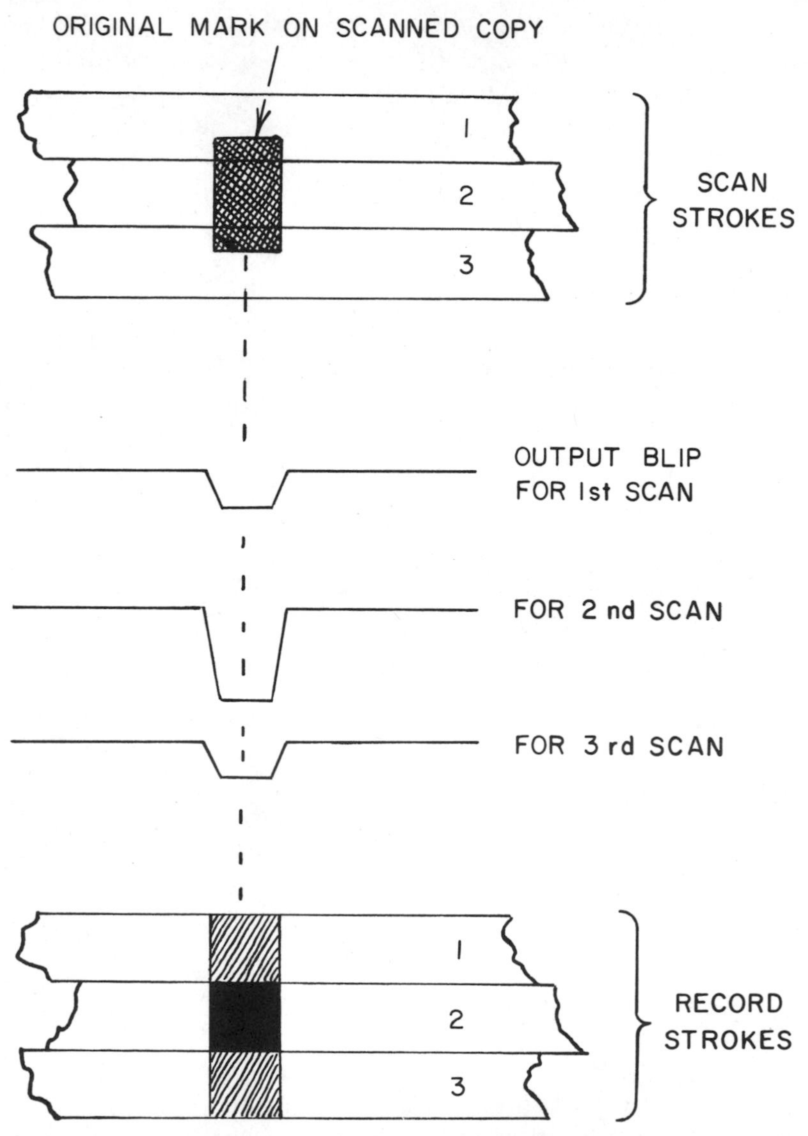

Fig. 5.5. A mark reproduced by a fax recorder will always occupy at least the full width of the recording stroke, regardless of the dimensions of the actual mark on the scanned original.

This should not be taken to mean that, where resolution along one axis is fixed and there is margin for improvement along the other, such improvement should not be undertaken. If, for example, the LPI of a system is preestablished (possibly for reasons of equipment compatibility), and there is bandwidth to spare, an increase in resolution along the scan axis is bound to result in improved output legibility—up to a point. The increase may

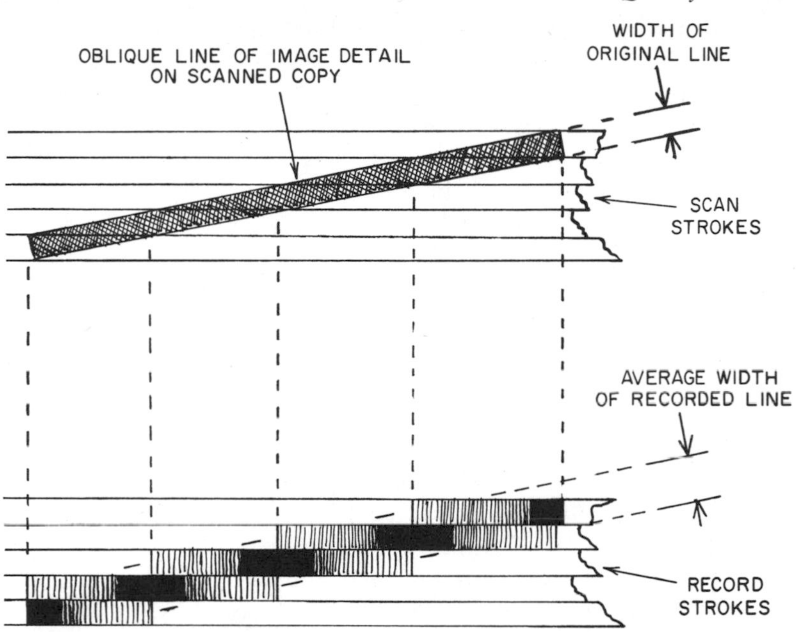

Fig. 5.6. Spreading, or "stepladder," effect in the reproduction of an oblique line of image detail has the effect of increasing the line's width.

be implemented by narrowing the scanning aperture, or, in a digital system, by stepping up the sampling rate (which may also require modification of the aperture). Unfortunately, there are no clear criteria for determining where the point is beyond which increased resolution would be wasted. Subjective tests have placed it anywhere from 25 to 100 percent over that required for square resolution.

There may also be cases where it is advantageous to reduce resolution along the scan axis relative to that along the cross-grain axis. For example, where bandwidth is more than adequate to satisfy the resolution requirements for certain types of documents, it may be expedient to increase the scan rate to obtain a speed advantage without altering the LPI. Depending on how much the balance is shifted, the result could be appreciably less resolution along the scan axis than at right angles to it. How fair an exchange this resolution imbalance would be for the ability to send and receive more rapidly is something that would have to be determined subjectively.

Another consideration that can affect squareness of resolution is the value we choose to place on *edge gradient,* or the fidelity with which sharp tonal transitions are reproduced. As has already been pointed out, transition fidelity along the scan axis is primarily a function of aperture width, and cannot be divorced from resolution in terms of maximum elements resolvable per scan stroke. Thus, the balancing of elemental resolution between the vertical and horizontal axes can impose an imbalance in fidelity.

In practice, a compromise is generally struck between square resolution and good fidelity by employing a scan aperture whose width is somewhat less than its height. (See 2. *Shape of Scan Aperture.*) Thus, rather than shape the aperture to impose square resolution as a limitation, the system is normally designed to afford resolution along the scan axis at least equal to that at right angles to it. In this way, allowance can also be made for losses in fidelity that may occur in the circuitry between scanner and recorder.

Technically, Kell factor should be considered, too, in the balancing of vertical and horizontal resolution. However, ignoring it will simply result in greater resolution along the scan axis than at right angles to it—which, as noted above, is an acceptable condition. A 96 LPI system, for example, will usually be designed to resolve at least 96 elements (48 cycles) along the scan axis. Applying Kell factor, the nearest the system could come to yielding true square resolution would be a matrix of 96 × 67 elements within a 1-inch square (67 being the product of 96 × 0.70, and therefore the actual cross-grain elemental resolution).

In any event, it can be argued that a loss along one axis is no reason for introduction of a compensating artificial loss (as it were) along the other, just to preserve true square resolution. The argument is certainly valid, but then a lot depends on where we start—and how we proceed—with the design of a system.

Kell factor is most effectively applied when a system is being designed from the very beginning and the required output resolution has been rigidly specified. Let us assume, for example, that we start with two specific requirements:

1. *Output Resolution* (minimum)—3.5 line pairs (spatial cycles) per millimeter, horizontally and vertically;[3]
2. *Transmission*—vestigial sideband amplitude modulation via the switched telephone network (effective bandwidth, about 400 to 2400 Hz).

At 25.4 millimeters per inch, 3.5 cycles/mm translates to 89 cycles—or 178 contiguous lines (or elements)—per inch. Taking Kell factor into account, the scan resolution necessary to reproduce 178 elements is 178 × 1/0.70, or 254 LPI.

For square resolution (ignoring losses other than Kell), the system must be capable of resolving 89 cycles per inch throughout the effective scan length, which we will assume to be 8.5 inches. Thus, the system must allow for 8.5 × 89 × 254, or a total of 192,151 cycles to be transmitted (and received) per vertical inch.

[3] A recommended minimum for assured legibility of $\frac{1}{16}$-inch-high characters is 3.5 cycles/mm of photographic resolution.

Now for bandwidth. For a system of this nature (AM vestigial sideband via the switched network),[4] the carrier frequency will have to be set at about 1800 Hz so that the maximum frequency transmitted (as determined by how much of a "vestige" of the upper sideband is retained) will be well within the 2400-Hz upper limit. Inasmuch as the carrier has to be somewhat higher than the maximum baseband frequency, the latter has to be limited to about 1400 Hz. At 756.5 cycles per scan line (89 cycles per inch × 8.5 inches), 1.85 lines can be transmitted per second, making the scan rate 1.85 × 60, or 111 lines per minute. At 254 LPI, an 11-inch-high document will require a total of 2794 scan strokes and 25 minutes of transmission time.

What we end up with is a system that is painfully slow, that may not give us good edge gradient along the scan axis, and that is subject to most of the transmission impairments discussed in Chapter 4. But, from the standpoint of straight elemental resolution, it is a system of optimal design. Such are the trade-offs that forever plague the fax system designer.

EFFECT OF "GAPS"

To say that a fax system transmits *x* number of scan lines within a given interval of time (e.g., 180 LPM, or three lines per second) is not to say that the interval is solidly filled with *x* lines' worth of picture information. Invariably there are gaps between the end of one line and the beginning of the next. In a conventional system, phasing or synchronizing pulses may occupy them, and, in an electronic flying-spot system, they represent the *blanking period* in which the scan spot is "flown" back to a new start position at the completion of each line.

To understand the effect that these gaps in signal continuity can have on resolution and bandwidth, it is necessary merely to remember that frequency is a rate, and not a quantity. For example, if the only activity within a scan line is a burst of ten black-white cycles at some point along the stroke, the quantity of transitions for that line is ten, but the rate is ten per *x* second. In a 180 LPM system, if the burst is evenly spaced and occurs within a $\frac{1}{4}$-inch segment of an 8.5-inch stroke, the ten cycles represent a frequency of 1020 Hz (ten cycles in $\frac{1}{34}$ of a stroke, at three full strokes per second (Fig. 5.7).

Accordingly, in the preceding example of an 8.5-inch scan line in which 756.5 cycles of spatial frequency are resolved, the 8.5 inches constitutes the *effective* or *available line length,* meaning that each line is followed (or preceded) by some finite gap. Assuming the gap to be $\frac{1}{2}$ inch, the 756.5 cycles occur not within a full line, but rather in 8.5/9 of a line. Thus, at 1.85 lines per second, the true maximum baseband frequency will be

$$\frac{9}{8.5} \times 756.5 \times 1.85 = 1481.8 \text{ Hz}$$

[4] See Chapter 4.

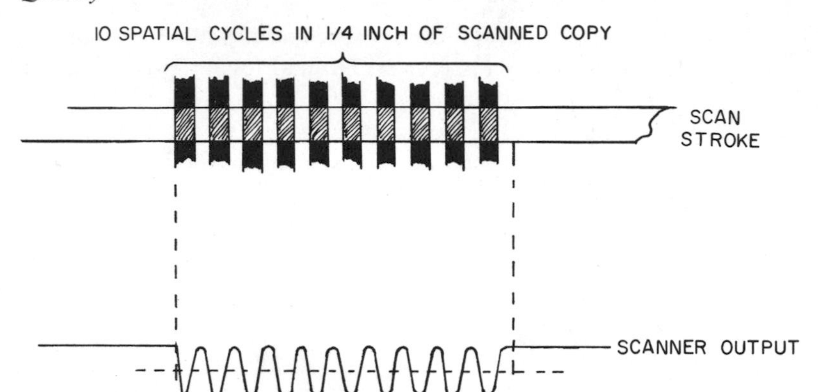

STROKE SPEED: 180 PER MINUTE (3 PER SECOND)

LENGTH OF EACH STROKE: 8.5 INCH

1/4 INCH = 1/34 OF 8.5 INCHES

3 STROKES X 34 X 10 = 1020 ELECTRICAL CYCLES GENERATED PER SECOND (1020 Hz)

Fig. 5.7. Relationship of spatial frequency to scanner output frequency. The former is fixed, whereas the latter will vary with scan rate.

In order to bring the system back to within the 1400-Hz baseband limitation, the cycles-per-line resolution would have to be reduced from 756.5 to 714.5, or the scan rate from 111 to 105 LPM.

In this example, the difference is slight. But it is plain that, as the scan rate increases, the effect of gaps on bandwidth—and, therefore, on the system's resolution capabilities—can become significant. Consider, for example, a 96 LPI system operating at a scan rate of 360 LPM. We will assume that the total scan line interval (total length between corresponding points on consecutive lines) is 9 inches, of which $\frac{1}{2}$ inch is a gap, and that the system is designed to resolve 48 cycles per inch along the scan axis. Taking only the effective scan length into consideration, the maximum baseband frequency of the scanner output, at six strokes per second, would be

$$48 \times 8.5 \times 6 = 2448 \text{ Hz}$$

However, taking the gaps into account, the maximum frequency becomes

$$48 \times 9 \times 6 = 2592 \text{ Hz}$$

Unfortunately there is no universal standard governing the length of gaps (or "dead sectors") or the percentage of line length they represent. Nor is there one governing whether the gap falls within the page width of the scanned subject copy or beyond it.

The percentage can range from zero to about 16, depending on the particular system. Five to seven percent is common for conventional fax systems, while 16 percent is relatively common for electronic "flyback" systems. As for location with respect to the copy, this, too, will vary from system to system. In some it is beyond the edge of the subject copy, while in others it falls within either the left or right margin.

Whatever the particular arrangement, the simple rule to follow in computing the resolution, bandwidth, or scan rate of a fax system—whichever of the three is (or are) variable—is that scan length always be taken as the *total* interval between corresponding points on consecutive lines (effective length plus gaps).

CONTRAST, GRAY SCALE, AND POLARITY

There was a time, before photoelectric devices had been developed to their present high state of refinement, that a fax scanner's ability to distinguish between image details and background of the scanned copy often left much to be desired—particularly if the copy consisted of anything other than black or blue on white. Modern scanners, by comparison, not only are capable of excellent color and gray scale discrimination, but also are usually designed to compensate automatically for varying background reflectances.

Despite these advances, contrast remains a factor in the faithfulness and clarity with which a fax recorder reproduces the subject copy. While it is true that modern electronics permits the boosting of weak contrast by the mere twist of a knob (or automatically, through special compensating circuits), the fact remains that contrast below a certain level can only be boosted at the expense of introducing excessive "noise" into a recording.

A certain amount of noise is always present in the output of a scanner, and a certain additional amount is bound to be picked up in transmission and in amplifier circuitry. The degree to which it degrades a recording depends largely on the ratio between it and the picture detail component of the signal fed to the recorder—i.e., the *signal-to-noise ratio* (more on this later).

The recording process and medium have already been briefly discussed as to their role in reproduction quality. For the most part, the fidelity of tonal rendition and contrast required at the output of a fax system is determined by the particular function the system serves. For the transmission of photographs, gray scale discrimination is important; for the transmission of messages, it is not.

MEASURING CONTRAST

Contrast may be assessed in various ways. That of a photographic negative, for example, can be measured in units of *transmission density* on a

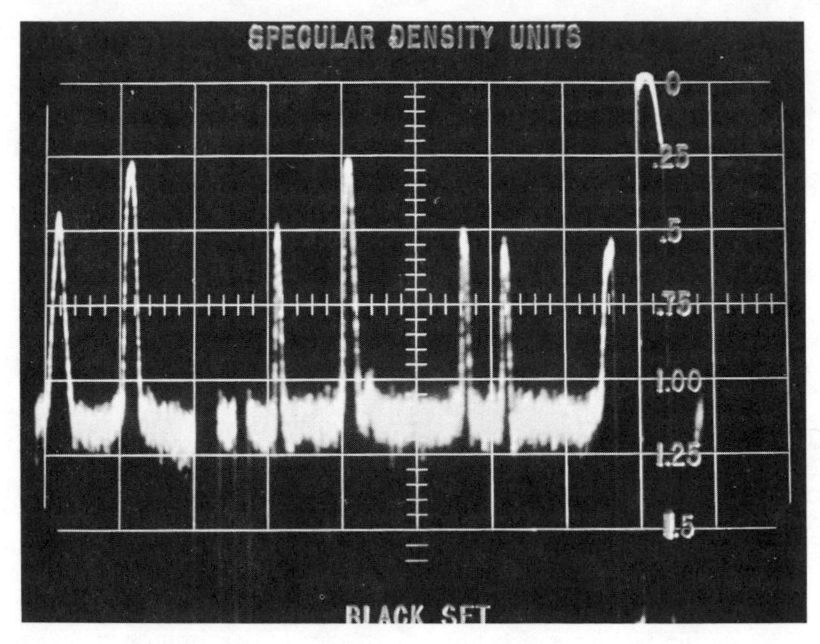

Fig. 5.8. Portion of a negative microimage of a line drawing analyzed for contrast on the screen of a scanning microdensitometer. The analyzed segment consists of "off-white" peaks averaging about 0.5 density unit, against an "off-black" background (broad white areas in the scope image) of about 1.10 density units.

photoelectric device known as a *densitometer.* Readings taken for representative areas of subject and background are compared, and the greater the difference, the better the contrast. Depending on the application, certain minimal standards may be set as a quality control. Scanning type densitometers make it possible to analyze contrast graphically as a spatial frequency waveform (Fig. 5.8).

Similarly, the contrast of opaque prints is measurable in units of *reflection density,* which correlates directly with transmission density. The instrument used for measurement is a *reflecting densitometer,* or *reflectometer.* Table 5.B shows the relationship between tone, reflectance (or transmission), and densitometer readings.

Table 5.B—*Relationship of tone, reflectance (or transmission), and densitometer readings*

Tone	*Percent Transmission or Reflectance*	*Densitometer Reading (Density Units)*
Black	1	2.00
Medium gray	50	0.30
White	100	0.00

Ordinarily, the contrast of a fax recording is gauged and evaluated by eye. The IEEE Test Chart (Fig. 5.2) contains patterns to aid in the assessment. The principal one appears near the top of the chart, between the vertical bar and repeating tri-bar resolution patterns. It is in the form of a *step tablet* containing two rows of 15 discrete tones, each row ranging from nearly pure white to nearly pure black. (Not all 15 are clearly distinguishable in the reproduction.) The extreme steps have reflection densities of approximately 0.00 and 1.85, respectively.

The continuous "wedge" (so-called) just above the step patterns represents a linear variation covering essentially the same range. It is useful for testing the quantization of gray levels in a digital fax system.

Gray levels approximating steps 6 and 11 of the step tablet are reproduced at the right-hand side of the chart as an aid in detecting level variations during recording (assuming horizontal scanning of the chart). Paired gray levels, approximating steps 1 and 6 in one case and 11 and 15 in the other, appear in the form of vertical bar resolution patterns at the very top of the chart. The latter are useful in checking the system's response to threshold contrast levels encountered in scanning.

The portrait photograph of the young lady contains approximately the same tonal range covered by the step tablet. To the discerning eye of one experienced in assessing fax recording quality, its highlights and shadows serve as an effective gauge of the system's tonal capabilities.

EFFECT OF CONTRAST ON RESOLUTION

Although little data exist in the way of specific correlations, there is substantial evidence that, within limits, for a given level of legibility, resolution and contrast can compensate each other. It is well established, for example, that the human eye's visual acuity—the ability to discern small objects or the separation between closely spaced objects—increases with an increase in overall subject illumination. The reason is that increased brightness causes a corresponding decrease in the size of the eye's iris opening (equivalent to lowering the *f*-stop of a camera lens), which results in improved resolving capability. Therefore, to the extent that contrast is improved by an increase in background reflectance of a dark-on-light document reproduction, legibility should also be improved—without having altered the resolution.

As for empirical data correlating contrast and resolution, the results of a study by Dr. C. E. Nelson are of particular interest. Based on a jury analysis of a large number of paper prints produced from microfilm images containing a variety of contrast/resolution relationships, Nelson's general conclusion was that "Satisfactory readability can be achieved with *moderate resolution and high contrast* or *high resolution and moderate contrast.*"[5]

[5] See C. E. Nelson, *Microfilm Technology*, New York, McGraw-Hill, 1965, pp. 303–304.

For the particular prints involved in the analysis, it was possible to establish a contrast/resolution relationship expressible as a simple equation:

$$\text{CR index} = D_b/D_l \times R$$

where D_b is the background density, D_l the line (or image detail) density, and R the resolution in line pairs (spatial cycles) per millimeter. All values are as read on the microfilm from which the test prints were produced.

According to Nelson, an index of 200 represented the threshold of legibility (prints produced from images for which the index was less than 200 proved consistently illegible). He points out, however, that the 200 index applies only to the particular materials and processes employed in this trial and cannot be applied universally.

Tests have also been conducted by H. C. Frey of Bell Telephone Laboratories, the results of which indicate that contrast may influence legibility to an even *greater* degree than does resolution. The tests were of limited scope, however, and the results must therefore be regarded as inconclusive.

Suffice it to say, for the time being, that there *is* a relationship between contrast and resolution (or contrast and legibility), and that an improvement in the contrast of a fax recording—with resolution remaining fixed—will almost certainly enhance legibility. There is simply no sufficiently definitive yardstick, as yet, to permit us to predict that if we increase the contrast by a given amount, we can do with *x* amount less resolution.

POLARITY

The tonal polarity of a fax recording—the dark/light relationship of detail to background—may be the same as that of the original (i.e., *positive*) or the reverse of it (*negative*), depending on application.

In systems intended for the production of photographic negatives of the subject copy, the signal to the recorder will have the same electrical polarity as the scanner output, prior to amplification. In other words, maximum signal will represent the *white* portions of the original. With a crater tube as the reproducer, maximum signal to the recorder will produce maximum light, which will be interpreted on the processed film as maximum density, or black. Systems designed to reproduce newspaper page proofs as printing masters at a branch plant are frequently arranged to work this way.

In most other applications, regardless of recording technique, the polarity of the output signal to the recorder is *opposite* that of the scanner output. Minimum signal at the scanner, representing black, therefore becomes *maximum* at the recorder, so that black signal components produce maximum marking current.

Polarity of the transmitted signal is partly a function of the number of amplifier stages between the scanner and the transmission facility. In any event it is determined by the reversals that take place in signal processing between the output of the scanning transducer and that of the transmitter as a unit.

In order to ensure compatibility between terminals within a system, it has been necessary to establish standards on transmission polarity. For message fax and other systems customarily employing direct recording techniques—e.g., weather map distribution systems—*negative modulation,* or *maximum signal on black,* is the standard. However, in systems customarily employing photorecording techniques (with the possible exception of those for the transmission of newspaper page masters), *positive modulation,* or *maximum signal on white,* is usually specified. These tonal-maximum signal relationships obviously assume amplitude modulation. In FM or Frequency Shift Keying (FSK) Systems, black may be represented by a higher or lower frequency than white, with no change in amplitude. As with AM, there is no universal standard. In any event, these standards are largely a matter of tradition and have nothing directly to do with recording polarity.

The effect of transmission polarity on output quality is difficult to assess. It is primarily a question of whether blemishes due to noise acquired in transmission will impair the background or image detail of a recording. If the blemishes are conspicuous, they are objectionable either way.

IMPAIRMENTS DUE TO DIGITIZING

It is sometimes advantageous to transmit fax signals in digital rather than analog form. (The particular advantages are discussed in Chapter 2.) Where subject copy consists essentially of only two contrasting tonal levels—e.g., black text on a white background—it may be desirable to use a two-level (mark-space; on-off) form of transmission. It is also sometimes practical, and may become more so as digital techniques become more prevalent, to transmit photographs and other halftone material digitally by *pulse-code modulation* (PCM) techniques, in which each of a number of discrete steps in the gray scale is assigned a binary code.

But, whether the digitizing is two-level or multilevel, there are two potential quality impairments inherent in the analog-to-digital conversion process. One is the possibility of errors in discrimination between one tonal level and another. The other is the displacement of marks that may occur in the recording due to slight differences between the scan rate and the digital sampling rate.

For the purposes of this book, it will suffice to confine the discussion to two-level quantization. The nature of the impairments is basically the same as for multilevel, with the exception that amplitude quantizing errors (sometimes called quantizing noise) are likely to be more conspicuous, and therefore more deleterious, in a two-level system.

AMPLITUDE QUANTIZING ERRORS

A basic step in two-level analog-to-digital conversion is the setting of a reference level, or *threshold,* for discrimination between image detail and

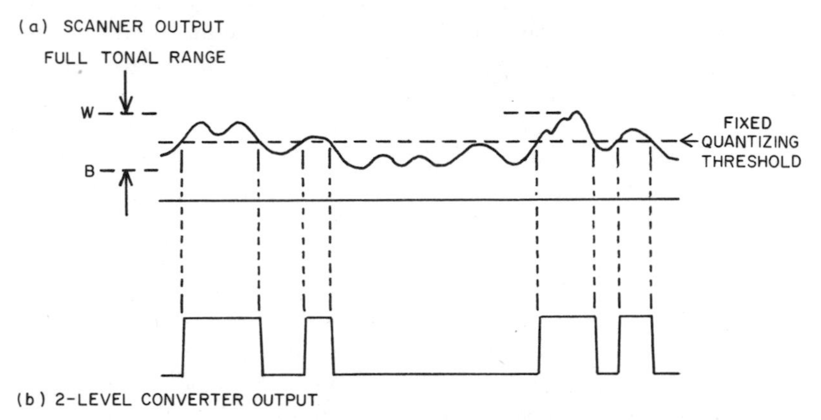

Fig. 5.9. Illustration of the amplitude quantizing problem inherent where contrast is lacking between image details and background. Several details are lost because fluctuations in signal strength are too weak to cross the quantizing threshold.

background. For high contrast originals, there is no problem. For moderate or low contrast originals, the probability of discrimination (or amplitude quantizing) errors occurring because of the small difference in level between background and detail will depend on how consistent the contrast is. One can appreciate the quantizing problem that could obtain where the subject copy consists of characters of various colors (convertible by the scanner to gray levels) on an off-white background. Figure 5.9 illustrates the nature of the problem.

Sophisticated converters have been developed in which discrimination is governed by a *"floating" threshold,* which constantly changes position, with variations in the average between maximum and minimum levels of the analog signal. For most applications, however, it is sufficient for the threshold to be essentially fixed but adjustable manually, as needed.

Figure 5.10 is a segment of a digital fax recording in which the effects of amplitude quantizing errors appear.

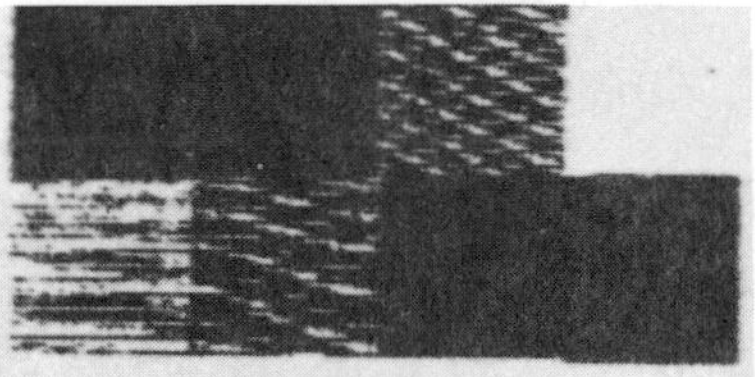

Fig. 5.10. Quantizing errors in a two-level reproduction of a halftone original. Specimen (left) was reproduced by an analog system; specimen (right) by a two-level digital (binary) system. Errors are particularly evident in the lower left square of the latter specimen, which, on the original, has the least contrast with the white background.

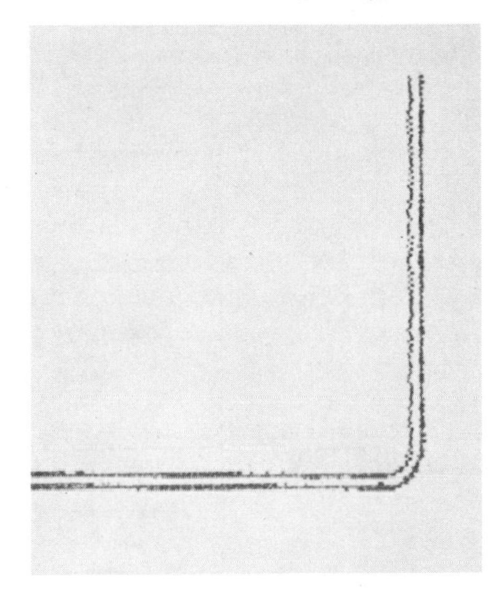

Fig. 5.11. Segment of a two-level fax recording in which jitter is evident. Defects in the horizontal segment are the result of the image line's not having been exactly coincident with the scan axis.

TIME QUANTIZING ERRORS ("JITTER")

"Jitter" is an effect occurring at right angles or oblique to the scan axis of a fax recording, the result of slight time and space inconsistencies between scan rate and digital sampling interval or between sampling interval and the angle of a line of picture detail. It can occur in analog systems as well, but is generally more common and of a slightly different character in digital systems. An actual sample of jitter appears in Fig. 5.11, and the effect is graphically analyzed in Fig. 5.12.

Sampling, in a digital system, is controlled by what is commonly called a *clock,* which is essentially a precision oscillator similar to those sometimes used for the generation of synchronous power to operate scanner and recorder drive motors. (See Chapter 3.) In effect, the clock pulses, occurring at regular intervals, momentarily connect the amplitude-quantized scanner output to a sensing circuit to determine whether an ON (mark) or OFF (space) condition prevails at that moment. If an ON condition is sensed, the carrier is shifted to mark level, where it remains until the sensor detects an OFF condition. Accordingly, if an OFF condition is sensed, the carrier is shifted back to space level, where it remains until the next ON sensing. The shifting may be in the form of amplitude, frequency, or phase changes, depending on the modulation technique employed.

The explanation is perhaps somewhat oversimplified, but it should help to explain Fig. 5.12.

Inasmuch as each *bit* (each ON or OFF pulse) is roughly equivalent to half an analog cycle, the sampling rate in bits per second will usually be at least twice the highest baseband frequency (in hertz) that the system is expected to accommodate. And, technically, the carrier frequency in hertz should at

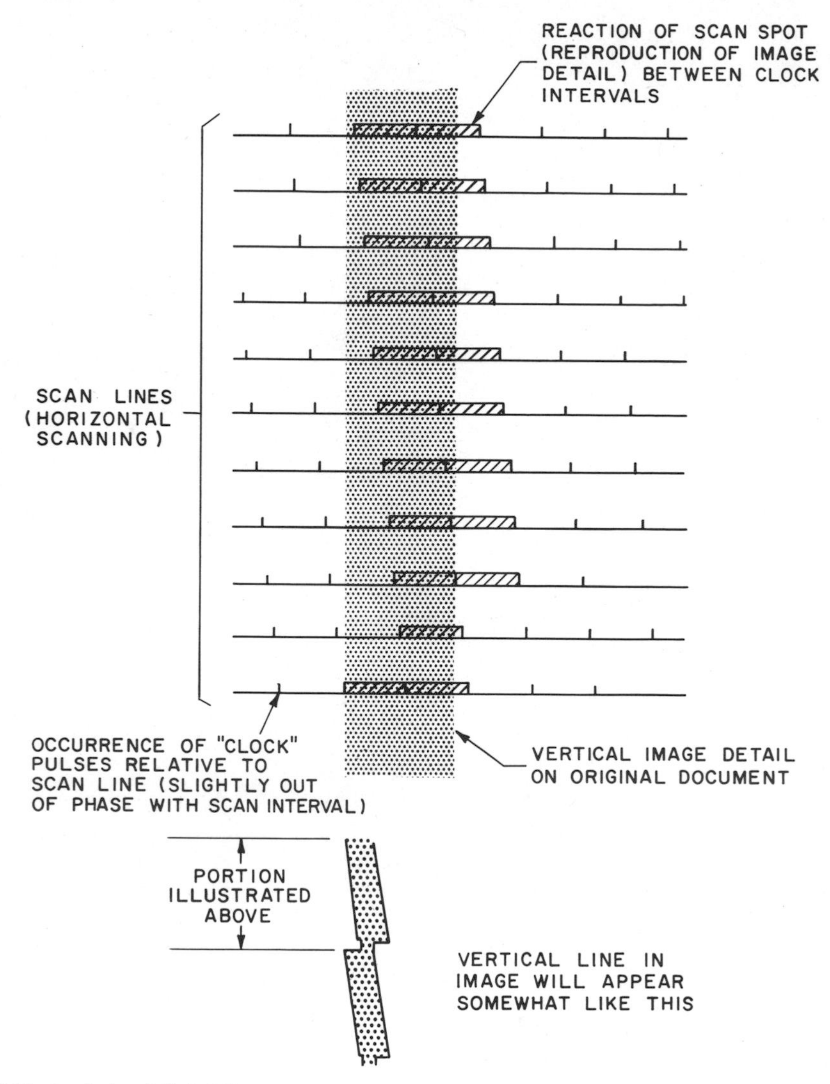

Fig. 5.12. Analysis of digital jitter.

least equal the sampling rate in bits per second, so that there is a full cycle of carrier for each bit of transmitted data.

Jitter can be minimized by designing the digital system so that the clock frequency, or sampling rate, is somehow synchronized with the drive motor frequency. But, even then, except for some improvement in uniformity, the effect will persist for oblique image lines. No degree of precision can entirely eliminate jitter.

But, while jitter may be unavoidable, controlled laboratory tests[6] have

[6] Specifically, those conducted by Erdmann and Neal (see reference at end of chapter).

indicated that there is little, if any, fundamental difference in character legibility between recordings produced by a two-level digital system and those produced by straight analog.

LEGIBILITY CRITERIA

The legibility of words or characters is often a key factor in the establishment of output quality requirements for a fax system. But before any specific end requirements can be set, a choice has to be made as to which of the following two basic objectives applies:

1. Individual letters of a word need not be positively identified so long as the word, as a whole, is legible;
2. Identity of the smallest significant individual character must be virtually assured.

Objective No. 1 might apply in the case of a conventional message fax system, the input to which is predominantly text type material, whereas objective No. 2 will apply where technical documents—graphs, specifications, etc.—or documents containing significant numerical data are involved. Figure 5.13 illustrates the distinction between word and character identification.

Having decided this basic objective, there are various criteria by which specific output resolution requirements can be set. Not all of those discussed below apply directly to fax systems, although, regardless of the language or the approach, there is general agreement among them as to the fundamental criteria for meeting either of the two basic legibility objectives.

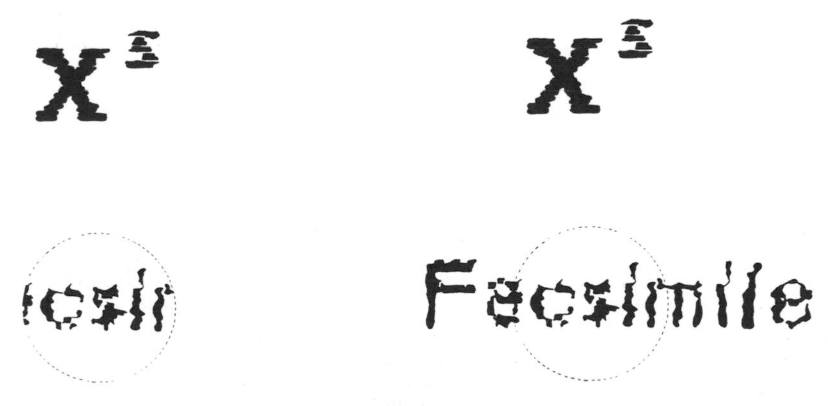

Fig. 5.13. Individual character vs word legibility. On the left, neither the exponent for the "x" nor the characters in the circle are clearly identifiable. On the right, the characters in the circle become identifiable in context, whereas the identity of the exponent remains in doubt. (These are hand-drafted copies of magnified fax recording specimens.)

SCAN LINES PER CHARACTER

The most direct approach to the design (or selection) of a fax system to meet a given legibility objective is to determine the minimum number of scan lines by which an individual character should be dissected. A number of experiments have been performed, by a number of researchers, in which subjects were asked to evaluate the comparative legibility for a varying number of scan lines per character. The collective result has been a more or less unanimous agreement that 10 scan lines is the minimum required for assured legibility of an individual character (objective No. 2).

Supplementing this, experience has shown that approximately half that number, a minimum of five lines, is required to meet objective No. 1 (word legibility), where individual characters need be identified only by inference from the supporting context. Figure 5.14 illustrates the comparative effects of a large and small number of scan lines per character.

Table 5.C interprets the above criteria as scan resolutions required for various minimum character heights. It bears mentioning here that the *point* designation for type size is somewhat deceptive, a point being $\frac{1}{72}$ inch. Typically, 6 pt. text characters range from about $\frac{1}{32}$ to $\frac{3}{64}$ inch in height; 8 pt. from $\frac{3}{64}$ to $\frac{1}{16}$; 10 pt. from $\frac{3}{64}$ to $\frac{5}{64}$; 11 pt. from $\frac{1}{16}$ to $\frac{3}{32}$; 12 pt.

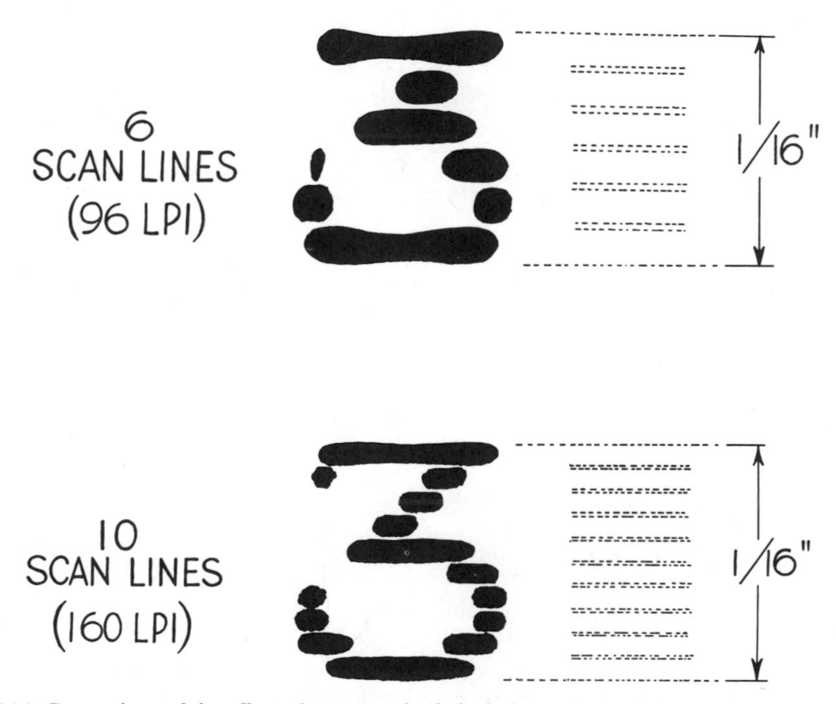

Fig. 5.14. Comparison of the effect of coarse and relatively fine scan resolution on reproduction of the number 3.

Table 5.C—*Scan resolutions required for various minimum character heights, based on five lines per character to identify words and 10 lines to identify individual characters.*

Minimum Character Height (inch)	*Approximately Equivalent Type Face*	*Minimum Scan Lines Per Inch (LPI)*	
		1. Identify Words	*2. Identify Individual Characters*
3/64	6–7 pt.	107	214
1/16	8–10 pt.	80	160
3/32	11–12 pt.	53	106
1/8	14–18 pt.	40	80
5/32	20–22 pt.	32	64

from $\frac{1}{16}$ to $\frac{7}{64}$; 14 pt. from $\frac{5}{64}$ to $\frac{1}{8}$; 18 pt. from $\frac{3}{32}$ to $\frac{9}{64}$; and 22 pt. from $\frac{7}{64}$ to $\frac{11}{64}$. These are based (loosely) on measurements of Caslon Old Style upper and lower case letters. Of the standard typewriter fonts, *elite* falls somewhere between 10 and 11 pt. type, and *pica* between 11 and 12 pt.

What Table 5.C shows, among other things, is that an LPI of 32 would be sufficient for assured *word* identification if the smallest letter ever to be encountered were $\frac{5}{32}$ inch high, or about 22 pt. upper case. It is difficult to conceive, however, of a text type application where letter height would be confined consistently to so comparatively large a dimension. A more realistic situation would be one in which characters are consistently $\frac{1}{8}$ inch high and require individual identification. This would be the case for most modern "drafted" documents, such as engineering drawings and specifications.

Drafting standards vary from one company to another, but a recent survey reveals that $\frac{1}{8}$ inch is a fairly universal minimum for character height, and that, for documents larger than 17 × 22 inches in size, the minimum is often upped to $\frac{5}{32}$ inch.

As for text type material—books, letters, forms, etc.—the minimum character height commonly encountered is likely to be closer to $\frac{1}{16}$ inch, which is a good minimum to allow for in any case, since it will give fair assurance of legibility for the common typewriter fonts as well as most 8 pt. and larger type faces.

The realistic lower limit for scan resolution, then, for drafted and text type material alike, is about 80 LPI. However, this should not be interpreted as implying that scan resolutions lower than 80 LPI are to be ruled out as unacceptable. By this particular criterion, lower resolutions will merely decrease the degree of *assurance* of output legibility for a given character size.

For individual character identification in text material, the lower limit figure would be doubled, to 160 LPI. And, where items set in 6 pt. or comparable size type—footnotes, exponents, column headings, etc.—are

Table 5.D—*Scan resolutions required at the film plane to meet the 5 and 10 lines per character legibility criteria in a microfilm input fax system.*

Minimum Character Height (inch)	*Minimum Scan Lines Per Inch (LPI) at Film Plane*							
	1. Identify Words				*2. Identify Individual Characters*			
	16×	*20×*	*24×*	*30×*	*16×*	*20×*	*24×*	*30×*
3/64	1712	2140	2568	3210	3424	4280	5136	6420
1/16	1280	1600	1920	2400	2560	3200	3840	4800
3/32	848	1060	1272	1590	1696	2120	2544	3180
1/8	640	800	960	1200	1280	1600	1920	2400
5/32	512	640	768	960	1024	1280	1536	1920

frequently encountered, it may be necessary to go to scan resolutions in excess of 100 and 200 LPI, respectively, depending on whether word or individual character identification is required.

In cases where the material is microfilmed, documents ranging from $8\frac{1}{2} \times 11$ to 17×22 inches in size may be reduced anywhere from 16× to 24× on film, while the larger ones will usually be reduced either 24× or 30×. These are *linear* reductions. In other words, at a 16× reduction, a line of image detail measuring 1 inch on the original will measure $\frac{1}{16}$ inch on the microimage.

Assuming a fax scanner has to be designed to scan a microimage directly at the film plane, the scan resolution (in LPI) required to meet the 5 or 10 lines/character legibility criterion can be derived simply by multiplying the LPIs in Table 5.C by the photographic reduction. These film plane LPIs have been worked out and are shown in Table 5.D.

MICROFILM PRINTBACK CRITERIA

In connection with its activities in the area of test standards for the reproduction of microfilmed drawings and documents, the National Bureau of Standards has devised the following equation as a guide in determining the resolution required for a given level of reproduction quality:

$$R = qr/e$$

As applied to microfilm, R is the resolution in spatial cycles per millimeter, as read on the film with the aid of a microscope; r is the linear reduction at which the original document was recorded on film; e is the height in millimeters of a lower case "e" on the original document, and q is an arbitrary quality index.

According to the NBS, q must be at least 8 when computing the resolution required for excellent copy, 5 when computing for medium quality copy, and 3 for marginal quality.

Applying the formula to facsimile, we will want R to represent resolution in scan lines per inch rather than spatial cycles per millimeter. The millimeter-to-inch conversion can be accomplished simply by expressing the character height e in inches; and the conversion from spatial cycles to scan lines simply requires the answer to be increased by a factor of 2. (There are two scan lines to a spatial cycle.) It might be argued that the conversion from resolvable spatial cycles to scan lines per inch should also take Kell factor into account by further multiplying the answer by 1/0.70. The NBS formula, however, already assumes certain magnification and reproduction losses, thereby making further compensation unnecessary.

In addition, since there is no reduction involved, we can simply eliminate r from the equation, which thus becomes

$$R = 2q/e$$

Computing R for a q of 5, which we may assume to represent the minimum quality required for *individual character* recognition, and letting $e = 1/16$ inch, we find that

$$R = \frac{10}{0.062} = 161$$

which agrees with the 10 lines/character criterion previously discussed.

Computing R for a q of 3, which we may assume to represent the minimum quality required for *word* recognition, we find that, for an e of $1/16$ inch,

$$R = \frac{6}{0.062} = 97$$

which is slightly higher than that required to meet the 5 lines/character criterion previously discussed.

Another generally accepted microfilm printback criterion is that, to be judged acceptable, a print must be capable of resolving 3.5 to 4 spatial cycles per millimeter. In other words, on a nonreduced print of a photographed NBS Microcopy Test Chart (Fig. 5.15), separate lines and spaces must be discernible in all patterns from the largest down to 3.6 or 4.0.

At 25.4 millimeters per inch, and at two scan lines per spatial cycle, 3.5 cycles/mm works out to 178 scan lines/inch—which is a bit higher than that required for independent recognition of $1/16$-inch characters (by the 10 lines/character criterion) and more than adequate for word recognition where characters are $3/64$ inch, or 6 point. Four cycles/mm works out to 203 scan lines/inch, just short of the minimum needed to ensure independent recognition of $3/64$-inch characters.

So, in general, the microfilm printback criteria agree with the rules governing the number of scan lines per character for good and for marginal legibility.

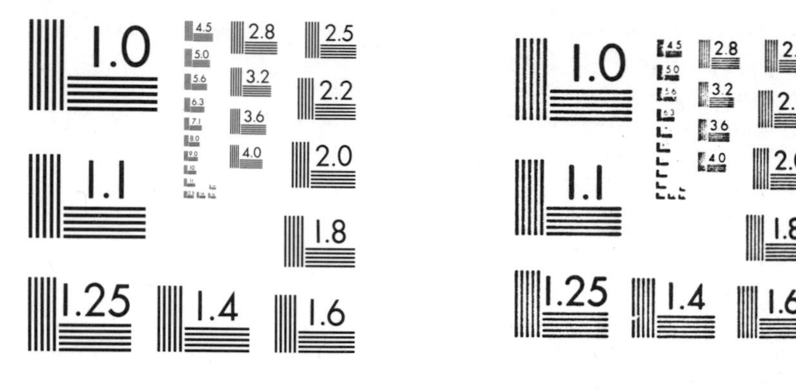

Fig. 5.15. Comparison of an actual NBS Microcopy Resolution Test Chart (left), with a near 1:1 reproduction of an enlarged, first-generation microfilm image of the same chart (right). Allowing for the slight reduction from original to print, there is approximately a 12-target loss from input to output—which is normal for the particular processes involved. (These reproductions also, of course, reflect losses inherent in the processes involved in the printing of this book.)

NMA-EIA COMMITTEE FINDINGS

The joint National Microfilm Association/Electronic Industries Association Microfilm-Facsimile Standards Committee, TR 29.1, conducted subjective tests in 1969 to determine minimum scan resolution requirements for engineering drawings and other technical documents requiring individual character identification. The 14 committee members, themselves (including the author), constituted the jury which analyzed the two specimens used in the trial—a segment of an engineering drawing that was judged "typical," and a slightly modified IEEE facsimile test chart—each of which was scanned at nominal resolutions of 100, 135, 150, 165, 180, and 200 LPI. The object was to subjectively evaluate the threshold of acceptability, both intuitively and with the aid of resolution test charts.

The results of the analysis were (a) a general conclusion that type sizes smaller than 6 pt. require a scan resolution in excess of 200 LPI for independent identification, and (b) a specific recommendation of 165 LPI as the standard scan resolution for engineering drawings.

LIBRARY APPLICATIONS

In tests conducted in 1966 by the University of Nevada Library (under a grant from the Council on Library Resources) it was determined that a 96/180 message fax system operating over the dial network via phone couplers was able to produce copies of a quality that was ". . . adequate for most library materials."[7] The materials that were legibly reproduced included printed pages of 8 point and larger type faces, typed pages (pica and elite), carbons of typed pages, line drawings, graphs, charts, and photos having good contrast.

As for printed matter specifically, the test results further indicated that most 6 pt. type faces and 8 pt. italics reproduced with border line legibility, while 6 pt. italics and most type faces smaller than 6 pt. generally reproduced illegibly. In addition, materials of very low contrast resulted in illegible recordings in most cases.

Referring to the previously discussed criteria, it will be seen that there is a fair degree of correlation with these library tests. By the 10 lines/character criterion, we observe that we can go as low as 80 LPI and still have marginal legibility of 8 pt. characters, and that an LPI of over 100 is necessary for legibility of 6 pt. characters. And, according to the NBS printback legibility equation, marginal legibility of 6 pt. characters requires a minimum of about 97 LPI.

PICTORIAL CRITERIA

So far, the discussion has been confined largely to alphanumerics, or symbols and characters of a more or less uniform construction, normally isolated from one another against a contrasting and uniform background. But what of graphics that are not so conveniently modular in character, such as handwriting and photographs? What sort of acceptability criteria applies to them?

Obviously, this category of graphics does not as readily lend itself to the establishment of acceptability thresholds. Nevertheless, there has been a certain amount of quasi-standardization that deserves mention.

HANDWRITING

The nearest thing to a resolution standard applying to handwriting is the establishment of 80 LPI as adequate scan resolution for the identification of signatures. This was the consensus of engineers and others who participated in the development of an experimental facsimile signature verification system by Bell Telephone Laboratories in the late 1950s.[8] The system was developed primarily for use by banks, where customer signature records are frequently filed at a central location and are therefore not readily accessible at branches.

One commercially available fax system for this purpose, produced by the Alden Company, uses a scan resolution of 100 LPI, which, of course, is

[7] Morehouse report (see reference at end of chapter).

[8] F. K. Becker, et al., "An Experimental Visual Communication System," *Bell System Technical Journal,* Vol. 38, January 1959, pp. 141–176.

Fig. 5.16. Handwriting specimen reproduced by a nominal 100 LPI fax system.

preferable to 80. (Higher resolution is always preferable, from a quality standpoint, in any graphic system.) A signature verification system is unique in that the area to be scanned is very limited, thus permitting a favorable trade-off of time and bandwidth for quality.

Though requiring a special 10-kHz circuit (or the nearest equivalent in standard facilities), the Alden system is able to transmit the contents of a 3 × 5-inch record card in 10 seconds. The Bell Labs experimental system was designed to transmit an area of $1\frac{1}{4} \times 5$ inches in 20 seconds via an ordinary telephone circuit, and five seconds via a special 5-kHz circuit.

A nominal 100 LPI fax recording of a handwriting specimen is reproduced in Fig. 5.16.

FINGERPRINTS

In law enforcement, the expediting of fingerprint records between outlying precincts and police record centers has proved a definite aid in the speedy identification of a criminal suspect and in the limiting of detention time. The fact that no two fingerprints are exactly alike is an indication of their complexity. Besides the three general pattern types—arch, loop, and whorl—there are numerous subclassifications, within each of which are subtle variations.

Experience has shown that a scan resolution of about 200 LPI is required to preserve all of the essential details of a fax-transmitted fingerprint. In addition, a reasonably good gray scale capability is desirable to ensure reproduction of very light or smudged prints. A 200 LPI fax recording of a fingerprint is reproduced in Fig. 5.17.

MAPS

It is characteristic of maps to range widely in complexity, thus making it somewhat impractical to generalize on fax resolution criteria. However, one type of map, the traditional weather map (Fig. 5.18), has been married to facsimile long enough now for its users to have agreed on what constitutes acceptable quality. The standard that has evolved is 96 LPI, the same as that for conventional message fax.

Limited use has been made of lower resolutions—as low as 48 LPI—where the maps are relatively simple and contain no fine detail. The reduction permits speedier transmission or use of lower grade (and therefore less expensive) transmission facilities. Likewise, higher resolutions are sometimes employed for particularly "busy" maps.

As for other types of maps, required resolution will depend on relative complexity and fineness of detail. A typical road map, for example, with its extensive use of comparatively small characters and symbols, would probably require a scan resolution in the neighborhood of 200 LPI. In addition, the liberal use of color in such maps would require that the system have a good gray scale capability in order to maintain the distinction between background and detail.

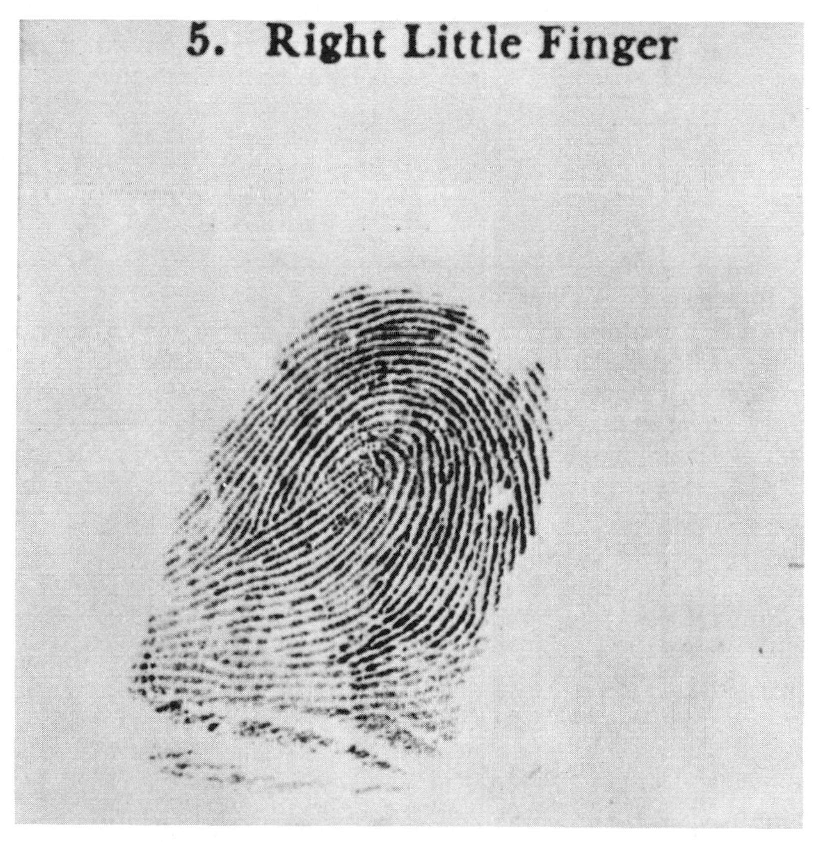

Fig. 5.17. Fax-transmitted fingerprint. (Courtesy Datalog Division, Litton Industries.)

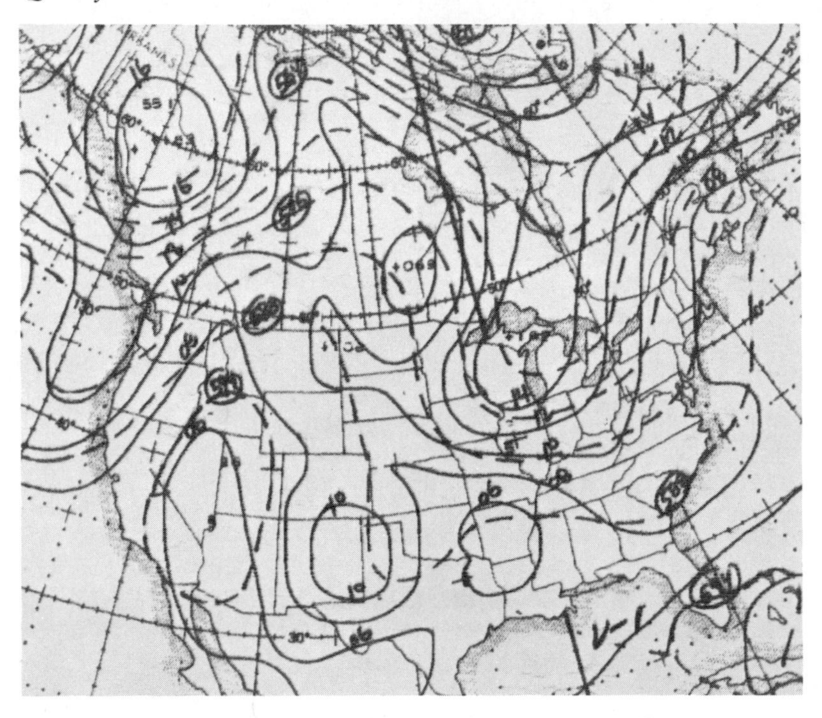

Fig. 5.18. Weather map reproduced by facsimile at 96 LPI. (Courtesy U.S. Weather Bureau.)

PHOTOGRAPHS

Photographs, like maps, can vary widely in complexity. While scan resolution requirements will usually vary according to the level of output quality required in a given application, the 100 LPI standard for the fax distribution of news photos has sufficed for a number of years for a wide variety of subject matter. Established about 1925, it remains the more or less official standard for modern telephotography.[9]

Press photos are usually transmitted as 8 × 10-inch enlarged prints of the photographers' camera negatives. Scanned at 100 LPI, the recorded result is a picture having approximately one and a half times the resolution of the best image obtainable on a 12-inch commercial TV screen. The received fax-recorded picture is usually reduced in size for publication, which has the effect of increasing its resolution somewhat (just as a smaller TV image appears sharper than a larger one). Much resolution is subsequently lost, however, in the halftone printing process.

In police facsimile systems, "mug shots" of criminal suspects are usually transmitted at a resolution of 200 LPI. But the real reason for the choice

[9] Actually, there are no universal standards for newspicture reception. Recorders are designed for a variety of resolutions up to 200 LPI.

is that these systems are geared to the transmission of fingerprints, which, as already pointed out, requires the higher resolution to preserve essential details.

Fax systems designed for the transmission of full-size newspaper page proofs to satellite printing plants, and which must be capable of faithfully reproducing halftone photos as well as text, employ scan resolutions as high as 1000 LPI. The choice is influenced primarily by the need to minimize the occurrence of *moiré,* or interference, patterns caused by the interaction of scan lines with the dot arrays constituting the halftone pictures.

Experience has shown that, to avoid moiré patterns completely in the fax reproduction of halftones, the scan resolution must be at least 10 times the halftone screen density in lines (or dots) per inch. Thus, if 65-line halftones are the finest used, a scan resolution of 650 LPI will suffice for moiré-free reproduction. Likewise, use of 100-line halftones will require 1000 LPI.

However, experience has also shown that, despite some occurrence of

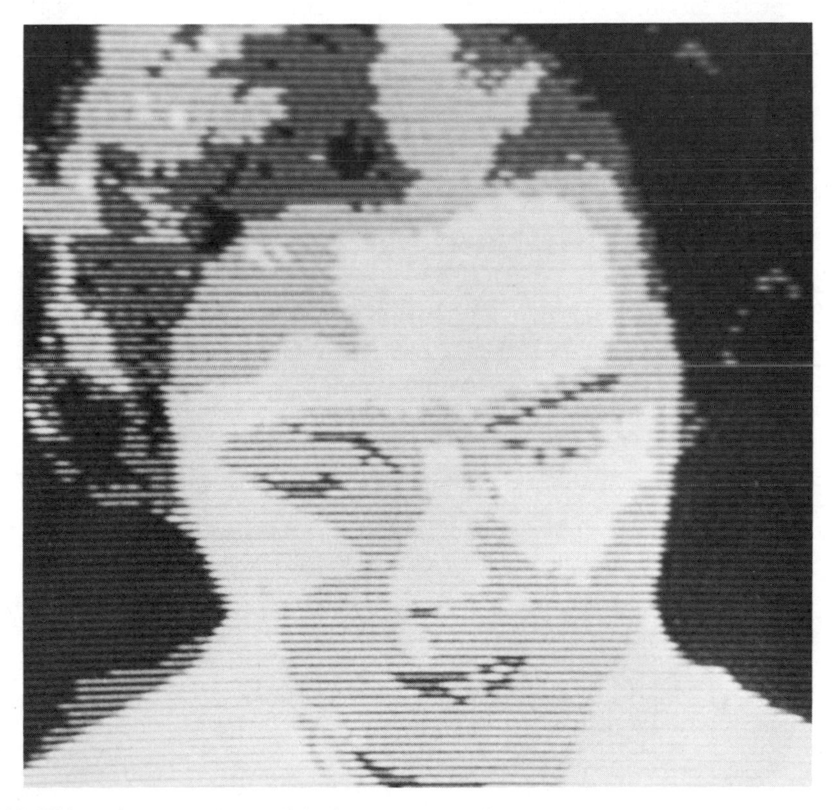

Fig. 5.19. Video picture produced digitally with only eight brightness levels, resulting in a "paint-by-numbers" effect. (Copyright 1970, Bell Telephone Laboratories, Inc. Reprinted by permission of the Editor, Bell Laboratories *Record.*)

moiré patterns, a scan resolution of only seven times the halftone screen density will afford acceptable reproduction. By this criterion, the scan resolutions for 65- and 100-line halftones can be reduced to about 450 and 700 LPI respectively. These page-proof fax systems are offered commercially with resolutions as low as 300 LPI, which, while offering no guarantee against the appearance of interference patterns in halftones, at least makes it possible for the system to operate at a reasonable speed over a comparatively inexpensive transmission facility: approximately six minutes per 16 × 24-inch page via a 48-kHz group circuit. (The higher resolution systems, to be competitive in terms of speed, require transmission facilities in the megahertz range.)

One final word on quality considerations affecting the fax transmission of photos and other halftone material: if a multilevel *digital* (PCM) system is being considered, experience has shown that a minimum of from 14 to 20 gray levels (including black and white) is required for reasonably "smooth" reproduction of tonal gradations. A larger number is, of course, preferable. Since each level may require as much as a 7-bit code for transmission, bandwidth requirements can be quite high. Figure 5.19 illustrates the effect when only eight levels are quantized.

BIBLIOGRAPHY

Arps, R. B., et al., "Character Legibility Versus Resolution in Image Processing of Printed Matter," *IEEE Transactions on Man-Machine Systems,* Vol. MMS-10, No. 3, Sept. 1969, pp. 66–71.

Baldwin, M. W., Jr., "The Subjective Sharpness of Simulated Television Images," *Bell System Technical Journal,* Vol. 19, Oct. 1940, pp. 563–586.

Becker, F. K., et. al., "An Experimental Visual Communication System," *Bell System Technical Journal,* Vol. 38, January 1959, pp. 141–176.

Costigan, D. M., "Resolution Considerations Affecting the Electrical Transmission of Technical Documents by Scanning Processes," *NMA Journal,* Spring 1968, pp. 99–115.

Erdmann, R. L., and A. S. Neal, "Character Legibility of Digital Facsimile Resolution," *Human Factors,* Oct. 1968, pp. 465–473.

Fink, D. G., *Television Engineering,* New York, McGraw-Hill, 1952.

———, *Television Standards and Practice,* New York, McGraw-Hill, 1943.

Goldsmith, A. N., et al., *Radio Facsimile,* Vol. I, New York, RCA Institutes Technical Press, 1938.

Hemingway, J. C., and R. A. Erickson, "Relative Effects of Raster Scan Lines and Image Subtense on Symbol Legibility on Television," *Human Factors,* Nov. 1969, pp. 331–338.

Hills, L., and T. J. Sullivan, *Facsimile,* New York, McGraw-Hill, 1949.

Jones, C. R., *Facsimile,* New York, Murray Hill Books, 1949.

Kell, R. D., et al., "A Determination of Optimum Number of Lines in a Television System," *RCA Review,* Vol. 5, July 1940, pp. 8–30.

———, "An Experimental Television System," *Proceedings of the IRE,* Vol. 22, Nov. 1934, p. 1247.

Luxenberg, H. R., and R. L. Kuehn, *Display Systems Engineering,* New York, McGraw-Hill, 1968.

Mayers, M. A., and R. D. Chipp, *Closed-Circuit Television System Planning,* New York, J. F. Rider, 1957.

Mertz, P., and F. Gray, "A Theory of Scanning and Its Relation to the Characteristics of the Transmitted Signal in Telephotography and Television," *Bell System Technical Journal,* Vol. 13, July 1934, pp. 464–515.

Morehouse, H. G., "Telefacsimile Services Between Libraries With the Xerox Magnavox Telecopier," Dec. 20, 1966; and "Equipment for Facsimile Transmission Between Libraries: a Description and Comparative Evaluation of Three Systems," Dec. 29, 1967 (studies prepared for Council on Library Resources, Inc., published by University of Nevada Library, Reno).

Nelson, C. E., *Microfilm Technology,* New York, McGraw-Hill, 1965.

Poole, H. H., *Fundamentals of Display Systems,* Washington, D.C., Sparton Books, 1966.

Shurtleff, D. A., "Studies in Television Legibility—A Review of the Literature," *Information Display,* Jan./Feb. 1967, pp. 40–45.

Thomas, A. G., and J. F. Verruso, "Fingerprint Identification and Facsimile Communications," *Technique* (Muirhead & Co., Ltd.), April 1967, pp. 11–16.

Wortman, L. A., *Closed-Circuit Television Handbook,* New York, Bobbs-Merrill, 1964.

6 *Economics*

CONSIDERING the combined effects of the accelerating pace of technological advances, the various new forces that are at work in the communications services market,[1] and the changing economic picture in general, it is virtually impossible to set down specific guidelines on facsimile economics that are likely to remain valid for any length of time. About the best this chapter can do is outline the basic elements and general philosophies governing fax system costs *at the time of writing.* Specific current cost data will be included only for the purpose of illustrating comparative weights of the various cost elements and the comparative costs of different basic system configurations.

In addition, certain current trends will be analyzed and projected in an effort to determine what their impact might be on facsimile's economic future.

Throughout the chapter, unless otherwise noted, references to "current" or "present" conditions, or to typical or specific costs, are to be interpreted as pertaining to the first quarter of the year 1971.

COST FACTORS

The various factors influencing fax economics can be grouped into three basic categories:

1. Terminal costs (the actual fax gear and accessories);
2. Material costs (recording paper, chemicals, etc.);
3. Transmission costs (common carrier charges).

There are also certain labor costs associated with the operation of fax systems, such as those of routine maintenance (e.g., reloading of recording

[1] Easing of interconnection restrictions, emergence of new sources of competition, changes in public attitude toward utilities, etc.

paper) and the placing of calls. But these probably amount to no more than the cost of filling and addressing envelopes, were the same documents to be sent by mail, and can therefore be generally disregarded. One labor cost that does warrant consideration is that of the manual processing of photographic recordings. However, since this will vary with locale, no attempt will be made here to set down any universal guidelines on this particular cost element.

1. TERMINAL COSTS

Fax gear—transmitters, receivers, and transceivers—can usually be either leased (rented) or purchased. At present, the typical message fax transceiver sells for a little over $2000 and leases for about $70 a month, while separate transmitters and receivers sell for an average of $2800 per unit and lease for about $100 a month per unit.

Systems capable of higher speeds and/or better resolution, or designed for special applications, may range from a few dollars to several thousand dollars higher in price than conventional message fax gear. Stewart-Warner's 900 line-per-minute *Datafax* system, for example, sells for about $6000 per send/receive pair (one transmitter, one receiver), and a basic Datalog (Litcom) *Pressfax* system, capable of up to 1000 LPI resolution and 2000 LPM, bears a price tag of about $60,000.

The question of whether to lease or purchase is largely one of preference on the part of the individual customer. There are pros and cons for each. It is true, for example, that for only two and a half years of rental payments a system could be purchased outright, but there is also the matter of maintenance costs to consider. Where complex and highly specialized electronic or electromechanical apparatus is concerned, servicing coverage can be a primary inducement for leasing.[2]

Another factor to be considered is the fast pace of technological change. Electronic equipment in particular is vulnerable to rapid obsolescence. There is always the chance, therefore, that a purchased fax system will become antiquated before its cost has even been amortized.

Beyond these practical considerations, the decision to lease or buy may be dictated simply by accounting practices, which will vary from one company to another.

The choice between a transceiver and separate transmit and receive units is often solely an economic one, but it may also be governed by system objectives. There are systems, for example, in which communication is strictly one way and which therefore require only a transmitter at one end and a receiver at the other (or multiple units, as the system requires). There are also systems in which transmission and reception must take place simultaneously. In such systems it would seem only logical to use separate trans-

[2]The words lease and leasing are used here in the sense of a customer leasing from a supplier.

mitters and receivers exclusively. However, from a purely economic standpoint, it might be expedient to use transceivers, even though half their capability may be wasted.

Another advantage of separate transmit and receive units is the facility they provide for monitoring and troubleshooting. The cause of poor copy at one end of a system can usually be isolated through a back-to-back hookup of the transmitter and receiver within a terminal.

Terminal costs may also include certain accessories. For example, where opposite ends of a system cross a commercial power grid boundary, a precision power supply may be required at each terminal (see Chapter 3). These can range in price from $500 to $3000 per unit, or $10 to $50 a month, leased. Other typical accessories are phone couplers ($100–$200, or $5 a month), and automatic document loaders ($400–$1000, or about $20 a month).

Although technically belonging under the heading of transmission interfaces, commercial data compression modems may be regarded as terminal accessories. Units capable of compression ratios of 2:1 and 3:1 can be purchased for $1400 to about $7000 per terminal, or leased for $50 to $175 a month per terminal.

2. MATERIAL COSTS

In many if not most fax systems in operation today, the only significant continuing material cost is that of recording paper. The major exception is photographic recording, widely used in the distribution of news photographs and the recording of cloud cover pictures from earth-orbiting weather satellites. The process consumes photographic processing chemicals, sensitized paper, and special recording lamps, and in many cases also requires the skill of a darkroom technician, which imposes yet another operational cost. The economics of the process have been improved somewhat with the introduction of photographic recorders featuring automatic processing within the machine.

There are also some electrostatic fax systems in operation which require processing chemicals and usually specially coated recording paper as well.

Of the various direct recording processes, electrolytic is generally the least expensive, the cost range being from two to three cents a copy. Impact (transfer) and electrostatic rank next with a range of from two-and-a-half to four cents a copy, and thermal recordings cost from four to six cents apiece.

An additional continuing material cost, peculiar to the electrolytic process, is that of printing electrodes. These tend to erode rather rapidly as a result of electrochemical action and must therefore be periodically replaced. Printing blades can cost from a few cents to several dollars apiece, and the useful life of each can range from two hundred to a few thousand copies, depending on the specific process involved. But, at worst, the consuming of printer electrodes adds only a fraction of a cent to the cost of an electrolytic copy and can therefore be generally disregarded.

The photographic process is by far the most expensive. In material costs alone, a photo recording can easily run to seven times the median per-copy cost for direct recording processes. Twenty-five to 30 cents a copy is typical.

3. TRANSMISSION COSTS

The first consideration in determining transmission cost is required bandwidth. Because of modulation, the maximum frequency to be transmitted is invariably higher than the maximum baseband frequency, the amount of margin depending primarily on the transmission scheme employed—i.e., FM, AM Single Sideband (SSB), AM Vestigial Sideband (VSB), or AM Double Sideband (DSB). The various aspects of bandwidth determination have been covered in preceding chapters.

Having determined bandwidth requirements, the next question is whether transmission is to be via the dial network or a leased private line. Without resorting to data compression techniques, the dial network (or public switched network) is limited to an effective maximum frequency of about 2400 Hz. For broader bandwidths or for better assurance of consistent transmission quality, a leased private line is usually required.

As pointed out in Chapter 4, there are two switched broadband services available from common carriers. One is Western Union's Broadband Exchange, or switched Schedule II (4-kHz) service, which the company plans eventually to expand to cover 48 kHz as well; and the other is the Bell System's switched 50-kilobit service, which is currently offered on a trial basis within and between four cities.

Another consideration in choosing between a switched network (voice or broadband) and a private line is whether transmission is to be in two directions simultaneously—*full-duplex*—or one direction at a time—*half-duplex.* Switched networks are customarily confined to the latter mode, whereas private lines can usually be leased in either mode, the rate for full-duplex being about 10 percent higher than that for half-duplex.

If the dial network is to serve as the transmission facility, an interface is required between the terminal gear and the line at each end of the system. The intent is to ensure that certain characteristics of the signal—particularly its level—are controlled so as not to cause interference with other circuits or damage to the network's switching gear and amplifiers. The customer has a choice of essentially four types of interface:

1. indirect, via an acoustic and/or inductive coupler;
2. a data compression modem;
3. a Data Access Arrangement (DAA);
4. the Bell System 602 Data Set, or equivalent.

The first two are supplied by the customer, and the latter two by the common carrier. Item 2 may additionally require one of the other three interfaces.

Even before interconnection restrictions were liberalized a few years ago, use of indirect phone couplers was generally permitted inasmuch as they did not require direct hookup to the line. Some modern fax terminal units feature built-in couplers of this type. Where they are not integrated with the terminal gear, the couplers can usually be purchased as an option, costing from $100 to over $500 apiece, or leased for about 5 dollars a month per unit.

Use of data compression modems or *any* noncommon-carrier interfaces requiring direct hookup to the line, is, at present, permitted only in conjunction with a common-carrier-supplied Data Access Arrangement (item 4). The latter is available for 2 to 6 dollars a month, depending on locale and on the automatic features provided. As previously noted, current prices for typical compression units available for fax use start at about $1400 per terminal (for 2:1 compression), and tend to rise rather precipitously as the compression ratio increases. Typical lease rates are $50 a month per terminal for 2:1, and $160 a month for 3:1 to 4:1.

Physically, the basic DAA consists of a small coupler unit, usually wall-mounted somewhere near the associated telephone set. Both the phone and the fax terminal gear—or noncommon-carrier modem—are wired to the coupler, and the phone is equipped with a selecting key to permit switching between the voice and data access modes.

The 602 Data Set is described in Chapter 4. All that need be said about it here is that it is basically an FM modem, aimed at tailoring the fax signal to a format compatible with the dial network. The lease rate varies with locale, but $35 a month is about average.

Where leased lines are concerned, the customer can connect fax terminal gear and noncommon-carrier interfaces directly to the line, provided the output of these devices is not such that it could pose a safety hazard to maintenance personnel or cause interference in adjacent lines. (Criteria are stated in FCC Tariff 260.) However, as of this writing, it is expected that the common carriers soon will be providing protective couplers for the purpose.

A big factor in transmission cost, regardless of whether the medium is a switched network or a leased line, is mileage. Some sample costs, illustrating the relationship of dollars to distance, are shown in Table 6.A.

Note that the costs shown reflect the *base rates* only. To complete the picture on transmission costs, there are various miscellaneous charges that must also be taken into account. The required ones are as follows:

1. 10% Federal excise tax on all toll calls;
2. Service Terminal charge of $12.50 per month at each termination of a Schedule 4 circuit (3002 channel) (In effect, this is the lease

Table 6.A—*Sample costs, illustrating relationship of dollars to distance, for a selection of transmission facilities and services. The costs shown reflect base rates only.*

	Mileage (Air Miles Between Terminals)							
Transmission Service	*10*	*25*	*50*	*100*	*250*	*500*	*1000*	*2000*
Three-minute toll call on dial net*	$0.17	0.35	0.40	0.60	0.85	1.00	1.15	1.35
Sched. 4 voice-grade leased line (per month)	$30	75	127.50	232.50	457.50	720	1095	1845
Sched. II "Telephoto" condit. leased line (per month)	$40	100	170	310	610	960	1460	2460
Three-minute toll call on W. U. broadband exchange service	$0.60	0.60	0.60	0.60	0.90	1.05	1.65	1.95
48-kHz leased "group" (per month)	$150	375	750	1500	3750	6375	10,125	17,625

* Based on interstate day rates.

charge for the "loop" between a customer's premises and the nearest telephone exchange);
3. Service Terminal charge of $60 per month at each termination of a Schedule II circuit (4002 channel);
4. Service charge of $30 per month at each termination of W.U. Broadband Exchange Service;
5. Station charge of $425 per month (including required modem) at each termination of a full 48-kHz "group" (8000 type channel).

In addition, it is usually recommended that Schedule 4 and Schedule II circuits be specially conditioned to ensure undistorted transmission of picture signals over long distances. At present, the applicable half-duplex conditioning charges are $19 a month per circuit ("C2" conditioning) for Schedule 4, and $30 a month per circuit for Schedule II.

One final note on transmission costs: in spite of the many separate cost elements that can enter the picture, there are conditions under which there is—ostensibly, at least—*no* transmission cost whatever. They are basically four:

1. when the transmitter is indirectly coupled to an existing phone, and transmission is confined *within* an exchange area;
2. when the transmitter is indirectly coupled to an existing phone, and transmission is via an existing tie line;
3. when the transmitter is indirectly coupled to an existing phone,

and transmission is via the Bell System's Wide Area Telephone Service (WATS),[3]

4. when the transmitter and receiver(s) are interconnected via a customer-owned, solid-wire circuit.

Obviously, there are hidden costs in all of these. For example, if an existing phone installation is used for fax transmission to the extent that an additional circuit becomes necessary to maintain the normal volume of voice communication, the cost of the first circuit—or at least part of it—must be regarded as a fax transmission cost. Thus the first three of the above conditions assume a modest fax transmission volume.

TRADE-OFFS

There is not much that can be said about the trade-offs between economy, speed, and quality that has not already been said elsewhere in this book. But perhaps this is a good point at which to review the basic considerations, with the emphasis on economics.

The general rules governing trade-offs can be summarized as follows:

To Increase . . .	*Must Sacrifice . . .*
quality[4]	speed and/or economy
speed	quality and/or economy
economy	quality and/or speed

Expanding on these slightly, it is well to note that increasing either speed or output resolution, without sacrificing one for the other, will invariably require an increase in channel bandwidth. Where the existing channel is already being utilized to capacity, this will mean either going to a broader bandwidth facility or adopting bandwidth compression techniques to enable transmission of the higher baseband frequencies over the existing facility.

Supplementing these technical fundamentals are certain economic "facts of life" that one should be aware of in planning or modifying a system:

1. In general, the two elements impacting most heavily on the cost of a fax system are *transmission distance* and *required bandwidth;*
2. In terms of common carrier standard offerings, the steps in which bandwidth may be increased are limited and, in most cases, represent sharp increases in rates;
3. The volume of copies transmitted in a system already operating at capacity may be increased in one of three ways:

[3] A long-distance service which permits the customer unlimited calls (or 10 hours of calls, depending on the arrangement chosen) within a given zone, at a fixed monthly rate.

[4] "Quality" pertains primarily to output resolution. (See Chapter 5.)

(a) by adding additional circuits,
(b) by adopting data compression techniques to permit increased transmission speed,
(c) by converting to a broader bandwidth facility to permit increased transmission speed.

The most economical choice of the three will vary with volume, distance, and comparative costs of terminal gear.

About all that can be said further about trade-offs from the economic standpoint is that, having tied down speed and quality requirements—and volume requirements to the extent that they can be predicted—the most economical system configuration can be determined only by an analysis of various combinations of the cost elements previously discussed. The charts at the end of the next section will be helpful in assessing comparative transmission costs.

COST PER COPY

A good basis for comparing the economics of different fax systems is to compute the cost per copy for each—assuming, of course, that the same size of original material applies in each case. In the case of a leased private line, the cost per copy will be the prorated share per copy of the total cost of the system within a given period. And, where the system utilizes an existing switched network, the cost per copy will be the prorated share of the fixed cost, *plus* the toll charge per "call."

Where terminal equipment is purchased outright, a determination must be made as to the period of time over which the total purchase is to be amortized. The purchase price is thus convertible to a continuing annual or monthly cost.

To avoid inconsistent results in the distribution of total costs, certain guidelines as to accounting procedure must be established before any computations are made. A question that must be resolved at the outset is whether all terminals of a system are to be financed from the same budget, or each from separate budgets.

Where the first condition—a single budget—applies, there is no problem. However, where each terminal is financed from a separate budget, which might well be the case where transmission is via a switched network, the total cost of a terminal must be confined to the incurred *by that terminal only*. Computation is complicated in the latter case by the question of how the send and receive costs per copy are to be distributed. The easy way would be to simply ignore receive costs, since they are relatively negligible anyway. But a better way is to base cost per copy on copies sent only, while including receive (material) costs as an *average* under continuing monthly costs.

Let us examine two hypothetical systems, one a single transceiver interfaced with the dial network by a phone coupler, and the other consisting of two transceivers interconnected by a leased, voice-grade, private line. Actually, System #1 is merely a terminal, which qualifies as a system only when it has linked up with a compatible terminal elsewhere on the dial network. For the sake of this example, we shall assume that it customarily communicates with a terminal (or terminals) located 50 air miles away.

System #1, Terminal A

1. Terminal costs: leased transceiver, \$115/mo. (incl. phone coupler)
2. Material costs: recording paper, \$0.03/ copy
3. Average daily copies sent: 10
4. Average daily copies received: 10
5. Transmission—
   Facility: public telephone (dial) network
   Distance: 50 miles
   Duration, per copy: 4.5 minutes
   Cost per call: \$0.78 (interstate day rate as of Feb. 1, 1971, incl. 10% Federal excise tax)

Cost per copy (assuming 22 working days per month)

$$\frac{\$115 + (22 \times 10 \times \$0.03)}{22 \times 10} + \$0.78 = \$1.33$$

System #2	*Terminal A*	*Terminal B*
1. Terminal costs (leased transceivers)	\$100/mo.	\$100/mo.
2. Material costs (recording paper)	\$0.03/copy	\$0.03/copy
3. Average daily copies sent	10	20
4. Average daily copies received	20	10

5. Transmission—
   Facility: schedule 4B leased line (type 4002, conditioned)
   Distance: 50 miles
   Duration, per copy: (does not apply—except to the extent that the volume of copies is sufficient to require additional circuits)
   Base rate (for 50 miles): \$127.50/mo.
   C_2 conditioning: \$19/mo.
   Service terminals: \$12.50/mo., each terminal

Fixed monthly system cost:

$$(\$100 + \$12.50) \times 2 = \$225;$$
$$\$225 + \$127.50 + \$19 + (22 \times 30 \times \$0.03) = \$391.30$$

(Note: 22 is the working days per month; 30 is the total copies per month, both terminals.)

Terminal A share of fixed monthly cost:

$$\tfrac{10}{30} \times \$391.30 = \$130.43$$

Terminal B share of fixed monthly cost:

$$\tfrac{20}{30} \times \$391.30 = \$260.87$$

$$\text{Cost per copy, Terminal A} = \frac{\$130.43}{22 \times 10} = \$0.59$$

$$\text{Cost per copy, Terminal B} = \frac{\$260.87}{22 \times 20} = \$0.59$$

Obviously, the cost per copy for System #2 can more readily be computed for the system as a whole, as follows:

$$\frac{\$225 + \$127.50 + \$19}{22 \times 30} + \$0.03 = \$0.59$$

The trap to avoid is that of splitting the total operating cost evenly between Terminals A and B, and then computing the cost per copy for each terminal on that basis, thus:

$$\$391.30 \div 2 = \$195.65$$

$$\text{Cost per copy, Terminal A} = \frac{\$195.65}{22 \times 10} = \$0.89$$

$$\text{Cost per copy, Terminal B} = \frac{\$195.65}{22 \times 20} = \$0.44$$

Average cost per copy (unweighted) = $0.67

Unfortunately, the trap may be difficult to avoid where separate terminals connected to the dial network are lumped together and treated as one system—and especially when each sends or receives a different volume of copies within a given period. Assume, for example, that System #1 is completed by a Terminal B, which sends 20—rather than ten—copies daily to Terminal A. It would seem a simple enough matter to split the total cost of the system equally between Terminals A and B, in which case cost per copy might compute as follows:

Total system cost per month:

$$(2 \times \$115) + 22 \times 30\ (\$0.78 + \$0.03) = \$764.60$$

Each terminal's share:

$$\$764.60 \div 2 = \$382.30$$

$$\text{Cost per copy, Terminal A} = \frac{\$382.30}{22 \times 10} = \$1.74$$

$$\text{Cost per copy, Terminal B} = \frac{\$382.30}{22 \times 20} = \$0.87$$

Average cost per copy (unweighted) = $1.30

Alternatively, the cost per copy can be computed on the basis of each terminal's own cost:

$$\text{Cost per copy, Terminal A} = \frac{\$115 + (22 \times 20 \times \$0.03)}{22 \times 10} + \$0.78 = \$1.36$$

$$\text{Cost per copy, Terminal B} = \frac{\$115 + (22 \times 10 \times \$0.03)}{22 \times 20} + \$0.78 = \$1.06$$

Average cost per copy (unweighted) = $1.21

But, as in the case of the leased line system, the *true* cost per copy is obtained by allocating a prorated share of the total system cost to each terminal—or simply by computing for the system as a whole, as follows:

$$\frac{2 \times \$115}{22 \times 30} + \$0.78 + \$0.03 = \$1.16$$

For comparison purposes, it would be well to select one method of computing cost per copy and apply it consistently, even if it does not produce true costs. In comparing a leased line system with a "detached" dial network terminal, for example, it is almost imperative that we treat each terminal as a separate entity, with the exception that, for the leased line system, we would have to allocate a share of the fixed transmission costs to each terminal under study.

So much for the mechanics of cost computation. With a little additional manipulation of the foregoing data, we can also illustrate a couple of basic economic distinctions between switched network and leased line systems in general (Table 6.B).

First, by reducing the average daily copy volume from 15 to 4 per terminal for our two systems (System #1, as modified, and System #2), we can demonstrate the relationship of copy volume to economic advantage. Both systems will naturally be less economical at the lower volume because of the larger share of the fixed terminal cost apportioned to each copy. But, whereas System #2 showed a decided economic advantage at the higher volume, System #1 will now be the more economical by a slight margin: $2.12 per copy versus $2.14 for System #2.

The general rule that reveals itself here is that in a switched system, transmission *duration* is generally the controlling economic factor, whereas in a leased line system, the greater the number of "calls," the more economical the system becomes. This assumes, of course, that the "calls" made in the switched system are toll calls, so that the longer their duration or the

Table 6.B—*Comparative costs per copy for a basic dial network fax system (System #1) and a basic leased line system (System #2) at two mileages and various copy volumes.*

	Avg. 4/Day per Term.	*Avg. 5/Day per Term.*	*Avg. 6/Day per Term.*	*Avg. 8/Day per Term.*	*Avg. 15/Day per Term.*
1. 50 Miles					
System #1	$2.12	1.85	1.68	1.46	1.16
System #2	$2.14	1.72	1.44	1.08	0.59
Percent difference	2	7.5	17	35	96
2. 100 Miles					
System #1	$2.37	2.10	1.93	1.71	1.41
System #2	$2.74	2.20	1.83	1.38	0.75
Percent difference	16	5	5	24	88

(Note: Percent difference figures are the approximate percentage by which the higher cost exceeds the lower for each daily volume.)

greater their number within a given period, the higher the total cost. In a nontoll situation, such as the use of existing tie lines, the rule would obviously not apply.

Now the influence of distance can be demonstrated by increasing the terminal separation from 50 to 100 miles for both systems. The effect on rates is an increase from $0.78 to $1.03 per five-minute call in the switched system, and from $127.50 to $232.50 per month for the leased line. At these higher rates, we find that the copies a day per terminal can be increased to *six* before System #2 again becomes more economical than System #1. What is indicated here is that increasing distance tends to have a somewhat greater economic impact on leased line systems than on switched systems.

The charts that follow will provide a more graphic picture of the ways in which copy volume, distance, bandwidth, and "call" duration interact to affect cost per copy in fax systems. Note that only transmission costs are reflected—including service terminals and conditioning where applicable—but *not* modems or other interfaces except in the case of the 48-kHz "Group" service, which normally includes required modems under a "station charge." Addition of terminal and material costs will affect the shape and crossover points of the various curves to a certain extent, but the basic interrelationships will remain essentially the same.

One additional note regarding the 48-kHz curves: it is usually possible, with Group service, to split the group into bands and share it with one or more other systems. On the charts, however, it is assumed that each of the leased services is devoted exclusively to a single fax system, even though the full bandwidth may not be utilized in all cases.

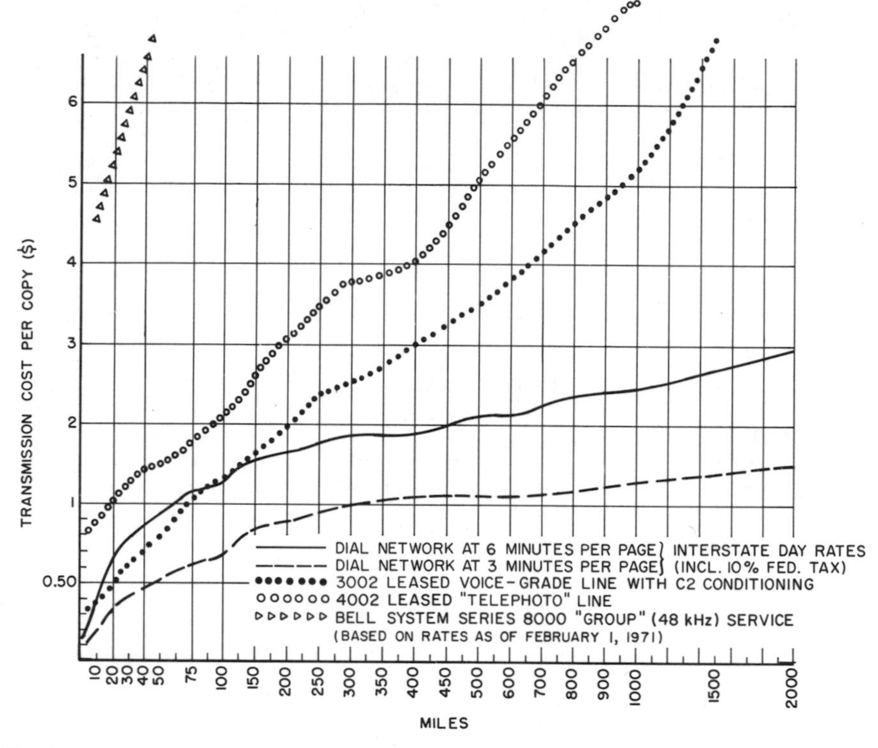

Fig. 6.1. Facsimile transmission costs at average volume of 10 copies a day.

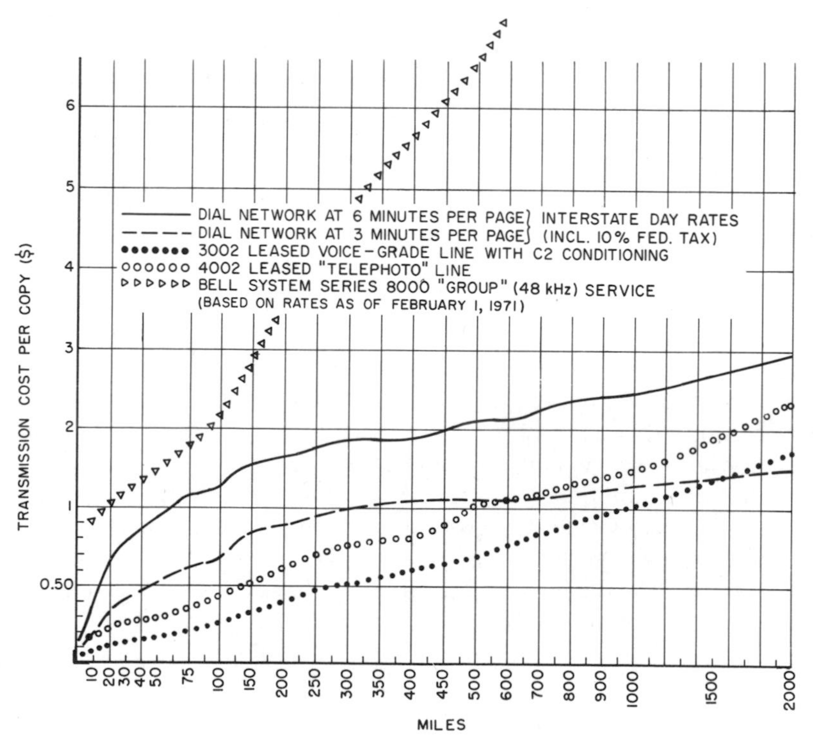

Fig. 6.2. Facsimile transmission costs at average volume of 50 copies a day.

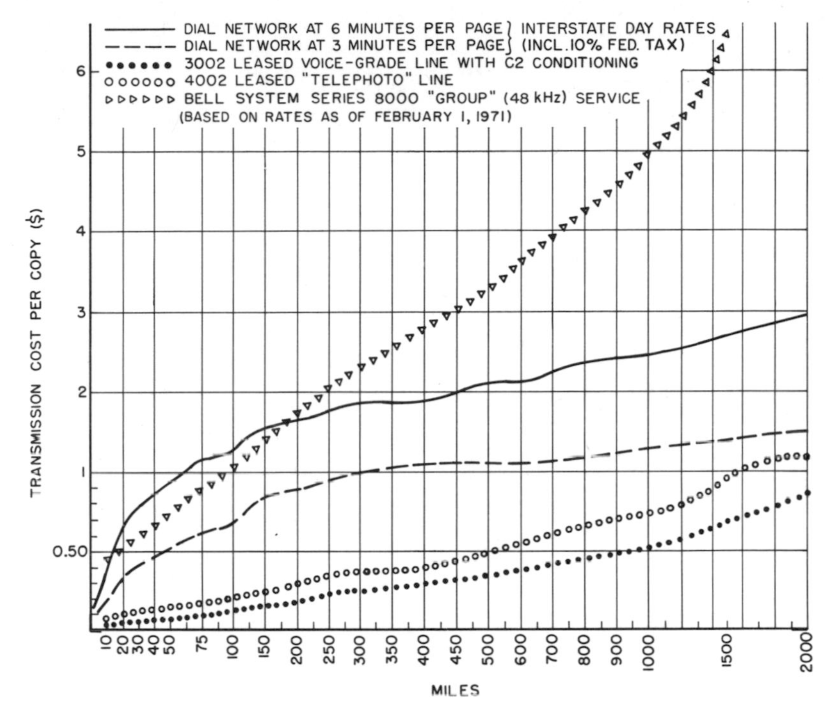

Fig. 6.3. Facsimile transmission costs at average volume of 100 copies a day.

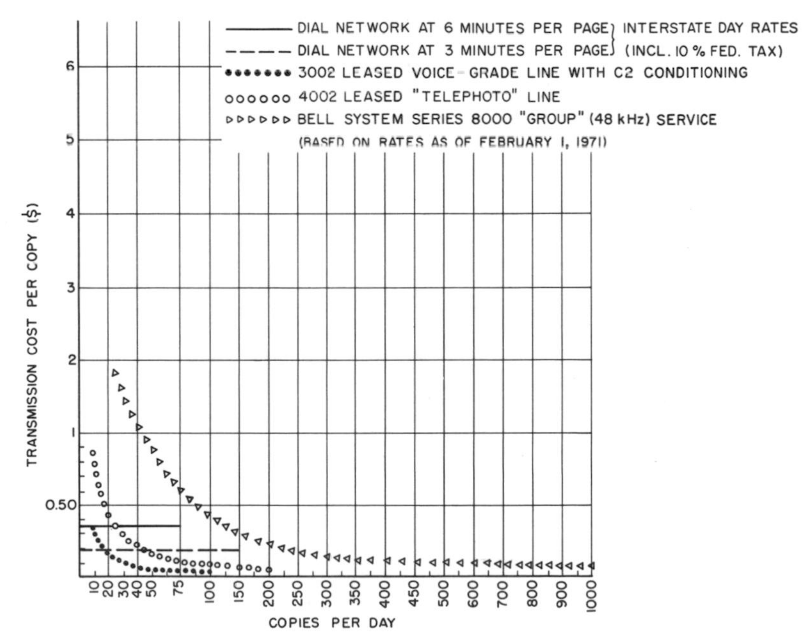

Fig. 6.4. Facsimile transmission costs for a 10-mile link.

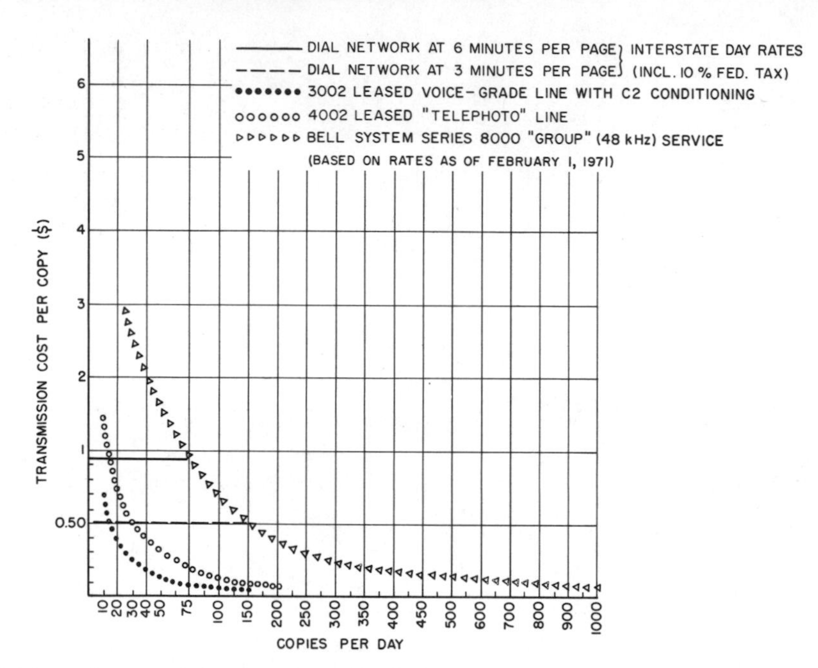

Fig. 6.5. Facsimile transmission costs for a 50-mile link.

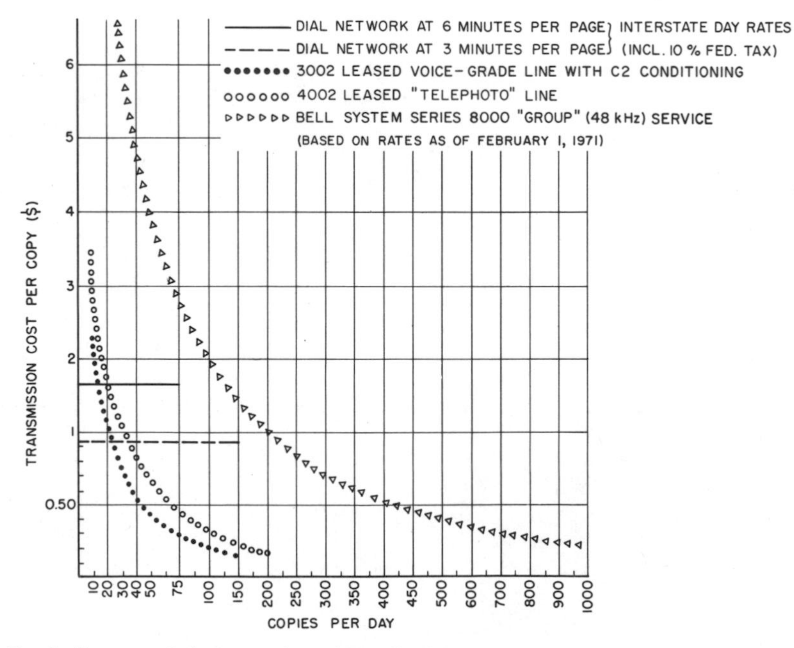

Fig. 6.6. Facsimile transmission costs for a 250-mile link.

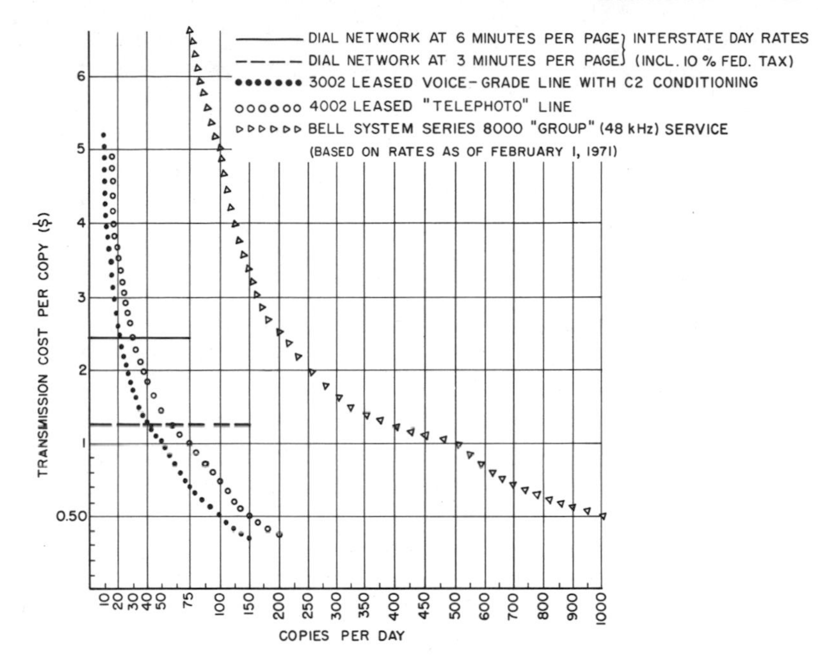

Fig. 6.7. Facsimile transmission costs for a 1000-mile link.

ECONOMIC TRENDS

In the light of current trends, what is the outlook for facsimile's economic future? And what are some of the trends that particularly bear watching?

From the author's point of view there is every indication that the economics of facsimile will continue to improve. Looking at the terminal gear market alone, we see new names constantly cropping up to enlarge the circle of competitors, each new entry contributing some attractive new improvement at a bargain price. The stimulation of competition among suppliers is naturally beneficial to fax customers by itself, but it is additionally encouraging that the improvements offered by each new competitor have not been superficial. The emphasis appears generally to be in the right place—on improved operating efficiency.

Early in 1969 there was only one device commercially available to permit the compression of fax signals for transmission economy. The number has since grown to four, and there are at least as many more being readied for introduction in the immediate future.

It seems only natural that, in order to compete, each new supplier to introduce a compression (or redundancy reduction) system will have to prove his product's superiority primarily in terms of *bit rate per dollar.* In other words, whether the customer wants increased speed for its own sake or more economical utilization of transmission facilities, the supplier who gets the order in most cases will be the one who can meet either requirement most economically.

But, re-formatting the fax signal at the terminals is just one way of effecting operational economics, and it has its limitations. A more important potential source of transmission economy is the transmission area itself.

One of the significant changes which the communications industry has undergone in the past few years has already resulted in certain economies. It is the easing of restrictions on the connection—or *interconnection*—of noncommon-carrier devices to the common carriers' lines. The immediate result has been the introduction of the Data Access Arrangement. For many fax users DAA has amounted to a substantial reduction in the monthly charges for terminal-to-line interfacing. Another result, one with more important long-range implications, is the competition that has been stimulated among commercial suppliers of modems aimed at increasing transmission efficiency.

Another change, perhaps better characterized as a "latent force," has been the increasing potential for competition in this lucrative market. The development of new radio communication technologies—notably microwave and spaceborne satellites—during the past two decades has opened the door to the formation of private communication networks with the potential for competing with the established common carriers. Here, as in the terminal gear market, increasing competition could have a favorable long-range effect on transmission costs.

Meanwhile, there is the prospect of certain self-imposed changes in common carrier services that should result in significant transmission economies for customers. One is the possible full-time adoption of a 1-minute charge basis for toll calls in place of the present minimum initial 3-minute unit. The 1-minute unit already applies after 11 p.m. on interstate calls, and, as this is being written, is being applied full-time on a trial basis in four cities—Louisville, Kentucky; Charlotte, North Carolina; Tulsa, Oklahoma; and Pine Bluff, Arkansas. Its official adoption on a national basis during normal business hours could have important implications on the economies obtainable with data compression terminal gear.

But the big change forthcoming from the common carriers is the conversion from analog to digital facilities. The digital mode of transmission not only lends itself to the use of compression techniques, but also affords the common carrier certain internal economies, which can, in turn, be passed on to the customer (see Chapters 2 and 4). It has already been determined that, ultimately, common carrier facilities will be almost exclusively digital.

There has also been much talk of fitting fax signals into unused time slots or channel space in existing communication systems, permitting operators of big networks—notably commercial broadcasters—to make more efficient use of their facilities. One proposed scheme, for example, would "piggyback" fax signals on top of TV sync pulses. At least two such systems have already been developed and tested, and have demonstrated their ability to send a document in as little as two and a half seconds.

These, then, are the most obvious current trends that are likely to influence facsimile's economic future. Others will be emerging that could either enhance or blemish this optimistic picture. Things can change fast, particularly in a field as competitive as facsimile has recently become.

7 *Standards*

WHENEVER a large number of like components are linked together to form a system, there has to be some degree of standardization to ensure compatibility. Home TV receivers, for example, may differ widely in size, layout of controls, circuit design, and overall appearance, but all are designed to accept the same input signal and to produce from it a 525-line, sound-accompanied picture, renewed at the rate of 30 frames a second. Needless to say, commercial TV could not exist as a system without this common bond.

Closed-circuit television, on the other hand, need not be similarly constrained. In fact, there can be any number of different CCTV standards, just so long as a given set of standards is applied within a system.

The same goes for facsimile. Each apparatus manufacturer is free to design to his own standards, but if he wants to sell to the U.S. National Weather Service or to a big news agency, or to any individual customer who has to rely on common carrier facilities for transmission, he has to observe the standards that have been set for the particular realm within which the apparatus is to function.

Within weather forecasting and telephotography networks, for example, even though various types and makes of equipment may be used, there are specific standards—strictly enforced—governing input, output, and transmission parameters. The systems could not otherwise function.

But within other realms, such as the exchanging of documents and sketches, on a private basis ("message fax") there is somewhat less incentive for strict adherence to a given set of standards. Recommended standards that do exist may be applied or ignored, as the manufacturer or customer sees fit.

There are, in fact, established standards affecting practically every facet of facsimile communication. There are separate domestic and international standards, and, domestically, there are both industry and government standards. There are standards outlining engineering specifics such as the duration of a phasing pulse, and there are standards establishing rates and classes of service. Common carriers offer certain standard transmission services that many facsimile systems have come to rely upon and that exert a strong influence on the design of most manufactured fax gear.

This chapter will concern itself chiefly with technical standards relating to engineering and transmission, and only with those that are established and have discernible influence. Standard common carrier transmission services are covered in Chapter 4, and quality standards (such as they are), in Chapter 5. Standards regarding rates for "message" services or for the leasing of transmission facilities will not be discussed since they are periodically subject to change.

Note: Throughout the remainder of this chapter, wherever the contents of specific standards or recommendations are reproduced, the wording and the arrangement may not be precisely that found in the actual documents. In the interests of consistency and of minimizing detail—and, in some cases, for clarification—the author has taken the liberty to abridge and rearrange as required. Words and data in brackets [ ] are, in all cases, the author's.

DOMESTIC STANDARDS

EIA STANDARDS

The Electronic Industries Association (EIA) is a trade association composed mainly of component and equipment manufacturers. Oldtimers may remember it as the RMA (Radio Manufacturers' Association), its name from 1924 to 1950, or as RETMA (Radio-Electronics-Television Manufacturers' Association), which it had become briefly before assuming its present identity in 1957.[1] Its Engineering Department publishes a number of recommended standards, among which are three that deal specifically with facsimile.

RS-328, titled *Message Facsimile Equipment for Operation on Switched Voice Facilities Using Data Communication Terminal Equipment,* is the standard that gives official recognition to the popular $^{96}/_{180}$ combination for scan resolution and rate. It also standardizes on eight additional design parameters, as follows:

Index of cooperation—805 to 889 (829 recommended)
Total line length—8.5 to 9.2 inches
Available line length—8.0 inches minimum (8.5 inches recommended)
Phasing time—15 seconds
Signal sense—Maximum on black

[1] It was also known briefly as RTMA, Radio-Television Manufacturers' Association.

Synchronization—(a) 60 (±0.5) Hz transmitted signal
(b) frequency standard accurate to one part in 100,000

Paper speed—1⅞ inches/minute (nominal)

Phasing pulse—25 (±3) mseconds; black signal interrupted by white pulse once per scan line, black-to-white transition occurring at right-hand edge of 8½-inch-wide sheet

The standard defines message facsimile as relating to ". . . equipments used for transmission of documents such as letters, charts, forms, drawings, graphs, etc., which do not require accurate reproduction of the grey tones between black and white."

In its present form, RS-328 dates back to 1966. However, as this is being written, plans for its reissue are being considered by the EIA's Facsimile Standards Committee, TR-29. In addition, a recently formed Subcommittee on Facsimile Equipment, TR 29.2, has announced plans to create a totally new, comprehensive fax equipment standard that will attempt to consolidate the objectives of existing industrial, military, and international standards.

RS-357, *Interface Between Facsimile Terminal Equipment and Voice Frequency Data Communication Terminal Equipment,* is the second EIA fax standard. As the title implies, it concerns itself with the various electrical and signaling considerations associated with the interconnection of an analog fax system with voice band transmission facilities by way of a so-called "data set," or modem. It specifies signal voltage levels, impedances, and general wiring arrangements. It is applicable to both switched network and private line systems.

Finally, there is RS-373, *Unattended Operation of Facsimile Equipment,* which specifies the minimum requirements for unattended operation of fax terminal equipment conforming to the preceding two standards. The requirements concern the sequence and duration of control signals necessary to permit one terminal to "call" another, send or receive a "message" (a document or whatever), and terminate the call—in that sequence.

The standard provides for two modes of unattended operation. One has the transmitter initiating the call, while the other provides for preloading of a transmitter and putting it on standby to commence transmission upon automatic receipt of a call initiated by the receive station.

Among other published EIA standards in the RS- series are a few that relate indirectly to facsimile. RS-269, for example, concerns signaling speeds for data transmission. RS-203, -210 and others concern microwave systems, and RS-247 has to do with analog-to-digital conversion. All of these standards are available, for a small fee, from the Engineering Department, Electronic Industries Association, 2001 Eye Street N.W., Washington, D.C. 20006.

IEEE STANDARDS

The Institute of Electrical and Electronics Engineers (IEEE) has worked closely with the EIA in the establishment of facsimile standards. Like the EIA, it publishes two standards dealing specifically with fax: No. 167, *Test Procedures for Facsimile* (formerly IRE Standard 43-9 S1), and No. 168, *Definitions of Terms for Facsimile* (formerly IRE Standard 56-9 S1).

In addition, there is the IEEE Facsimile Test Chart, the 1970 update of which (illustrated in Chapter 5) is the result of recommendations by a joint EIA/National Microfilm Association Committee: TR 29.1. The charts are produced by the Eastman-Kodak Company and are obtainable from the EIA.

IEEE No. 168 is the basis for terms used in EIA Standard RS-328, and the test procedures outlined in No. 167 are, in turn, arranged to reflect the various parameters standardized in RS-328.

No. 167 is divided into three sections, each of which is quite comprehensive. The three are *Equipment Specifications, Distortions from Facsimile Equipment,* and *Distortions from Transmission Medium.* Among the specific items for which tests are outlined within the sections are scanning line length, stroke speed, spot dimensions, halftone characteristics, effective band, index of cooperation distortion, skew, jitter, delay distortion, echo, noise (random, impulse, and single frequency), and Kendall effect.

No. 168 includes all of these parameters among the total of 117 terms it defines. However, in its present form (January 1971), it is by no means complete. Having been compiled in the mid-1950s, it is lacking in several terms that one would expect an up-to-date facsimile glossary to include—terms like data set, digital transmission, Kell factor, modem, quantizing (amplitude and time), and run-length encoding. Some if not all of these are expected to be included in future updates of this standard.

Two other IEEE standards that may be of interest inasmuch as they relate indirectly to fax transmission are No. 170, *Definitions of Terms for Modulation Systems* (Formerly IRE Standard 53-11 S1), and No. 269, *Method for Measuring Transmission Performance of Telephone Sets.* Copies of all of these standards are purchasable from the Institute of Electrical and Electronics Engineers, 345 East 47th Street, New York, N.Y. 10017.

FCC

In its ten published volumes of *Rules and Regulations* the Federal Communications Commission covers everything from the acquisition of telephone companies to technical requirements for wire and radio transmission systems. Included are certain standards regarding facsimile systems, specifically, those involving radio broadcasting. These are to be found in Volume III, principally in Part 73, which concerns radio broadcast services in general and deals with facsimile in connection with both commercial and noncommercial (educational) FM broadcasting. Following are the basic fax engineering standards, as excerpted from subsection 73.318:[2]

(a) Rectilinear scanning, left to right and top to bottom;
(b) Index of Cooperation [IEEE]: 984;
(c) Scan rate: 360 LPM;
(d) Line-use ratio: $\frac{7}{8}$ or 315 degrees of full scanning cycle [total scan line interval];
(e) Remaining $\frac{1}{8}$ or 45 degrees divided into three equal parts: white-black-white [usable as a phasing pulse];
(f) Max. 12 seconds interval between pages of subject copy;
(g) Amplitude or frequency (shift) modulation of subcarrier;
(h) Approximately linear relationship of signal variations to optical density variations on subject copy;
(i) Negative modulation: maximum on black [This applies to both amplitude for subcarrier AM and instantaneous frequency for FM.];
(j) Subcarrier noise level maintained at least 30 dB below max. modulation level at radio transmitter input;
(k) Subcarrier frequency range: 22 to 28 kHz. (AM: 25 kHz, ±3 kHz for sidebands; FM: 22 kHz white, 28 kHz black.); . . .

These standards apply to both commercial and noncommercial FM broadcasting, and are essentially the same ones that were authorized in 1948 for limited fax broadcasting via commercial FM outlets. The 1948 standards (contained in Order No. FCC 48-1655, authorized June 9, 1948) were applied briefly by a small number of pioneering manufacturers and broadcasters who were soon forced, by lack of public acceptance, to abandon the whole fax-in-the-home idea.

The chief distinction between the present and earlier standards is that the latter included specific scan resolution and line length recommendations—105 LPI and 9.37 inches, respectively—which were consistent with the 984 Index of Cooperation.

Part 74 of the *Rules and Regulations* also deals directly with facsimile—specifically, experimental facsimile broadcast stations (Subpart B)—though not in the same technical detail as Part 73. It is concerned chiefly with administrative procedures, licensing policies, and operating requirements. About the only specific technical standard contained is the requirement that transmitter operating power not exceed 5 percent above the maximum power authorized.

Fax is also dealt with briefly, and in a general manner, in various other parts of the *Rules and Regulations*—notably 21 (Domestic Public Radio Services) and 23 (International Fixed Public Radio Communication Services). Subsection 21.703 of Part 21 provides for fax transmission on a "shared" basis (with mobile radio repeater stations, for example) in point-

[2]Abridged and restated as required. See Note preceding this section.

to-point microwave service, and Subsection 23.21 of Part 23 provides for press and meteorological fax applications.

Fax transmission is frequently referred to in FCC documents as A4 or F4 emission, the number 4 being the code for facsimile in the international classification of radio transmission modes, the A signifying AM, and the F, FM.

MILITARY

The principal standards for U.S. military fax systems are contained in two Defense Department documents—MIL-STD-188C, "Military Communication System Technical Standards," and Defense Communication Agency (DCA) Manual 330-175-1, "Defense Communication System Engineering-Installation Standards Manual." The basic distinction between the two is that MIL-STD-188C is pertinent only to tactical communications, whereas the DCA document stresses global or long-haul systems. Moreover, the DCA manual tends to go into greater technical detail in describing the terminal equipment to be used in a system.

MIL-STD-188C is prepared by the U.S. Army Electronics Command at Fort Monmouth, New Jersey, and approved by the Department of Defense (DOD) as "mandatory" for use by all its Departments and Agencies. (In the development of new equipment, adherence to the standards is mandatory only to the extent that it does not inhibit advances in communications technology.) It contains basic technical specifications for all types of electronic communication systems and facilities. Those for fax systems are covered in Subsection 6.3, which is quite comprehensive in itself, even though it represents only a small segment of the entire document.

Two basic types of fax system are covered: meteorological and general purpose ("message") fax. As will be seen further on, except for relative flexibility of certain parameters, the DOD specifications are generally compatible with the international standards recommendations of the World Meteorological Organization and International Telecommunications Union. Moreover, those for general purpose systems are substantially in agreement with EIA Standard RS-328.

Following is a condensation of Subsection 6.3 of MIL-STD-188C:

6.3.1 Meteorological Equipment—

Copy Size, drum scanner: 18⅝″ (473 mm) × 12″ (305 mm)
Copy Size, flat-bed scanner: 18⅝″ (473 mm) × at least 2″
Scan Line Length (total): 18.85″ (478.8 mm)
Scan Direction: "normal" (corresponding to left-hand helix) [L–R]
Dead Sector: 0.5″ [approx. 2.5% of total scan]
Scan Speeds: 60, 90, 120 LPM, selectable by manual control
Line Advance: $\frac{1}{96}$ inch (0.25 mm) [96 LPI]
Index of Cooperation [CCITT]: 576 [IEEE: 1809]
Signal Output Impedance: 600 Ω

Carrier: sinusoidal, 2400 Hz, accurate to 3 parts in 10^6
Signal Contrast [and Signal Sense]: 20 dB, + 2 dB; max. on black (desirable to have black *or* white transmission provided for on a selectable basis)
Signal Halftone Characteristic (voltage output/copy density relationship): nominally linear
Synchronization: scan rate controlled by self-contained frequency standard maintained at assigned frequency (300 Hz, or integral multiple thereof) within 3 parts in 10^6
Control Functions: (1) "start" command, (2) phasing signal, (3) "stop" command. (Phasing signal is black, interrupted by white of min. 2.5%, max. 5% of total scan length, and coincident with leading edge of dead sector.)
Recorded Copy Size, drum recorder: 18⅝″ × 12″ (or integral multiples thereof)
Recorded Copy Size, flat-bed recorder: 18⅝″, 400-ft. roll
Receiver Input Impedance: 600 Ω

6.3.2 "Small Format" [8½″ copy width] Meteorological Receiver—
Recorder Type: continuous
Resolution Capability: 200 LPI
Recording Medium: stable, indefinite storage life, nonfading on exposure to light
Recorded Copy Size: 8½″, 400-ft. roll
Scan Line Length (total): 8.64″ (220 mm)
Scan Direction: "normal" [L–R]
Scan Speeds: 60, 90, 120, or 180 LPM, selectable by manual control
Line Advance: $1/_{209.5}$ or $1/_{96}$ inch, selectable by manual control [209.5 and 96 LPI, respectively]
Index of Cooperation: 576 and 264 [CCITT] [IEEE: 1809 and 829, respectively] (264 will serve for charts transmitted at an index of 288. Dimensional distortion will be negligible.)
Receiver Input Impedance: 600 Ω
Synchronization: [same as 6.3.1.]

6.3.3 General Purpose (Black/White) Facsimile Equipment—
Copy Size: max. 8½″ × any length
Scan Line Length (total): 8.64″
Scan Direction: "normal" [L–R]
Dead Sector: 2% of total scan line duration; black signal
Scan Speeds: 90 or 180 LPM
Line Advance: $1/_{96}$ inch (0.26 mm) [96 LPI]
Resolution Within Total Scan Line: min. 800 elements
Index of Cooperation: 264 [CCITT] [IEEE: 829]
Signal Output Impedance: 600 Ω
Signal Types:
(1) AM— 2400-Hz carrier, linear voltage output/copy density relationship
(2) FM— frequency variable from 1500 Hz for white to 2300 Hz for black

(3) Digital (4-level)— 11 for white; 10 for light gray; 01 for dark gray; 00 for black. (1 = +6 volts; 0 = −6 volts)
[Digital Standard Interface (low-level), specified elsewhere in the document, operates with 4-kHz analog channels.]

Synchronization: scan rate controlled by self-contained frequency standard maintained at assigned frequency within 3 parts in 10^6 (For digital operation, system should be capable of synchronization by external "clock" as well as by self-contained frequency standard.)

Recorder Type: continuous

Recording Medium: preferably plain paper

Recorded Copy Size: 8½″, min. 150-ft. roll

In DCA Manual 330-175-1, fax standards are covered in subsection 3.4.2, which, like its MIL-STD counterpart, is several pages in length. The subsection begins with the observation that fax systems separate into two broad categories: real-time, and storage and release (store-and-forward).[3] But the distinction is not further explored. The basic subdivision of the standard is between signal characteristics and equipment performance, with meteorological, telephotographic, and general purpose systems being lumped together for the most part.

Following is a condensation of subsection 3.4.2:

3.4.2.2 Signal Characteristics—

Synchronization: self-contained frequency standards in transmitter and receiver—multiple or submultiple of 300 Hz, accurate to 1 part in 160,000 [approx. 6 parts in 10^6]—capable of independent or master-slave operation, the transmitter serving as master in the latter mode

Modulation:

Baseband—0–11 v.d.c. (max.); max. frequency: 60% of carrier.

AM—Vestigial sideband (VSB)

FM—Indirect (phase/time) or direct (frequency deviation); max. modulation index of 2 in either case

3.4.2.3 Equipment Performance—

Aspect Ratio (copy width to copy length): 3 : 4
[No specific copy sizes are given.]

Scanner [Transducer] Characteristics: approx. panchromatic spectral response; linear relationship of illumination variations to d.c. output, max. output on white. [max. white or max. black outputs selectable by manual control after amplification.]

Scanning Ordinates [Scan Direction]: Left to right across narrow dimension of copy; top to bottom ["normal"]

Scan Speeds: 60 and 90 LPM, and multiples and submultiples thereof.

Skew: max. 0.125″ in 12″ of copy

[3] "Store-and-forward" denotes magnetic recording of the received fax signals for read-out into a fax recorder at a later time. It is sometimes utilized in relay stations, for example, when transmission in one of the links of the system has been temporarily curtailed.

Resolution: 96 LPI, vertically & horizontally
Index of Cooperation:
  Weather systems [CCITT]: 576 [IEEE: 1809]
  Other [CCITT]: 264 [IEEE: 829]
Signal Output Impedance: 600 Ω
Modulator: Two separate inputs, one for picture baseband and one for transmitted synch.; input sensitivity as follows—
  AM—2.5 v.d.c. = 100% modulation
  FM—5.0 v.d.c. = 75% of max. permissible deviation
Carrier:
  AF Subcarrier—1800 or 2400 Hz
  HF Carrier—70 MHz
Signal Sense:
  General (incl. meteorol.)—max. on black
  Photo Copy (telephoto.)—max. on white
Reproduction Capability (Tonal Response) of Recorder:
  General (incl. meteorol.)—density variations of 0% (white), 18%, 75%, and 90% (black)
  Photo Copy (Telephoto.)—linear progression of densities, 5% to 90% (black to white)
  [Note: In this standard, recording densities relate to signal sense. Thus the reversal of density-tonal relationships between general and photo copy systems.]
Sync Signal: pulses of min. 5 picture elements duration [min. 5/96 inch] between scans. [Freq. of sync pulse as specified under 3.4.2.2.]
Receiver Input Impedance: 600 Ω

WEATHER

The effective dissemination of weather data obviously requires a measure of standardization. Accordingly, the U.S. National Weather Service has standardized on the following basic criteria for its voice-grade fax nets:

Scan Speed: 120 LPM
Resolution: 96 LPI
Index of Cooperation (CCITT): 576
Signal Characteristics: double sideband AM, 2400-Hz carrier
Start Signal: 300 Hz
Phasing Signal: black signal interrupted by 12.5 msec white pulse twice per second prior to start of recording
Stop Signal: 450 Hz

In certain instances, speeds and resolutions higher or lower than those specified may be used. For example, where bandwidth compression is employed, the standard 120 LPM speed may be doubled to 240.

As for the reception of cloud cover pictures from weather satellites, there are no published standards per se, but there are certain basic NASA specifications on satellite signals to which receiving equipment must obviously conform. These are as follows:

Scan Speed: 240 and 48 LPM (the lower speed for nighttime infrared readouts)
Resolution: 100 LPI
Index of Cooperation (CCITT): 267
Input Signal Characteristics: 2400 Hz, AM
Start Signal: 300 Hz

Standards for the international dissemination of weather data are controlled by the World Meteorological Organization, with headquarters in Geneva. These will be examined in the next section.

INTERNATIONAL STANDARDS

Standards regarding international facsimile and telephotography (phototelegraphy) transmissions are chiefly the province of the International Telecommunications Union (ITU),[4] which was formed in 1932, in Madrid, as the successor to the International Telegraph Union. The latter had its origins in Paris and Berne in the late 1860s. The present ITU became a special agency of the United Nations in November 1947.

The specific organizations responsible for fax standards within the ITU are the Comité Consultatif International Télégraphique et Téléphonique (CCITT) and the Comité Consultatif International des Radio Communications (CCIR). Both are permanent organs of the parent organization, and both are, in turn, divided into study groups, one of which (for each organization) is concerned specifically with facsimile and telephotography.[5]

Another special UN agency of more recent origin, the World Meteorological Organization (WMO), is involved with international facsimile standards relating specifically to the exchange of weather data (maps, etc.). It has collaborated closely with the ITU in establishing standards for the format and speed of transmissions of weather charts by facsimile and for the remote control signals employed in transmission and reception. The WMO was created directly as a UN agency in 1950.

The CCIR's standard for the transmission of weather maps by radio is confined to recommendations regarding frequency shift limitations and transmission polarity in FM systems, in which respects it matches the WMO standards.

Standards activities of all three organizations—CCITT, CCIR, and WMO—consist of the studying of questions and the making of recommendations, as opposed to the establishment and enforcement of rigid

[4] Official name: Union Internationale des Télécommunications (UIT).
[5] CCITT Study Group XIV, and CCIR Study Group 3.

standards (as is usually the case within national governments). The recommendations do, however, have the semblance of rules or directives, which, while not mandatory, are generally observed by all concerned.

CCITT

The fax standards of the Comité Consultatif International Télégraphique et Téléphonique are contained in the Committee's "White Book," Volume VII, as "Series T" Recommendations: *Apparatus and Transmission for Facsimile Telegraphy.* Most of the basic technical standards are contained in Recommendations T.1, T.2, and T.16, which are outlined below. Unless otherwise noted, the Recommendations reflect revisions made at the Fourth Plenary Assembly in Mar del Plata, Argentina, in 1968.

Recommendation T.1, "Standardization of Phototelegraph Apparatus"

1. Scanning track: message area should be scanned in "negative" direction at transmitter; "negative" direction at receiver for "positive" reception; "positive" direction at receiver for "negative" reception. ["Negative" *direction* means right to left; "negative" *reception* means production of a photographic negative at the recorder, in which case a mirror image of the subject copy is desired for subsequent contact printing.]
2. Index of Cooperation:
   Normal—352; preferred alternative—264 [These are equivalent to IEEE-defined indices of 1105 and 829, respectively. The International Index of Cooperation = drum diameter × scan lines per unit length of copy, or $1/_{\pi}$ times the IEEE-defined index (total scan length in inches × LPI).]

3.1. Dimensions affecting drum scanning:
   Drum diameters—66, 70, and 88 mm [approx. 2.6, 2.75, and 3.5 inches, respectively]
   Width of "dead sector"—max. 15 mm [approx. 0.6 inch]

3.2. Dimensions affecting flat-bed scanning:
   Total scan line lengths—207, 220, and 276 mm [approx. 8.15, 8.66, and 11 inches, respectively]
   Width of "dead sector"—max. 15 mm [approx. 0.6 inch]

3.3. Scanning densities:
   3, 3.77, 4, 5, and 5.3 lines/mm [approx. 76, 96, 100, 127, and 135 LPI, respectively]

5.1. Drum rotation speeds (normal):
   60 RPM [LPM] for Index of Cooperation 352
   90 RPM [LPM] for Index of Cooperation 264

7. Synchronization:
   (a) Standard frequency maintained within 5 parts in 10^6, or
   (b) a.c. sync tone of 1020 Hz transmitted to receiver [5 parts in 10^6 amounts to 0.5 parts in 100,000, as compared with 1 part in 100,000, as specified in EIA Standard RS-328.]

10.1. Modulation parameters—AM:
Level of output greatest for white and least for black (ratio of nominal white to nominal black: 30 db)
Carrier freq. for regular telephone lines: 1300 Hz
Carrier freq. for conditioned telephone lines: 1900 Hz

10.2. Modulation parameters—FM:
Mean [center] freq.—1900 Hz; white freq.—1500 Hz; black freq.—2300 Hz.

Recommendation T.2, "Standardization of Black-and-White Facsimile Apparatus"—

1. Scanning track: message area should be scanned in "positive" direction at transmitter *and* receiver
2. Index of Cooperation: nominal—264 [IEEE 829]
3. Dimensions:
   (a) normal drum diam.—68.5 mm [approx. 2.7 inches]
   (b) width of "dead sector"—15 mm [approx. 0.6 inch]
   (c) total scan length for flat-bed scanners—215 mm (incl. "dead sector") [approx. 8.5 inches]
   (d) width of paper in continuous recorders—210 mm [approx. 8.25 inches]
4. Scanning density: normally 3.85 lines/mm [approx. 98 LPI]
7. Definition: same horizontally and vertically
8. Scanning line frequency [scan rate]:
   120 and 180 LPM, held within 10 parts in 10^6 of the nominal figure
11. Modulation:
   (a) AM—signal level higher for black and lower for white.
   carrier freq. range: 1300—1900 Hz, depending on circuit characteristics
   (b) FM—
   mean freq. (fo) for switched ckts—1700 Hz.
   mean freq. (fo) for leased ckts—1300–1900 Hz, depending on circuit characteristics.
   freq. shift for black—fo − 400 Hz.
   freq. shift for white—fo + 400 Hz.

Recommendation T.16, "Facsimile Transmission of Meteorological Charts Over Radio Circuits" (CCIR, Oslo, 1966) [This is a combined CCIR and CCITT Recommendation]

1. Center frequency— 1900 Hz
   Freq. corresponding to black— 1500 Hz
   Freq. corresponding to white— 2300 Hz
2. Frequency characteristics for direct FM transmission:

2.1. HF (decametric) circuits
Center frequency (assigned freq.)— fo
Freq. corresponding to black— fo − 400 Hz
Freq. corresponding to white— fo + 400 Hz

2.2. LF (kilometric) circuits

Center frequency (assigned freq.)—	fo
Freq. corresponding to black—	fo − 150 Hz
Freq. corresponding to white—	fo + 150 Hz

Other recommendations in the T Series, none of which need be outlined here, are T.4, "Remote Control of Black-and-White Facsimile Apparatus"; T.10, "Black-and-White Transmissions on Telephone-Type Circuits Permanently Used for Facsimile Service (Leased Circuits)"; T.10 bis, "Black-and-White Facsimile Transmissions in the General Switched Telephone Network"; T.11, "Phototelegraph Transmissions on Telephone-Type Circuits" (Geneva, 1964); T.12, "Range of Phototelegraph Transmissions on a Telephone-Type Circuit" (Geneva, 1964); T.15, "Phototelegraph Transmission Over Combined Radio and Metallic Circuits." Some of these repeat the same basic parameters given in the three recommendations outlined above. Others consist of details that go somewhat beyond the scope of this book.

One remaining CCITT recommendation that bears mentioning is T.20, "Standardized Test Chart for Facsimile Transmissions." In it, the recommended international test chart is described and reproduced (at a slight reduction). The actual chart measures 110 × 250 mm (approx. 4.3 × 10 inches) and contains the following test patterns, symbols, etc.:

Two tone scales, each containing 15 density steps (ranging from black to white);
Three wedge-type resolution patterns: black and white, gray and white, gray and black;
Letters, digits, and punctuation marks in various styles;
Photograph (portrait of an Argentine boy in latest edition);
Miscellaneous patterns.

The second (latest) edition of the chart is shown in Fig. 7.1.

CCIR

In addition to the combined CCITT/CCIR Recommendation T.16, regarding meteorological chart transmissions, the Comité Consultatif International des Radio Communications has issued its own general standard, the latest version of which is Recommendation 344-2, "Standardization of Phototelegraph Systems for Use on Combined Radio and Metallic Circuits" (New Delhi, 1970).

At the outset, the standard lists its purposes, among which are (and these are paraphrased):

(a) to facilitate interworking of systems for long-distance telephotograph transmission via HF (decametric) radio circuits;

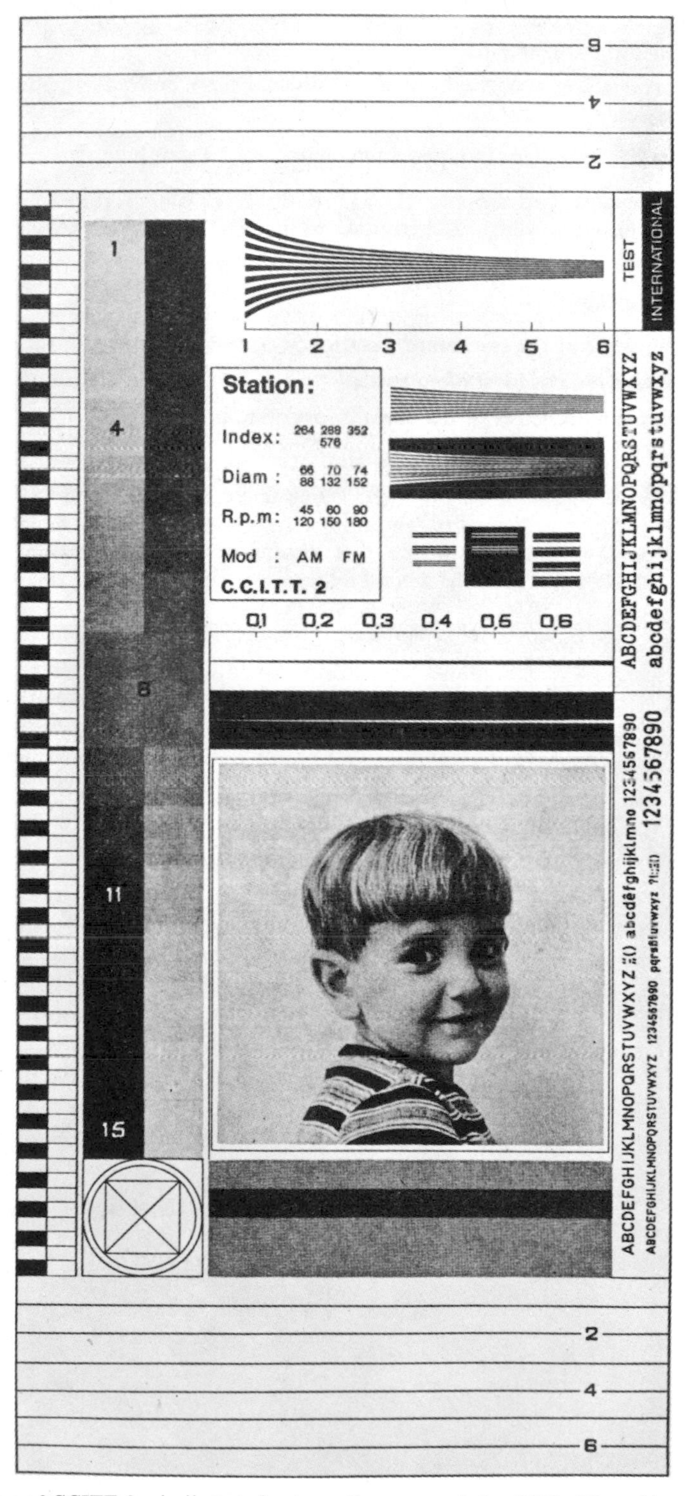

Fig. 7.1. Second edition of CCITT facsimile test chart, per Recommendation T.20. (*Note:* this reproduction of the chart cannot be used for actual tests.) (Courtesy CCITT.)

(b) to standardize certain characteristics of the systems so as to make them equally suitable for use with wire circuits;

(c) to better secure the advantages of FM techniques by standardizing certain modulation parameters.

The specific recommendations are as follows:

1. "that over the radio path, . . . the preferred method of transmission of halftone pictures is by subcarrier frequency-modulation, of a single-sideband or independent-sideband emission with reduced carrier. . . ."

   [The specific recommendations for subcarrier FM are the same as in CCITT Recommendation T.1, item 10.2; and those for direct FM are the same as those in T.16, item 2.1, but with the black and white frequencies reversed. In addition, 344-2 recommends that the higher frequency in each case also be used for phasing. It also specifies limits on frequency deviations within the various sections of a combined radio and wire circuit.]

2. "that, for the present, the following alternative characteristics should be used:

	a	*b*
index of cooperation	352	264
speed of rotation of drum in r.p.m.	60	90/45

   In due course, characteric b will become obsolete."

3. "that frequency-modulation or amplitude-modulation may be used in the metallic portions of the combined circuit. When conversion from amplitude-modulation to frequency-modulation (or vice versa) is required, the conversion should be such that the deviation of the frequency-modulated carrier varies linearly with the amplitude of the amplitude-modulated carrier. . . ."

WMO

The World Meteorological Organization's recommended standards for the collection and exchange of meteorological data by facsimile are contained in WMO Publication No. 9.TP.4, Volume C—Transmission (October 1966), excerpts from which follow:

3.1. Index of Cooperation:
576, for min. black or white picture elements of 0.4 mm, [about 1.5 mils]; and
288, for min. picture elements of 0.7 mm [about 3 mils] [These are equivalent to IEEE-defined indices of 1809 and 904, respectively.]

3.2. Drum speed:
60, 90, 120 revolutions [or strokes] per minute
Note: If speeds greater than 120 rpm are used, they should be multiples of 60 rpm.

3.3. Diameter of drum:
152 mm [approx. 6 inches]. In the case of flat-bed scanners this will be the length of the scanning line (including the dead sector) divided by π.

3.4. Scanning density:

$$\text{Scanning density} = \frac{\text{Index of cooperation}}{\text{Diameter of drum}}$$

It is approximately:
4 lines per mm [about 100 LPI] for index 576
2 lines per mm [about 50 LPI] for index 288.

3.5. Length of the drum:
at least 55 cm [about 22 inches].

3.6. Direction of scanning:
At the transmitter, left to right, commencing in the left hand corner at the top and finishing in the right hand corner at the bottom.

3.7. Dead sector:
4.5 percent ± 0.5 percent of length of scan line; signal transmitted during passage of "dead sector" should correspond to white, but a black pulse may be transmitted within, and not exceeding, one half the length of dead sector.

3.8. Synchronization:
Scanning speed should be maintained within 5 parts in 10^6 of its normal value.
[Same as CCITT *Recommendation T.1,* item 7(a).]

3.9. Remote control signals transmitted:
[Means for remotely controlling selection of Index of Cooperation, speed, starting of recorders, phasing, adjustment of recording levels, and stopping of recorders are specified.]

3.10. Modulation characteristics:
(a) AM— Max. carrier amplitude should correspond to signal black. Value of carrier freq.: about 1800 Hz.
(b) FM— Center freq.: about 1900 Hz; black freq.: 1500 Hz; white freq.: 2300 Hz.

3.11. Levels of signals for AM:
Receiving equipment should accept any level between +5 db and −20 db, zero reference level corresponding to one milliwatt dissipated in a resistance of 600 ohms.

3.12. Contrast ratio: between 12 and 25 db (same for picture and control signals in any one transmission.)

4.2. Frequency characteristics for direct FM—or Frequency Shift Keying (FSK):
[Same as CCITT *Recommendation T.16,* item 2.]

In addition to these recommendations, the WMO also has, in the making, a facsimile test chart designed specifically for meteorological applications. As this is being written, a limited printing of the chart is in process, but copies are not yet available for reproduction.

In calling the current WMO standards recommendations to the author's attention in June 1970, Dr. G. K. Weiss, Chief of the organization's Networks and Telecommunications Division, pointed out that studies had already been initiated regarding ways of speeding up the exchange of processed meteorological information by use of digital transmission techniques. It is therefore likely that, in the next few years, additional technical specifications will be adopted to permit transmission of weather maps at approximately double the present maximum speed.

STANDARDS CONVERSION

In spite of all the effort that has gone into the development of domestic and international standards, certain incompatibilities have persisted, in some cases necessitating the adoption of elaborate measures to accommodate them. A case in point is the transmission of Associated Press Wirephotos between Europe and the United States. For years these had to be received on a machine meeting the sender's standards, and the processed picture then retransmitted via the local system. Needless to say, the procedure was costly, time-consuming, and detrimental to output quality.

Only recently was this crude, two-step process replaced by something more sophisticated. But it took the brain power of a team of MIT scientists[6] and the development of a highly complex electronic converter to do it.

At the root of the problem is the fact that there are differences in drum speed, scanning density, and direction of scanning between the U.S. and European systems. In the specially developed standards converter, called the CIWP (Computer Interface Wirephoto), which was built by the Shintron Company of Cambridge, Massachusetts, and has been in operation in New York City since January 1968, these differences are resolved automatically by a combination of analog-to-digital conversion, buffering, and core storage. The electronics of the system consists of some 2000 integrated circuits. A block diagram is shown in Fig. 7.2.

Apart from its having simplified the interfacing of international and domestic systems, improving output quality in the process, CIWP has also

[6]Donald E. Troxel, William F. Schreiber, and Charles L. Seitz.

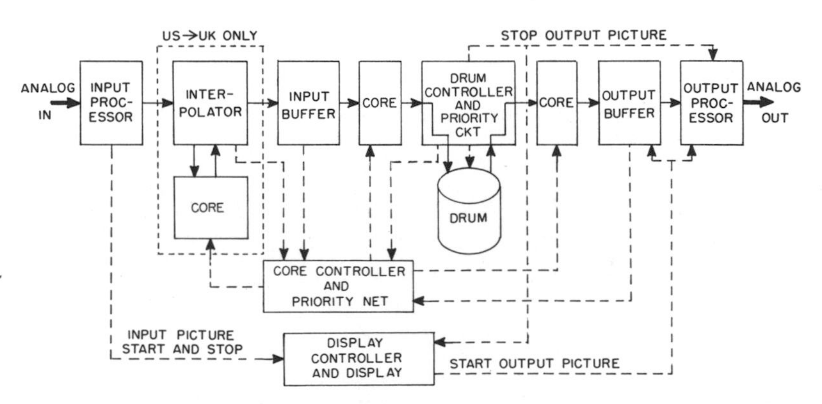

Fig. 7.2. This block diagram of the CIWP illustrates the complexities of standards conversion. Thin black lines denote digital signals, and dotted lines denote control signals. (Courtesy IEEE.)

Table 7.A—*Areas of general agreement in international standards.*

		General Purpose			Meteorological			Photo	
Item		*EIA*	*DOD**	*CCITT*	*DOD**	*CCITT*	*WMO (& CCIR)†*	*DOD**	*CCITT*
Copy width (drum circumf. or tot. scan length, inches)		8.5–9.2	8.5	8.5	18.6, 8.5	–	18.75	–	8.1, 8.5, 11
Scan direction		–	L–R	L–R	L–R	–	L–R	L–R	Neg. (R–L)
Signal sense		Max black	Max black	Max black	Max black	Max black	Max black	Max white	Max white
Index of cooperation	IEEE	829	829	829	1809/829		1809/904	829	1105/829
	CCITT	264	264	264	576/264	–	576/288	264	352/264
Line feed (LPI)		96	96	98	96/209	–	–	96	76, 96, 100, 127, 135
Scan rate (LPM)		180	90/180	120/180	60, 90, 120, 180	–	60, 90, 120	60, 90 (& mults.)	60/90
FM freq. swing (Hz)		–	1500–2300	1500–2300	–	1500–2300	1500–2300	–	1500–2300

* MIL-STD-188C and/or DCA 330-175-1.
† Where applicable.

greatly enhanced the practicality of exchanging *color* pictures internationally. Separate transmissions must still be made for each primary color, but now only once for each, rather than twice, as before. The separate recordings have to be superimposed to obtain a full-color reproduction, and in the old system of retransmission there was always the prospect of cumulative registration errors, which could considerably degrade reproduction quality.

When one considers the economic problems, alone, in trying to achieve complete international compatibility of the many independent facsimile systems operating around the globe, the progress that has been made to date is commendable. In the case of the news agencies (for example), bringing a domestic system into line with international standards could mean the scrapping and replacement of millions of dollars' worth of existing equipment—a price that no private business is going to pay willingly unless it is necessary for its survival.

But, in spite of the incompatibilities that give rise to such dilemmas, there is, in fact, substantial agreement on most of the fundamental design parameters affecting international compatibility of fax systems. A review of the various standards outlined in this chapter will bear this out. Table 7.A summarizes the areas of general agreement.

The evolution of international standards satisfactory to all concerned is a long and tedious process. As noted, appreciable progress has been made, but there are still a few gaps to be closed.

BIBLIOGRAPHY

Bell, E. J., and R. Everett, *Facsimile Transmission and Reception of Weather Charts by Radio* (booklet), Muirhead & Co., Ltd., 1965.

CCIR Recommendation 344-2, New Delhi, 1970 (Comité Consultatif International des Radio Communications, Geneva, Switzerland).

CCITT "White Book," Vol. VII, "Series T" Recommendations, Mar del Plata, 1968 (Comité Consultatif International Télégraphique et Téléphonique, Geneva, Switzerland).

DCA Manual 330-175-1 (Defense Communication Agency, Washington, D.C.).

EIA Standards RS-328, -357, and -373 (Electronic Industries Association, Washington, D.C.).

FCC *Rules and Regulations,* Vol. III (Federal Communications Commission, Washington, D.C.).

Feldman, S., "Facsimile is Coming of Age," *Electronic Industries,* May 1964, pp. 38–42.

IEEE Standards No. 167 and 168 (Institute of Electrical and Electronics Engineers, New York, N.Y.)

Jones, C. R., *Facsimile,* New York, Murray Hill Books, 1949 (Chapter XI, Facsimile Standards, pp. 164–183).

MIL-STD-188C (Department of Defense, Washington, D.C.).

Troxel, D. E., et al., "Wirephoto Standards Converter," *IEEE Transactions on Communication Technology,* Vol. COM-17, No. 5, Oct. 1969, pp. 544–533.

Vermillion, C. H., "Constructing Inexpensive Automatic Picture-Transmission Ground Stations" (NASA Report SP-5079, 1968, National Aeronautics and Space Administration, Washington, D.C.).

WMO Publication No. 9.TP.4, Vol. C, Transmission, Oct. 1966 (World Meteorological Organization, Geneva, Switzerland).

8 *Commercial Hardware and Systems*

UP to this point the book has covered all essential facets of the facsimile art. But so far there has been only passing mention of specific commercial apparatus that is available to implement various system objectives. The purpose of this chapter, therefore, is to provide the reader with descriptions of a representative sampling of commercially available fax systems or terminal gear.

The descriptions are concise, providing only the most essential data and, in most cases, including pictures of the apparatus described. They have been grouped into four system categories, as follows:

Section 1. "Message," or general purpose: low-speed to medium-speed
Section 2. General purpose: high-speed (and multispeed)
Section 3. Telephotographic (phototelegraphic or photofacsimile)
Section 4. Special purpose and miscellaneous:

Section 1 is confined to systems capable of speeds *up to three minutes* per $8\frac{1}{2} \times 11$-inch page via ordinary voice-grade transmission facilities, and Section 2 to systems capable of anything *faster than three minutes* per page, via either voice-grade *or* broadband facilities. Section 3 is self-explanatory, and Section 4 contains those systems that do not properly fit any of the other three categories.

There is considerable overlapping. The first two sections, for example, both deal exclusively with systems designed primarily for the interchange of conventional documents, business forms, sketches, etc.; and some of the multispeed systems in Section 2 rightfully belong in Section 1 as well. Similarly, the systems in the latter two sections may be either voice-grade or broadband; low- or high-speed. Further, both 3 and 4 contain systems that can serve general applications as well, and both contain photographic systems.

In compiling a representative sampling of commercial items, the most difficult task always is that of determining where to draw the line between inclusion and exclusion. One expedient loosely applied in this case was to include only the latest version of systems that have undergone an evolution of model changes over a period of time and the earlier versions of which have remained commercially available along with their successors. Other than that, the line was drawn pretty much at the author's discretion, and it is likely that some perfectly worthy equipment items have been excluded from each category. This is unavoidable, and the author trusts that manufacturers of items or systems not included will understand.

No distinction is made between domestic and foreign products, other than that the country of origin is noted for all items except those originating in the United States. The distinction has become increasingly vague in recent years for commercial products in general and is not particularly significant anyway. Information on domestic fax gear was generally easier to obtain than that on foreign products. As a result, the variety of makes available abroad may not be covered to the same extent.

One more point before proceeding with the specific data: suppliers can be expected to have mixed feelings about having their products anatomized side by side with those of their competitors, particularly with regard to prices. Those whose products appear to be relatively inexpensive for the particular category will have no objection, whereas those with products bearing higher price tags may feel disadvantaged.

The reader should bear in mind that prices are based in large part on features and capabilities, not all of which are listed on the data sheets. Each customer for a fax system has his own set of requirements (or should have). Some may be very basic, in which case price may be the chief determinant in the choice of one system over another, while other customers may be willing to pay extra for features that the less expensive systems do not provide.

In any event, the author wishes to emphasize, at this point, that the purpose of this chapter is merely to show a representative sampling of the variety of systems and equipment items commercially available at the time of writing, along with approximate costs. (Within a year of publication, this information may only have historical value.) Any apparently unfavorable comparison of one product with another in a given category is unintentional, and the reader is especially urged not to consider price alone in assessing the relative worth of the various systems described.

Section 1

"MESSAGE," OR GENERAL PURPOSE: LOW- TO MEDIUM-SPEED SYSTEMS

Item (and Manufacturer) *Page*

Copyphone 300 and 300D (Telautograph), 194
Datafax Series 3600 (Stewart-Warner), 195
Dex 180 (GSI), 196
"Electronic Mailbox" (Stewart-Warner), 197
400 Telecopier® (Xerox), 198
Hellfax HF 146 (Hell), 199
KD-111 Remotecopier® (Matsushita), 200
M4-2 and M4-3 (International Scanatron), 201
Magnafax® 860 (Magnavox), 202
Messagefax (Datalog), 203
Mufax "Courier" 240 and 300 (Muirhead), 204
Qix® 503 (Shintron), 205
Speed-O-Fax (ETS), 206
Telecopier® III (Xerox), 207
TF-4501/RS-451 (NEC), 208

Product Name (or Number)

COPYPHONE 300 and 300D

Manufacturer—Telautograph Corporation, Los Angeles, Calif.

General Description—General purpose fax system for operation over telephone circuits. Separate transmit and receive units. Sends letter-size document in approx. 3 minutes.

Max. Input Size—$8\frac{1}{2}$ inches × any length

Transmission

- Mode: analog (AM)
- Bandwidth: 3 kHz (nom.)
- Facility: voice-grade private line (300), or dial net. (300D)

Scan Resolution or Line Feed (Lines Per Inch)—83.3

Scan Rate (speed, in Lines Per Minute)—300

Scanner Type—flat-bed (slot-load); continuous feed

Recorder Type—flat-bed (roll-load); continuous feed

Recording Technique—electrolytic

Synchronization Method—automatic, via common power grid

Index of Cooperation—CCITT: 225 IEEE: 708

Dimensions

- Transmitter: $16\frac{1}{2}$"W × 19"D × 15"H
- Receiver: $16\frac{1}{2}$"W × $13\frac{1}{2}$"D × 15"H

Special Features

- Recorded copies automatically cut to size at recorder.
- Can operate completely automatically.

Approx. Prices, as of October, 1970

- Transmitter: $2700 (purchase); $105/mo. (lease)
- Receiver: $2700 (purchase); $105/mo. (lease)

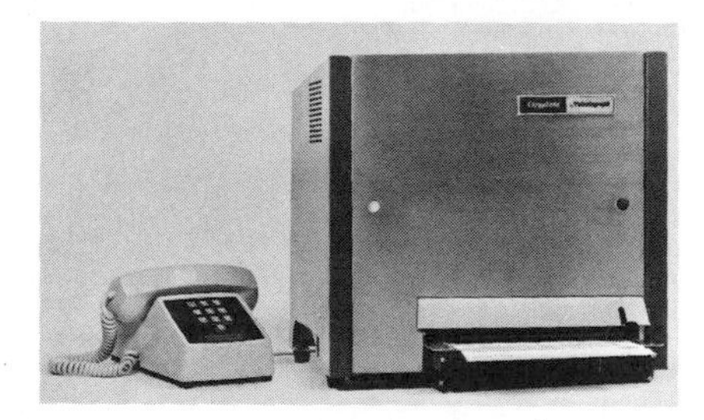

Fig. 8.1. Copyphone 300 Transmitter

Fig. 8.2. Copyphone 300 Receiver

Product Name (or Number)

DATAFAX SERIES 3600

Manufacturer—Stewart-Warner Corp., Chicago, Ill.
General Description—General purpose fax system for operation over voice-grade circuits. Separate transmit and receive units. Sends letter-size documents in approx. 3 minutes.
Max. Input Size—9 inches × any length
Transmission
  Mode: analog (AM)
  Bandwidth: 3 kHz (nom.)
  Facility: conditioned voice-grade circuit.
Scan Resolution or Line Feed (Lines Per Inch)—96
Scan Rate (speed, in Lines Per Minute)—360
Scanner Type—flat-bed (slot-load); continuous feed
Recorder Type—flat-bed (roll-load); continuous feed
Recording Technique—electrolytic
Synchronization Method—automatic, via common power grid
Index of Cooperation—CCITT: 279 IEEE: 876
Dimensions
  Transmitter: 16½"W × 19½"D × 15½"H
  Receiver: 15⅛"W × 19½"D × 15"H
Special Features
  Can operate completely automatically.
Approx. Prices, as of September 1970
  Transmitter: $2990 (purchase); $109/mo. (lease)
  Receiver: $2570 (purchase); $98/mo. (lease)

Product Name (or Number)

DEX (Decision EXpediter) 180

Manufacturer—Graphic Sciences, Inc., Danbury, Conn.
General Description—General purpose two-speed fax transceiver for operation over telephone circuits via built-in acoustic coupler. Sends letter-size documents in 3 or 6 minutes, depending on scan rate.
Max. Input Size—9 × 14 inches
Transmission
Mode: analog (AM)
Bandwidth: 3 kHz (nom.)
Facility: dial net., or any suitable voice-grade facility
Scan Resolution or Line Feed (Lines Per Inch)—88
Scan Rate (speed, in Lines Per Minute)—150/300
Scanner Type—cylinder (drum); auto-load, single sheets
Recorder Type—cylinder (drum); auto-load, single sheets
Recording Technique—electrothermal
Synchronization Method—built-in frequency standard
Index of Cooperation—CCITT: 266 IEEE: 835
Dimensions—22″W × 15″D × 5″H
Special Features
Compact.
Built-in phone coupler.
Selective scanning of portions of documents.
Uses special compression technique at high speed.
Approx. Price, as of November 1970
$4000 (purchase); $95/mo. (lease for 6 mos.), $85/mo. (1 unit for 2 yrs., or 2 or more units for 1 yr.)

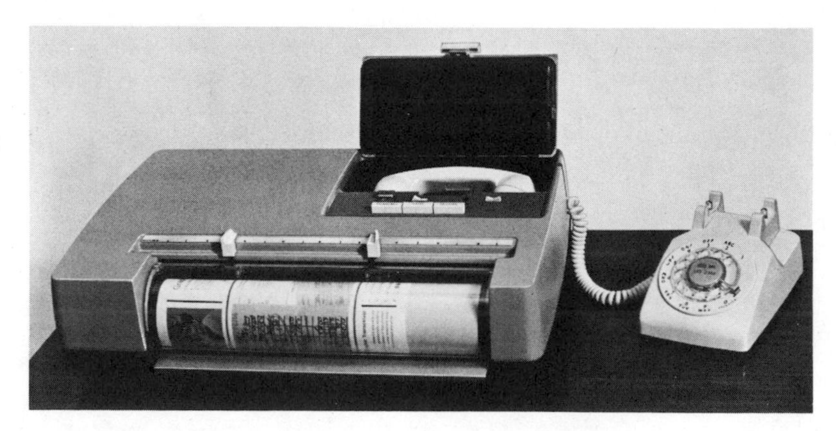

Fig. 8.3. DEX (Decision EXpediter) 180

Product Name (or Number)

"ELECTRONIC MAILBOX"

Manufacturer—Stewart-Warner Corp., Chicago, Ill.
General Description—General purpose fax transceiver for operation over telephone circuits. Sends letter-size document in approx. $4\frac{1}{2}$ minutes.
Max. Input Size—9 inches × any length
Transmission
  Mode: analog (FM)
  Bandwidth: 3 kHz (nom.)
  Facility: dial net., or any suitable voice-grade facility
Scan Resolution or Line Feed (Lines Per Inch)—96
Scan Rate (speed, in Lines Per Minute)—240
Scanner Type—flat-bed (slot-load); continuous feed
Recorder Type—flat-bed (roll-load); continuous feed
Recording Technique—electrolytic
Synchronization Method—automatic, via common power grid
Index of Cooperation—CCITT: 279 IEEE: 876
Dimensions—15″W × 21″D × 12″H
Special Features
  Can operate completely automatically.
Approx. Price, as of September 1970 (dial net. unit for use with DAA)
  \$3800 (purchase); \$99/mo. (lease)

Fig. 8.4. "Electronic Mailbox"

Product Name (or Number)

400 TELECOPIER®

Manufacturer—Xerox Corporation

General Description—General purpose, portable fax transceiver arranged for indirect telephone coupling. Sends letter-size documents in 4 or 6 minutes, depending on LPI.

Max. Input Size—8½ × 11 inches

Transmission

Mode: analog (FM)

Bandwidth: 3 kHz (nom.)

Facility: dial net., or any suitable voice-grade facility

Scan Resolution or Line Feed (Lines Per Inch)—64/96

Scan Rate (speed, in Lines Per Minute)—180

Scanner Type—cylinder (drum); semiautomatic loading, single sheets

Recorder Type—cylinder (drum); semiautomatic loading, single sheets

Recording Technique—electrothermal

Synchronization Method—built-in frequency standard

Index of Cooperation—CCITT: 178/267 IEEE: 560/840

Dimensions—18⅜″W × 13⅜″D × 4⅝″H

Special Features

Selective scanning of portions of documents.

Lightweight (18 lbs.).

Built-in phone coupler.

Self-test capability.

Approx. Price, as of November 1970

$50/mo. (lease for 1–10 units; lower rates for larger quantities)

Fig. 8.5. 400 Telecopier®

Product Name (or Number)

HELLFAX HF 146

Manufacturer—Dr.-Ing. Rudolf Hell, Kiel, West Germany
General Description—General purpose fax transceiver for operation over telephone circuits. Sends letter-size document in approx. 6 minutes.
Max. Input Size—8½ × 11½ inches
Transmission
Mode: analog (AM or FM)
Bandwidth: 3 kHz (nom.)
Facility: dial net., or any suitable voice-grade facility
Scan Resolution or Line Feed (Lines Per Inch)—100
Scan Rate (speed, in Lines Per Minute)—180
Scanner Type—cylinder (drum), single sheets
Recorder Type—cylinder (drum), single sheets
Recording Technique—wet ink offset on ordinary paper
Synchronization Method—built-in frequency standard
Index of Cooperation—CCITT: 288 IEEE: 904
Dimensions—21½″W × 15¾″D × 6¾″H
Special Features
Compact.
Records on ordinary paper.
Approx. Price, as of November 1970
$1200 F.O.B. Kiel

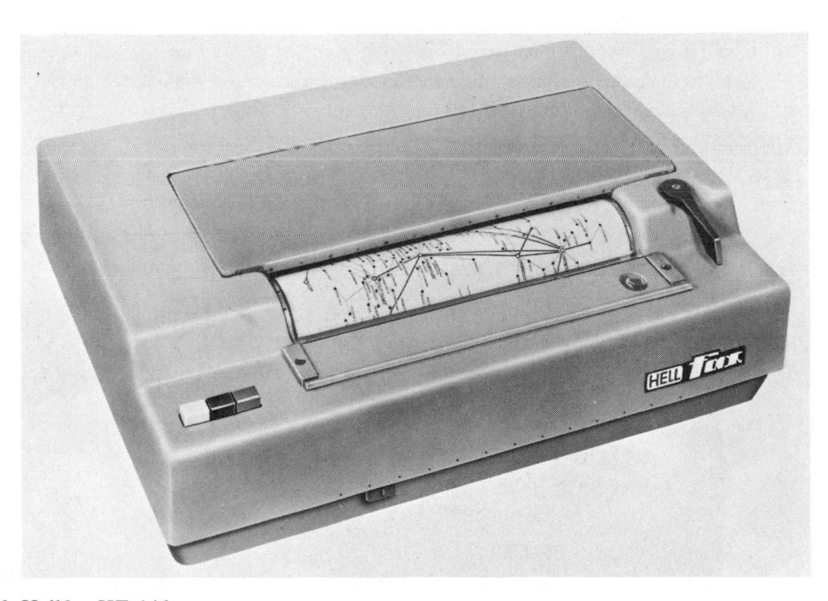

Fig. 8.6. Hellfax HF 146

Product Name (or Number)

KD-111 REMOTECOPIER®

Manufacturer—Matsushita Graphic Communication Systems, Inc. (formerly Toho-Denki Co., Ltd.), Tokyo, Japan

General Description—General purpose fax transceiver featuring separate send and receive circuitry to permit simultaneous transmission and reception. Available in various resolution/speed combinations. Can send letter-size document in 3.4 minutes.

Max. Input Size—$8\frac{1}{2} \times 14$ inches

Transmission

Mode: analog (FM)

Bandwidth: 3 kHz (nom.)

Facility: dial net., or any suitable voice-grade facility

Scan Resolution or Line Feed (Lines Per Inch)—96

(84 and 75 LPI also available)

Scan Rate (speed, in Lines Per Minute)—choice of 180, 240, or 300

Scanner Type—flat-bed (slot-load); continuous feed

Recorder Type—flat-bed (roll-load); continuous feed

Recording Technique—electrostatic

Synchronization Method—built-in frequency standard

Index of Cooperation—CCITT: 267 IEEE: 840

Dimensions—20″W × 16″D × 11″H

Special Features

Send and receive sections can operate back-to-back as a copier, or to facilitate servicing.

Can be adjusted for compatibility with other makes of transceiver.

Selective scanning of portions of documents.

Unattended reception.

(Price data unavailable at time of writing.)

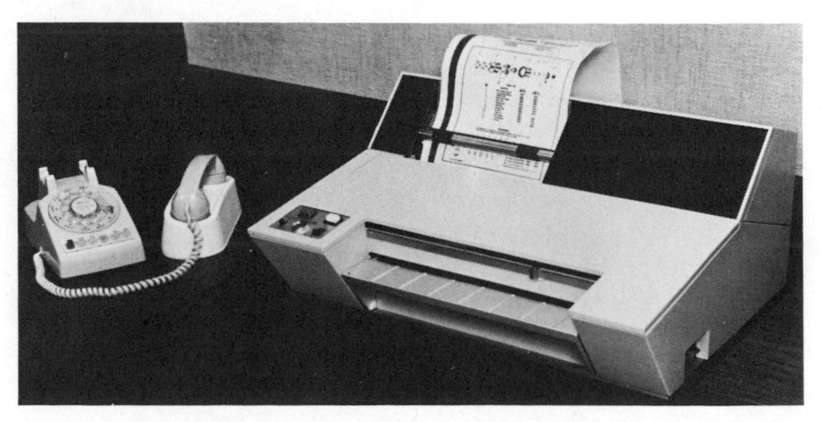

Fig. 8.7. KD-111 Remotecopier®

Product Name (or Number)

M4-2 and M4-3 BUSINESS FACSIMILE SYSTEMS

Manufacturer—International Scanatron Systems Corp., Wyandanch, N.Y.
General Description—Two-speed voice-grade fax system with bandwidth compression capability. Separate transmit and receive units. Sends letter-size documents in from 3 to 9.2 minutes, depending on LPM.
Max. Input Size—$9\frac{1}{8}$ inches × any length
Transmission
    Mode: analog, or special signal format (AM, FM, or baseband)
    Bandwidth: 3 kHz (nom.)
    Facility: dial net., or any suitable voice-grade facility
Scan Resolution or Line Feed (Lines Per Inch)—100
Scan Rate (speed, in Lines Per Minute)—M4-2: 120/240; M4-3: 180/360
Scanner Type—modified flat-bed (slot-load); continuous feed
Recorder Type—flat-bed (roll-load); continuous feed
Recording Technique—electrolytic
Synchronization Method—built-in frequency standard
Index of Cooperation—CCITT: 291   IEEE: 913
Dimensions
    Transmitter: $15\frac{3}{4}$″W × 18″D × 13″H
    Receiver: $15\frac{3}{4}$″W × 18″D × $13\frac{3}{4}$″H
Special Features
    Special bandwidth compression technique.
    Can operate completely automatically.
    Also available in three higher speed configurations (see Section 2).
Approx. Prices, as of September 1970
    Transmitter: $1900
    Receiver: $1900

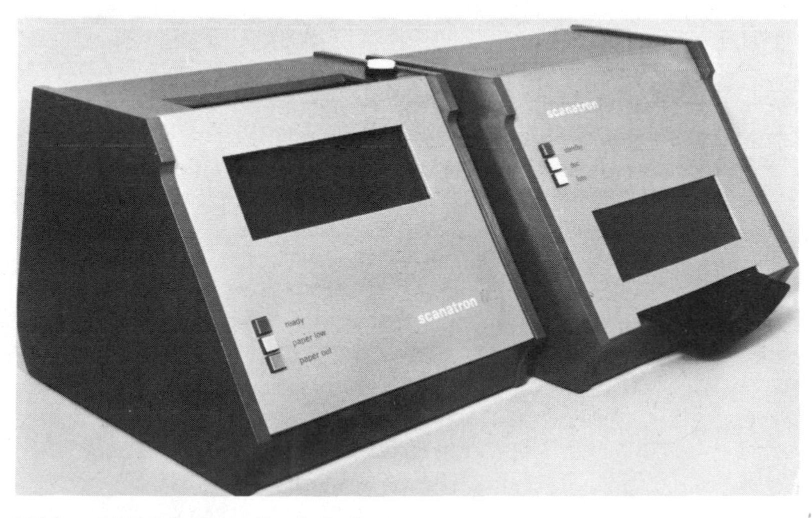

Fig. 8.8. M4-2 and M4-3 Business Facsimile Systems

Product Name (or Number)

MAGNAFAX® 860

Manufacturer—Magnavox Co., Torrance, Calif.

General Description—General purpose fax transceiver for operation over telephone circuits. Sends letter-size documents in from 3 to 6 minutes, depending on scan rate.

Max. Input Size—$8\frac{1}{2}$ inches $\times$ any length

Transmission

Mode: analog (FM) at 6-min. speed; special signal format at 3-min. speed

Bandwidth: 3 kHz (nom.)

Facility: dial net., or any suitable voice-grade facility

Scan Resolution or Line Feed (Lines Per Inch)—96

Scan Rate (speed, in Lines Per Minute)—180/360

Scanner Type—modified flat-bed; door-load; continuous feed

Recorder Type—modified flat-bed; door-load; continuous feed

Recording Technique—electropercussive

Synchronization Method—built-in frequency standard

Index of Cooperation—CCITT: 267 IEEE: 840

Dimensions—$18\frac{1}{2}''$W $\times$ $20''$D $\times$ $15\frac{1}{2}''$H

Special Features

Special bandwidth compression technique for higher speed.

Unattended reception (with roll-feed accessory).

Records on ordinary paper.

Simultaneous duplicate recordings producible on single machine.

Approx. Price, as of November 1970

\$3595 (purchase); \$90/mo. (lease for 1 yr., 1–14 units; lower rates for larger quantities)

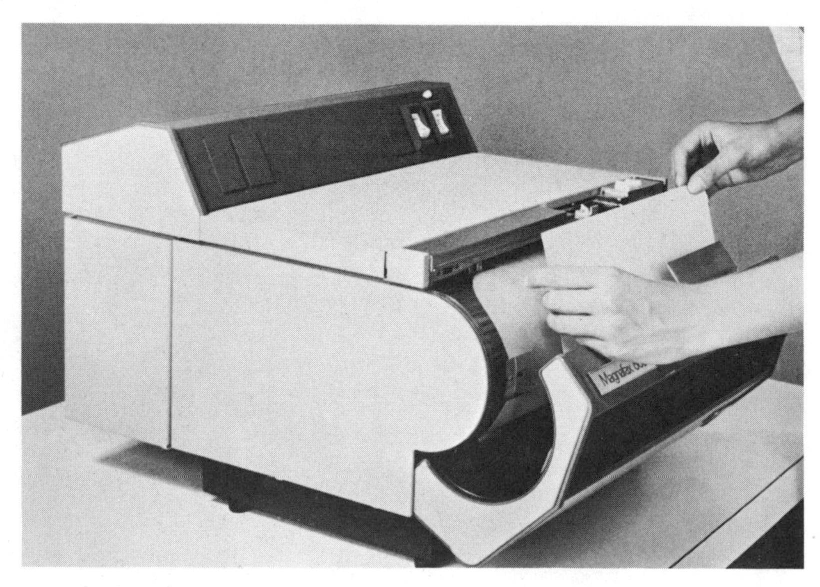

Fig. 8.9. Magnafax® 860

Product Name (or Number)

MESSAGEFAX

Manufacturer—Datalog Div., Litton Industries, Melville, N.Y.

General Description—General purpose fax system for operation over telephone and other voice-grade circuits. Separate transmit and receive units, capable of stacking. Sends letter-size document in 3.3 or 5.5 minutes, depending on scan rate.

Max. Input Size—$8\frac{1}{2} \times 14$ inches

Transmission

Mode: analog (FM for 180 LPM; AM for 300 LPM) or special compressed sig. format at 300 LPM (FM)

Bandwidth: 3 kHz (nom.)

Facility: dial net. for 180 LPM; any suitable voice-grade facility for 300 LPM

Scan Resolution or Line Feed (Lines Per Inch)—91

Scan Rate (speed, in Lines Per Minute)—choice of 180 or 300

Scanner Type—cylinder (drum); auto-load; single sheets

Recorder Type—flat-bed; roll-load; continuous feed

Recording Technique—electrolytic

Synchronization Method—automatic, via common power grid

Index of Cooperation—CCITT: 264 IEEE: 829

Dimensions

Transmitter: $21\frac{1}{4}$"W × $17\frac{7}{8}$"D × $6\frac{3}{8}$"H

Receiver: $21\frac{1}{4}$"W × $17\frac{7}{8}$"D × $6\frac{1}{2}$"H

Special Features

Receiver is "stackable" atop transmitter.

Unattended reception.

Bandwidth compression optional at extra cost.

Approx. Prices, as of November 1970

Transmitter: $2200 (purchase); $75/mo. (lease)

Receiver: $2200 (purchase); $75/mo. (lease)

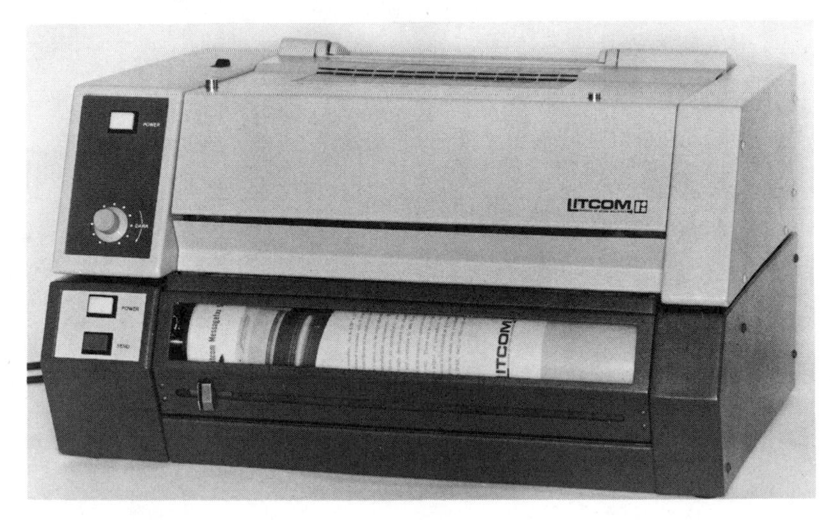

Fig. 8.10. Messagefax (transmitter bottom, receiver top)

Product Name (or Number)

MUFAX "COURIER" 240 and 300

Manufacturer—Muirhead & Co., Ltd., Beckenham, Kent, England
General Description—Business fax system arranged for operation over telephone circuits. Separate transmit and receive units. Sends letter-size document in 3.3 or 4.1 minutes, depending on scan rate.
Max. Input Size—8⅝ inches × any length
Transmission
  Mode: analog (FM)
  Bandwidth: 3 kHz (nom.)
  Facility: dial net., or any suitable voice-grade facility
Scan Resolution or Line Feed (Lines Per Inch)—90
Scan Rate (speed, in Lines Per Minute)—choice of 240 or 300
Scanner Type—flat-bed (slot-load); continuous feed
Recorder Type—flat-bed (roll-load); continuous feed
Recording Technique—electrolytic
Synchronization Method—built-in frequency standard (each unit)
Index of Cooperation—CCITT: 264   IEEE: 829
Dimensions
  Transmitter: 16″W × 16″D × 10″H
  Receiver: 15¾″W × 12¾″D × 12¾″H
Special Features
  Can operate completely automatically.
Approx. Prices, as of November 1970
  Transmitter: 240—$1960, 300—$1850 (purchase); 240—$120/mo., 300—$115/mo. (lease)
  Receiver: 240—$1835, 300—$1725 (purchase); 240—$120/mo., 300—$115/mo. (lease)

Fig. 8.11. Mufax "Courier" 240 and 300

Product Name (or Number)

QIX® 503

Manufacturer—Shintron Co., Inc., Cambridge, Mass.
General Description—Portable fax transceiver arranged for indirect telephone coupling. Sends letter-size document in approx. 4½ minutes.
Max. Input Size—8½ × 11 inches
Transmission
    Mode: analog (AM)
    Bandwidth: 3 kHz (nom.)
    Facility: dial net., or any suitable voice-grade facility
Scan Resolution or Line Feed (Lines Per Inch)—89
Scan Rate (speed, in Lines Per Minute)—216 (norm.); 142 (alt.)
Scanner Type—cylinder (drum); auto-load, single sheets
Recorder Type—cylinder (drum); auto-load, single sheets
Recording Technique—electrothermal
Synchronization Method—transmitted signal
Index of Cooperation—CCITT: 244 IEEE: 766
Dimensions—19½″W × 14¾″D × 5¼″H
Special Features
    Special optical "image-enhancing" technique.
    Margin adjustments permit sending only portion of original.
    Lightweight: 20 lbs.
Approx. Price, as of October 1970
    $1795 (purchase); $65/month per unit (lease)

Fig. 8.12. QIX® 503

Product Name (or Number)

SPEED-O-FAX

Manufacturer—Electronic Transmission Systems, Inc., New York, N.Y.

General Description—General purpose fax system arranged for direct telephone coupling via Data Access Arrangement (DAA). Separate transmit and receive units. Sends letter-size documents in approx. 6 minutes.

Max. Input Size—$8\frac{1}{2} \times 11$ inches

Transmission

- Mode: analog (FM)
- Bandwidth: 3 kHz (nom.)
- Facility: dial net., or any suitable voice-grade facility

Scan Resolution or Line Feed (Lines Per Inch)—105

Scan Rate (speed, in Lines Per Minute)—180

Scanner Type—cylinder (drum); auto-load; single sheets

Recorder Type—flat-bed (roll-load); continuous feed

Recording Technique—electrothermal

Synchronization Method—automatic, via common power grid

Index of Cooperation—CCITT: 284 IEEE: 893

Dimensions

- Transmitter: $18\frac{1}{2}''$W $\times$ $12\frac{1}{2}''$D $\times$ $9\frac{3}{4}''$H
- Receiver: $15''$W $\times$ $17''$D $\times$ $10\frac{3}{4}''$H

Special Features

- Selective scanning of portions of documents.
- Unattended reception.
- Transmitter can be stopped remotely from receiver.

Approx. Prices, as of November 1970

- Transmitter: \$2850 (purchase); \$100/mo. (lease)
- Receiver: \$3000 (purchase); \$100/mo. (lease)

Product Name (or Number)

TELECOPIER® III

Manufacturer—Xerox Corporation
General Description—General purpose fax transceiver for operation over telephone circuits. Sends letter-size documents in 4 or 6 minutes, depending on LPI.
Max. Input Size—$8\frac{1}{2}$ inches × any length
Transmission
  Mode: analog (FM)
  Bandwidth: 3 kHz (nom.)
  Facility: dial net., or any suitable voice-grade facility
Scan Resolution or Line Feed (Lines Per Inch)—64/96
Scan Rate (speed, in Lines Per Minute)—180
Scanner Type—modified flat-bed; door-load; continuous feed
Recorder Type—modified flat-bed; door-load; continuous feed
Recording Technique—electropercussive
Synchronization Method—built-in frequency standard
Index of Cooperation—CCITT: 178/267 IEEE: 560/840
Dimensions—$19\frac{3}{4}$"W × 17"D × $11\frac{1}{4}$"H
Special Features
  Unattended reception (with roll-feed accessory).
  Records on ordinary paper.
  Simultaneous duplicate recordings producible on single machine.
Approx. Price, as of November 1970
  $2500 (purchase); $55/mo. (lease)

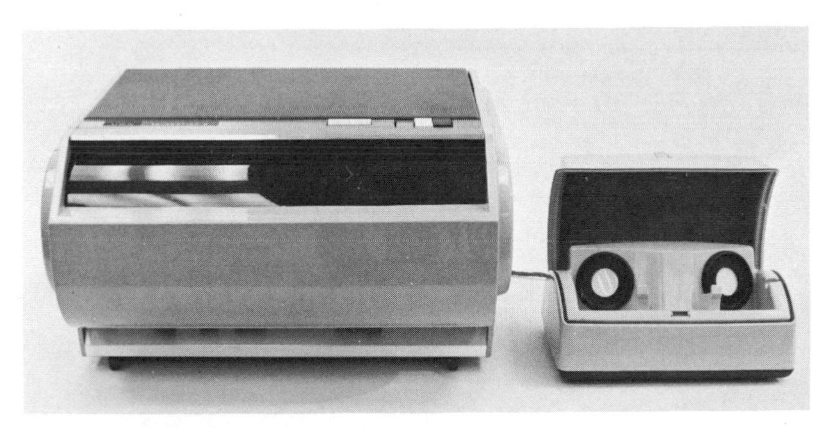

Fig. 8.13. Telecopier® III

Product Name (or Number)

TF-4501/RS-451

Manufacturer—Nippon Electric Co., Ltd., Tokyo, Japan
General Description—General purpose fax system for operation over voice-grade circuits. Separate transmit and receive units. Sends letter-size documents in from 3.8 to 5.6 minutes, depending on LPI.
Max. Input Size—8½ inches × any length
Transmission
  Mode: analog
  Bandwidth: 3 kHz (nom.)
  Facility: dial net., or any suitable voice-grade facility
Scan Resolution or Line Feed (Lines Per Inch)—102/127
Scan Rate (speed, in Lines Per Minute)—295
Scanner Type—flat-bed (platen-load); continuous feed
Recorder Type—flat-bed (roll-load); continuous feed
Recording Technique—electrostatic
Synchronization Method—
Index of Cooperation—CCITT: 264/330 IEEE: 829/1036
Dimensions (approx.)
  Transmitter: 15½″W × 18½″D × 12¾″H
  Receiver: 14½″W × 16″D × 18½″H
Special Features
  Unique fiber-optic scanning system.
  Transmits pages in bound books without removal.
  Can operate completely automatically.
  Electrolytic recorder also available.
(Price data unavailable at time of writing.)

Fig. 8.14. TF-4501 Transmitter

Section 2

General Purpose: High-Speed (and Multispeed) Systems

Item (and Manufacturer) *Page*

Bandcom 1000 (Graphic Transmission Systems), 210
Comfax 60 (Comfax/Computerpix), 211
Copyphone 900 (Telautograph), 212
Dacom 111 (Dacom), 213
Datafax Series 9000 (Stewart-Warner), 214
LDX® (Xerox), 215
M4-4, M4-6, and M4-9 (International Scanatron), 216
Mufax "Courier" 500 (Muirhead), 217
Telikon 1000 (A-M Corp.), 218
Videofax (Matsushita/Datalog), 219
Videograph (A. B. Dick), 220

Product Name (or Number)

BANDCOM 1000

Manufacturer—Graphic Transmission Systems, Inc., Hanover, N.J.
General Description—Compression fax system arranged for direct telephone coupling via Data Access Arrangement (DAA). Separate transmit and receive units. Sends letter-size documents in approx. 2½ minutes.
Max. Input Size—8½ × 11 inches
Transmission
  Mode: special signal format (FM)
  Bandwidth: 3 kHz (nom.)
  Facility: dial net., or any suitable voice-grade facility.
Scan Resolution or Line Feed (Lines Per Inch)—96
Scan Rate (speed, in Lines Per Minute)—450
Scanner Type—flat-bed (slot-load); continuous feed
Recorder Type—flat-bed (roll-load); continuous feed
Recording Technique—electrostatic
Synchronization Method—transmitted signal
Index of Cooperation—CCITT: approx. 260   IEEE: approx. 816
Dimensions—16½″W × 18½″D × 11½″H (each unit)
Special Features
  Special bandwidth compression technique.
  Unattended reception.
Approx. Prices, as of September 1970
  Transmitter: $2250 (purchase); $90/mo. (lease)
  Receiver: $2250 (purchase); $90/mo. (lease)

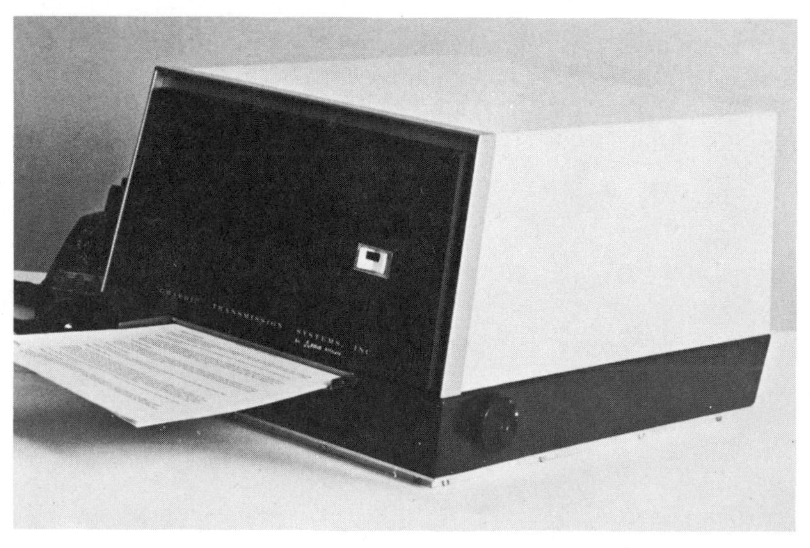

Fig. 8.15. Bandcom 1000 Transmitter

Product Name (or Number)

COMFAX 60

Manufacturer—Comfax/Computerpix Corporation, New York, N.Y.
General Description—Compression fax transceiver for general purpose applications. Can send letter-size documents in 1 minute or less (depending on content) via ordinary telephone circuits.
Max. Input Size—$8\frac{1}{2} \times 14$ inches
Transmission
  Mode: special signal format (AM, FM)
  Bandwidth: 3 kHz (nom.)
  Facility: dial net., or any suitable voice-grade facility
Scan Resolution or Line Feed (Lines Per Inch)—96/166
Scan Rate (speed, in Lines Per Minute)—variable, 300 to 10,000 (average: 1100)
Scanner Type—flat-bed (slot-load); continuous feed
Recorder Type—flat-bed (roll-load); continuous feed
Recording Technique—electrostatic
Synchronization Method—transmitted signal
Index of Cooperation—CCITT: IEEE:
Dimensions—$35\frac{1}{2}''$W $\times$ $20\frac{1}{2}''$D $\times$ $40\frac{1}{8}''$H
Special Features
  Variable velocity redundancy reduction technique.
  Uses advanced electronic scanning and recording techniques.
  Arranged for automatic stack-feeding of originals in SEND mode.
  Recorded copies automatically cut to size and delivered to basket.
  Unattended reception.
(This unit is expected to be commercially available by sometime in 1971, at an estimated monthly lease of $240.)

Product Name (or Number)

COPYPHONE 900

Manufacturer—Telautograph Corp., Los Angeles, Calif.

General Description—General purpose fax system arranged for operation over broadband circuits. Separate transmit and receive units. Sends letter-size documents in approx. 1.2 minutes.

Max. Input Size—$8\frac{1}{2}$ inches × any length

Transmission

Mode: analog (AM)

Bandwidth: 15 kHz (nom.)

Facility: "group" service, or any suitable broadband facility

Scan Resolution or Line Feed (Lines Per Inch)—100

Scan Rate (speed, in Lines Per Minute)—900

Scanner Type—flat-bed (slot-load); continuous feed

Recorder Type—flat-bed (roll-load); continuous feed

Recording Technique—electrolytic

Synchronization Method—automatic, via common power grid

Index of Cooperation—CCITT: 271 IEEE: 850

Dimensions

Transmitter: $16\frac{1}{2}$"W × 19"D × 15"H

Receiver: $16\frac{1}{2}$"W × $13\frac{1}{2}$"D × 15"H

Special Features

Recorded copies automatically cut to size at recorder.

Can operate completely automatically.

Approx. Prices, as of October 1970

Transmitter: $3000 (purchase); $115/mo. (lease)

Receiver: $3000 (purchase); $115/mo. (lease)

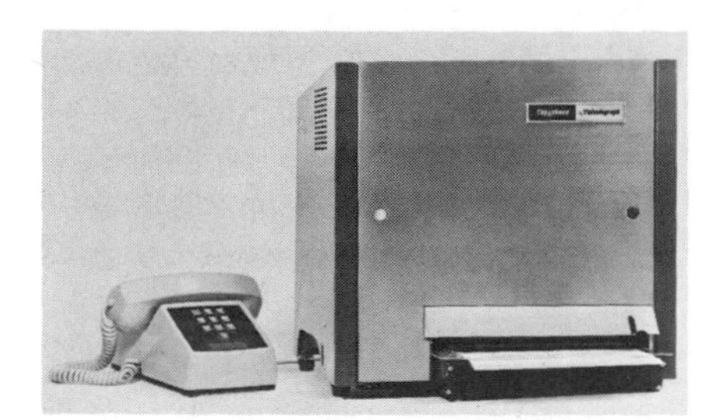

Fig. 8.16. Copyphone 900 Transmitter

Fig. 8.17. Copyphone 900 Receiver

Product Name (or Number)

DACOM 111

Manufacturer—Dacom, Inc., Sunnyvale, Calif.
General Description—Compression fax system arranged for direct telephone coupling via Data Access Arrangement (DAA). Can send letter-size documents in 1 minute or less, depending on content.
Max. Input Size—8½ inches × any length
Transmission
 Mode: digital
 Bandwidth: 3 kbits/sec. (nom.)
 Facility: dial net., or any suitable voice-grade facility.
Scan Resolution or Line Feed (Lines Per Inch)—choice of 80 or 100
Scan Rate (speed, in Lines Per Minute)—approx. 900
Scanner Type—flat-bed (slot-load); continuous feed
Recorder Type—flat-bed (roll-load); continuous feed
Recording Technique—electrolytic
Synchronization Method—transmitted signal
Index of Cooperation—CCITT: 217/260 IEEE: 680/816
Dimensions—24″W × 18½″D × 46″H (each unit)
Special Features
 Plug-in chassis design.
 Special redundancy reduction technique.
 Can operate completely automatically.
Approx. Prices, as of November 1970
 Transmitter: $7850 (purchase); $195/mo. (1-yr. lease); $175/mo. (2-yr. lease)
 Receiver: $7380 (purchase); $195/mo. (1-yr. lease); $175/mo. (2-yr. lease)

Fig. 8.18. Dacom 111 Receiver

Product Name (or Number)

DATAFAX SERIES 9000

Manufacturer—Stewart-Warner Corp., Chicago, Ill.
General Description—General purpose, high-speed fax system for operation over broadband circuits. Separate transmit and receive units. Sends letter-size documents in approx. 1 minute.
Max. Input Size—9 inches × any length
Transmission
Mode: analog (AM)
Bandwidth: 10 kHz (nom.)
Facility: "group" service, or any suitable broadband facility
Scan Resolution or Line Feed (Lines Per Inch)—96
Scan Rate (speed, in Lines Per Minute)—900
Scanner Type—flat-bed (slot-load); continuous feed
Recorder Type—flat-bed (roll-load); continuous feed
Recording Technique—electrolytic
Synchronization Method—automatic, via common power grid
Index of Cooperation—CCITT: 279 IEEE: 876
Dimensions
Transmitter: 16½"W × 19½"D × 15½"H
Receiver: 15½"W × 19½"D × 15"H
Special Features
Can operate completely automatically.
Approx. Prices, as of September 1970
Transmitter: $3250 (purchase); $124/mo. (lease)
Receiver: $2780 (purchase); $119/mo. (lease)

Product Name (or Number)

LDX® (Long Distance Xerography)

Manufacturer—Xerox Corporation

General Description—High-speed, high-resolution electronic fax system for operation over broadband circuits. Separate transmit and receive units. Sends letter-size documents in from 0.09 to 1.14 minutes, depending on LPI/LPM combination.

Max. Input Size—$9\frac{1}{2}$ inches × any length

Transmission

Mode: two-level digital (synchronous)

Bandwidth: 48 kHz for 1800 or 2520 LPM; 240 kHz for 9000 or 12,600 LPM

Facility: "group," "supergroup," or other suitable broadband facilities

Scan Resolution or Line Feed (Lines Per Inch)—100, 115, 135, or 190

Scan Rate (speed, in Lines Per Minute)—choice of 2520 or 12,600 at up to 135 LPI; choice of 1800 or 9000 at 190 LPI.

Scanner Type—flat-bed (slot-load); continuous feed

Recorder Type—flat-bed (roll-load); continuous feed

Recording Technique—electrostatic

Synchronization Method—transmitted signal

Index of Cooperation—CCITT: 270, 311, 366, 514 IEEE: 850, 978, 1148, 1615

Dimensions

Transmitter: 24″W × 46″D × 46″H

Receiver: $25\frac{1}{2}$″W × 33″D × 59″H

Special Features

Recorded copies automatically cut to size at recorder.

Records on ordinary paper.

Uses advanced electronic scanning & recording techniques.

Approx. Prices, as of November 1970, base rental (up to 2500 ft. of copy per mo.):

Transmitter: $550/mo.

Receiver: $650/mo.

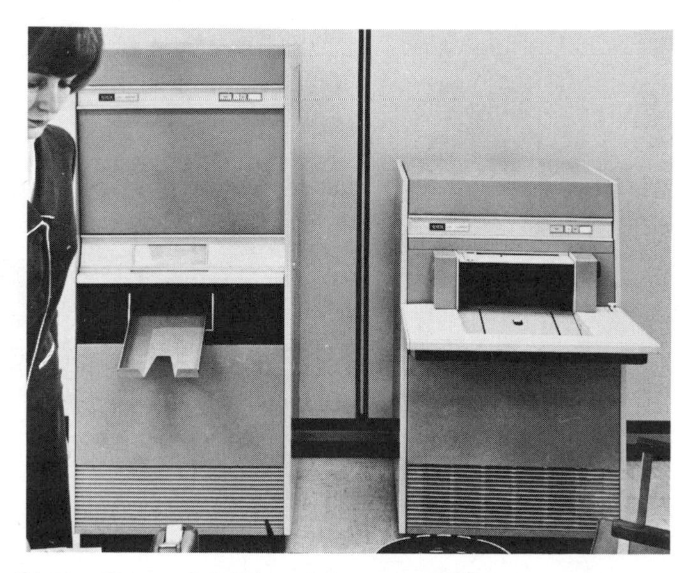

Fig. 8.19. LDX (Long Distance Xerography) (printer left, scanner right)

Product Name (or Number)

M4-4, M4-6, and M4-9 BUSINESS FACSIMILE SYSTEMS

Manufacturer—International Scanatron Systems Corp., Wyandanch, N.Y.
General Description—Two-speed fax system with bandwidth compression capability. Separate transmit and receive units. Sends letter-size documents in from 1.1 to 4.5 minutes (depending on LPM) via voice-grade or broadband facilities, as required.
Max. Input Size—$9\frac{1}{8}$ inches × any length
Transmission
  Mode: analog, or special signal format (AM, FM, or baseband)
  Bandwidth: 3 kHz (nom.) up to 600 LPM. Higher for 960 LPM.
  Facility: dial net., or any suitable voice-grade or broadband facility.
Scan Resolution or Line Feed (Lines Per Inch)—100
Scan Rate (speed, in Lines Per Minute)—M4-4: 240/480, M4-6: 300/600, M4-9: 480/960.
Scanner Type—modified flat-bed (slot-load); continuous feed
Recorder Type—flat-bed (roll-load); continuous feed
Recording Technique—electrolytic
Synchronization Method—built-in frequency standard
Index of Cooperation—CCITT: 291 IEEE: 913
Dimensions
  Transmitter: $15\frac{3}{4}$″W × 18″D × 13″H
  Receiver: $15\frac{3}{4}$″W × 18″D × $13\frac{3}{4}$″H
Special Features
  Special bandwidth compression technique.
  Can operate completely automatically.
  Also available in two lower-speed configurations (See Section 1).
Approx. Prices, as of September 1970
  Transmitter: $1900
  Receiver: $1900

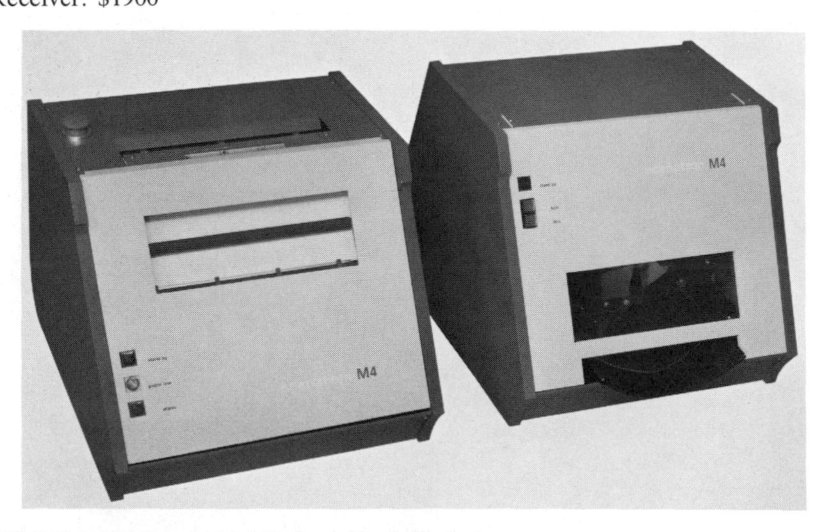

Fig. 8.20. M4-4, M4-6, and M4-9 Business Facsimile Systems

Product Name (or Number)

MUFAX "COURIER" 500

Manufacturer—Muirhead & Co., Ltd., Beckenham, Kent, England
General Description—High-speed business fax system arranged for operation over short-haul solid wire circuits. Separate transmit and receive units. Sends letter-size document in approx. 2 minutes.
Max. Input Size—$8\frac{5}{8}$ inches × any length
Transmission
  Mode: analog (baseband)
  Bandwidth: 3 kHz (nom.)
  Facility: solid wire circuit
Scan Resolution or Line Feed (Lines Per Inch)—90
Scan Rate (speed, in Lines Per Minute)—500
Scanner Type—flat-bed (slot-load); continuous feed
Recorder Type—flat-bed (roll-load); continuous feed
Recording Technique—electrolytic
Synchronization Method—built-in frequency standard (each unit)
Index of Cooperation—CCITT: 264 IEEE: 829
Dimensions
  Transmitter: 16″W × 16″D × 10″H
  Receiver: $15\frac{3}{4}$″W × $12\frac{3}{4}$″D × $12\frac{3}{4}$″H
Special Features
  Can operate completely automatically
Approx. Prices, as of November 1970
  Transmitter: $1850 (purchase); $115/mo. (lease)
  Receiver: $1725 (purchase); $115/mo. (lease)

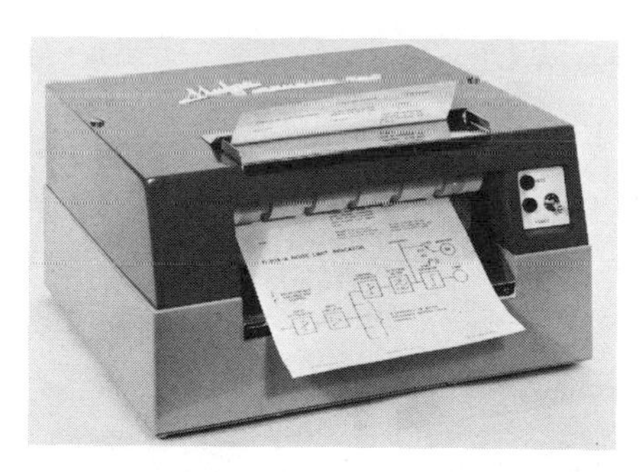

Fig. 8.21. Mufax "Courier" 500 Transmitter

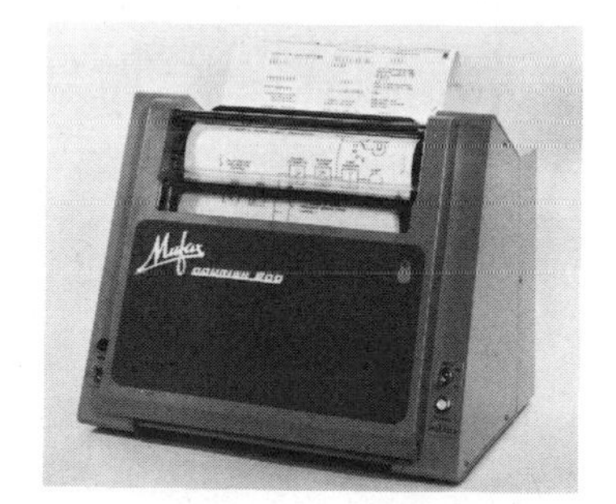

Fig. 8.22. Mufax "Courier" 500 Receiver

Product Name (or Number)

TELIKON 1000

Manufacturer—Addressograph-Multigraph Corp.
General Description—Compression fax transceiver for operation over telephone circuits. Uses laser beam for recording. Can send letter-size documents in 1 minute or less, depending on content.
Max. Input Size—9 × 17 inches
Transmission
Mode: special digital format
Bandwidth: 3 kHz (nom.)
Facility: dial net., or any suitable voice-grade facility
Scan Resolution or Line Feed (Lines Per Inch)—100 (200 bits per inch along scan axis)
Scan Rate (speed, in Lines Per Minute)—variable according to content of subject copy
Scanner Type—flat-bed (slot-load); automatic feed
Recorder Type—flat-bed (cut sheets); automatic feed
Recording Technique— electrostatic (laser beam)
Synchronization Method—transmitted signal
Index of Cooperation—CCITT: 278 IEEE: 875
Dimensions—63″W × 32″D × 34″H
Special Features
Special compression technique.
Laser beam recording.
Sending unit automatically stopped by receiver in the event of circuit failure or when error rate is high.
Operates completely automatically.
(Price data not available at time of writing. *Note:* the Telikon system has been undergoing field tests for some time, and is expected to be commercially available by the time this book goes to press.)

Product Name (or Number)

VIDEOFAX

Manufacturer—Matsushita Graphic Communication Systems, Inc., Tokyo, Japan (Distributed in U.S. by Datalog Division, Litton Industries)

General Description—High-speed electronic fax system for operation over broadband circuits. Separate transmit and receive units. Sends 7 × 10-inch documents in from 0.2 to 0.5 minute, depending on LPI/LPM combination.

Max. Input Size—7.2 × 10.2 inches

Transmission

Mode: analog (AM); digital (alt.)

Bandwidth: 48 kHz (nom.); 50kB/s (nom.)

Facility: "group" or comparable broadband facility; broadband digital facilities

Scan Resolution or Line Feed (Lines Per Inch)—75/150

Scan Rate (speed, in Lines Per Minute)—3000 or 3600

Scanner Type—flat-bed (slot-load)

Recorder Type—flat-bed (roll-load); continuous feed

Recording Technique—electrophotographic

Synchronization Method—transmitted signal

Index of Cooperation—CCITT: 173/345 IEEE: 543/1084

Dimensions

Transmitter: 19″W × 30″D × 48″H

Receiver: 22½″W × 28½″D × 48″H

Special Features

Scanner uses advanced fiber-optic technique.

Can operate completely automatically.

Approx. Prices, as of November 1970

Transmitter: $8,470 (purchase); $305/mo. (lease)

Receiver: $23,100 (purchase); $835/mo. (lease)

(*Note:* selling prices are F.O.B. Melville, N.Y.)

Fig. 8.23. Videofax (transmitter left, receiver right)

Product Name (or Number)

VIDEOGRAPH

Manufacturer—A. B. Dick Co.

General Description—General purpose fax system for operation over broadband circuits. Separate transmit and receive units. Sends letter-size documents in approx. 0.1 minute.

Max. Input Size—$8\frac{1}{2}$ inches × any length

Transmission

Mode: two-level

Bandwidth: 200 kHz

Facility: "supergroup" service, or comparable broadband facility

Scan Resolution or Line Feed (Lines Per Inch)—96

Scan Rate (speed, in Lines Per Minute)—approx. 10,000

Scanner Type—flat-bed (slot-load); continuous feed

Recorder Type—flat-bed (roll-load); continuous feed

Recording Technique—electrostatic (CRT)

Synchronization Method—transmitted signal

Index of Cooperation—CCITT: IEEE:

Dimensions—24″W × 56″D × 40″H (each unit)

Special Features

Recorded copies automatically cut to size at recorder.

Uses advanced high-speed scanning and recording techniques.

Unattended reception.

(*Note:* although still available on a special order basis, this is essentially a discontinued item as of late 1969. No price information available.)

Fig. 8.24. Videograph (printer left and scanner right)

Section 3

TELEPHOTOGRAPHIC (PHOTOTELEGRAPHIC OR PHOTOFACSIMILE) SYSTEMS

Item (and Manufacturer) *Page*

FT-64B (NEC), 222
FT-68T Transmitter (NEC), 223
FT-69 (NEC), 224
FT-77 (NEC), 225
FT-1001 AR (NEC), 226
K-221 Transmitter (Muirhead), 227
K-300-A Recorder (Muirhead), 228
Photofax (Datalog), 229
Unifax TFR-3M Recorder (UPI), 230

Product Name (or Number)

FT-64B

Manufacturer—Nippon Electric Co., Ltd., Tokyo, Japan

General Description—Medium/high resolution photofacsimile transceiver for operation over voice-grade circuits. Sends 8 × 10-inch picture in 12 or 19 minutes, depending on LPI.

Max. Input Size—$8\frac{5}{8} \times 10\frac{1}{4}$ inches

Transmission

Mode: analog (AM)

Bandwidth: 3 kHz (nom.)

Facility: conditioned telephone circuit, or any suitable voice-grade facility

Scan Resolution or Line Feed (Lines Per Inch)—127/203

Scan Rate (speed, in Lines Per Minute)—115.3

Scanner Type—cylinder (drum); single sheets

Recorder Type—cylinder (drum); single sheets

Recording Technique—photographic

Synchronization Method—automatic, via common power grid

Index of Cooperation—CCITT: 350/560 IEEE: 1099/1785

Dimensions—$32\frac{1}{4}$"W × $18\frac{1}{8}$"D × $22\frac{1}{2}$"H

Special Features

Modular construction.

(Price data unavailable at time of writing.)

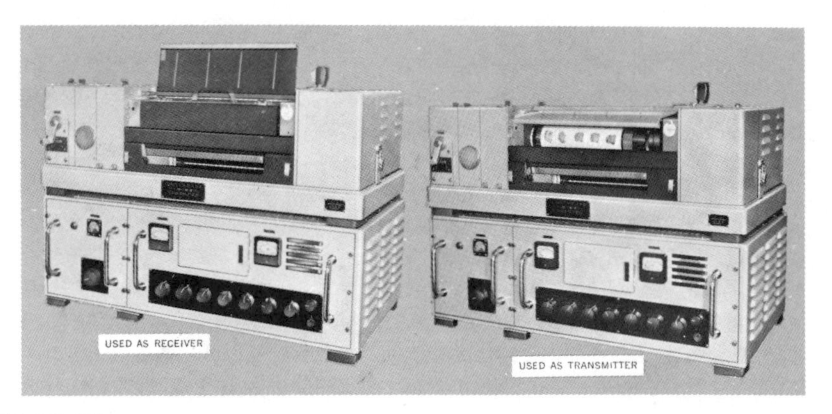

Fig. 8.25. FT-64B

Product Name (or Number)

FT-68T

Manufacturer—Nippon Electric Co., Ltd., Tokyo, Japan
General Description—Portable photofacsimile transmitter for operation over voice-grade circuits. Sends 5 × 7-inch picture (with caption) in approx. 7 minutes.
Max. Input Size—$5\frac{1}{8}$ × 8 inches
Transmission
Mode: analog (AM)
Bandwidth: 3 kHz (nom.)
Facility: conditioned telephone circuit or any suitable voice-grade facility
Scan Resolution or Line Feed (Lines Per Inch)—120
Scan Rate (speed, in Lines Per Minute)—90
Scanner Type—cylinder (drum), single sheets
Recorder Type—(not applicable)
Recording Technique—(not applicable)
Synchronization Method—frequency standard
Index of Cooperation—CCITT: 296.6 IEEE: 931.3
Dimensions—$16\frac{1}{2}$″W × $11\frac{1}{4}$″D × 7″H
Special Features
Ease of maintenance.
Provision for picture caption.
(Price data unavailable at time of writing.)

Fig. 8.26. FT-68T

Product Name (or Number)

FT-69

Manufacturer—Nippon Electric Co., Ltd., Tokyo, Japan

General Description—Medium-speed photofacsimile system for use by news agencies, etc. Sends 8 × 10-inch picture in approx. 6 minutes over conditioned telephone circuit.

Max. Input Size—8 × 10¼ inches

Transmission

Mode: analog (AM)

Bandwidth: 3 kHz (nom.)

Facility: Schedule II, or other suitably conditioned voice-grade circuit

Scan Resolution or Line Feed (Lines Per Inch)—120

Scan Rate (speed, in Lines Per Minute)—200

Scanner Type—cylinder (drum), single sheets

Recorder Type—cylinder (drum), single sheets

Recording Technique—photographic

Synchronization Method—frequency standard

Index of Cooperation—CCITT: 296.6 IEEE: 931.3

Dimensions—31½″W × 23⅝″D × 47¼″H (each unit)

Special Features

Removable drums for ease of loading.

(Price data unavailable at time of writing.)

Fig. 8.27. FT-69

Product Name (or Number)

FT-77

Manufacturer—Nippon Electric Co., Ltd., Tokyo, Japan
General Description—Fax system for use with Polaroid self-processing film. Sends 3 × 4-inch picture in approx. 2.5 minutes over a voice-grade circuit.
Max. Input Size—3.3 × 4.4 inches
Transmission
 Mode: analog (AM)
 Bandwidth: 3 kHz (nom.)
 Facility: dial net., Schedule II, or other suitably conditioned voice-grade circuit
Scan Resolution or Line Feed (Lines Per Inch)—127
Scan Rate (speed, in Lines Per Minute)—225
Scanner Type—cylinder (drum), single sheets
Recorder Type—flat-bed (Polaroid film pack)
Recording Technique—photographic
Synchronization Method—automatic, via common power grid
Index of Cooperation—CCITT: 200 IEEE: 628
Dimensions
 Transmitter: 13¼″W × 8½″D × 5″H
 Receiver: 22⅝″W × 23⅝″D × 20″H
Special Features
 Lightweight transmitter (only 19 lbs.).
(Price data unavailable at time of writing.)

Product Name (or Number)

FT-1001 AR

Manufacturer—Nippon Electric Co., Ltd., Tokyo, Japan
General Description—Fully automatic photofacsimile receiver for operation over voice-grade circuits. Records 5 × 8-inch picture in approx. 9 minutes; 8 × 10-inch in approx. 11 minutes.
Max. Input Size—8 × 10¼ inches
Transmission
 Mode: analog (AM)
 Bandwidth: 3 kHz (nom.)
 Facility: dial net., Schedule II, or other suitably conditioned voice-grade circuit
Scan Resolution or Line Feed (Lines Per Inch)—120
Scan Rate (speed, in Lines Per Minute)—116/145
Scanner Type—(not applicable)
Recorder Type—cylinder (drum); auto-load from cassette
Recording Technique—photographic
Synchronization Method—built-in frequency standard
Index of Cooperation—CCITT: 296.6 IEEE: 931.3
Dimensions—40⅛"W × 43¼"D × 58⅞"H
Special Features
 Fully automatic loading, reception, and processing.
 Selectively receives large or small pictures.
 Produces 500 photo recordings on a single loading.
(Price data unavailable at time of writing.)

Product Name (or Number)

K-221 TRANSMITTER

Manufacturer—Muirhead & Co., Ltd., Beckenham, Kent, England
General Description—Fax transmitter intended for sending photographs via phone lines. Sends 10 × 10-inch picture in approx. 8 minutes.
Max. Input Size—10 × 10½ inches
Transmission
Mode: analog (AM)
Bandwidth: 3 kHz (nom.)
Facility: Schedule II, or any suitably conditioned voice-grade facilities
Scan Resolution or Line Feed (Lines Per Inch)—100/150
Scan Rate (speed, in Lines Per Minute)—60/120
Scanner Type—cylinder (drum), single sheets
Recorder Type—(not applicable)
Recording Technique—(not applicable)
Synchronization Method—frequency standard
Index of Cooperation—CCITT: 352/528 IEEE: 1105/1658
Dimensions—21¾″W × 14¾″D × 7¾″H
Special Features
Other models available for resolutions of 135, 200, and 220 LPI.
Approx. Price, as of November 1970
$4345 (purchase); $185/mo. (lease)

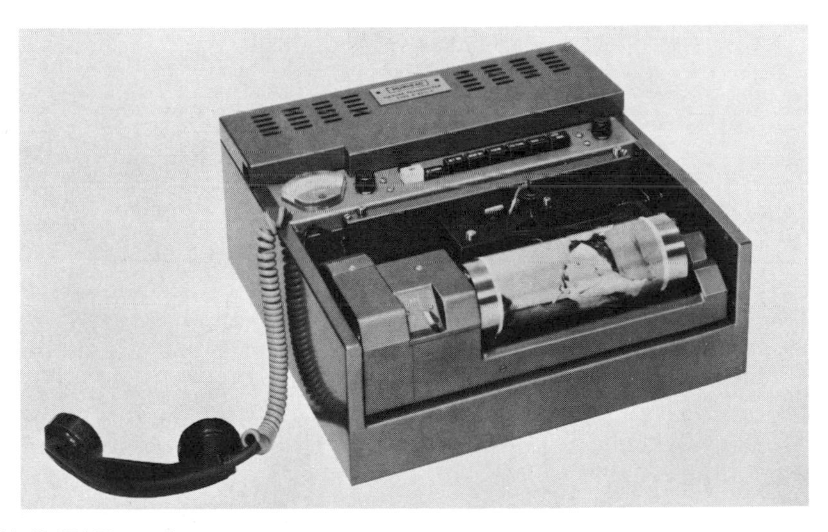

Fig. 8.28. K-221 Transmitter

Product Name (or Number)

K-300-A RECORDER

Manufacturer—Muirhead & Co., Ltd., Beckenham, Kent, England
General Description—Automatic-processing photographic fax recorder. Arranged for automatic reception of cloud cover pictures from weather satellites.
Max. Input Size—(not applicable)
Transmission
Mode: analog or two-level (AM)
Bandwidth: 3 kHz (nom.)
Facility: any suitable voice-grade wire or radio link
Scan Resolution or Line Feed (Lines Per Inch)—100
Scan Rate (speed, in Lines Per Minute)—240
Scanner Type—(not applicable)
Recorder Type—roll-load; continuous feed
Recording Technique—photographic
Synchronization Method—built-in frequency standard
Index of Cooperation—CCITT: 267 IEEE: 838
Dimensions—28″W × 24½″D × 50″H
Special Features
For weather satellite reception, recorder actions are controlled by satellite-transmitted signals.
Fully automatic processing.
Similar recorder (K-300-D/F) available for 200 LPI resolution.
Approx. Price, as of November 1970
$7920 (purchase); $340/mo. (lease)

Fig. 8.29. K-300-A Recorder

Product Name (or Number)

PHOTOFAX

Manufacturer—Datalog Division, Litton Industries, Melville, N.Y. (Recorder manufactured by Hell of West Germany)
General Description—High-resolution photographic fax system.
Max. Input Size—8 × 8 inches
Transmission
 Mode: analog (AM)
 Bandwidth: 3 kHz (nom.)
 Facility: dial net., or any suitable voice-grade facility
Scan Resolution or Line Feed (Lines Per Inch)—192
Scan Rate (speed, in Lines Per Minute)—120
Scanner Type—cylinder (drum); single sheets
Recorder Type—cylinder (drum); auto-load of cut sheets from cassette
Recording Technique—photographic
Synchronization Method—automatic, via common power grid
Index of Cooperation—CCITT: 528 IEEE: 1659
Dimensions
 Transmitter: 21″W × 17⅞″D × 6″H
 Receiver: 31½″W × 24½″D × 42⅛″H
Special Features
 Recorder features automatic processing.
 Unattended operation.
Approx. Prices, as of November 1970
 Transmitter: $2825 (purchase); $95/mo. (lease)
 Receiver: $12,500 (purchase); $190/mo. (lease)

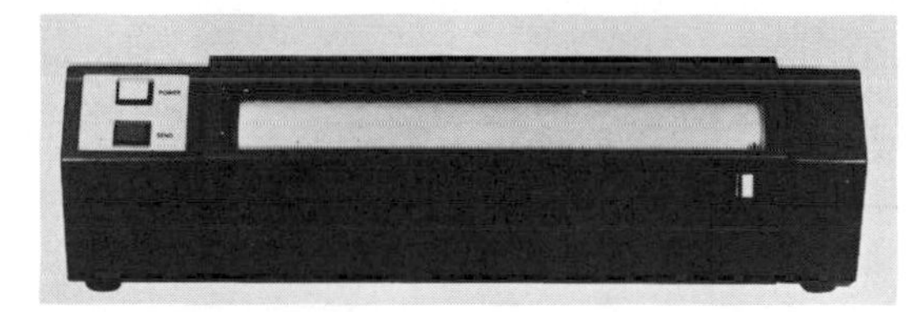

Fig. 8.30. Photofax Transmitter

Fig. 8.31. Hell Automatic Recorder used in Datalog Photofax system

Product Name (or Number)

UNIFAX MODEL TFR-3M RECORDER

Manufacturer—United Press International (Engineering Laboratory), Maywood, N.J.
General Description—Electrolytic continuous-tone facsimile recorder for news-picture use.
Max. Input Size—(variable)
Transmission
  Mode: analog (AM)
  Bandwidth: 3 kHz (nom.)
  Facility: Schedule II, or other suitably conditioned voice-grade circuit
Scan Resolution or Line Feed (Lines Per inch)—150
Scan Rate (speed, in Lines Per Minute)—120
Scanner Type—(not applicable)
  Recorder Type—flat-bed (roll-load); continuous feed
Recording Technique—electrolytic
Synchronization Method—built-in frequency standard
Index of Cooperation—CCITT: 440 IEEE: 1382
Dimensions—15″W × 14″D × 56″H
Special Features
  Unattended reception.
  Automatic fail-safe switch.
(Not offered for sale; used only on UPI domestic newspicture net.)

Section 4

SPECIAL PURPOSE AND MISCELLANEOUS SYSTEMS

Item (and Manufacturer) *Page*

Alden 2 (Alden), 232
Alden 11 Docufax (Alden), 233
Alden 18 Alpurfax (Alden), 234
Alden 35mm Microfilm Scanner (Alden), 235
Alden 600 (Alden), 236
Colorfax (Matsushita/Datalog), 237
Computerpix Micro 60 Transmitter (Comfax/Computerpix), 238
Dacom 212 (Dacom), 239
DEX V (GSI), 240
FH-94R Receiver (NEC), 241
FT-76 (NEC), 242
Hellfax BS 110 MD Recorder (Hell), 243
Hellfax FA 124 Transmitter (Hell), 244
Hellfax WF 205 Transmitter (Hell), 245
Hell-Pressfax (Hell), 246
K-500/1 Color Equipment (Muirhead), 247
Mercury IV (Muirhead), 248
Mercury V (Muirhead), 249
Newspaper Page Facsimile System (Muirhead), 250
Pressfax 501 (Matsushita/Datalog), 251
Radarfax (Datalog), 252
Weatherfax LD-40 Recorder (Matsushita/Datalog), 253
Weatherfax RJ-6 Recorder (Datalog), 254
Zetfax (Hell), 255

Product Name (or Number)

ALDEN 2

Manufacturer—Alden Electronic & Impulse Recording Equipment Co., Inc., Westboro, Mass.

General Description—Fax system for narrow documents. Used principally for signature verification. Sends 3 × 5-inch card in approx. 10 seconds via broadband channel.

Max. Input Size—7 inches × any length

Transmission

 Mode: analog (AM)

 Bandwidth: approx. 15 kHz

 Facility: "group" service, or any suitable broadband facility

Scan Resolution or Line Feed (Lines Per Inch)—100

Scan Rate (speed, in Lines Per Minute)—3600

Scanner Type—flat-bed (slot-load); continuous feed

Recorder Type—flat-bed (roll-load); continuous feed

Recording Technique—electrolytic

Synchronization Method—automatic, via common power grid

Index of Cooperation—CCITT: 80 IEEE: 250

Dimensions

 Transmitter: $15\frac{1}{2}$″W × $15\frac{3}{4}$″D × 40″H

 Receiver: $11\frac{1}{2}$″W × $7\frac{1}{2}$″D × 7″H

 Receiver Electronics: 10″W × $8\frac{7}{8}$″D × 12″H

Special Features

 Unattended reception.

 Selectively scans any 2.25-inch portion of documents up to 7 inches wide.

Approx. Prices, as of November 1970

 Transmitter: $5000

 Receiver: $3000

Fig. 8.32. Alden 2 Transmitter

Product Name (or Number)

ALDEN 11 DOCUFAX

Manufacturer—Alden Electronic & Impulse Recording Equipment Co., Inc., Westboro, Mass.

General Description—Fax system for 11-inch-wide documents (charts, engineering drawings, etc.). Separate transmit and receive units. Sends 11 × 17-inch document in from 1.7 to 23.5 minutes, depending on LPI/LPM combination.

Max. Input Size—28 inches × any length (scans 10-inch-wide portion at a time)

Transmission
- Mode: analog (AM)
- Bandwidth: 3–24 kHz (nom.)
- Facility: any suitable voice-grade or broadband facility, as required

Scan Resolution or Line Feed (Lines Per Inch)—96/166

Scan Rate (speed, in Lines Per Minute)—choice of 120/240 or 120/240/480/960

Scanner Type—flat-bed (slot-load); continuous feed

Recorder Type—flat-bed (roll-load); continuous feed

Recording Technique—electrolytic

Synchronization Method—automatic, via common power grid

Index of Cooperation—CCITT: 328/576 IEEE: 1029/1809

Dimensions
- Transmitter: 30″W × 21″D × 50″H
- Receiver: 24″W × 18″D × 50″H

Special Features
- Selectively scans any 10-inch-wide portion of input document.
- Also available with 16-mm microfilm scanner.
- Unattended reception.

Approx. Prices, as of November 1970
- Transmitter: 2-speed: $6460 (purchase); $140/mo. (lease)
  4-speed: $7950 (purchase); $359/mo. (lease)
- Receiver: 2-speed: $3850 (purchase); $110/mo. (lease)
  4-speed: $8550 (purchase); $357/mo. (lease)

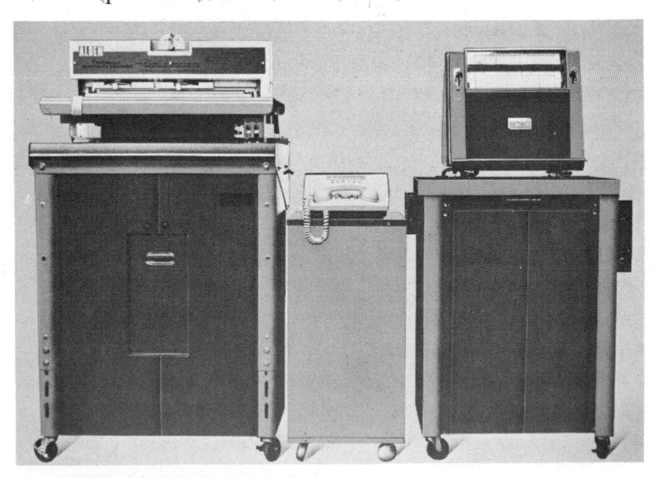

Fig. 8.33. Alden 11 Docufax (transmitter left, receiver right)

Product Name (or Number)

ALDEN 18 ALPURFAX

Manufacturer—Alden Electronic & Impulse Recording Equipment Co., Inc., Westboro, Mass.

General Description—Fax system for 18-inch-wide documents (charts, engineering drawings, etc.). Separate transmit and receive units. Sends 18 × 24-inch drawing in from 2.4 to 66.4 minutes, depending on LPI/LPM combination.

Max. Input Size—60 inches × any length (scans 18-inch-wide portion at a time)

Transmission

Mode: analog (AM)

Bandwidth: 3–48 kHz (nom.)

Facility: any suitable voice-grade or broadband facility, as required

Scan Resolution or Line Feed (Lines Per Inch)—48/96/166

Scan Rate (speed, in Lines Per Minute)—choice of 60/120, 120/240, 480/960, or 120/240/480/960

Scanner Type—flat-bed (slot-load); continuous feed

Recorder Type—flat-bed (roll-load); continuous feed

Recording Technique—electrolytic

Synchronization Method—automatic, via common power grid

Index of Cooperation—CCITT: 576 IEEE: 1809 (96 LPI)

Dimensions

Transmitter: 34″W × 22″D × 56″H

Receiver: 35″W × 22″D × 55″H

Special Features

Selectively scans any 18-inch-wide portion of input document.

Also available with 35-mm microfilm scanner.

Unattended reception.

Approx. Prices, as of August 1970

Transmitter: $6460–$9800 (purchase); $210/mo.–$440/mo. (lease)

Receiver: $2900–$9500 (purchase); $140/mo.–$464/mo. (lease)

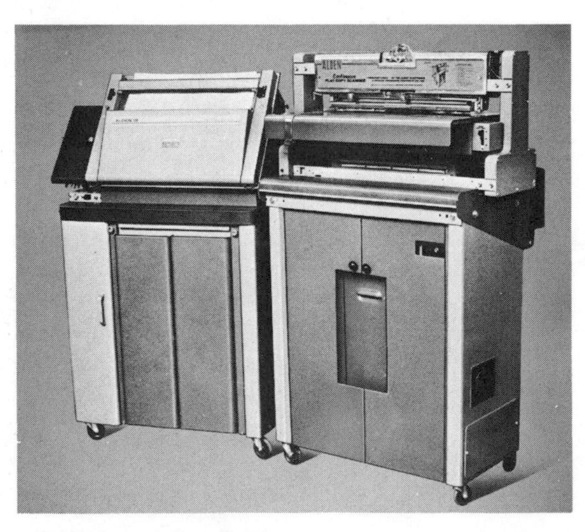

Fig. 8.34. Alden 18 Alpurfax (receiver left, transmitter right)

Product Name (or Number)

ALDEN 35-mm MICROFILM SCANNER

Manufacturer—Alden Electronic & Impulse Recording Equipment Co., Inc., Westboro, Mass.
General Description—Fax scanner for 35-mm microfilm mounted in tab cards. Sends 16× reduced 18 × 24-inch drawing in from 2.4 to 38.4 minutes, depending on scan rate.
Max. Input Size—tab card containing frame of 35-mm film
Transmission
  Mode: analog (AM)
  Bandwidth: 3–24 kHz (nom.)
  Facility: dial net., or any suitable voice-grade or broadband facility, as required
Scan Resolution or Line Feed (Lines Per Inch)—1459 (at film plane)
Scan Rate (speed, in Lines Per Minute)—choice of 60/120, 120/240, or 120/240/480/960
Scanner Type—flat-bed (slot-load)
Recorder Type—(not applicable)
Recording Technique—(not applicable)
Synchronization Method—automatic, via common power grid
Index of Cooperation—CCITT: 576 IEEE: 1809
Dimensions—31″W × 21″D × 49″H
Special Features
  Capable of legibly transmitting microfilm images of nom. 16× reduction. Produces equivalent 96 LPI enlarged image on 18-inch recorder.
Approx. Prices, as of November 1970
  2-speed (#9207A): $9,000 (purchase); $320/mo. (lease)
  4-speed (#9240): $13,800 (purchase); $508/mo. (lease)

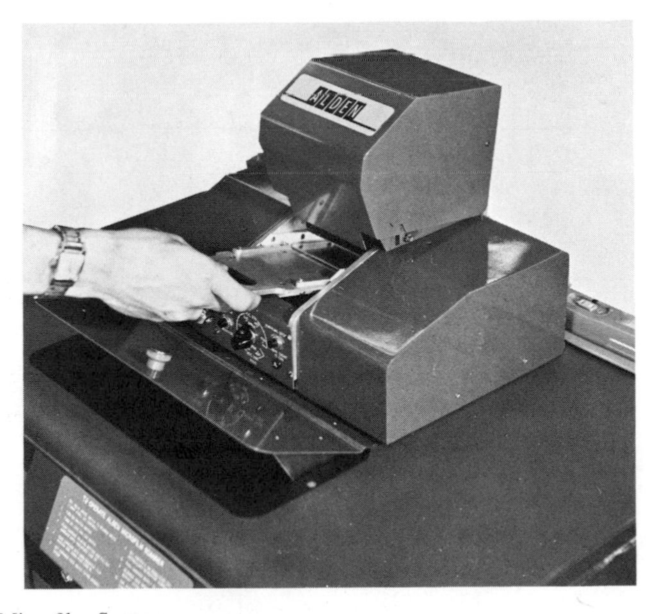

Fig. 8.35. Alden 35-mm Microfilm Scanner

Product Name (or Number)

ALDEN 600

Manufacturer—Alden Electronic & Impulse Recording Equipment Co., Inc., Westboro, Mass.
General Description—Fax system for 6 × 8-inch forms or 6-inch segments of larger documents. Separate transmit and receive units. Sends 6 × 8-inch form in from 24 seconds to 3.3 minutes, depending on scan rate.
Max. Input Size—11 inches × any length (scans 6-inch-wide portion at a time)
Transmission
 Mode: analog (AM)
 Bandwidth: 3–16 kHz (nom.)
 Facility: dial net., or any suitable voice-grade or broadband facility, as required
Scan Resolution or Line Feed (Lines Per Inch)—96
Scan Rate (speed, in Lines Per Minute)—choice of 225, 450, or 1800
Scanner Type—flat-bed (slot-load); continuous feed
Recorder Type—flat-bed (roll-load); continuous feed
Recording Technique—electrolytic
Synchronization Method—automatic, via common power grid
Index of Cooperation—CCITT: 183 IEEE: 576
Dimensions
 Transmitter: 18″W × 25″D × 22″H
 Receiver: 14¼″W × 15″D × 9¼″H
Special Features
 Selectively scans any 6-inch-wide portion of input document.
 Can operate completely automatically.
Approx. Prices, as of November 1970
 Transmitter: $4500 (purchase); $140/mo.–$150/mo. (lease)
 Receiver: $2500–2750 (purchase); $100/mo.–$155/mo. (lease)

Fig. 8.36. Alden 600 (scanner left, recorder right)

Product Name (or Number)

COLOR FACSIMILE (COLORFAX)

Manufacturer—Matsushita Graphic Communication Systems, Inc., Tokyo, Japan (Distributed in U.S. by Datalog Division, Litton Industries)
General Description—Fax system for transmission of black and white or color pictures over voice-grade circuits. Sends "snapshot-size" black and white pictures in 2.3 minutes; color in 7 minutes.
Max. Input Size—$2\frac{3}{4} \times 3\frac{7}{8}$ inches
Transmission
  Mode: analog (AM)
  Bandwidth: 3 kHz (nom.)
  Facility: dial net., or any suitable voice-grade facility
Scan Resolution or Line Feed (Lines Per Inch)—120
Scan Rate (speed, in Lines Per Minute)—150
Scanner Type—cylinder (drum); single sheets
Recorder Type—fiber optic (plane)
Recording Technique—photographic, on Polaroid self-processing film
Synchronization Method—built-in frequency standard
Index of Cooperation—CCITT: 204 IEEE: 537
Dimensions
  Transmitter: $13\frac{1}{4}$"W × 8"D × 19"H
  Receiver: $26\frac{1}{2}$"W × $18\frac{1}{2}$"D × $16\frac{1}{2}$"H
Special Features
  Full-color recordings produced by line-sequential color filtering at scanner.
Approx. Prices, as of November 1970
  Transmitter: $5870 (purchase); $215/mo. (lease)
  Receiver: $10,900 (purchase); $425/mo. (lease)
    (Note: selling prices are F.O.B. Melville, N.Y.)

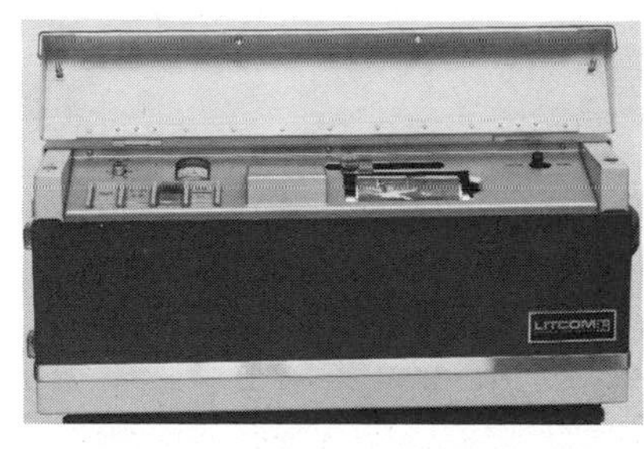

Fig. 8.37. "Colorfax" Transmitter

Fig. 8.38. "Colorfax" Receiver

Product Name (or Number)

COMPUTERPIX MICRO 60 TRANSMITTER

Manufacturer—Comfax/Computerpix Corporation, New York, N.Y.

General Description—Compression fax terminal for transmission of microfilmed documents and graphics. Accepts most standard microforms (reels, cartridges, cards, and fiche). Sends average page of information in approx. 1 minute via ordinary telephone circuits. Compatible with Comfax 60 transceiver (see Section 2) as the receiving terminal.

Max. Input Size—8½ × 14 inches, reduced 12× to 70× on microfilm

Transmission

Mode: special signal format (AM, FM)

Bandwidth: 3 kHz (nom.)

Facility: dial net., or any suitable voice-grade facility

Scan Resolution or Line Feed (Lines Per Inch)—equivalent of 96 or 166 on original (selectable)

Scan Rate (speed, in Lines Per Minute)—variable, 300 to 10,000 (average: 1100)

Scanner Type—electro-optical (CRT); microfilm remains stationary during scanning

Recorder Type—(not applicable; see Comfax 60 in Section 2)

Recording Technique—(not applicable; see Comfax 60 in Section 2)

Synchronization Method—transmitted signal

Index of Cooperation—CCITT: IEEE:

Dimensions—35½″W × 20½″D × 52″H

Special Features

Variable velocity redundancy reduction technique.

Uses advanced electronic scanning technique.

Built-in viewing screen provides enlarged image of input.

Input images may be negative or positive. Recorder will produce positive copy in either case.

(This unit is expected to be commercially available by sometime in 1971, at an estimated purchase price of $10,000.)

Product Name (or Number)

DACOM 212

Manufacturer—Dacom, Inc., Sunnyvale, Calif.
General Description—Two-speed compression fax system for high resolution applications, available in transceiver or individual unit configurations. Sends letter-size documents in from 2 to 5 minutes, depending on desired resolution.
Max. Input Size—$8\frac{1}{2} \times 14$ inches
Transmission
  Mode: digital
  Bandwidth: 3 kbits/sec. (nom.)
  Facility: dial net., or any suitable voice-grade facility
Scan Resolution or Line Feed (Lines Per Inch)—96/200
  (Resolution within scan line is approx. 200 LPI, regardless of line feed.)
Scan Rate (speed, in Lines Per Minute)—approx. 400
Scanner Type—cylinder (drum); single sheets
Recorder Type—cylinder (drum); single sheets
Recording Technique—electrosensitive
Synchronization Method—transmitted signal
Index of Cooperation—CCITT: 428/890 IEEE: 1344/2800
Dimensions—Transceiver: 24″W × 18″D × 48″H (includes cabinet)
Special Features
  Special redundancy reduction technique.
  Recorded copy can serve as stencil master or projection transparency.
Approx. Price, as of September 1970
  $13,000 (projected price for transceiver)

Product Name (or Number)

DEX (Decision EXpediter) V

Manufacturer—Graphic Sciences, Inc, Danbury, Conn.
General Description—High-resolution fax transceiver arranged for direct telephone coupling via Data Access Arrangement (DAA). Sends letter-size document in approx. 17 minutes.
Max. Input Size—9 × 14 inches
Transmission
  Mode: analog (AM)
  Bandwidth: 3 kHz (nom.)
  Facility: dial net., or any suitable voice-grade facility
Scan Resolution or Line Feed (Lines Per Inch)—176
Scan Rate (speed, in Lines Per Minute)—120
Scanner Type—cylinder (drum); auto-load, single sheets
Recorder Type—cylinder (drum); auto-load, single sheets
Recording Technique—electrothermal
Synchronization Method—transmitted signal
Index of Cooperation—CCITT: 532 IEEE: 1672
Dimensions—22″W × 15″D × 5″H
Special Features
  Selective scanning of portions of documents.
  Compact.
Approx. Price, as of November 1970
  $3900 (purchase); $125/mo. (lease)

Product Name (or Number)

FH-94R RECEIVER

Manufacturer—Nippon Electric Co., Ltd., Tokyo, Japan
General Description—Weather chart receiver for large charts. Receives complete $18\frac{7}{8} \times 22$-inch chart in from 9 to 36 minutes, depending on LPI/LPM combination.
Max. Input Size—$18\frac{7}{8} \times 22$ inches
Transmission
    Mode: two-level
    Bandwidth: 3 kHz (nom.)
    Facility: weather net. drop, or HF radio channel
Scan Resolution or Line Feed (Lines Per Inch)—48/96
Scan Rate (speed, in Lines Per Minute)—60/120
Scanner Type—(not applicable)
Recorder Type—flat-bed (roll-load); continuous feed
Recording Technique—electrolytic
Synchronization Method—built-in frequency standard
Index of Cooperation—CCITT: 288/576   IEEE: 904/1809
Dimensions—$29\frac{1}{2}''$W $\times$ 15″D $\times$ 22″H
Special Features
    Designed to include HF radio receiver as an option.
(Price data unavailable at time of writing.)

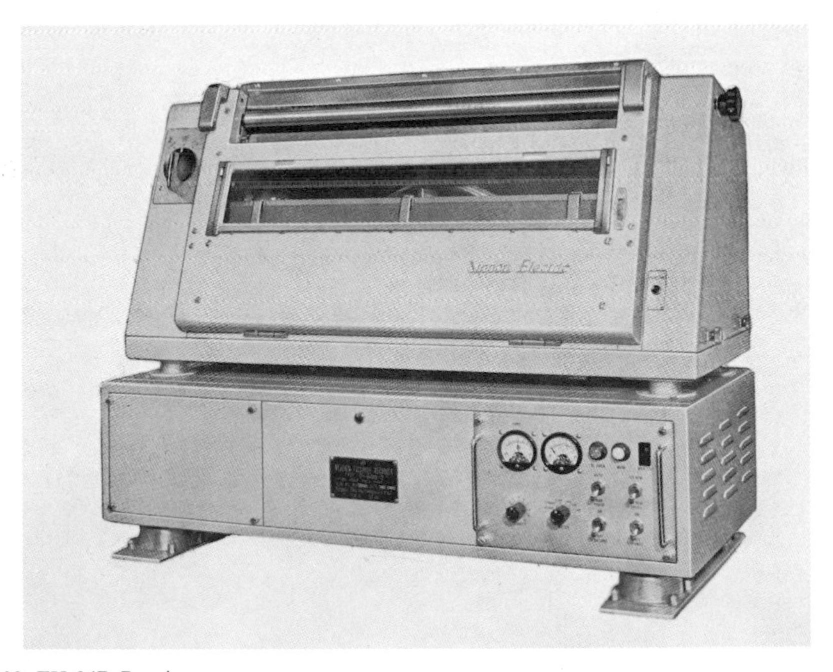

Fig. 8.39. FH-94R Receiver

Product Name (or Number)

FT-76

Manufacturer—Nippon Electric Co., Ltd., Tokyo, Japan

General Description—Newspaper page facsimile system for operation over broadband channels. Sends "standard" size newspaper page (16 × 23 inches) in from 7 to 10 minutes, depending on LPI/LPM combination.

Max. Input Size—16⅛ × 23 inches

Transmission

Mode: analog (AM) (digital optional)

Bandwidth: 120 kHz (nom.)

Facility: "supergroup," or comparable broadband facility

Scan Resolution or Line Feed (Lines Per Inch)—320/399

Scan Rate (speed, in Lines Per Minute)—600/750 (other speeds available up to 3000 LPM)

Scanner Type—cylinder (drum), single sheets

Recorder Type—cylinder (drum), single sheets

Recording Technique—photographic

Synchronization Method—frequency standard

Index of Cooperation—CCITT: 2380/2970 IEEE: 7473/9326

Dimensions—47¼″W × 27½″D × 47¼″H (transmitter or receiver)

Special Features

Automatic/unattended operation.

Recordings may be positive or negative; paper or film.

(Price data unavailable at time of writing.)

Product Name (or Number)

HELLFAX BS 110 MD RECORDER

Manufacturer—Dr.-Ing. Rudolf Hell, Kiel, West Germany

General Description—Continuous recorder for large-size weather charts. Records in ink on 18-inch-wide roll of ordinary paper. Records 18 × 22-inch chart in from 9 to 36 minutes, depending on LPI/LPM combination.

Max. Input Size—(not applicable)

Transmission

Mode: analog or two-level (AM)

Bandwidth: 3 kHz (nom.)

Facility: any suitable voice-grade wire or radio link

Scan Resolution or Line Feed (Lines Per Inch)—48/96

Scan Rate (speed, in Lines Per Minute)—60/90/120

Scanner Type—(not applicable)

Recorder Type—flat-bed (roll-load); continuous feed

Recording Technique—wet ink offset on ordinary paper

Synchronization Method—frequency standard

Index of Cooperation—CCITT: 288/576 IEEE: 904/1809

Dimensions

Receiver: 33½″W × 20″D × 17″H

Companion power unit: 20″W × 11″D × 8″H

Special Features

Provision for tuning in on transmission from the various international weather services.

Unattended reception.

Records on ordinary paper.

Approx. Price, as of November 1970

$4500 F.O.B. Kiel

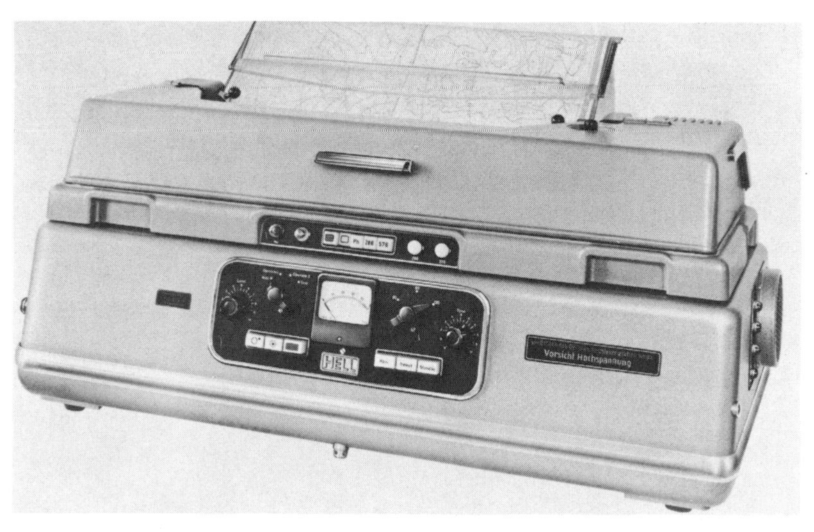

Fig. 8.40. Hellfax BS 110 MD Recorder

Product Name (or Number)

HELLFAX FA 124 TRANSMITTER

Manufacturer—Dr.-Ing. Rudolf Hell, Kiel, West Germany
General Description—Fax transmitter for small weather charts. Sends $8\frac{1}{4} \times$ 12-inch chart in 7 or 10.5 minutes, depending on scan rate.
Max. Input Size—$8\frac{1}{2} \times$ any length
Transmission
 Mode: analog (AM)
 Bandwidth: 3 kHz (nom.)
 Facility: any suitable voice-grade wire or radio link
Scan Resolution or Line Feed (Lines Per Inch)—108
Scan Rate (speed, in Lines Per Minute)—120 or 180
Scanner Type—flat-bed (slot-load); continuous feed
Recorder Type—(not applicable)
Recording Technique—(not applicable)
Synchronization Method—frequency standard
Index of Cooperation—CCITT: 288 IEEE: 904
Dimensions
 Transmitter: 19″W × 16″D × $7\frac{1}{2}$″H
 Companion sync unit: 20″W × 11″D × 8″H
Special Features
 Lightweight: 27 lbs.
 Can operate completely automatically.
Approx. Price, as of November 1970
 \$3000 F.O.B. Kiel

Product Name (or Number)

HELLFAX WF 205 TRANSMITTER

Manufacturer—Dr.-Ing. Rudolf Hell, Kiel, West Germany

General Description—Fax transmitter for large-size weather charts. Sends 18 × 22-inch chart in from 9 to 36 minutes, depending on LPI/LPM combination.

Max. Input Size—18 × 22 inches

Transmission

Mode: analog or two-level (AM)

Bandwidth: 3 kHz (nom.)

Facility: any suitable voice-grade wire or radio link

Scan Resolution or Line Feed (Lines Per Inch)—48/96

Scan Rate (speed, in Lines Per Minute)—60/90/120/ (180 opt.)

Scanner Type—cylinder (drum); single sheets

Recorder Type—(not applicable)

Recording Technique—(not applicable)

Synchronization Method—built-in frequency standard

Index of Cooperation—CCITT: 288/576 IEEE: 904/1809

Dimensions—33½″W × 18½″D × 18½″H

Special Features

Adjustable to three carrier frequencies.

Receiver starts automatically.

Approx. Price, as of November 1970

$6000 F.O.B.Kiel

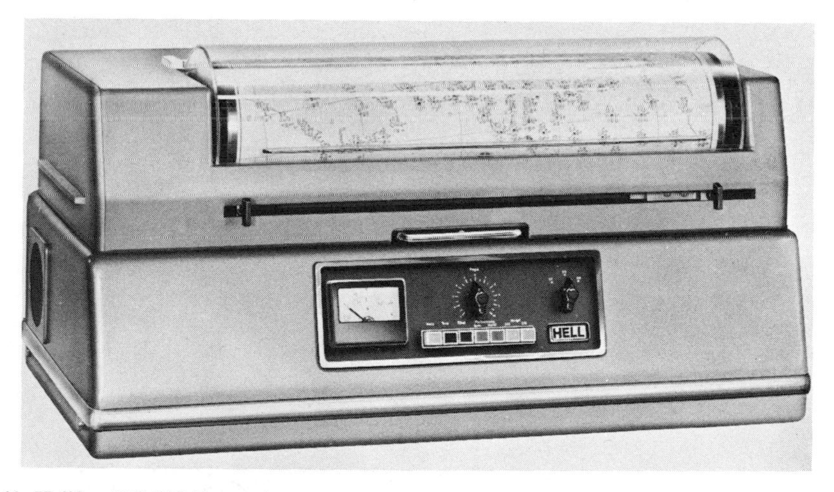

Fig. 8.41. Hellfax WF 205 Transmitter

Product Name (or Number)

HELL-PRESSFAX

Manufacturer—Dr.-Ing. Rudolf Hell, Kiel, West Germany

General Description—Transceiver for master proofs of newspaper pages. Sends 16 × 23-inch proofs in from 2 to 40 minutes via broadband facilities, the speed depending on the LPI/LPM combination.

Max. Input Size—$17\frac{3}{4} \times 25\frac{1}{2}$ inches

Transmission

 Mode: analog (AM) (2-level compressed signal optional)

 Bandwidth: 48 kHz to 1 MHz (3 kHz for special applications)

 Facility: "group," "supergroup," or TV

Scan Resolution or Line Feed (Lines Per Inch)—100 to 1000

Scan Rate (speed, in Lines Per Minute)—300 to 3600

Scanner Type—cylinder (drum); single sheets

Recorder Type—cylinder (drum); single sheets

Recording Technique—photographic

Synchronization Method—built-in frequency standard

Index of Cooperation—CCITT: 828–8280 IEEE: 2600–26,000

Dimensions—58″W × 26″D × 52″H

Special Features

 Automatic/unattended operation.

 Recordings may be positive or negative; paper or film.

 Bandwidth compression option reduces transmit time by 50%.

 Also available in separate transmitter/receiver configuration.

Approx. Price, as of November 1970—$62,500

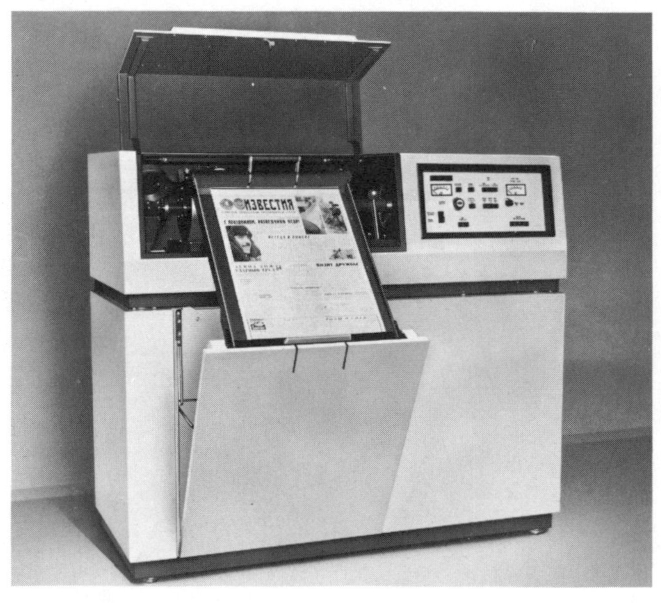

Fig. 8.42. Hell-Pressfax Transceiver

Product Name (or Number)

K-500/1 COLOR EQUIPMENT

Manufacturer—Muirhead & Co., Ltd., Beckenham, Kent, England
General Description—Color facsimile system for operation over voice-grade circuits. Separate transmit and receive units. Sends 8 × 10-inch color print (plus 2-inch caption) in from 13 to 18 minutes, depending on transmission mode.
Max. Input Size—8 × 12 inches
Transmission
Mode: analog (AM or FM)
Bandwidth: 3 kHz (nom.)
Facility: Schedule II, or other suitable voice-grade facilities
Scan Resolution or Line Feed (Lines Per Inch)—92.1 or 100
Scan Rate (speed, in Lines Per Minute) 45 for FM; 60 for AM
(*Note:* 45 LPM is actually 135 LPM, with three successive scans per line.)
Scanner Type—cylinder (drum); single sheets
Recorder Type—flat-bed (roll-load); continuous feed
Recording Technique—photographic
Synchronization Method—built-in frequency standard
Index of Cooperation—CCITT: 352 IEEE: 1105
Dimensions (approx.)
Transmitter: 20″W × 18″D × 12″H
Receiver: 28″W × 22″D × 50″H
Special Features
Recorded copies automatically cut to size; put into cassette for processing.
Approx. Prices, as of November 1970
Transmitter: $6000
Receiver: $14,000

Product Name (or Number)

MERCURY IV

Manufacturer—Muirhead & Co., Ltd., Beckenham, Kent, England

General Description—Mobile fax system for operation over vehicle radio communication systems. Recorder mounts beneath dashboard of vehicle. Sends 4.5-inch-wide graphic materials (including photos) at 4 inches per minute.

Max. Input Size—4.5 inches × any length

Transmission

Mode: analog (FM)

Bandwidth: 3 kHz (nom.)

Facility: any standard vehicle radio communication system

Scan Resolution or Line Feed (Lines Per Inch)—90

Scan Rate (speed, in Lines Per Minute)—375

Scanner Type—flat-bed (slot-load); continuous feed

Recorder Type—flat-bed (roll-load); continuous feed

Recording Technique—electrolytic

Synchronization Method—built-in frequency standard

Index of Cooperation—CCITT: 122 IEEE: 383

Dimensions

Transmitter:	16½″W × 17¾″D × 10″H
Receiver electronics:	12¼″W × 10½″D × 6½″H
Recorder:	10½″W × 5½″D × 3¼″H

Special Features

Receiver electronics mounted separately from recorder in vehicle.

Voice and pictures can be sent simultaneously over same channel.

Transmitter can serve any number of vehicles simultaneously.

Unattended reception.

Approx. Prices, as of November 1970

Transmitter: (est.) $1800

Receiver: (est.) $1000

Product Name (or Number)

MERCURY V

Manufacturer—Muirhead & Co., Ltd., Beckenham, Kent, England
General Description—Ground-to-air fax system for operation over standard HF radiotelephone channels. Sends 4-inch-wide graphic materials at approx. 4.25″ per minute. May be used air-to-air and air-to-ground as well.
Max. Input Size—4 inches × any length
Transmission
  Mode: two-level (SCFM)
  Bandwidth: 3 kHz (nom.)
  Facility: standard HF radio-telephone facilities
Scan Resolution or Line Feed (Lines Per Inch)—90
Scan Rate (speed, in Lines Per Minute)—380
Scanner Type—flat-bed (slot-load); continuous feed
Recorder Type—flat-bed (roll-load); continuous feed
Recording Technique—electrolytic
Synchronization Method—transmitted signal
Index of Cooperation—CCITT: 113   IEEE: 355
Dimensions
  Transmitter: 16½″W × 18⅛″D × 10″H
  Receiver Electronics: 12¾″W × 12″D × 6¼″H
  Recorder 12¾″W × 12″D × 6¼″H
Special Features
  Receiver electronics mounted separately from recorder.
  Voice and pictures can be sent simultaneously over same channel.
  Transmitter can serve any number of receivers simultaneously.
  Unattended reception.
(Price data not available at time of writing.)

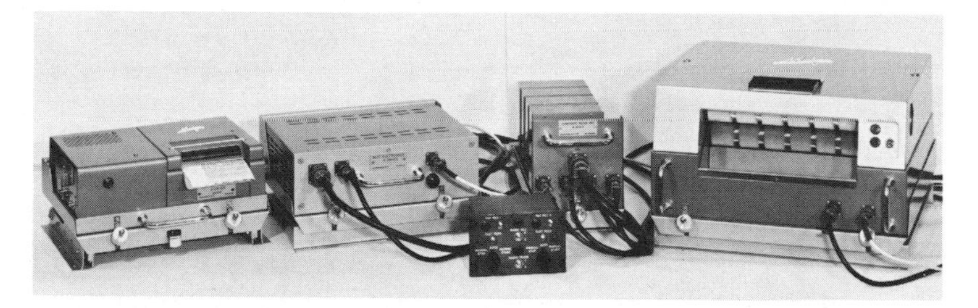

Fig. 8.43. Muirhead Mercury V equipment

Product Name (or Number)

NEWSPAPER PAGE FACSIMILE SYSTEM

Manufacturer—Muirhead & Co., Ltd., Beckenham, Kent, England
General Description—Fax system for transmission and high-quality reproduction of newspaper page proofs. Sends one page in from 2 to 40 minutes, depending on LPI/LPM combination.
Max. Input Size—17 × 24 inches
Transmission
Mode: analog (AM); digital
Bandwidth: 48 kHz to 1 MHz; 50 kbits/sec. to 1.34 Mbits/sec.
Facility: "group" or TV; broadband digital facilities
Scan Resolution or Line Feed (Lines Per Inch)—300–1000
Scan Rate (speed, in Lines Per Minute)—300–3600
Scanner Type—cylinder (drum); single sheets
Recorder Type—cylinder (drum); single sheets
Recording Technique—photographic
Synchronization Method—built-in frequency standard, each terminal
Index of Cooperation—CCITT: 2400–8000 IEEE: 7536–25,120
Dimensions
Mechanical unit: 34″W × 28″D × 45″H
Electronic console: 32½″W × 26″D × 58″H
Applies to both send and receive terminals
Special Features
Automatic/unattended operation.
Recordings may be positive or negative; paper or film.
Approx. Price, as of November 1970
$30,000 to $35,000 per terminal

Fig. 8.44. Newspaper Page Facsimile System Transmitter

Fig. 8.45. Newspaper Page Facsimile System Receiver

Product Name (or Number)

PRESSFAX 501

Manufacturer—Matsushita Graphic Communication Systems, Inc., Tokyo, Japan (modified and distributed by Datalog Division, Litton Industries)

General Description—Fax system for transmission and high-quality reproduction of newspaper page proofs. Sends one page in from 2.5 to 33 minutes, depending on LPI/LPM combination.

Max. Input Size—$16\frac{1}{2} \times 23$ inches

Transmission

Mode: analog (AM); digital

Bandwidth: 48 kHz to 1 MHz; 50 kbits/sec. to 1.34 Mbits/sec.

Facility: "group," "supergroup," or TV; broadband digital facilities

Scan Resolution or Line Feed (Lines Per Inch)—300/400/600

Scan Rate (speed, in Lines Per Minute)—300/400/2000

Scanner Type—cylinder (drum); single sheets

Recorder Type—cylinder (drum); single sheets

Recording Technique—photographic

Synchronization Method—built-in frequency standard, each terminal

Index of Cooperation—CCITT; 2302, 3069, 4604 IEEE: 7232, 9642, 13,463

Dimensions

Mechanical unit: $44\frac{1}{2}''$W $\times$ $27''$D $\times$ $47\frac{1}{2}''$H

Electronic unit: $24''$W $\times$ $27''$D $\times$ $47\frac{1}{2}''$H

Applies to both send and receive terminals

Special Features

Automatic/unattended operation.

Recordings may be positive or negative; paper or film.

Approx. Price, as of November 1970

$30,000 per terminal

Fig. 8.46. Matsushita/Datalog Pressfax 501 Transmitter

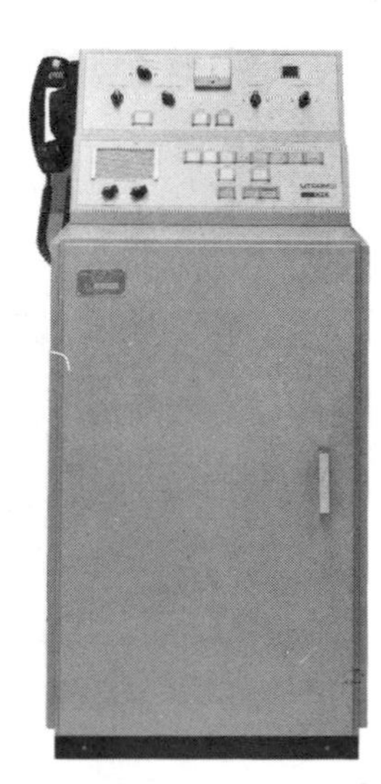

Fig. 8.47. Pressfax 501 Electronic Console (send station)

Product Name (or Number)

RADARFAX

Manufacturer—Datalog Division, Litton Industries, Melville, N.Y.
General Description—Records image of weather radarscope display transmitted by slow-scan TV. Full frame is recorded in 100 seconds.
Max. Input Size—(not applicable)
Transmission
  Mode: analog (AM) (FM alt.)
  Bandwidth: 3 kHz (nom.)
  Facility: dial net., or any suitable voice-grade facility
Scan Resolution or Line Feed (Lines Per Inch)—91
Scan Rate (speed, in Lines Per Minute)—480
Scanner Type—(not applicable)
Recorder Type—flat-bed (roll-load); continuous feed
Recording Technique—electrolytic
Synchronization Method—frequency standard (separate)
Index of Cooperation—CCITT: 264   IEEE: 829
Dimensions—$21\frac{1}{4}$"W $\times$ $17\frac{7}{8}$"D $\times$ $6\frac{1}{2}$"H
Special Features
  Completely automatic reception.
Approx. Prices, as of November 1970
  Receiver: $2825 (purchase); $128/mo. (lease)
  Frequency standard: $600 (purchase); $15/mo. (lease)

Fig. 8.48. Radarfax

Product Name (or Number)

WEATHERFAX LD-40 RECORDER

Manufacturer—Matsushita Graphic Communication Systems, Inc., Tokyo, Japan (distributed in U.S. by Datalog Division, Litton Industries.)
General Description—weather chart recorder
Max. Input Size—(not applicable)
Transmission
Mode: LD-40 W: AM (wire); LD-40 R: FSK (radio)
Bandwidth: 3 kHz (nom.); 3 kHz (nom.)
Facility: weather net. drop, or conditioned voice channel: HF radio channel
Scan Resolution or Line Feed (Lines Per Inch)—96
Scan Rate (speed, in Lines Per Minute)—120/240
Scanner Type—(not applicable)
Recorder Type—flat-bed (roll-load); continuous feed
Recording Technique—electrostatic
Synchronization Method—frequency standard
Index of Cooperation—CCITT: 576 IEEE: 1809
Dimensions—28¾"W × 18¾"D × 19¼"H
Special Features
Unattended reception.
Approx. Price, as of November 1970
$4800 (purchase); $140/mo. (lease)

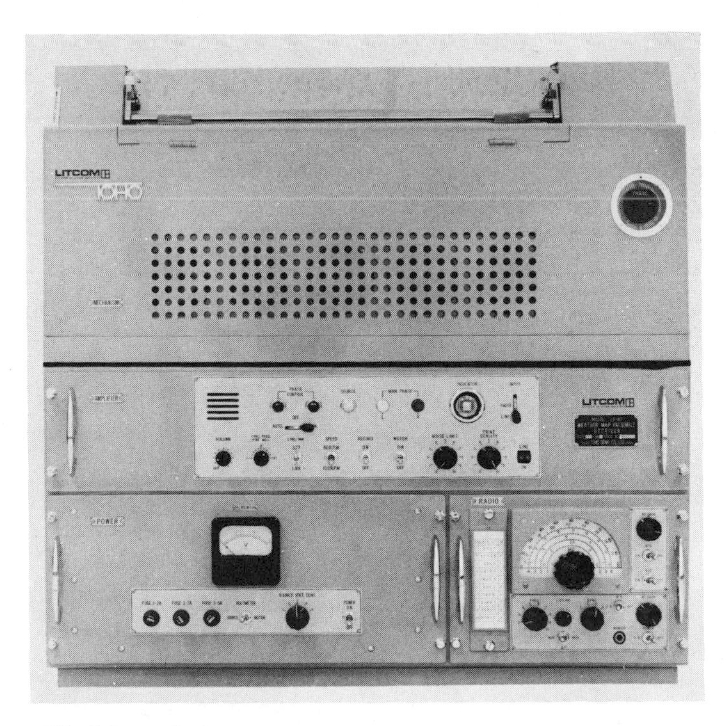

Fig. 8.49. Weatherfax LD-40 Recorder

Product Name (or Number)

WEATHERFAX RJ-6 RECORDER

Manufacturer—Datalog Division, Litton Industries, Melville, N.Y.
General Description—Weather chart recorder. Records high-resolution, small format ($8\frac{1}{2}$-inch) weather charts at about $\frac{5}{8}$ inch a minute.
Max. Input Size—(not applicable)
Transmission
    Mode: analog (AM)
    Bandwidth: 3 kHz (nom.)
    Facility: weather net. "drop" or conditioned voice channel
Scan Resolution or Line Feed (Lines Per Inch)—213
Scan Rate (speed, in Lines Per Minute)—120/240
Scanner Type—(not applicable)
Recorder Type—flat-bed (roll-load); continuous feed
Recording Technique—electrolytic
Synchronization Method—frequency standard (separate)
Index of Cooperation—CCITT: 576 IEEE: 1809
Dimensions—$21\frac{1}{4}$"W × $17\frac{7}{8}$"D × $6\frac{1}{2}$"H
Special Features
    Completely automatic reception.
Approx. Prices, as of November 1970
    Receiver: $2825 (purchase); $128/mo. (lease)
    Frequency standard: $600 (purchase); $15/mo. (lease)

Fig. 8.50. Weatherfax RJ-6 Recorder

Product Name (or Number)

ZETFAX

Manufacturer—Dr.-Ing. Rudolf Hell, Kiel, West Germany

General Description—Fax system for messages graphically formed on paper tape. Messages are handwritten in a "window" on the transmitter. Sends 1-inch-wide messages at $1\frac{1}{16}$ inches a minute.

Max. Input Size—1 × 6 inches (max. window size) (Input medium is integral to the transmitter: 328 feet of paper tape per loading.)

Transmission

Mode: analog (AM)

Bandwidth: 3 kHz (nom.)

Facility: dial net., or any suitable voice-grade facility

Scan Resolution or Line Feed (Lines Per Inch)—102

Scan Rate (speed, in Lines Per Minute)—920

Scanner Type—flat-bed (roll-load); continuous feed

Recorder Type—flat-bed (roll-load); continuous feed

Recording Technique—ink on paper tape

Synchronization Method—automatic, via common power grid

Index of Cooperation—CCITT: approx. 32 IEEE: approx. 102

Dimensions

Transmitter: $14\frac{1}{4}$″W × $13\frac{1}{2}$″D × $5\frac{1}{2}$″H

Receiver: 8″W × 12″D × 6″H

Special Features

Compact.

Unattended reception.

Records on ordinary paper.

Approx. Prices, as of November 1970

Transmitter: $1500 F.O.B. Kiel

Receiver: $1200 F.O.B. Kiel

9 *The Future*

HAVING examined the present status of the facsimile art from practically all angles, we can now round out the picture by looking ahead at what may be in store for it in the next decade or so. A knowledge of future possibilities is always helpful in testing the validity of present decisions.

We did some speculating on fax's future in Chapter 6, but only from an economic standpoint. This chapter will focus on technological advances and, to a certain extent, on prospective new applications.

SPEED

One thing that can be said with absolute confidence about tomorrow's typical facsimile system is that it will be a much faster system than today's. As this is being written, there is a vigorous race going on among manufacturers of fax terminal gear to capture a bigger share of the market (or to retain their present share) by offering the fastest system at the lowest cost. Some are going the "compression" route, employing special electronic techniques to re-format the transmitted signal so that more efficient use is made of channel space; others are merely reducing resolution to permit a purely mechanical speed-up. Both are acceptable approaches, depending, of course, on the customer's end requirements and on how he balances desired output quality against finances.

Unfortunately, as a result of this race, we see the clashing of two equally desirable trends. On the one hand there is the growing popularity of the "detached terminal" approach to fax communication: the desk-top transceiver coupled to an existing telephone set and utilizing the switched voice network to communicate with other, compatible, terminals within a wide radius. And, on the other hand, there is the increasing speed of transmission, which—desirable trend that it is, per se—has resulted in the further deterioration of an already grim standardization picture. Without standards, phone-coupled fax gear of different makes is not likely to be compatible, and so the use of such gear, with all of its valuable potential, is handicapped.

We can only hope that the situation resolves itself in due time, which it undoubtedly will. The manufacturers, themselves, recognize the problem, and some have already expressed a willingness to get together and seek a solution. But there also has to be a willingness to make concessions. *Post facto* standardization invariably requires sacrifices.

The development of high-speed facsimile systems dates back many years. RCA's *Ultrafax*® for example, which combines the technologies of fax and TV to achieve transmission speeds of 480 pages a minute, or better, dates back to the 1940s. Other high-speed systems have been developed since then, and today there are several—though none as fast as Ultrafax—that are available commercially (Xerox's LDX® and A. B. Dick's Videograph, to mention just two).

With the promised extension of true digital transmission facilities by common carriers, the availability of terminal gear capable of data compression ratios in the area of 10:1 will fast become a practical reality. Speeds of a page per half-minute over ordinary telephone lines, at prices that the average facsimile customer can afford, are by no means an exaggerated forecast, nor very remote in terms of time.

FAX IN THE HOME

The idea of a fax receiver in every home, automatically receiving printed newspapers by radio, is generally regarded as having died and been entombed at about the time commercial TV had begun to dominate the postwar American consumer market of the late 1940s. But apparently it is still very much alive in some quarters, both here and abroad.

For some time now, at least three large Japanese electronics firms have been engaged in the development of inexpensive fax recorders for the purpose. The efforts of one of the firms, Toshiba, in collaboration with the Tokyo newspaper *Asahi Shimbun,* culminated in the public demonstration of an experimental system at the United Nations Pavilion of Japan's *Expo 70* in March 1970.

The Toshiba system, designated "AT3," features a receiver the size of a conventional TV set, designed to market for about $100 (or the Japanese equivalent thereof). The scan resolution is 8 lines per millimeter—about 200 LPI—and it takes five minutes to receive a full, electrostatically recorded, 12 × 18-inch newspaper page. Present scheduling calls for commercial licensing of the system for use in homes and places of business by about 1975.

In this country, authorities in the fields of electronic graphic systems and information retrieval are predicting that home facsimile systems will become a commercial reality sometime during the 1970s. However, the purpose of such systems will not be merely to receive newspapers, but to provide a variety of other services as well, such as the dissemination of financial and medical data to appropriate professionals, library research services, and, in general, the receipt (or exchange) of anything presently distributed in printed form.

One obstacle to the implementation of such systems is the question of how authors, publishers, libraries, etc., will be reimbursed for the materials so disseminated. How, for example, will the copyright situation be handled when such items as the pages of published books and magazines are electronically distributed by facsimile—in some cases to many homes and offices simultaneously?

But, while there are obstacles to cope with, there are also some intriguing developments taking shape in the transmission area that promise to greatly enhance the technical and economic feasibility of such systems. One is the steady growth of CATV (Community Antenna TV), or "cable TV," as it is sometimes called. Another is a system that permits fax signals to fill the "dead space" represented by blanking pulses in a TV signal.

The significance of CATV is that it is expected eventually to provide a supplementary communications network that will, in a sense, take up where the present commercial networks leave off. As a purchased service, CATV represents a kind of compromise between the free reception of sponsored broadcasts on the one hand, and the leasing of a private communications link on the other. Authorities on information dissemination see CATV as having the potential for becoming a kind of general information "pipeline," carrying such diversified materials as mail, library books, newspapers, magazines, press releases, and information distributed according to subscriber profiles. Speculation is that, by the early 1980s, such materials will be receivable in the home or office at the rate of a page a second, at costs comparable to 1970 postal rates.[1]

As for the "piggybacking" of fax signals on commercial TV blanking pulses, systems to accomplish this have already been perfected by RCA in this country, and by Philips of the Netherlands and Matsushita of Japan.

The RCA-developed system is capable of producing electrostatic recordings at the rate of 10 seconds a page (at something less than 100 LPI resolution). The Philips system boasts somewhat higher transmission speeds and does its recording by photographing a CRT image. The Matsushita system is slower than the other two—30 seconds to a minute per page—and records on sensitized paper, using a special, fiber-optic CRT. As of this writing, all three systems have been successfully tested and are practically ready for implementation.

[1] According to a recent article in *Inforum,* a publication of the Information Industry Association. See reference, "Knowledge . . . ," at end of chapter.

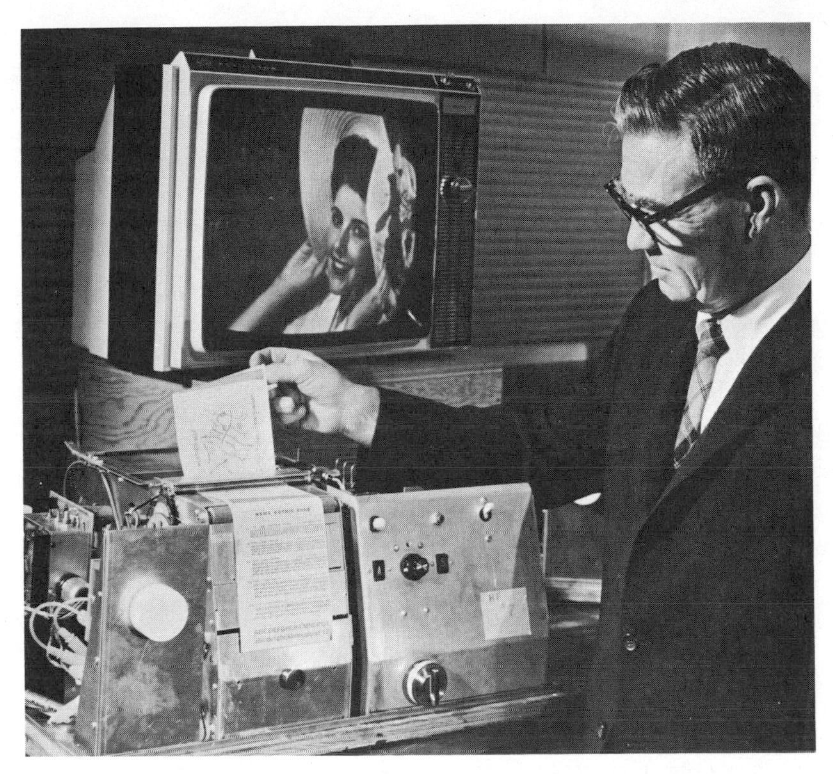

Fig. 9.1. RCA experimental home facsimile system sends fax signals in "spurts" over commercial TV channels during the brief blanking intervals that occur every $\frac{1}{60}$th of a second. An electrostatic graphic recording emerges from the fax receiver while a TV show, broadcast simultaneously over the same channel, proceeds without interruption. (Courtesy RCA.)

One particularly significant thing about these developments—the TV blanking pulse technique and the evolution of a CATV information network—is that they involve communications services that are already widely and economically available to home owners and businessmen. Moreover, they both connote more efficient use of existing facilities, which should have a favorable effect on economics.

So, in view of these several promising developments, and in spite of the various obstacles, it is a safe bet that fax will eventually join radio, TV, and hi-fi as a home entertainment and information medium, and possibly even as a supplement to the telephone as a communications medium.

FAX IN COLOR

The earliest example of color facsimile that has come to the author's attention is to be found in the frontispiece to an article by Dr. H. E. Ives, et al., in the April 1925 issue of *The Bell System Technical Journal.* It shows a fax-recorded reproduction of a colorful painting depicting the installation of a cross-country telephone line. It is actually a composite of three separate fax recordings of the same picture, each produced with a different color filter in the scanner's optical path. The process was crude and time-consuming, but the result is impressive.[2]

The same basic technique, automated somewhat, was later used by Finch Telecommunications in prototype fax equipment specially designed to reproduce pictures in color. In 1939 the Associated Press transmitted a full color picture via its Wirephoto network, and in August 1945 a color photograph of Truman, Stalin, and Atlee at the Potsdam Conference in Germany was successfully transmitted by radio from Europe to Washington, D.C.

Color facsimile has not enjoyed anything resembling spectacular growth, but its use by the news wire services has gradually increased over the years, and equipment for the purpose is now commercially available to anyone who has a need for it and can afford it. There is, for example, the equipment manufactured by Matsushita Graphic Communication Systems (formerly Toho-Denki) of Japan, which records by modulated light on Polaroid self-processing color film. It is marketed in this country by Litton's Datalog Division (formerly Litcom) and is called *Colorfax.* Muirhead of England has also produced color facsimile equipment, primarily for use by the news wire services.

As for the future of color facsimile, a lot depends on the degree to which speed of transmission can be economically increased, or more efficient use can be made of transmission channel capacity. There are, at present, basically two ways of sending pictures in color by facsimile, both of which have in common the technique of separating colors by optical filtration (which is fundamental to all color reproduction processes) at the scanner.

One way is to send the three primary colors sequentially, which, without degrading resolution, requires three times the transmission time necessary for straight black-and-white reproduction (or four times, if black is included). The other way is to send separate signals for each color simultaneously, which, without degrading resolution or increasing transmission time, requires a broader bandwidth channel.

Thus the key to the success of color facsimile—as it is to the continued success of the fax art in general—is *increased transmission efficiency.* And the prospects of that, as previously discussed, are good. If by 1985 we can realize the prediction of black and white copy at the rate of a page a second on a home receiver that everyone can afford, let us hope that we are not so spoiled by then as to reject a slight slowdown—to maybe three seconds a page—as an expedient for color reception.

Of course there is also the possibility that by the end of the present decade someone will have adapted present color TV techniques to facsimile, per-

[2] See reference, "Ives . . . ," at end of chapter.

mitting the transmission of color within the same bandwidth and at the same speed as black and white. In any event, it is reasonable to expect that both the economic and technological advances necessary to strengthen the feasibility of color facsimile are forthcoming, and that it is but a matter of time before color facsimile becomes commonplace.

THE QUESTION OF PAPER

No discussion of the future—of anything—is complete nowadays without some thought being given to the implications of the new ecological awareness. Pollution is a growing issue, and one of the things frequently cited as an environmental pollutant is paper. Not only does its production result in the pollution of streams in the vicinity of the paper mills, but its increasing consumption has resulted in the so-called "paper explosion," a side effect of which has been the increasing pollution of earth and air through disposal of paper waste.

In a typical application, a present-day fax recorder is a consumer of paper—or a "generator" of it if you view it from within the office environment. We can, of course, rationalize that, as a substitute for mail, fax eliminates the need for envelopes and stamps, and thus reduces paper waste. But, being realistic about it, the probability that the war on pollution will intensify with the passage of time, and that the use of paper may diminish as a result of it, raises a question of what new form, or forms, facsimile recording may take in the years ahead.

There are already very fine lines separating the facsimile process from certain other information retrieval/reproduction processes, notably Computer Output Microfilming (COM) and video recording.

COM is the outputting of manipulated, computer-stored data in the form of visual images on microfilm. The device that produces the film consists basically of a CRT, on whose face symbols and lines are reproduced in response to the computer's coded output signal; and a camera, which photographs the face of the CRT. There is, of course, also the logic necessary to translate a rapid stream of ON-OFF pulses, as outputted by the computer, into properly constructed and accurately positioned symbols on the face of the CRT.

A COM device has many of the attributes of a fax recorder, and can, in fact, be arranged to function as one. We therefore have microfilm as one possible substitute for paper in a fax system. It is a strong possibility in any event because of its steadily expanding use as an information storage and distribution medium, as was pointed out in Chapter 2.

Video tape recording, usually associated mainly with commercial TV broadcasting, has also proved itself an effective information storage and retrieval technique. A TV camera can be arranged to "snap" a picture of a subject by going through just one complete "framing" cycle (one complete raster) and recording its output as a kind of latent image on magnetic tape. In this manner many documents can be stored sequentially within a relatively short length of tape.

Retrieving a specific video-recorded document is then a matter of selecting the segment of tape containing the desired frame, and reading out the recorded data into a *buffer* (a recycling magnetic recorder). The buffer functions to "hold" the selected image on a CRT screen for as long a period as is necessary for viewing or reading—or reproduction.

Whether either of these techniques will influence the design of future fax systems is a matter for conjecture. However, there is a strong possibility that the fax gear produced only a few years from now will bear little resemblance to that which is currently typical. The world is changing at an accelerating rate, and, in order to survive, people, things, and systems will have to change with it.

BIBLIOGRAPHY

Bond, D. S., and V. J. Duke, "Ultrafax," *RCA Review,* Vol. 10, Mar. 1949, pp. 99–115.

"Facsimile Paper?" (item), *Industrial Research,* Aug. 1967, p. 29.

"Filling the Blanks" (item), *Electronics,* Nov. 13, 1967, p. 305.

Ives, H. E., et al., "The Transmission of Pictures Over Telephone Lines," *The Bell System Technical Journal,* April 1925, pp. 187–214.

"Japanese Firms Develop Home Facsimile Prototypes" (item), *Business Automation,* Nov. 1969, p. 141.

"Japan's Telenewspaper Shown at Expo 70" (item), *Graphic Communications Weekly,* Mar. 31, 1970, p. 7.

Jones, C. R., *Facsimile,* New York, Murray Hill Books, 1949, pp. 105–106, 282–286 (color facsimile).

Kane, J. N., *Famous First Facts* (3rd ed.), New York, H. W. Wilson, 1964, p. 500.

"Knowledge Industry Report" (as reprinted in *Inforum,* a publication of Information Industry Association, Mar. 1970, pp. 3–4.)

Index

Page numbers in italics indicate picture only.

A. B. Dick Co., 220, 257
Acme Newspictures, 8
Acme (Telectronix), 8, 9
Acoustic coupling. *See* Couplers, phone
Acuity. *See* Visual acuity
Adaptive encoding, 113
Ader, Clement, 3
Addressograph-Multigraph Corp., 11, 111, 218
Alden (Electronic & Impulse Recording Equipment Co.), 10, 42, 58, 124, 147–148, 232–236
Alden equipment (descriptions), 232–236
Alfax paper, 58
Allen D. Cardwell Electronics Production Corp., 10
AM. *See* Amplitude Modulation
American Telephone & Telegraph (AT&T), 4, 6, 7–8, 83
Amplification, 54–55, 66–67, *68*
  direct coupling, 67, *68*, 87
Amplitude Modulation (AM), 82, 93, 137, 157
  single sideband, 84, 157
  vestigial sideband, 84, 130–131, 157, 179
  double sideband, 98, 157, 180
Analog Signal, 4, 34, 41, 79, 106, 138
Analog-to-digital conversion, 115, 137–141, 170, 174, 188
ANPA Research Institute, 31*n*
Aperture, scanning, 49–50
  shape of, 124–125, 130
Aperture distortion, 124
Archival (quality), 58
Asahi Shimbun, 21, 257
Associated Press (AP), 7–8, 13, 36, 101, 188–190, 260
Atmospheric disturbances, 91, 100
"AT3" system, 257
Automatic feed, 32–33, 42
Automatic loading, 52
Automatic photographic recorder, 14, 65, 156
Automatic picture transmission (APT), 101
Automatic retrieval. *See* Information retrieval
Automation. *See* Facsimile automation

Bain, Alexander, 2, 58
Bain system, 2, 3, *4*, *5*, 58, 69, 74
Baird, John, 1
Bakewell, Frederick, 3
Balancing network, 95
Bandcom, 41, 210
Bandwidth compression, 16, 103, 109–110, 180
  See also Data compression and Redundancy Reduction
Bar Harbor, Maine, 3
Bartholomew and Macfarlane, 4
Bartlane system, 4
Baseband, 81, 106, 132, 139, 157
Becker, F. K., 147 *n*
Bell System Technical Journal, The, 6*n*, 147*n*, 259
Bell Telephone Laboratories (Bell Labs), 6, 8, 109, 136, 147–148
Bell (Telephone) System, 8, 10, 105, 106, 157, 160, *166–169*
Bits (binary digits)
  vs cycles, 139–140
  vs image elements, 122–123
"Blanking" period, 131, 258–259
Britain, 1, 3
Broadband Exchange service (WU), 99–100, 157, 159
Broadcasting. *See* Facsimile broadcasting
Buffer, 110, 112, 113, 114, 262
"Burn-off" process. *See* Recording, electrothermal
Business applications. *See* Facsimile in business
Business Week, 21

Carrier swing, 86, 105
Carrier systems, 91–92, 92*n*, 101
Carson, John R., 83
Caselli, Giovanni, 3
Cathode ray techniques, 40, *53*, 55–56, 61, 62, 63, 261–262
Cathode Ray Tubes (CRTs), 35, 53, 55–56, 61, 62, 63, *111*, 261–262
CATV, 258–259
Change orders, transmission of, 22
Character vs word legibility. *See* Legibility
Chicago *Tribune*, the, 9
CIWP (Computer Interface Wirephoto), 188–190
Clock, electric, 2
Color discrimination, 48, 133, 138, 149
  See also Spectral sensitivity
Color facsimile. *See* Facsimile in color
Colorfax, 237, 260
Comfax-Computerpix (Corp.), 11, 42, 111, 211, 238
  facsimile system, 42, 111, 211, 238
Comfax 60, 211
Comité Consultatif International des Radio Communications (CCIR), 181, 183, 184, 186, 189
Comité Consultatif International Télégraphique et Téléphonique (CCITT), 181–184, *185*, 186, 187, 189
Commercial equipment. *See* Facsimile equipment, commercial
Common carriers, 41, 97, 101, 102, 116–117, 154, 158, 160, 170, 172–173
Communication, facsimile. *See* Facsimile
Communications, graphic. *See* Facsimile
Compatibility, 37, 172, 256–257
Computer, 27, 29, 107, 110, 261
  mini-, *40*
  -plotters, 14
Computer output microfilming (COM), 261
ComputerPix Micro, 60, 238
Conditioning, 159, 162, 165–169
Contrast, 133–136
  effect on resolution, 135–136
  effect on thresholding, 138
Cooley, Austin, 9
Copyphone, 194, 212
Copyright situation, 258
Costs. *See* Facsimile economics; Terminal costs; Transmission costs
Council on Library Resources, 146
Couplers
  hard-wired (direct), 103
  phone (indirect), 38, *39,* 102–103, 157, 158, 162
CR index, 136
Crater tube, 63, 66, 136
Crosstalk, 85, 91–92
CRT. *See* Cathode Ray Tubes
"Cylinder-and-screw", 3, *5*
Cylinder type machine, 3, *5*, *7*, 50–52

Dacom, 112–114, 213, 239
Data access arrangement (DAA), 103, *104*, 157, 158, 170
  See also Couplers, hard-wired
Data compression, 21, 40–41, 103, 109, 156, 157, 158, 161, 169–170, 256–257
  See also Bandwidth compression and Redundancy Reduction
Datafax, 10, 41, 155, 195, 197, 214
  See also Stewart-Warner Corp.
Datalog. *See* Litton Industries
Data sets, 102, 105–108, 157, 158, 174, 175
Data transmission, 12, 29, 30–31, 33, 173, 174
  See also Digital transmission
d.c. component, 80
"Dead sector", 80, 132, 177–178, 182–183, 187
Decitron Communications Systems, Inc., 11
Defense Communication Agency (DCA), 177, 179–180
Delay distortion. *See* Envelope delay distortion
Demodulation (Detection), 89–91, 105–106
Densitometer, 134
Density
  reflection, 134–135
  transmission, 133–134
Department of Defense, U.S. (DOD), 177–179, 189
Desk-Fax, 7, 26
Detection. *See* Demodulation
Dex, 52, 196, 240
"Dial-a-Document", 42
Dial network, 37, 44, 84–85, 102–103, 105 130–131, 157, 158, 161, 162, 163, 164, 165–169, 173, 256–257
Digital transmission, 12, 29, 31, 35, 41, 106–108, 109, 110–117, 129, 135, 137–141, 152, 170, 187–188, 257
  See also Data transmission; Pulse Code Modulation
"Digitizing", 30, 41, 137–141
Direct recording, 14, 44, 57, 58–65, 126, 156–157
Distortion, 41, *74*, 125, 175
  aperture, 124
  delay, 95–96, *97*
  geometric, 76–78
  See also Skew; Transmission impairments
Drafting standards, 143
Drive motors, 70–74, 140
Dudley, Homer, 109
Dynodes. *See* Photomultiplier

Echo, 93–95, *96*, 175
Suppression, 95
Economics. *See* Facsimile economics
Edge gradient, 129, 131
"8000 type" channel (group), 99, 106, 108, 159, 165–169
Electrolytic paper. *See* Paper, recording
Electronic Industries Association, 37, 81*n*, 146, 173–175, 177, 182
"Electronic Mailbox", 197
Electronic Transmission Systems, Inc., 11, 206
Electron microscopes, 28
Electrosensitive paper.
See Paper, recording
Engineering drawings & sketches, transmission of, 21–22, 42, 146, 233–235
England, 11, 23
Envelope delay distortion, 95–96, *97*, 175
Equalization, 95–96, 98
of amplitude peaks, 113
Erdmann, R. L., 140*n*
Error immunity, 30–31
Error (rate), transmission, 12, 18, 30–31, 41
Expo 70, 257

Facsimile,
definition of, 1–2
high-speed, *17*, 18, 27, 56, 97, 99, 113, 191, 209–220, 232, 236, 238, 239, 242, 246, 250–252, 255, 256–257
invention of, 2–3. *See also* Facsimile history
message, 1, 2, 7, 10, 44, 81*n*, 98, 99, 105, 172, 173–174, 177, 191, 193–220
definitions of, 23, 25, 174
military, 28, 177–180, 189
Facsimile applications, 12–28, 44
Facsimile automation, 32–33, 42, 174
Facsimile broadcasting, 8–9, 10, 175–177
Facsimile economics, 154–171. *See also* Terminal costs; Transmission costs
cost-per-copy, 161–165
charts, 166–169
labor costs, 154–155
material costs, 156–157, 161, 165
terminal costs, 155–156
trade-offs, 160–161
transmission costs, 157–160
trends, 169–171
Facsimile equipment, commercial, 9–11, *16–19*, *21*, *28*, *32*, *33*, *39*, *40*, 42, *43*, 52, *57*, *61*, *64*, *65*, 99, 111, 112, 113, 115, 124, 147–148, 155, 191–255
See also Foreign facsimile equipment, commercial; Special purpose facsimile systems, commercial
Facsimile flexibility, 33–34
Facsimile history, 1–11, 12, 14, 19, 21, 23, 26, 38, 57, 58, 59, 60, 69, 87–88, 101, 105, 115, 150, 257, 259–260
Facsimile in banking, 19–20, 147
Facsimile in business, 16–23
Facsimile in color, 190, 237, 247, 259–261
commercial equipment for, 237, 247, 260
Facsimile in libraries, 26–27, 146–147, 258
Facsimile in the home, 1, 8–9, 176, 257–259
Facsimile limitations, 34–37
Facsimile makers (current), 9–11
Facsimile networks (message), 43–44
Facsimile newspaper, 8–9, 257, 258
standards for, 176
Facsimile pioneers
(individuals), 1–9, 259–260
(firms) 1, 4, 6–11, 176, 257, 260
Facsimile principles, 47–78
Facsimile quality, 119–153
Facsimile standards. *See* Standards
Facsimile test chart, IEEE, 121–122, 175
See also Test charts
Facsimile transmission, 79–118
Facsimile trends, 37–44, 169–171, 256–262
Facsimile users, 12–28
Facsimile virtues, 28–34
Facsimile weather networks. *See* Weather networks
Fading, 86, 93, 100
Fairchild Camera & Instrument Corp., 9, 11
"Fax," 2. *See also* Facsimile
Fax by phone, 38, 102, 157, 158, 159, 162, 165–169, 172–175, 194–208, 210, 211, 213, 216, 218, 233–240, 252, 255, 256–257
See also Transmission, voice-grade; Voice communication
FAXpaper®, 10
FCC *Rules and Regulations*, 175–177
Federal Communications Commission (FCC), 9, 101, 158, 175–177
FH-94R receiver (NEC), 241
Fidelity, 82, 84, 124, 129–130, 133
Finch Telecommunications, 8, 10, 260
Fingerprint transmission, 23, 148, *149*, 151
Flexibility, 29–30
FM. *See* Frequency Modulation
"Foreign" devices, 38
Foreign facsimile equipment, commercial, 9, 11, *21*, *64*, *65*, 199, 200, 204, 208, 217, 219, 222–228, 237, 241–251, 253, 255
Ft. Monmouth, N.J., 177
"Framing" cycle, 262
France, 3
Freight expediting, 17–18
Frequency Modulation (FM), 9, 35, 85, 93, 101, 105–106, 137, 157, 158, 176–177, 189
Frequency Shift Keying (FSK), 101, 137, 187

Frequency standard, 71, *72*
Frey, H. C., 136
FT-series equipment (NEC), 222–226, 242
Full-duplex, 157
Future of facsimile, 256–262

General Electric (Co.), 10
General purpose facsimile systems. *See* Facsimile, message
Germany, 3, 11, 23
Glow modulator tube, 66
See also Crater tube
"Governor," inductive, 73
Graphic communications. *See* Facsimile
Graphic Sciences, Inc. (GSI), 10, 52, 196, 240
Graphic Transmission Systems, Inc., 11, 210
Gray, F., 124*n*
Gray scale, 48, 122, 133–135, 137, 138, 148, 149
"Grouped" circuits, 99, 106, 108
Grundig, 116
Half-duplex, 157
Half-group, 99, 108
Halftone, 6, 122, 151–152, 175, 178
Handwriting legibility, 147–148
Harmonics, 82–83
Harris-Intertype Corp., 115
HELAC Electronics, 115*n*
Helix-and-blade, 58–59, 156–157
Hell, Dr. -Ing. Rudolf, 11, 63, 199, 229, 243–246, 255
Hellfax, 57, 63–65, 199, 243–245
Hell-Pressfax, 246
Hertz, 121, 139–140
History. *See* Facsimile history
Hogan Faximile, 10
Hogan, John V. L., 8
Hogan Laboratories, 10

Impact recording. *See* Recording, electropercussive
Impedance matching, 94–95
Impression recording. *See* Recording, electropercussive
Index of cooperation, 75–78, 96, 173, 175–178, 180–183, 186, 189
CCITT, 75*n*
CCITT-IEEE conversion, 75*n*, 182
Info-Fax 100 (WU), 44
Information explosion, 27
Information retrieval, 27, 35, 43, 257–258, 261–262
Inforum, 258*n*
Institute of Electrical & Electronic Engineers (IEEE), 47*n*, 121, 126, 135, 146, 175
"Interconnection," 102, 154*n*, 158, 170
Interference, external, 30, 91–92, 102–103
International News Service, 9
International Scanatron (Systems Corp.), 11, 115, 201, 216
International Telecommunications Union (ITU), 177, 181
International Telegraph Union, 181
Interlibrary loans, 26–27
IRE, 175
IRE Transactions, 112*n*
Ives, Dr. Herbert, 6, 259, 260*n*
Ives, Frederic, 6

Japan, 11, 21, 26, 257, 258, 260
Jenkins, C. F., 7
Jitter, 139–141, 175

Kell factor, 127, 130, 145
Kell, R. D., 127*n*
Kendall effect, 82, 83, 96, 175
Kerr cell, 66
Keyboard type equipment, 29, 32
See also Teletype(writer)
Kilobits, 123
Kodak (Eastman-) Co., 42, 175
Korn, Dr. Arthur, 3
K-series equipment (Muirhead), 227, 228, 247
KSTP (St. Paul), 8

Laser beam, 111, 124
"Lathe-style"scanning, 50
Law enforcement, 23, *24*, 148, *149*, 150–151
See also Fingerprint transmission; "Mug shot" transmission.
LDX, 61, 99, 215, 257
Legibility, 141–147
character vs word, 141–146
library applications, 146–147
microfilm printback criteria, 144–145, 147
NMA/EIA Committee findings, 146
Scan lines per character, 142–144
Level fluctuations, 93, *94*
Library systems, 26–27, 43, 146–147
See also Facsimile in libraries
"Light pipe" (Fiber optic), *61*, 62, *63*, 65
Light valve, 3, 66
Limiter (FM), 91, 105
Line advance (line feed), 177–178, 189
Line length, scan, 131–133, 173, 175, 189
Litton Industries, 9
Litcom (Datalog) Division of, 10, 23, 52, 155, 203, 219, 229, 237, 251–254, 260

M4 system, 201, 216
Madrid, 181

Magnafax®, 11, 56, 60, 71, 202
See also Magnavox Co.
Magnavox Co., The, 10–11, 56, 60, 202
Mail, 17–18, 29, 44, 261
costs, 44
Manufacturers. *See* Facsimile makers
Map transmission, 148–149
See also Weather maps
Mar del Plata, Argentina, 182
"Mark and space". *See* Two-level signal
Massachusetts Institute of Technology (MIT), 27, 43, 188–190
Matsushita Graphic Communication Systems (Toho-Denki), 11, 200, 219, 237, 251, 253, 260
"Mercury" systems (Muirhead), 248, 249
Mertz, P., 124*n*
"Message block" ("message board"), 2, 3
Message facsimile. *See* Facsimile, message
Messagefax, 52, 203
Miami *Herald*, The, 9
Microfacsimile, 27, 42–43, 56, 122, 144, 261
"Microfiche", 42
Microfilm facsimile. *See* Microfacsimile
Microfilm printback, 135–136, 144–145, *146*
Microfilm Technology, 135*n*
Micron, 124
Microphotography, 122
Microwave, 44, 100–101, 170, 174, 177
Military facsimile. *See* Facsimile, military
Missing person dispatch, *24*
Mobile systems, 23, *24*, 176, 248
Modems, 103, 105–106, 108, 114, 116, 156, 157–158, 170, 174, 175
Modulation, 81–91, 157, 175–180, 186–187
negative vs positive, 136–137
See also Polarity, tonal; Signal sense
schemes, 87–89, 105
Modulation index, 87, 179
Modulator-demodulator. *See* Modems
Modulators, 87–89, 180
Ring, 88–89
Multivibrator, 89
Moiré patterns, 122, 124*n*, 151–152
Morehouse report, 147*n*
Mufax "Courier," 204, 217
"Mug shot" transmission, 23, 150–151
Muirhead (& Co., Ltd.), 11, 21, 23, 204, 217, 227, 228, 247–250, 260

NASA, 180–181
National Weather Service, 16, 115, 172, 180
National Bureau of Standards (NBS), 122, 144–145
National Meteorological Center (NMC), 14, 16
National Microfilm Association, 146
NEA-Acme, 9
Neal, A. S., 140*n*
Nelson, Dr. C. E., 135–136
Networks. *See* Dial network, Facsimile networks, Weather networks
News Wire Services. *See* Associated Press and United Press International
Newspaper Page Facsimile System, 250
See also Pressfax; Proofs, transmission of
Newspictures, 1, 4, 6, 12–14, 29, 56, 98, 150, 156
New York *Sun*, *6*
New York *Times*, the, 9
New York *World*, 3
Nippon Electric Co., 11, 52, 208, 222-226, 241, 242
Nippon Telegraph & Telephone Corp., 26
Noise, 35, 41, 48, 85–86, 133, 137, 175
internal, 93, 133
quantizing, 137
See also Distortion; Transmission impairments
"Normal" scanning, 127

Optical Character Recognition (OCR), 29
Order dispatching, 18–20

Pacfax, 41, 115
Palmer Newspapers, the, 21
Paper as a pollutant, 261
Paper "explosion," 261
Paper, recording
cost of, 156–157
electrolytic, 56, 58–59, 156–157
Electrosensitive, 3, 7, 59, 60, 61, 62, 156
Patriot-Ledger, the, 20
Pendulum, 2, 3, *4*, *5*, 69
Pennsylvania State University, 26–27
Phasing, *5*, 69–70, *71*, 173, 174, 176, 180, 186
coincident pulse, 69–70
stop-start, 69
Philadelphia *Inquirer*, the, 9
Photocell, 47, 48, 53, 54
three-element, 53*n*
Photoelectric scanning, 3
See also Scanning
Photoelectric transducer. *See* Photocell, Photomultiplier, and Scanning
Photofacsimile. *See* Phototransmission; Picture transmission; Recording, photographic: Telephotography
Photofax, 229
Photomultiplier, 47, 48, 53–54
Phototelegraphy. *See* Telephotography
Phototransmission, 7
See also Picture transmission; Recording, photographic; and

Phototransmission (*Continued*)
Telephotography
Pictorial quality criteria, 147–152
fingerprints, 148, *149*
handwriting, 147–148
maps, 148–149, *150*
photographs, 147, 150–152
Picture editor, 14
Picture transmission, 1, 3, 4, 6, 7, 188–190
See also Phototransmission; Recording, photographic; Telephotography
"Piggyback" system, 170–171, 258–259
Pigment transfer recording. *See* Recording, electropercussive
Points (type face), 142–143, 146–147
Polarity, tonal, 136–137
See also Signal sense
Polaroid film, 65, 260
Polaroid (photos), 28
Police facsimile. *See* Law enforcement
Pope Pius XI, 3
Portability, 38–40
"Positive" scanning, 127
Post Office Dept., U.S., 44
Power line induction, 85, 91
See also Single frequency interference
Pressfax, 155, 246, 251
Proceedings of the IRE, 8*n*, 127*n*
Project Intrex, 27, 43
Proofs, transmission of, 20–21, 151–152, 246, 250, 251
Pulse Code Modulation (PCM), 4, 116, 137, 152
See also Digital transmission

Qix, 205
Quality, output. *See* Facsimile quality
Quantizing,
amplitude, 35, 107, 135, 137–138, *151*, 152
errors, 137–141
time, 139–141
Queuing, 26

RACE, 115
Radarfax, 252
Radiation, Incorporated, 115
Radio Corporation of America (RCA), 1, 4, 6, 7, 8, 10, 101, 127*n*, 257
Radio facilities, 100–101, 175–177
Radiofacsimile, 1, 7, 8–9, 19, 101, 175–177, 181, 183–186, 257
Radio Inventions, Inc., 8, 10
Radiophoto, 6, *13*, 101
Randomness (of fax signal), 66, 79, 107, 109
Recording, 56–66, *67*, 111, 124, 126, 127, 136–137, 156–157, 178–180
cylinder, 56, *60*

Recording (*Continued*)
direct, 57, *59*, *60*, *61*, *62*, *63*, *64*, 126
electrolytic, 56, 58–59, 156–157
electromechanical, 56–65
electron beam, 56, 66, *67*, 124
electropercussive, 60–61
electrostatic, 57, 61–63, 156
electrothermal, 59–60, 156
flat bed, 56, *59*, *61*, *62*, *63*, *64*, 127
ink vapor, 57
laser, 111, 124
optical fiber, 62, *63*
photographic, 56, 65–66, 126, 136–137, 156, 157
roll feed, 56, *57*, *59*, *62*, *63*, *64*
wet ink offset, 57, 63–65
Recording quality, 125–126
Recording speed, 56
See also Scan rate
Redundancy (transmission), 34–35
Redundancy reduction, 35, 41, 108–117, 169–170
See also Bandwidth compression; Data compression
Reflectometer, 134
Remotecopier®, 200
Resolution, 75, 119–133, 135–136, 178, 180–183, 187
definition of, 120
effect of contrast on, 135–136
effect of "gaps" on, 131–133
elemental, 122–123, 127
lines, "line pairs," elements and cycles, 120–123
scan (density), 75, 120, 178, 180–183, 187
"square," 127–131
Resolution determinants, 123–131
Resolution test charts. *See* Test charts
RETMA, RMA, 173
R.I. Bulletin, 31*n*
Ridings, G.H., 26
RTMA, 173*n*
Run length encoding, 111–112, 113

St. Louis *Post-Dispatch*, The, 9
Sampling, 111–113, 139–141
adaptive, 112
Scan axis, 126–127
Scan density, 75, 120, 182–183, 187
See also Resolution, scan
Scan "grain," 120, 125, 127
Scan pitch, 123
See also Scan density; Scan "grain"; Resolution, scan.
Scan rate, 33–34, 37, 40, 56, *75*, 81, 131–133, 176–183, 186, 188, 189
Scan speed. *See* Scan rate

Scanning, 47–56
contact, 2, 3, 6, 53
cylinder, 50–52
electromechanical, 50–52
electronic (CRT), 52, 53, 55–56, 131, 133
electronics of, 53–56
flat bed, 50, 52
flood, 49–50
"flying spot," 52, 53, 55–56, 131
optical fiber, 52
spot, *48*, 49–50
"Schedule II" facilities. *See* Telephoto facility
Schreiber, Wm. F., 188*n*
Seitz, Charles L., 188*n*
"Self-testing," 36
Series 3002 facility, 98, 158–159, 166–169
Service terminal, 158–159, 162
See also "Station charge"
Servicing difficulties, 36, 101
Shintron Co., the, 10, 188, 205
Sidebands, 82–83, *84*, *87*
Suppression of, 83–84, 108–109
Signal magazine, 26*n*
Signal, picture, 53–56, 66–67, 79–84, 89–91, 105–106, 113
Signal sense, 173, 180, 189
Signal, sync, 70–71, 73–74, 105, 107, 113
Signal-to-noise ratio, 133
Signature verification, 19, 147–148
Single frequency interference (SFI), 91, 92
See also Power line induction
Skew, 71, 175, 179
"Slaving," 73
"Slope" filtering, 90
Solid state, 38–40, 88
Spatial cycles. *See* Spatial frequency
Spatial frequency, 120–121, 122, 131, *132*, 145
Special purpose facsimile systems, commercial, *19*, *21*, 42, *43*, 124, 147–148, 155, 231–255
Spectral sensitivity, 48, 179
Speed-O-Fax, 206
Spot size, 123–124, 125, 175
Spreading effect, 127, *128*, *129*
Standards, 36–37, 172–190, 256–257
domestic, 37, 173–181, 189
EIA, 173–174, 189
IEEE, 175
FCC, 175–177
military, 177–180, 189
weather, 180–181
drafting, 143
international, 181–188, 189
CCITT, 182–184, *185*, 189
CCIR, 184, 186, 189
Standards (*Continued*)
WMO, 186–188, 189
lack of, 36–37, 256–257
Standards conversion, 188–190
"Station charge," 99, 108, 159
See also Service terminal
Stencil-maker, 27–28
"Step wedge," 135
Stewart-Warner Corp., 10, 155, 195, 197, 214
Store-and-forward, 179
Study groups (CCIR & CCITT), 181
Subaudio frequencies, 80
Subcarrier, 100, 101, 176, 186
Subject copy, 47
Supergroup, 99, 106, 108
Switched ("dial-up") broadband, 98–100, 157, 159
See also Broadband Exchange service
"Switched network," limitation of, 84–85
See also Dial network
Synchronization, 3, 69, 70–75, 174, 178–180, 182, 187
methods, 3, 70–74
Synchronizing "clocks," 107, 139–141, 179
Systems planning, 91–262

Tape transmission, 4, 35, 42, 179*n*, 261–262
Telautograph Corp., 10, 194, 212
Telecopier®, 10–11, 56, 60, 198, 207
See also Xerox Corp.
Teledeltos®, 7, 59–60
"Telefacsimile," 26
Telegraph, printing, 3
Telemetry, 29, 113
Telephone bandwidth, 80, *81*, 105, 125, 130, 157
Telephone couplers. *See* Couplers, phone
Telephone network. *See* Dial network
Telephone rates, 33, 158–160, 162–169, 170
"Telephoto," 6, 9, *13*
Telephoto facility, 98–99, 157, 159, 162, 165–169
Telephotography, 12–14, 172, 179, 181–182, 184, 186, 191, 221–230
See also Phototransmission; Picture transmission; Recording, photographic
"Telepix," 6
Teletype (writers), 17–18, 19
Television, 1, 6, 9, 12, 120, 127, 150, *151*, 171, 172, 257, 260–262
closed-circuit, 12, 116, 172
slow-scan, 12
See also CATV
Telikon, 111, 218
Terminal costs, 34, 44, 155–156, 158, 159, 161–165, 194–208, 210–220, 222–229, 232–255

Terminal equipment. *See* Couplers; Data Sets; Facsimile equipment, commercial; Modems
Test charts
IEEE, *92*, *96*, *97*, 121–122, *126*, 135, 146, 175
NBS microcopy, 122, 145, *146*
CCITT, 184, *185*
WMO, 187
TF-4501/RS-451 system, 208
"Theory of Scanning, A," 124*n*
Thermal recording. *See* Recording, electrothermal
Three-level digital, 114–115
Threshold, 137–138
Ticket reservation, 28
Times Facsimile Corp., 8, 9
Toho-Denki. *See* Matsushita . . .
Tonal latitude, 126, 135
Toner, 61–62
Toshiba, 257
Trade-offs, 33–34, 131, 148, 160–161
Training, operator, 12, 31–32
Transmission,
broadband, 98–102, 106–108, 148, 157, 159, 161, 191
voice-grade, 26, 83–87, 91–98, 115, 116, 148, 157, 173, 174, 175, 180, 191
See also Fax by phone; Voice communication
Transmission costs, 98–100, 111, 157–169
Transmission distance (mileage), Cost of, 98, 99, 100, 158, 160, 162, 165–169
Transmission facilities, 97–101
Transmission impairments, 35, 41, 91–96, *97*, 137–141
Trends. *See* Facsimile economics and Facsimile trends
Troxel, Donald E., 188*n*
Type 4002 facilities. *See* Telephoto facility
Type sizes, 142–143, 146–147
Typewriter fonts, 143
Two-level (black-white) signal, 41, 106–108, 114, 122–123, 137–141

Ultrafax®, 257
Unattended operation. *See* Facsimile automation
Unifax, 230
Union Internationale des Telecommunications (UIT), 181*n*. *See also* International Telecommunications Union (ITU)
United Nations (UN), 181, 257
United Press Associations, 9
United Press International (UPI), 9, 13, 36, 101, 230
U.S. Army Electronics Command, 177
University of California, 26–27
University of Nevada, 26, 146–147

Variable velocity scanning, 110–111, 112
Videofax, 219
Videograph, *62*, 220, 257
Video tape recording, 261–262
Vidicon, 101
Visual acuity, 135
Vocoder, 109, *110*
Voice communication, 33, 34, 35, 95, 102–103, 158, 175

Wall Street Journal, the, 20–21
Weather charts. *See* Weather maps.
Weatherfax, 253, 254
Weather forecasting, 7, 14–16, 101, 172
Weather maps, 7, 14, 16, 29, 101, 148–149, 177–178, 181, 183–184, 186–188
Weather networks, 14, *15*, 16, 36, 172, 180
Weather satellites, 14, 36, 101, 156, 180–181
Weiss, Dr. G. K., 187
Wente, E. C., 4
Western Electric Co., 6, 8, 9
Western Union (Telegraph Co.), 4, 6, 7, 8, 10, 23, 25–26, 44, 58*n*, 59, 97, 98, 100, 157, 159
Westrex, *8*, 9
"White Book" (CCITT), 182
Wide Area Telephone Service (WATS), 160
"Wirephoto", 7, *13*, 188–190, 260
WOR (New York), 8
World Meteorological Organization (WMO), 16, 177, 181, 186–188, 189
Wyle, H., 112*n*

Xerography,
direct, 61, 62
transfer, 61, 63
Xerox Corp., 10, 56, 60, 61, 99, 198, 207, 215, 257
X-rays, transmission of, 28

Zetfax, 255

ABOUT THE AUTHOR

Daniel M. Costigan is associated with Bell Telephone Laboratories, where, for the past several years, he has been engaged in the planning and evaluation of information systems with emphasis on studies relating to the electronic dissemination of engineering drawings via facsimile and other systems. He is Bell's representative on the Electronic Industries Association Facsimile Subcommittee. As a technical writer, he has published a number of articles in various fields. His most recent, on *Microfacsimile: A Status Report*, appeared in the May 1971 issue of *The Journal of Micrographics*. Mr. Costigan is a graduate of RCA Institutes and of New York University. He lives in Edison, New Jersey.